# BLACKS
# IN THE LAW

Geraldine R. Segal

# BLACKS
# IN THE LAW
Philadelphia and the Nation

Foreword by Judge A. Leon Higginbotham, Jr.

University of Pennsylvania Press
Philadelphia
1983

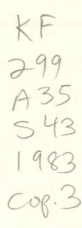
**Library of Congress Cataloging in Publication Data**

Segal, Geraldine R.
  Blacks in the law.

    Revision and updating of the author's thesis
(Ph.D.—University of Pennsylvania, 1978) originally
presented under title: Blacks in the law in Philadelphia.
    Bibliography: p.
    Includes index.
    1. Afro-American lawyers—Pennsylvania—Philadelphia.
2. Afro-American judges—Pennsylvania—Philadelphia.
3. Law students—Pennsylvania—Philadelphia.    4. Law
teachers—Pennsylvania—Philadelphia.    5. Afro-American
lawyers.    6. Afro-American judges.    I.    Title.

KF299.A35S43    1982        349.748'11'08996073        82-60304
ISBN    0-8122-7854-2        347.4811008996073

Printed in the United States of America

To Bernie, my inspiration

# Contents

# Tables

# Appendices

Judge A. Leon Higginbotham, Jr.

# Foreword

In 1896 while an Assistant Instructor[1] at the University of Pennsylvania, Dr. W. E. B. Du Bois wrote one of the early classics in American sociology, *The Philadelphia Negro: A Social Study.*[2] Gunnar Myrdal, in his seminal work, *An American Dilemma,*[3] paid tribute to Du Bois by stating "We cannot close this description of what a study of a Negro community should be without calling attention to the study which best meets our requirements, a study which is now all but forgotten."[4] Myrdal was referring to W. E. B. Du Bois' *The Philadelphia Negro,* published in 1899. Eighty-six years after Du Bois' extraordinary pioneer study, another classic sociological study of Philadelphia, in keeping with the Du Bois tradition, has been produced from the Sociology Department of the University of Pennsylvania: Dr. Geraldine Segal's dissertation[5] and book, *Blacks in the Law: Philadelphia and the Nation.* Though her study of the black legal community is more narrowly focused than Du Bois' study of the Philadelphia Negro, I predict that, like Du Bois' earlier work, Dr. Segal's book will be for decades the standard by which future studies of minority lawyers, and indeed other professions, are measured.

Having read many dissertations and sociological treatises over the years, my instinctive reaction most often is: "While interesting, what is it's relevance? Who benefits from the study other than the author, who rejoices in seeing his or her words in print? Will the quality of life be improved anywhere in this nation or in the world after one has collected, analyzed, or read the data discussed?"

Such questions do not disturb me when reading Dr. Segal's book because the relevance of her work is obvious. She deals with the profound question which Frederick Douglass asked almost a century ago:

> [Can] American justice, American liberty, American civilization, American law, and American Christianity . . . be made to include and protect alike and forever *all* American citizens in the rights which have been guaranteed to them by the organic and fundamental laws of the land?[6]

In many respects, Dr. Segal's work is an inquiry, in Douglass' words, into "American justice, American liberty, American civilization, American law and American [Religions]." *Blacks in the Law* is not merely a study of either black lawyers as the victims of racial discrimination or the pervasive methodologies used to exclude and deter blacks. Perhaps equally, if not more importantly, it reveals the values of the "people in charge" of the legal and political systems in America. It reflects their prejudices, their biases, their tolerances, and their fleeting moments of fairness. Just as the history of slavery tells us as much about the masters and those who profited from that inhuman institution as it does the blacks who were denigrated and dehumanized,[7] similarly, the statistics on blacks in the law reflect the degrees of exclusion, levels of hatred, and plateaus of intolerance perpetuated by the leaders and foot soldiers of the legal profession.

Professors Eulau and Sprague observe that lawyers have been "the high priests of politics."[8] Of the 52 signers of the Declaration of Independence, 25 were lawyers, as were 31 of the 56 members of the Continental Congress. Of the 40 American presidents, 25 have been lawyers. Between 1877 and 1934, 70 percent of the American presidents, vice-presidents, and cabinet members were lawyers.[9] Thus the long-term and persistent underrepresentation of blacks in the legal system reflects in itself the absence of blacks with power and the absence of advocates who could identify most with the problems of blacks when critical decisions were being made about the direction and destiny of society. The increased representation of blacks within the legal profession during the 1970s reveals that when those in charge truly cared about pluralism within their profession, they could make a difference—a difference not merely in rhetoric but in results. Yet, as I read the nation's priorities in the 1980s, it seems that the quest for affirmative action and racial pluralism is at best slowing down and at worst being eviscerated, and, as in the past, lawyers are playing a major role in slamming closed the doors to better options for blacks.

In the final analysis, however, America will be judged more by results than by rhetoric. Dr. Segal's work gives us an opportunity to evaluate past results by providing a statistical history of the victims and the occasional victors. Her probing study provides a reasonably accurate index of the progress made and the distance yet to be traveled. While her work focuses on Philadelphia, I would predict that her findings would be replicated in other major northern cities. There has never been as careful and precise a comparative analysis as her sixteen-city study of blacks in the law.

Dr. Segal's work has another important dimension, one almost on an inspirational level. She reveals many of the frustrations, challenges, disappointments, and joys of the blacks who dared to enter the profession, and the factors which motivated them. In my view, too often some minority law students seem overwhelmed by their perception of the present barriers. Some wonder whether the demand for persistent excellence will be worth the wear and tear of consistent effort, frequent frustration, and occasional failures. But anyone who reads the biographical sketches Dr. Segal has written on the hundreds of lawyers in sixteen cities must realize that great barriers have been hurdled in the past and that the future is brighter than ever for minority law students.

In every city there will be complaints as to why other persons were not named and perhaps why some were included. But the important message is that many blacks, despite pervasive obstacles, made it. If throughout the biographical sketches in part 2, one reflects on the challenges and attainments of the many who excelled despite extremely hostile environments, no one today should retreat or give up when confronted by present challenges. These brief biographies prove that many did "overcome" even though we are not told how tortuous the path was that they were required to travel. Thus, in addition to its sociological soundness and scholarship, Dr. Segal's book is a refreshing volume. It describes the past, documents the present and, if read with wisdom, can give us hope for the future.

If I were to note that area of the law in which, from my view, there has been the greatest rigidity, and perhaps the least racial progress, it would not be the law firms, the corporations, the judiciary, or the government. I submit that the greatest rigidity in the legal field has been within the teaching profession. At first glance, this result seems quite surprising because law professors have often been the staunchest advocates of affirmative action for others. They have often been the severest critics of courts, corporations, legal practitioners, and the profession generally. Yet, in many ways, their credibility today is as much on the line as anyone else's in our profession—that is, if they are to be measured by results and not by rhetoric. One of the most urgent challenges for the future will be to increase significantly the number of talented blacks with tenure on law school faculties.

The legal profession will remain eternally indebted to Dr. Segal for her pioneering study. With sensitivity and thoroughness she has reviewed the record, noting both our successes and our failures. What will lawyers do to improve the present record? Lawyers and judges wield disproportionate power in shaping the destiny of our nation. We give advice to many others in our society. If we can be as adroit in evaluating ourselves as we are in assessing and advising others, if we can be as constructive in correcting our own deficiencies as we are in demanding reform from others, then equal justice under the law may yet be more than a hollow aspiration.

Of course, a study of blacks in the law must be read as merely one facet of the challenges within the black community. By scanning the data of Dr. Segal's book, it is easy to overestimate the significance of the changes which have occurred. One must be mindful of the fact that we are studying only one aspect of the problem. Dr. Segal's data, demonstrating progress in the legal profession, must be balanced against 1981 data which reveal that the unemployment rate for blacks is still twice that of whites, and that the unemployment rate of black teenagers in some inner city areas ranges as high as 70 percent. The data on substandard housing, inadequate health care, deficient educational systems, and the high incidence of crime pushes the optimistic viewer to feel nothing less than despair.[10]

In recent years there has been a significant bifurcation within the black community, resulting in extremely improved options for the very talented and the status quo or even retrogression for most other blacks. This problem has been exacerbated for the masses of blacks who have been abandoned, forgotten, or deterred by deteriorating urban public school systems. The problem has been exacerbated as well by some of those who in the past, when the problems seemed more simple because they involved merely protesting racial discrimination at restaurant counters and voting booths, were the allies of blacks, but who now are the foes of affirmative action.

On his seventieth birthday, in *Dusk of Dawn,* Dr. Du Bois wrote: "I have essayed in a half century three sets of thought centering around the hurts and hesitancies that hem the black man in America. The first of these, 'The Souls of Black Folks,' written 37 years age, was a cry at midnight thick within the veil, when none rightly knew the coming of the day. The second, 'Darkwater,' now twenty years old, was an exposition and militant challenge,[11] defiant with dogged hope." His third book, "Dusk at Dawn," was started "to record dimly but consciously that subtle sense of coming day which one feels of early mornings even when mist and murk hang low." Du Bois concluded his Introduction in "Dusk of Dawn" by noting that the significance of his own life developed out of "the central problem of the world's greatest democracies and so the problem of the future world, . . . of which the concept of race is today one of the most unyielding and threatening."

Perhaps in many ways *Blacks in the Law* exemplifies the "early mornings even when mist and murk hang low." If we understand the significance of Geraldine Segal's book, perhaps in the future the concept of race will become less unyielding and less threatening because of the continuous effort to eradicate the sequellae of centuries of racism in the American legal process.

## Notes

1. There is a substantial debate as to what was the significance of Dr. Du Bois' title as an assistant instructor at the University of Pennsylvania. Dr. Du Bois wrote of his experience at the University of Pennsylvania as follows:

There must have been some opposition, for the invitation was not particularly cordial. I was offered a salary of $800 for a period limited to one year. I was given no real academic standing, no office at the University, no official recognition of any kind; my name was even eventually omitted from the catalogue; I had no contact with students, and very little with members of the faculty, even in my department. With my bride of three months, I settled in one room over a cafeteria run by a College Settlement, in the worst part of the Seventh Ward. We lived there a year, in the midst of an atmosphere of dirt, drunkenness, poverty and crime. Murder sat on our doorsteps, police were our government, and philanthropy dropped in with periodic advice.

I counted my task here as simple and clear-cut: I proposed to find out what was the matter with this area and why. I started with no "research methods" and I asked little advice as to procedure. The problem lay before me. Study it. I studied it personally and not by proxy. I sent out no canvassers. I went myself. Personally I visited and talked with 5000 persons.

W. E. B. Du Bois, "My Evolving Program for Negro Freedom" in Rayford W. Logan, ed., *What the Negro Wants* (Chapel Hill: The University of North Carolina Press, 1944), p. 44. Professor E. Digby Baltzell writes:

These are bitter words. And apparently Du Bois was not quite true to the facts of the case. There was no evidence in the minutes of the University's Board of Trustees of any "opposition" to the appointment. On a request for information on the case from a DuBois biographer, the late Professor Lindsay replied that DuBois was "quite mistaken about the attitude of the Sociology Department. It was quite friendly, I am sure, and as far as I know that was true of the entire Wharton School faculty."

W. E. B. Du Bois, *The Philadelphia Negro: A Social Study* (1899) (reprinted by Shocken Books, Inc., 1967). From the Introduction by E. Digby Baltzell, p. xix.

2. Du Bois, *The Philadelphia Negro: A Social Study.*

3. Gunnar Myrdal, *An American Dilemma,* (New York: Harper and Brothers Publishers, 1944).

4. Ibid., p. 1132.

5. This book is not merely a summary of Dr. Segal's excellent dissertation. Most of part 2 represents extensive additional research data and thought on issues which were not covered in her original dissertation.

6. R. Logan, *The Betrayal of the Negro,* pp. 9–10 (1965) (quoting Frederick Douglass).

7. See generally, A. L. Higginbotham, Jr., *In the Matter of Color: Race and the American Legal Process* (New York: Oxford University Press 1978).

8. H. Eulau & J. Sprague, *Lawyers in Politics,* pp. 11–30 (1964).

9. Ibid., p. 11.

10. Perhaps the current plight of blacks is summarized most presisely by the National Urban League in the important volume, *The State of Black America 1982,* p. 265:

At the end of 1981, the country was in a recession, black unemployment had reached a record high of 15.5%, 24.2% of black workers had been out of a job at some point during the year, teenage unemployment peaked at 45.7% during the summer and then fluctuated around 40% in the remaining months of the year, and blacks were disproportionately represented as participants in those social service programs which bore the brunt of budget reductions. In almost every black community in America there was a feeling that the rug had been pulled out and times would get worse before they got any better.

Dr. Bernard E. Anderson in his paper, "Economic Patterns in Black America," that appears in this publication, looked forward to 1982 and made this forecast.

"Because of recent shifts in economic policy, the current environment is less likely to be hospitable to further (black) progress than at any time in the recent past. There is no assurance that the job creation that might emerge from current policies will help narrow the employment gap between black and other workers, but it is almost certain that broad budget cuts for social programs will greatly reduce the opportunities for the disadvantaged to become prepared to make a productive contribution to society."

So in essence, many black Americans, along with others, are caught between a rock and a hard place. On one side unemployment is going up, and on the other side many of the programs that could help reduce the unemployment numbers and ease some of the hardships that follow in the wake of joblessness have been curtailed or abandoned.

11. W. E. B. Du Bois, *Dusk of Dawn,* (Harcourt, Brace World, Inc., 1940, reprinted Schocken Books, 1968), pp. vii-viii.

# Preface

After my graduation from college during the Depression, my first employment was as a social worker in a largely black and Filipino neighborhood in Philadelphia. There I observed on a daily basis the frustrations and anxieties of families and lone individuals trying to cope with unemployment and inadequate relief funds. I spent four years working in this neighborhood, until my marriage to a lawyer whose concern for minorities and civil rights inspired me to continue my interest in these subjects.

When, later in life, I returned to the University of Pennsylvania to pursue graduate studies, I chose Human Relations as the subject of my master of arts degree, selecting the life of Charles Houston, certainly the most noted black lawyer of his time, as the topic of my master's thesis.[1]

My dissertation for a Ph.D degree in sociology was entitled "Blacks in the Law in Philadelphia" and was completed in 1978. The dissertation, revised and brought up to date, is the source of the material on the Philadelphia situation in this book.[2]

The main purpose of this book is to examine the history and current status of blacks in the law in Philadelphia—law students, law teachers, practicing lawyers, and judges—and to place these findings in a national setting.

Until the present decade, very little was written about the black lawyer in Philadelphia. In order to trace the history of black membership in the Philadelphia Bar, information was gathered from the Black History Museum, the Philadelphia NAACP Library, the Philadelphia Free Library, the Van Pelt Library of the University of Pennsylvania, the Biddle Law Library of the University of Pennsylvania Law School, the Historical Society of Pennsylvania, the Jenkins Law Library of the Philadelphia Bar Association, the Philadelphia Social History Project, and the Library of Congress. These sources, however, did not provide answers to many important questions concerning the backgrounds, attitudes, and generational differences among black lawyers. In order to obtain answers to these ques-

1. Geraldine R. Segal, *In Any Fight Some Fall* (Rockville, Md.: Mercury Press, 1975).
2. Chapters 1 through 8. Portions of the dissertation on more general subjects have been transferred to chapters other than those on Philadelphia.

tions, I sent questionnaires to the 212 black members of the Philadelphia Bar in 1978 and subsequently conducted personal interviews with many of these black attorneys and also with black judges in Philadelphia.

In attempting to place the Philadelphia data in a national perspective, I recognize that national studies of blacks in the legal profession also have been extremely limited and have provided little information on developments during the important period of the past ten to fifteen years. The difficulty of obtaining information in the face of this dearth of detailed studies was exacerbated by the lack of racial-distribution information available from bar associations and other professional organizations and from boards of law examiners, as well as by the reluctance of some law firms to publicize information concerning the number of their black partners and associates. The only sources of nationwide statistics on blacks in the law are the American Bar Association (ABA) Section on Legal Education and Admissions to the Bar, the Association of American Law Schools (AALS), the National Bar Association (NBA), the Bureau of Labor Statistics (BLS), the Council on Legal Education Opportunity (CLEO), the Howard University Law School, the Law School Admissions Council (LSAC), and the Library of Congress. Unfortunately, none of these sources could provide a detailed survey of the professional activities of black lawyers nationwide.

In order to collect representative data on the situation of black lawyers nationally, I selected the one hundred largest law firms listed by the *National Law Journal* in 1979 and added another seven firms of approximately the same size in order to have a more representative study of the cities in which they are located. These firms were concentrated in seventeen cities (including Philadelphia), in sixteen of which there are two or more such firms.[3] Thus the study deals with sixteen key cities that provide a fair geographic and demographic representation of urban America: Atlanta, Boston, Chicago, Cleveland, Columbus, Detroit, Houston, Los Angeles, Milwaukee, Minneapolis, New York, Philadelphia, Pittsburgh, Richmond, San Francisco, and Washington, D.C.

It is my hope that the discussion of the black lawyers, judges, and law teachers who have achieved distinction or significant progress in various fields of professional endeavor within these cities, together with statistical data on the current employment of blacks in law firms, law schools, and the judiciary, will put the Philadelphia story into a larger perspective and will be a fair representation of the national situation of blacks in the legal profession.

3.   In order to have no firm specifically identified, Omaha, Nebraska, which has only one large firm, has had to be omitted from the statistical survey. All the sixteen cities included have two or more such firms. However, a statement concerning the Omaha firm does appear in this book.

# Acknowledgments

My grateful appreciation goes to those who gave unstintingly of their time and effort to make this study possible. I wish it were feasible to acknowledge the contribution of everyone who was instrumental in enabling me to obtain the requisite historical and current data on blacks in the legal profession across the nation, because so little of such data has been otherwise recorded.

This book had its inception in my dissertation, *Blacks in the Law in Philadelphia,* which had the benefit of the supervision of three distinguished faculty members of the Sociology Department of the University of Pennsylvania—Dr. Renée C. Fox, whose gentle persuasiveness induced me to continue the project; Dr. E. Digby Baltzell, whose keen analysis and pointed questions made me think things through; and Judge A. Leon Higginbotham, Jr., whose encouragement and guidance kept me from faltering along the way.

In preparing the dissertation, which is the basis for the Philadelphia portion of the book, I conducted personal interviews with a cross-section of Philadelphia black lawyers and judges, who graciously gave of their time, and provided me with source material and personal observations. Included among them were Judges William H. Hastie and A. Leon Higginbotham, Jr., Justice Robert N. C. Nix, Jr., Judges Matthew W. Bullock, Jr., Curtis C. Carson, Jr., James T. Giles (a practicing lawyer at the time), Doris M. Harris, Lawrence Prattis, Harvey N. Schmidt, and Juanita Kidd Stout; attorneys Sadie T. M. Alexander, Charles Bowser, William H. Brown III, William T. Coleman, Jr., Alvin Echols, Ragan A. Henry, and Austin Norris. Although much time has passed since those interviews were held, I repeat my thanks for the help that was so generously forthcoming.

With the broadening of the study to the black legal profession across the nation, the scope of investigation was enormously extended. Soon it became evident that published and other recorded sources of data were scarce and at best fragmentary. I found it necessary to rely on individuals as sources of information, and this meant men and women spanning the nation. Wade H. McCree, Jr., former United States Circuit Judge and Solicitor General, presently Professor at the University of Michigan Law School, provided an invaluable chart listing relevant data on every black federal judicial appointee in our history, and he was also a fertile source of information both nationally and specifically on the situation in Detroit. Judge Edward B. Toles of the United States Bankruptcy Court for the Northern District of Illinois, noted black legal historian, forwarded to me an account of the history of the National Bar Association as well as considerable data concerning Chicago's past and present black lawyers and judges. Professor Ralph R. Smith of the University of Pennsylvania Law School was the best single source for data concerning black faculty. He conscientiously took the time to draft a comprehensive report on the subject and to assure the updating of the directory of black law faculty members across the country. J. Clay Smith, Jr., until recently acting Chairman of the Equal Employment Opportunity Commission, not only broadened my vision with his articles and speeches, but also offered helpful advice to guide me in the preparation of the manuscript. Others who made available to me information on a variety of pertinent subjects were Edward B. McConnell, Director of the National Center for State Courts, who with Marilyn M. Roberts, Florence M. Leonard, and Erick Low of the Center, constituted an invaluable source for statistics and other data pertaining to state and local court judges; William Hildebrand, President of Martindale-Hubbell, Inc., for statistical information on, and wise guidance respecting, lawyer populations in various cities; Professor Gilbert Ware of Drexel University, for supplying relevant materials and directing me to others available elsewhere; John Crump, Executive Director of the National Bar Association, for essential details concerning the National Bar Association and its membership; Professor James P. White of the Indiana University School of Law, Consultant on Legal Education to the American Bar Association, for critical data pertaining to the accreditation of law schools and bar examination results; Linda Flores, Executive Director, and Gretchen G. Wessell, Admissions Analyst for the Council on Legal Education Opportunity, for charts and textual material pertaining to the work and accomplishments of that highly significant agency.

When I started to explore the situation of blacks in the law as it existed in the sixteen cities, historically and currently, I found that the sources of published or recorded data were extremely sparse, indeed nonexistent in many areas. Accordingly, the number of lawyers, judges, law teachers, and private citizens who entered the spirit of the undertaking and telephoned, wrote, or briefed me in person was very substantial. In some areas, the amount of assistance rendered was phenomenal. In Pittsburgh, Judge Justin M. Johnson of the Superior Court of Pennsylvania, in order to ascertain the data available to the most knowledgeable black members of the legal profession in that city, first consulted with a distinguished black veteran of the bar, Richard F. Jones, and then assembled a group of black lawyers, judges, and other citizens urging them to supplement with their recollections my story of Pittsburgh. He then prepared for me a detailed account of the facts and suggestions developed at the meeting. Those who attended the meeting were Judge Paul A. Simmons, of the United States District Court for the Western District of Pennsylvania; Judges Thomas A. Harper, Livingstone M. Johnson, Henry R. Smith, Jr., and J. Warren Watson, of the Court of Common Pleas of Allegheny County; attorneys Burrell A. Brown, Byrd R. Brown, Wendell Freeland, Richard F. Jones, Garland H. McAdoo, Everett E. Utterback; and Mr. Clarence B. Clark.

San Francisco presented especially difficult problems, and Judge Cecil F. Poole, of the United States Court of Appeals for the Ninth Circuit, although at home convalescing from surgery, gave generously of his time and energy to analyze my account of San Francisco, to offer valid criticism, and to add helpful comments and suggestions. A friend of mine, Robert D. Raven, of the San Francisco bar, referred to me Shelley E. Wheeler, Assistant United States Attorney for the Northern District of California, who undertook the research of past and present black members of the San Francisco bar. Mr. Raven continued his interest and was always available when I called.

In Detroit, Otis M. Smith, Vice-President and General Counsel of General Motors Corporation, gave generously of his time, and provided lawyers in his department (Dennis Davenport and David A. Collins) to supply facts and check information. He met at length with Wade H. McCree, Jr., and together they furnished me with excellent suggestions and data concerning the Detroit situation.

In Boston, my friend of long standing, Robert W. Meserve, of the Boston bar, former President of the American Bar Association, arranged for his partner, Daniel R. Coquillette, to assist me with the Boston data. Mr. Coquillette analyzed meticulously the suggestions on Boston, adding, amending, and updating the article as well as checking the account historically. His then associate, Francis E. Ackerman, worked with him assiduously on the project.

In New York City, Judge Lawrence W. Pierce, of the United States Court of Appeals for the Second Circuit and Hope R. Stevens, a member of the New York bar, working separately, provided facts for many years in succession concerning the local black bench and bar and gave me valuable suggestions for my account of New York City. I am indebted to Jack Greenberg, Director-Counsel of the NAACP Legal Defense and Educational Fund for advising me to consult Mr. Stevens and for referring me to other sources in the New York area.

I am most grateful to my friend Leonard S. Janofsky of the Los Angeles bar, former President of the American Bar Association, for putting me in touch with Assistant Dean Lola M. McAlpin-Grant of the Loyola Law

School, Loyola Marymount University, who did considerable research and provided valuable data on Los Angeles. Mr. Janofsky generously stayed in touch with my work on the Los Angeles situation and made numerous valuable suggestions.

In Houston, my friend Leon Jaworski of that bar, former President of the American Bar Association, enlisted for me the aid of his young partner, A. Martin Wickliff, Jr., who assembled and interviewed a group of knowledgeable Texans and supplied considerable data on black lawyers who had practiced and were still practicing in that city. A valuable source of information was also his father, Aloysius M. Wickliff, Sr., of the Houston bar, as was Frank M. Wozencraft of that bar, who thoughtfully made certain that I was always up-to-date on the additions of black lawyers to the large Houston firms.

In Washington, D.C., Charles T. Duncan, former Dean of the Howard University School of Law and now a partner in a substantial firm in that city, was of immense assistance in sorting out the complicated situation in a city with so many black lawyers in both government and private practice. He and his young associate, Amy Applegate, amassed a large amount of material relevant to my topic. Dean Wiley A. Branton of the Howard University School of Law and Professor John A. Bauman, Executive Director of the Association of American Law Schools, were valuable sources of information in their respective spheres.

In Atlanta, Frank C. Jones of that bar most kindly enlisted for me the services of his partner, Larry D. Thompson, who in turn called upon Isabelle Gates Webster, an Assistant City Attorney of Atlanta. She recommended Atlanta attorney, Flora Devine, who contributed to the Atlanta source material. Mr. Thompson remained in constant touch with the ongoing research in Atlanta and was extremely helpful.

In the two Ohio cities, Cleveland and Columbus, I was fortunate to know people who could refer me to appropriate sources. Peter B. Roper, now Executive Director of the Pennsylvania Bar Association but formerly in that same post for the Bar Association of Greater Cleveland, referred me to his successor, Thomas J. Brady, who secured excellent staff help for me and himself participated in the assembling of useful material, including a history of the Cleveland Bar that told me a great deal about its black members over the years. He also sent to me a large supply of clippings from the *Cleveland Press* and the *Cleveland Plain Dealer* relating to black members of the Cleveland bar. In Columbus, my friend Earl F. Morris, former President of the American Bar Association, secured staff assistance for me and remained in touch to make sure that my needs in that city were satisfied.

In Richmond, Harvey Chappell, Jr., of the bar of that city, enthusiastically entered into the spirit of the research, forwarding to me both facts and suggestions that were of great help in constructing my report on blacks in the law in Richmond. It was he who enlisted the aid of Oliver W. Hill, highly respected black veteran of the Richmond Bar, who was good enough to share with me his memories and his current information concerning the black bar of that city.

In Minneapolis, another friend, David R. Brink of the bar of that city, President of the American Bar Association, interested Anna W. Shavers, an associate in a large Minneapolis firm, in assembling for me data concerning the local black bar, and she did a very good job indeed.

In Milwaukee, my friend John A. Kluwin, a member of that city's bar, engaged staff assistance to answer my questions and conduct the investigations required.

Finally, I return to Philadelphia. I found that considerable updating was necessary since much time had elapsed since I researched the material for my dissertation. Many people were helpful to me in my native city. William H. Brown III was a constant source for facts concerning the black bench and bar of Philadelphia. James D. Crawford and Deena J. Schneider assisted me in the analysis of bar examination data. The deans of the three law schools in the Philadelphia area—James O. Freedman of the University of Pennsylvania, Peter J. Liacouras of Temple University, and J. Willard O'Brien of Villanova University—provided or arranged for me to receive the necessary information on law student enrollment in their respective institutions, a constantly changing situation. At Pennsylvania, Rae L. Di-Blasi, Assistant to the Dean, and Ernie Gonsalves, Registrar, and at Villanova, Miriam J. McFadden, Registrar, promptly supplied whatever information I requested. At Temple, Dean Liacouras, who was of enormous help to me on numerous substantive questions, usually provided the data himself. He became President of Temple University July 1, 1982.

I had excellent staff help from Sheila F. Segal, a professional editor, who provided me with superb editorial help; Karen Porter, a young lawyer, now general manager of the *Pennsylvania Law Journal—Reporter* supplied high-quality research assistance; and Martha Aleo, another young attorney, devoted much of her attention to the footnotes. Librarians who graciously responded to my needs, which were many, included Nancy I. Arnold, Reference Librarian of the Biddle Law Library of the University of Pennsylvania, and Librarian Susanne E. Hahn and Assistant Librarian Patricia Johnson at the law firm of Schnader, Harrison, Segal & Lewis. Don M. Knerr, Comptroller of the same law firm, analyzed and frequently corrected the many statistics found in the book; assisting him was Linda Hall. Others associated with the law firm who provided staff assistance to me were Ellen M. Briggs, Esquire, who worked extensively on the footnotes; Susan Fishbein and Alison Irving, former legal assistants, who performed research and did considerable work on the footnotes; Patricia Bosak, who cheerfully and conscientiously typed and retyped endless pages of the manuscript; Carol Beal, in charge of duplicating, who did an excellent job, along with her assistant Joseph Di Sciasco; Una Scanlon, in charge of word processing, who, assisted by Theresa A. Kulakowski and Mary E. Kain, always seemed able, effortlessly, to process and reprocess the manuscript with its many corrections, in almost no time at all; Rhoda Tessler and Linda Young, who proofread extensively and were always letter perfect; and George Nedzbala and his staff for excellent messenger service. Barbara Thomas was at all times prepared to provide help where it was needed and did so graciously.

I shall never be able to express my gratitude to Jane Traphoner, executive secretary, my trusted friend for many years, who was constantly on hand to attend to every detail and who was deeply concerned about each aspect of the manuscript and its accuracy.

Harris Wofford, Counsel to Schnader, Harrison, Segal and Lewis, spent many hours checking and editing the manuscript, calling to my attention a new fact here, an oversight there, and always with good humor. How does one express gratitude for such a selfless undertaking?

For their patience and understanding and for their gentle guidance and encouragement, I am deeply indebted to Maurice English, Director, and Ingalill Hjelm, Managing Editor, of the University of Pennsylvania Press.

My son, Richard M. Segal, then Assistant Dean of Student Affairs of Princeton University, kept abreast of the progress of the book and offered valuable suggestions as I went along, and with his superb command of the language, he assisted in the drafting of the epilogue. I shall always be grateful.

My daughter and son-in-law, Loretta and Bruce A. Cohen and their children, Marc and Jennifer, were understanding as to why I could not make the usual frequent visits to their family and encouraged me in my project.

The one person who made it all possible and for whom adequate words fail me is the inspiration for this book, my husband, Bernard G. Segal, to whom I shall always be indebted for his dedication, devotion, and never-ending help all along the way.

# Introduction
# Facing the Obstacles

Throughout the first half of the twentieth century, and even beyond, to become a black lawyer in America required an extraordinary measure of courage, determination, and vision. To most blacks it was a goal that seemed to defy social and economic realities. Indeed, at the turn of the century W. E. B. Du Bois found that physicians and lawyers together comprised only 1.5 percent of the black population. According to the 1910 United States census, there were then only 798 black lawyers in the country, and by 1940 there were a mere 1,925—one black lawyer for every 13,000 blacks in America.

During those years blacks who did manage to become lawyers found themselves in a profession that was pervaded by racism and fundamentally segregated. Until 1937 there was no black federal judge in the nation, and even then it was a term appointment in the Virgin Islands; until 1949, none on a United States Circuit Court; until 1961, none on a United States District Court; and until 1967, none on the United States Supreme Court. Until 1936, blacks were not admitted to "white" law schools. Until 1943 color had to be stated on applications to the American Bar Association. Until 1946 there was no black teacher on the faculty of predominantly white law schools. Thus the picture of the legal community was a sobering one to black hopefuls; black role models in the legal profession were few, and the disincentives to blacks were many.

## Legal Education

For blacks seeking to become lawyers, the fundamental discouragement has been the difficulty of obtaining a legal education, especially during the period 1900 to 1930. Since the states individually began to require a law degree for the practice of law at the turn of the century, the racial and economic barriers to a legal education have posed a continuing problem for blacks. Realizing that the requirements of white law schools would severely restrict their entrance into the profession, blacks had already, during the last half of the nineteenth century, begun to establish their own law schools. However, eighteen of the nineteen black law schools established prior to 1900 did not prosper and had to be discontinued.

1

The only surviving black law school, and still the foremost black law school in the United States, is Howard University Law School in Washington, D.C., founded and chartered by the federal government in 1869 and named for General Oliver O. Howard, head of the Freedmen's Bureau.[1] Because of the demoralizing conditions created by the resurgence of racism when Reconstruction ended, Howard University had to close its doors for a year in 1876. Between 1877 and 1935 Howard was the only substantial source of legal education for blacks in the United States. During this period no black could obtain a legal education in an approved law school anywhere south of Washington, D.C.[2]

During the next twelve years three other currently functioning accredited black law schools, all state institutions and all in the South, came into existence. The first of these was North Carolina Central University Law School in Durham, North Carolina, founded in 1939. The next two, both founded in 1947, were Texas Southern University Law School in Houston, Texas, and Southern University Law School in Baton Rouge, Louisiana.[3] Howard and these three state black law schools have trained the majority of black lawyers in the nation.[4]

Not content with the perpetuation of a situation that limited blacks to black law schools, skilled black advocates instituted suits beginning in the middle 1930s on the reasoning that blacks were entitled to a common educational forum with whites if they were to practice the same law.[5] Under the leadership of Charles H. Houston, and later Thurgood Marshall, and under the auspices of the NAACP Legal Defense and Educational Fund, a series of lawsuits were filed to obtain for blacks the right to attend predominantly white southern law schools.[6] When Houston and Marshall took up the fight to enable Donald Murray, a 1934 black graduate of Amherst College, to enter the University of Maryland Law School,[7] legal barriers restricting admission of blacks to white law schools began to fall, but only after persistent and effective advocacy produced court orders mandating this result. It was to be many years before the white academic legal community became fully aware of the extent of the problems faced

---

1. Harold R. Washington, "History and Role of Black Law Schools," *Howard Law Journal*, vol. 18, no. 2 (1974), p. 389.

2. John P. Davis, ed., *The American Negro Reference Book* (Englewood Cliffs, N.J.: Prentice-Hall, 1966), p. 584; Washington, "History and Role," p. 390.

3. Washington, "History and Role," pp. 399, 401, 404.

4. Kellis E. Parker and Betty J. Stebman, "Legal Education for Blacks," *Annals of the American Academy of Political and Social Science*, vol. 407 (May 1973), p. 146.

5. See, e.g., *Missouri ex rel. Gaines v. Canada*, 305 U.S. 337, 345 (1938).

6. Parker and Stebman, "Legal Education," p. 146, n. 7 (citing *Missouri ex rel. Gaines v. Canada*, 305 U.S. 337 (1938); *Sipuel v. Board of Regents of University of Oklahoma*, 332 U.S. 631 (1948); *McLaurin v. Oklahoma State Regents*, 339 U. S. 637 (1950); *McKissick v. Carmichael*, 187 F.2d 949 (4th Cir. 1951).

7. *Pearson v. Murray*, 168 Md. 478, 182 A. 590 (1936).

by blacks who dreamed of becoming lawyers and began to correct its own discriminatory practices.

With the passage of civil rights legislation in the early 1960s, there was a dramatic turnabout in national concern for the rights of minorities, and this change was notable within the academic legal community. Although a number of white law schools still continued to adhere to policies of racial exclusion,[8] there were some that recognized their responsibilities to potential black law students and began to take meaningful steps toward cure. In 1962, for instance, members of the faculty of the University of Pennsylvania Law School, spurred on by a black lawyer's criticism of the pitifully small number of black Penn law graduates, contributed $12,000 to help finance black applicants admitted to the school. The following year that law school admitted five black students instead of the usual one.[9]

However, it was not until 1964, some 147 years after formal legal education in the United States began, that the Association of American Law Schools' Committee on Racial Discrimination could state for the first time that no member school reported denying admission to any applicant on grounds of race or color.[10]

Undoubtedly, the decision of the United States Supreme Court in *Brown v. Board of Education,*[11] handed down in 1954, had some significant impact on the thinking of white law schools. This case held that segregation of white and Negro children in the public schools of a state solely on the basis of race, pursuant to state laws permitting or requiring such segregation, denies Negro children the equal protection of the laws guaranteed by the Fourteenth Amendment, even though the physical facilities and other "tangible" factors of white and Negro schools may be equal. Thus *Brown v. Board of Education* overruled the "separate but equal" doctrine approved by the Supreme Court in 1896 in *Plessy v. Ferguson,*[12] which had provided legal support for segregated school systems for fifty-eight years. While no one informed on the subject would doubt that the denial of admission to black students continued in 1964 and after in a substantial number of AALS law schools,[13] at least by 1964 no such institution was willing to admit that it engaged in such conduct.

8. Walter J. Leonard, "Foreword," *Harvard Law School Bulletin,* vol. 22 (February, 1971), p. 7.
9. Interview with a black lawyer in the senior age-group.
10. *AALS Proceedings,* Part One: Reports of Committees, 1964, p. 159.
11. 347 U.S. 483 (1954).
12. 163 U.S. 537 (1896).
13. Of approximately 700 black students enrolled in ABA-approved law schools in the academic year 1964–65, one-third, or 267, were students in five predominantly black law schools. Thus, throughout the United States there were only 433 black students in predominantly white law schools. "Report of the Philadelphia Bar Association Special Committee on Pennsylvania Bar Admission Procedures—Racial Discrimination of Pennsylvania Bar Examinations," *Temple Law Quarterly,* vol. 44, no. 2 (Winter 1971), pp. 141, 182.

After this milestone was reached, changes came more rapidly. The efforts of some to overcome the history of systematic exclusion of blacks from the legal profession became the efforts of many. By the late 1960s most law schools,[14] spurred on by the civil rights legislation and by the argument that minority lawyers could benefit the country in numerous ways, had initiated minority recruitment and admissions programs. First, it was thought that they would empathize with individuals of minority groups who were in need of legal representation.[15] Second, many argued that the increase in black lawyers would to some extent diminish prejudice, enhance the image of blacks, and reduce black resentment and self-hatred.[16]

Overt policies of racial discrimination in admissions were not the only barriers that potential black law students had to overcome. Many blacks grew up in deprived environments and did not receive in early life the educational opportunities that would allow them to compete in higher education. Further, few families or friends offered strong encouragement to the black would-be lawyer. In 1959, G. Franklin Edwards, using a predominantly southern group as a sample, wrote that the "law has not been regarded as a desirable profession among members of the Negro group." It was referred to as a "starvation profession." Parents deliberately discouraged their children from entering the legal profession. They were skeptical of the black lawyer's ability to obtain justice in the courts; they realized that a large proportion of the black community chose white lawyers to represent them; and they knew that black lawyers frequently had to associate themselves with white lawyers and split fees if they wanted clients.[17]

The discouragement facing potential black lawyers graphically appears in the advice given to Malcolm X when he discussed his career plans with his high-school teacher and adviser:

". . . Malcolm, you ought to be thinking about a career. Have you been giving it thought?"

". . . I've been thinking I'd like to be a lawyer."

". . . Malcolm, one of life's first needs is for us to be realistic. . . . You've got to be realistic about being a nigger. A lawyer—that's no realistic goal for a nigger."[18]

14. Ernest J. Gellhorn, "The Law Schools and the Negro," *Duke Law Journal,* vol. 1968, no. 5 (October 1968), p. 1069.

15. Charles A. Penderhughes, "Increasing Minority Group Students in Law Schools: The Rationale and the Critical Issues," *Buffalo Law Review,* vol. 20 (1971), p. 447.

16. Henry W. McGee, Jr., "Black Lawyers and the Struggle for Racial Justice in the American Social Order," *Buffalo Law Review,* vol. 20 (1971), p. 423.

17. G. Franklin Edwards, *The Negro Professional Class* (Glencoe, Ill.: Free Press, 1959), p. 135.

18. Alex Haley, *The Autobiography of Malcolm X* (New York: Grove Press, 1964), pp. 36–37.

In addition to family opposition, educational handicaps, and humiliating conditions diverting blacks from a career in the law, there was the problem of the high costs of both undergraduate and law school education. Edwards's study disclosed that blacks entering the legal profession had the least financial support from their families, the median income of black parents being lower than that of any other group. Even where black parents could afford to help their children to study law, they hesitated to do so because they saw no future for blacks in that profession.[19]

Prior to the 1960s few scholarships were available and universities had not yet launched their large-scale recruitment programs for disadvantaged students.[20] In the mid-1960s a number of philanthropic organizations attempted to spur the interest of blacks in becoming lawyers by making grants to reduce the financial barriers to their entering law school. Notable among such endeavors was the 1964 Ford Foundation grant of $1,800,000 to the Howard University Law School, $900,000 of which was to be used for scholarships and other forms of student aid. In the late 1960s some of the other large foundations and many private donors followed this lead by making additional pioneering grants to fund programs, such as the NAACP Legal Defense Fund Project, the Earl Warren Legal Training Program, and other local efforts[21] to ensure a larger enrollment of black students in law schools.[22]

However, despite these efforts to reduce financial obstacles, most blacks desiring to become lawyers were still unable to embark upon a legal education by the end of the decade. This nationwide problem alarmed both educators and government officials. Accordingly, with the encouragement of the United States Office of Economic Opportunity, the Council on Legal Education Opportunity was formed. This organization, known as CLEO, was chartered in 1968 and was sponsored by the Association of American Law Schools, the American Bar Association, the National Bar Association, and the Law School Admissions Test Council.[23] Its purpose was to help remedy the underrepresentation of disadvantaged groups in the legal profession by expanding their opportunities to study and practice law.[24]

In 1968 CLEO started a drive to double black enrollment in law schools within five years.[25] To accomplish this goal, it initiated pre-law

19. Edwards, *Negro Professional Class*, p. 135.

20. Marion S. Goldman, *A Portrait of the Black Attorney in Chicago* (Chicago: American Bar Foundation, 1972), p. 13.

21. Parker and Stebman, "Legal Education," pp. 150–51.

22. Ibid., p. 149 (citing the American Bar Endowment, the Carnegie Corporation of New York, the Field Foundation, the Ford Foundation, and the Rockefeller Brothers Fund).

23. Parker and Stebman, "Legal Education," p. 148.

24. Ibid. (Citing Nancy Fulop, "1969 CLEO Reports: A Summary," *University of Toledo Law Review*, 1970.) P. 633.

25. Parker and Stebman, "Legal Education," p. 148.

summer institutes intended to assess the participants' prospects for success as law students, provide additional motivation for them to become lawyers, and generally ease their transition to law school. The first institutes were so successful that every year since 1970 seven have been conducted in law schools around the nation for a total of about two hundred students each summer. CLEO assists the successful students in obtaining scholarships or loan funds covering full tuition and has also provided $1,000 per year for each student's living expenses during law school. The Ford Foundation and the Carnegie Corporation of New York gave material assistance at the start, but since then CLEO's funds have come from the federal government. CLEO continues to provide assistance to black students and to students of other racial minorities, as well as to economically disadvantaged white students,[26] although its 1982 budget was cut by 4 percent. The fate of its 1983 program is hanging in the balance, along with that of many programs which may be drastically reduced or closed down by federal budget cuts. Professor Ralph Smith, of the University of Pennsylvania Law School, comments, "At a time when so few things work, the CLEO model stands out as one which deserves continued support, expansion and replication."[27]

That the increased financial aid and remedial programs detailed above were successful to a significant degree is clear from the dramatic increases in black enrollment in law schools all over the country during the late 1960s and early 1970s. In 1965, Harvard Law School estimated that of the approximately 65,000 law students in accredited law schools in the nation, there were no more than 700 black students, or approximately 1 percent.[28] By 1972 the 4,423 black students constituted 4.3 percent[29] of all students attending accredited law schools in the country, and by the 1976–77 school year there were 5,503 black students, or about 4.7 percent of the total, in approved law schools.[30]

In the succeeding three school years, however, black enrollment leveled off instead of continuing its prior record of steady growth. Although total law student enrollments in approved law schools had been climbing

26. Statistical facts pertaining to CLEO participants from the program's inception in 1968 through December 1979, compiled by CLEO in its offices in Washington, D.C., are contained in Appendix 5.

27. Ralph R. Smith, "The CLEO Experience: A Success by Any Measure," *Howard Law Journal,* vol. 22, no. 3 (1979), p. 408.

28. Parker and Stebman, "Legal Education," p. 147.

29. Ibid.

30. Association of American Law Schools, *A Review of Legal Education in the United States —Fall 1978: Law Schools and Admission to the Bar Requirements* (ABA Section of Legal Education and Admissions to the Bar, 1979), p. 60. (Figures were not available for the 1970–71 school year.)

steadily from the 1969–70 through the 1976–77 academic years, the number of black law students in the 1977–78, 1978–79, and 1979–80 academic years was below that of 1976–77; in the 1980–81 academic year black enrollment resumed its climb and slightly exceeded 1976–77, and a further increase took place in 1981–82. These developments are reflected in Table 1, below.[31]

Whether there is any significance in the resumption of the increase of black enrollments in law schools during the 1980–81 school year, in contrast to the decline during the period from 1977–78 through 1979–80, cannot yet be determined. At best the increase is modest, and only a single year is involved, but at least the development reverses a three-year trend. Now the question is to what extent government cutbacks will affect the situation.

There has been some speculation that the Supreme Court's 1978 decision in *Regents of the University of California v. Bakke*,[32] a case involving a challenge to a medical school's affirmative-action program, had a chilling effect on black applications to law schools. In *Bakke* the court did not declare it unconstitutional for a state university to attempt to rectify past discrimination by favoring the members of minority groups in its admis-

Table 1
**Black American Students Enrolled in J.D. and LL.B. Programs in Approved Law Schools**

| Year | Black Students |
|---|---|
| 1969–70 | 2,128 |
| 1971–72 | 3,744 |
| 1972–73 | 4,423 |
| 1973–74 | 4,817 |
| 1974–75 | 4,995 |
| 1975–76 | 5,127 |
| 1976–77 | 5,503 |
| 1977–78 | 5,304 |
| 1978–79 | 5,350 |
| 1979–80 | 5,257 |
| 1980–81 | 5,506 |
| 1981–82 | 5,789 |

31. Ibid.; ABA Section of Legal Education and Admissions to the Bar, Memorandum QS 8182-28 from James P. White, Consultant on Legal Education to the American Bar Association, to Deans of ABA Approved Law Schools, "Minority Group J.D. and LL.B. Candidate Enrollment in Approved Law Schools 1971–1981," June 1982.
32. 438 U.S. 265 (1978).

sions process. However, by upholding Mr. Bakke in his challenge of one school's affirmative-action program, it did throw serious doubt on the permissible means to accomplish these goals in the future. Although the decision is subject to widely varying interpretations, it has been claimed that it has caused numerous law schools to reassess their commitment to affirmative action (not including, however, such leading law schools as Harvard, Yale, Columbia, Pennsylvania, and Stanford, but a sufficient number to cause real concern). Thus, in December 1978, Junius W. Williams, then President of the National Bar Association, noted that in response to *Bakke:*

> [A] disappointing 25 colleges and universities across the nation have dropped their affirmative action programs. In general, every law school is reevaluating its program, possibly looking for loopholes. As a result, circumstances are looking bleaker for those minority students who have dreams of matriculating at a major university.[33]

Following the *Bakke* decision, the American Bar Association Board of Governors appointed the Task Force for Improvement of Legal Education and Professional Opportunities for the Disadvantaged, chaired by Erwin N. Griswold, former Harvard Law School dean, later United States Solicitor General. The committee recommended that the ABA continue to expand its efforts to increase the number of minority and disadvantaged students in law schools. As a result, the ABA Section on Legal Education and Admissions to the Bar, after considerable study and debate, recommended to the ABA House of Delegates, and the house adopted in 1980, a new Standard 212 of the Standards for the Approval of Law Schools, which requires law schools, in order to qualify for approval, to

> demonstrate, or have carried out and maintained, by concrete action, a commitment to providing full opportunities for the study of law and entry into the profession by qualified members of groups (notably racial and ethnic minorities) which have been victims of discrimination in various forms. This commitment would typically include a special concern for determining the potential of such applicants through the admission process, special recruitment efforts, and a program which assists in meeting the unusual financial needs of many such students, provided that no school is obligated to apply standards for the award of financial assistance different from those applied to other students.[34]

33. *National Bar Bulletin,* vol. 10, no. 8 (December 1978), p. 2.
34. ABA Proposed Standard 212, August, 1980. While the House of Delegates approved the Section's original recommendation as quoted above, it also approved a somewhat watered-down substitute proposed by the Board of Governors which merely states that "law

Although minority spokesmen have criticized the new standard as vague, it does demonstrate a continuing commitment to affirmative action in legal education.

Regardless of the effectiveness of the standard, however, it seems probable that factors other than the elimination or reduction of enforcement of vigorous affirmative-action programs have played a large part in causing the recent lack of growth in black enrollments, factors such as the increasing shortage of funds needed to finance legal education today. In an address before the Old Dominion Bar Association in 1979, Dr. J. Clay Smith, Jr., at the time a member of the Equal Employment Opportunity Commission (EEOC) and later President of the Federal Bar Association, postulated that "one of the greatest deterrents to increased ranks of blacks as lawyers in the work force may be the growing cost of tuition in state and private colleges," accompanied by fewer available loan and scholarship funds, lack of legal positions for law school graduates, and, perhaps of the greatest overall effect, the current nationwide recession and the continuing inflation.[35]

It is also apparent that some gifted black youths are choosing other careers, such as business, banking, or government, over the practice of law as more promising and lucrative. The high black failure rate in bar examinations, which has received considerable publicity, may also have been a significant deterrent to blacks considering applying to law school. At the same time, law schools may well have been raising their admissions standards as a reaction to the relatively low number of blacks who were passing the state bar examinations. This was certainly true of the University of Connecticut Law School, whose dean stated that admissions standards were raised in 1975 after it was realized that a "disproportionate" number of blacks were failing the Connecticut bar examination.[36]

The assumption that LSAT scores, grade-point averages, and even the bar examination itself are accurate indicators of potential legal skills has been vigorously attacked. One of the law school deans who has questioned the objectivity of such admissions criteria comments, "We do not have . . . neutral admissions standards. . . . They tend to be artificial, exclusionary standards. They are standards not positively correlated to lawyering even if they may be predictors of how well one will perform on first year tests in law school and multiple choice bar exams." For, he asks, "What do law school admissions standards based solely on GPA [grade-point average]

---

schools are *urged to demonstrate, by* concrete action, *a commitment to expanding* opportunities. . . ." Ibid. (Changes from the original recommendation indicated by italics.)

35. J. Clay Smith, Jr., Speech at Annual Convention of the Old Dominion Bar Association, Lynchburg, Va., May 26, 1979, "The Future of the Black Lawyer in America."

36. *New Haven Register,* June 27, 1977.

and LSAT have to do with selecting each of those applicants who, taken as an individual whole, will probably become good lawyers? Without proof of that premise, how can we be convinced that by lowering the GPA and LSAT requirements we necessarily are lowering achievement standards and aptitude for lawyering?"[37]

Statistics compiled on black law students who entered law school under the CLEO program tend to support this dean's opinion. The figures show that the majority of participants successfully maintained good academic standing in law school, graduated, and then passed a bar examination. These results were achieved despite the fact that their numerical indicators, particularly their LSAT scores, ordinarily would have made their admission to law school unlikely. In addition, a survey of the present employment of participants shows that they are serving in legal roles of social significance, including service as judges, law professors, and directors of legal projects focusing on the legal needs of previously underrepresented segments of the population.[38] Other studies even question the proposition that LSAT scores, in particular, are good predictors of law school grades and hypothesize that heavy reliance on LSATs results in denying admittance to black applicants well qualified to succeed in law school.[39]

Alternative admission models to grade-point averages and LSAT scores are currently in use at Temple University School of Law and in the Urban Legal Studies Program at City College of New York.[40] These models give considerable weight to the racial composition of the student body, personal characteristics of applicants not reflected in test scores and grades, and career goals that coincide with legal needs of the community.

## Admission to the Bar

Ever since the adoption of rules barring any indication of the color of applicants in state bar application and examination records, it has been

37. "Symposium: The Minority Candidate and the Bar Examination," *Black Law Journal,* vol. 5, no. 1 (1977), pp. 156–57.

38. Wade J. Henderson and Linda Flores, "Implications for Affirmative Action in Legal Education After Bakke: Analysis of Academic and Bar Performance by Council on Legal Education and Opportunity Fellows, 1968–1978," in *Towards a Diversified Legal Profession: An Inquiry into the Law School Admissions Test, Grade Inflation, and Current Admission Policies,* ed. David White (San Francisco: Julian Richardson Associates for the National Council of Black Lawyers, 1981).

39. Allan Nairn, "Standardized Selection Criteria and a Diverse Legal Profession"; David M. White, "An Investigation into the Validity and Cultural Bias of the LSAT"; and Joseph L. Gannon, "College Grads and LSAT Scores," in *Towards a Diversified Legal Profession.*

40. Susan E. Brown and Eduardo Murenco, Jr., "Innovative Models for Increasing Minority Access to the Legal Profession," in *Towards a Diversified Legal Profession.*

difficult to obtain racial breakdowns on those passing or failing bar examinations in particular states.[41] The information available establishes that black lawyers have failed at a greater rate than white candidates. A number of studies in the early 1970s, before indicia of color were eliminated, brought to light the seriousness of the problem. The data in Table 2, extracted from a 1973 study by Lani Guiner, a member of the National Conference of Black Lawyers,[42] is illustrative of the general problem black lawyers have faced in state bar examinations.

Table 2
**State Statistics on Failing Rate of Black Candidates for Bar Examinations**

| | |
|---|---|
| California (no year given) | 56% of blacks and Latins failed<br>24% of nonminorities failed |
| District of Columbia June 1973 | 184 of 200 blacks failed (92%) |
| Georgia 1972 | 41 of 41 blacks failed (100%) |
| Illinois August 1972 | 30 of 40 blacks failed (75%) |
| March 1973 | 12 of 16 blacks failed (75%) |
| Nebraska June 1972 | 5 of 10 blacks failed (50%) |
| January 1973 | 1 of 9 blacks failed (11%) |
| Ohio 1973 | 11 of 29 blacks failed (38%) |
| Virginia 1970 | 24 of 30 blacks failed (80%) |

The results of the 1972 Georgia bar examination demonstrated that even blacks graduating from top-ranking "Ivy League" law schools did not fare well:

The results show that all 41 blacks who took the bar failed—while 50 percent of whites passed compared to 0 percent of the blacks.

All of the white Yale law school graduates who took the Georgia test passed, but the two black Yale graduates failed. All of the white Harvard law school graduates passed and the one black Harvard person failed.

41. When contacted, the National Conference of Bar Examiners reported that it maintains no data on the pass rates of blacks taking bar examinations and is unable to identify any other source for this information. Letter from National Conference of Bar Examiners, November 28, 1979.

42. "Symposium: The Minority Candidate," pp. 124–26. Several states other than those whose data are reported here were also analyzed.

All of the white Columbia law students passed and the three black graduates from Columbia failed.[43]

As disturbing as these fail rates of black candidates are, there is evidence that, after a temporary improvement in the mid-1970s, the problem is again increasing. The *National Law Journal* reported in 1980 that while pass rates on bar examinations among all students have been decreasing in recent years, black pass rates have fallen especially low. Recent pass rates in bar examinations for students at Howard, for instance, have fallen to 25 percent, and this is said to reflect the national pass rate for blacks.[44]

Several possible reasons have been suggested for the high black failure rate on state bar examinations. First among these is the lowering of admission standards at law schools since the late 1960s in order to attract more black law students. Dean William Warren of the University of California School of Law (UCLA) elaborated on this issue at a symposium in May 1976:

We have minority students in every quartile of the class and the same is true of the bar. We find that minority students that come to us with LSAT scores of 520 and over and undergraduate grade point averages of 3.20 and over are doing as well on the bar as regular students with LSAT scores of 150 points higher. In short, before we change what we are doing in law school instruction to get more minority students through the bar, let's be sure there is something wrong with the instruction now. If minority students will do as well as anglo students with the same qualifications, I submit the problem is not instruction, but admissions. If we simply raised our floor of admission to a 500 LSAT and a 3.00 GPA we should probably have very few people who would not get by the bar on at least the second time. We haven't been willing to do that because we have been willing to take high risks because we want more minority lawyers, but the fact that we will take greater risks does not mean that we are failing in our task of teaching students.

The sad, cruel lesson we learned at UCLA is that if people with low admission standards are admitted, however strong their motivation, however good the remedial teaching, they are going to have a great deal of trouble on the bar. Their chances on the bar are going to be from one in five to one in ten. I question if this is a rational allocation of our scarce resources.[45]

43. Ibid., p. 127.
44. Jonathan M. Winer, "It's Harder to Become a Lawyer," *National Law Journal,* August 25, 1980. p. 12.
45. "Symposium: The Minority Candidate," p. 151.

Dissatisfaction with the high failure rate has given rise to complaints against bar examinations ranging from the charge that the type of question and the system of grading inherently operate to the prejudice of the black applicant, to the charge of intentional discrimination. These accusations have generated litigation that has spanned the nation.[46]

One such case, *Tyler v. Vickery*,[47] was filed after slightly more than half the black candidates failed the 1972 and 1973 Georgia bar examinations, compared with roughly one-quarter of the white examinees. The argument of discrimination based on the use of "Black English" by black examinees was rejected by the United States Court of Appeals for the Fifth Circuit for several reasons: (1) the dialect was found to be one not limited to blacks but shared by southern whites as well; (2) graders were unlikely to spot use of "Black English" on examinations; and (3) blacks did not do well on the multiple-choice portion of the examination, which could not betray linguistic differences because of its objective answer form.[48] The court further held that the Georgia bar examinations did not discriminate against blacks in violation of the Equal Protection clause of the Fourteenth

46. Alabama: *Parrish v. Board of Commissioners*, 533 F.2d 942 (5th Cir. 1976). Arizona: *Murray v. Superior Court*, No. 72-2101 (9th Cir. Aug. 29, 1973). California: *Burge v. Committee of Bar Examiners*, No. C-741010SAW (N.D. Calif. June 11, 1976). Colorado: *Pacheco v. Pringle*, No. C-5219 (D. Colo. June 19, 1975). Connecticut: *Robinson v. Nair*, No. 123126 (New Haven Co. Super. Ct. Sept. 12, 1978). District of Columbia: *Feldman v. Gardner*, No. 78-0957 (D. D. C. Oct. 24, 1978); *Harper v. District of Columbia Committee on Admissions*, 375 A.2d 25 (D.C. App. 1977). Florida: *Marmol v. Adkins*, No. 76-1541 Vickery, 517 F.2d 1089 (5th Cir. 1975), *cert. denied*, 426 U.S 940 (1976); *Atwell v. Georgia*, No. C-78-1612A (N.D. Ga. Feb. 13, 1979). Illinois: *Whitfield v. Illinois Board of Law Examiners*, 540 F.2d 474 (7th Cir. 1974); *Ktsanes v. Underwood*, 467 F. Supp. 1002 (N.D. Ill. 1979). Kansas: *Murphy v. Fatzer*, No. 76-1265 (10th Cir. June 6, 1977). Kentucky: *Conley v. Kentucky State Board of Law Examiners*, No. 22-7922 (Jefferson Cir. Ct. Ky., Sept. 12, 1977), *aff'd* 582 F.2d 869 (1978). Louisiana: *Singleton v. Louisiana State Bar Association*, 413 F. Supp. 1092 (E.D. La. 1971); *Harris v. Louisiana State Supreme Court*, 334 F. Supp. 1289 (E.D. La. 1971). Maryland: *Marshall v. Murphy*, No. B-78-873 (D. Md. May 11, 1979); *Pettit v. Gingerich*, 427 F. Supp. 282 (D. Md. 1977), aff'd 582 F.2d 869 (1978); Michigan: *Oehmke v. Michigan*, No. 5532 (D. Mich. Apr. 18, 1974). Mississippi: *Lile v. Zant*, No. 74-89 (S.D. Miss. Dec. 12, 1977). Missouri: *Newsome v. Dominique*, 455 F. Supp. 1373 (E.D. Mo. 1978). Montana: *Hoffman v. Montana Supreme Court*, 372 F. Supp. 1175 (D. Mont. 1974), *aff'd* 419 U.S. 955 (1974). New Mexico: *In Re Pacheco*, 85 N.M. 600, 514 P.2d 1297 (1973); *Melendex v. Burciaga*, No. 78-2138 (Santa Fe County Dist. Ct., N.M., Dec. 20, 1978). North Carolina: *North Carolina Association of Black Lawyers v. Board of Law Examiners*, No. 4483-1973 (E.D. N.C. Jan. 11, 1978). Ohio: *Lewis v. Hartsock*, No. 73-16 (S.D. Ohio, Mar. 9, 1976), *aff'd* No. 76-1184 (6th Cir. Feb. 28, 1978). South Carolina: *Richardson v. McFadden*, 563 F.2d 1130 (4th Cir. 1977), *cert. denied*, 435 U.S. 978 (1978). Virginia: *Woodward v. Virginia Board of Bar Examiners*, 420 F. Supp. 211 (E.D. Va. 1976), *aff'd* 598 F.2d 1345 (4th Cir. 1979); *Lee v. Kuykendall*, No. 505-72-R (E.D. Va. Jul. 20, 1973).

47. 517 F.2d 1089 (5th Cir. 1973).

48. Ibid., pp. 1094–95. See also "Constitutional Law—Georgia's Bar Exam Does Not Unconstitutionally Discriminate on the Basis of Race," *Mercer Law Review*, vol. 27, no. 4 (Summer 1976), p. 1189.

Amendment and that traditional constitutional tests, rather than the stricter EEOC guidelines, are the appropriate standards by which the constitutionality of the examinations must be judged. The court held that standards derived from Title VII of the Civil Rights Act of 1964 do not apply. *Tyler* became an important precedent, cited by many courts in subsequent decisions.

In 1976, in the case of *Richardson v. McFadden,* [49] the United States Court of Appeals for the Fourth Circuit rejected a challenge by black applicants failing the South Carolina bar examination. The court found no evidence of *de jure* discrimination and agreed with the court in *Tyler* that job-relatedness standards derived from Title VII were not applicable in the bar examination context. [50]

In *Parrish v. Board of Commissioners,* another 1976 case, the plaintiff challenged the Alabama bar examination. The United States Court of Appeals for the Fifth Circuit reaffirmed its holding in *Tyler* that Title VII standards are not applicable to bar examinations. However, the court did remand *Parrish* for consideration of whether a photograph could be required as part of the application to take the bar examination. The court indicated that the use of photographs, by itself, did not establish discrimination but only "an opportunity to discriminate. . . ." [51]

In *Pettit v. Gingerich* the plaintiffs, challenging the Maryland Bar admission process, did not question the job relatedness of the bar examination but did charge cultural bias by the examiners as well as lack of scientific validation of the examination. It was alleged that while approximately 50 percent of all whites taking the examination between 1962 and 1972 had passed, the black pass rate had been only 6 percent, and that in 1973 half the whites had passed, in contrast to 12 percent of the blacks. [52] The Maryland District Court found that the "Board has no opportunity to discriminate in either the preparation, administration or grading of the Maryland bar examination." The court further noted that the procedures of the Maryland examiners "conclusively insure the anonymity of bar examination candidates and concomitantly, the impossibility of discrimination." [53]

The latest decision was issued in *Delgado v. McTighe* [54] by the Uni-

---

49. 540 F.2d 744 (4th Cir. 1976).

50. Ibid., p. 748. See Also, "Recent Decisions: Constitutional Law—Fourteenth Amendment—Challenging the South Carolina Bar Exam," *Marquette Law Review,* vol. 60, no. 4 (Summer 1977), p. 1134; "Recent Decisions: Civil Rights—State Bar Held Constitutional Despite Disproportionate Failure Rate of Minority Applicants—*Richardson v. McFadden,*" *Maryland Law Review,* vol. 36, no. 4 (1977), p. 886.

51. 533 F.2d 942 (5th Cir. 1976), p. 950.

52. 427 F. Supp. 282 (D. Md. 1977), p. 290 and n. 4.

53. Ibid., p. 292.

54. Discussed below, Chapter 5, pp. 63–74.

ted States District Court for the Eastern District of Pennsylvania on August 10, 1981.[55] Denying the claims of plaintiffs—three blacks and two Hispanics—that changes in passing grades were made arbitrarily and with intent to discriminate against minorities, and that the bar examination was not rationally related to determining minimum competence to practice law, Judge Raymond Broderick entered judgment for the defendants, the Pennsylvania Board of Law Examiners and its individual members.

In his supporting Memorandum, Judge Broderick goes into great detail concerning total average pass rates and pass rates for blacks, but he concludes: "In setting the passing grade on the Pennsylvania bar examination, the Board has always been concerned exclusively with determining what grade in its view demonstrated minimum competence to practice law."[56]

The cases above are only a sampling of court decisions from all over the country, but they represent the trend of adhering to the following legal principles:

> Intentional discrimination must be proved against bar examiners if an equal protection claim is to succeed; racial discrimination will not be inferred from statistics demonstrating adverse impact alone.
> Professional validation of bar examinations in accord with the EEOC Guidelines is not required where constitutional claims are advanced; the proper judicial stance is deferral to the "considered judgment" of bar examiners as to examination content and use.[57]

Another reason for the high black failure rate in bar examinations was advanced by Herbert O. Reid, then Acting Dean of the Howard Law School, who in 1974 rejected out of hand the charge of "conscious discrimination." He added that there "is probably more of a disposition to admit blacks than at any time in my memory—they've got some dirty work that has to be done, serving poor people." Dean Reid also said that he "suspects that at least a part of the explanation lies in [the] psychological upheaval black students (and black Americans generally) went through during the 1960s."[58]

> The period we went through made a lot of blacks question the system instead of learning it. . . . Educated and gifted blacks have always been subject to a downward pull from the rest of the community. . . . One result is a "sort of anti-intellectualism"—an attitude that says that they are qualified because they are here and their people need them

55. 522 F. Supp. 886 (E.D. Pa. 1981).

56. Ibid., p. 890.

57. Linda Greene, Introductory Presentation to Panel Three, "Search for Solutions," published in *Black Law Journal*, vol. 5, no. 1 (1977), pp. 186–87.

58. William Raspberry, contributing to the topic "The Painful Problem of Blacks and Legal Education," in *Student Lawyer*, April 1974, pp. 33–37.

. . . without recognizing the highly competitive nature of the profession they have chosen."[59]

While few minority plaintiffs have been successful in proving discrimination by bar examiners, it seems that bar examination litigation nonetheless has stimulated closer scrutiny of the examinations by bar examiners for fairness and for potential bias. Moreover, there is a growing trend toward questioning the ability of the bar examination as currently constituted to identify those who are qualified to become good practicing attorneys. For instance, one commentator questions the assumption that attorneys in every field of law need a certain degree of standard English proficiency. He also raises the question whether the use of a stylistically different, though not necessarily incorrect, form of English should be viewed so negatively as to submerge other qualities possessed by the examinee and to outweigh society's great need for black lawyers who in other respects are qualified for the practice of law.[60]

In response to criticism of examinations, California bar examiners in July 1980 gave an experimental test to selected applicants on such practical lawyering skills as trial advocacy, client counseling, and legal research. The applicants were permitted to substitute favorable evaluation of these skills for either the multiple-choice portion or the essay portion of their ordinary bar examination. There is evidence of considerable interest in this special examination designed to eliminate cultural bias against minorities. Bar examiners in other states are considering the California experiment as a possible model, and the costs of the experimental tests have been partially subsidized by the National Conference of Bar Examiners. It has been asserted that if the experiment is successful in California, this may result in diminishing or even eliminating the current high minority failure rates.

In his exhaustive Memorandum supporting his decision in *Delgado v. McTighe,* United States District Judge Broderick, after rejecting the claims of the minority plaintiffs of discrimination against them by the Pennsylvania Board of Law Examiners, and the inappropriateness of the bar examinations, states: "Although affirmative action policies in admitting minorities to law schools are now affording more minorities the opportunities to take the Pennsylvania bar examination, the record of their disproportionate failures cries out for an in-depth study to ascertain the reasons."[61]

59. Ibid., pp. 34–35.
60. "Symposium: The Minority Candidate," p. 186.
61. 522 F. Supp. 886, 898 (1981); Stuart Silverstein, "Bar Exam Makes Some 'More Equal,'" *National Law Journal,* August 18, 1980, p. 3.

## Professional Associations

Although blacks have not yet achieved anything near proportional representation in the legal profession, the situation has improved markedly
since *Brown v. Board of Education* (1954). Before that legal turning point, black
attorneys were virtually isolated professionally. Opportunities to work
with white colleagues or to represent white clients were almost nonexistent. Moreover, many blacks who needed legal representation feared that
black lawyers would be unsuccessful against a white lawyer and before a
white judge, regardless of the ability or the quality of the performance of
the black lawyers. Those blacks who did retain black lawyers were usually
too poor to furnish a lucrative practice. Black lawyers were largely confined to petty criminal cases and were rarely given the opportunity to
prove their ability in other areas of the law.

   In varying degrees this problem of professional segregation has beset
black lawyers throughout the century. In 1912, racism within the legal
community was so rampant that a storm arose over the "inadvertent"
election of the first three black attorneys to the American Bar Association
by its Executive Committee. When the Executive Committee discovered
that it had unknowingly elected three members "of the colored race," the
committee rescinded its prior action, stating that "the settled practice of
the Association has been to elect only white men to membership." It
reported the matter to the association at its 1912 annual meeting without
recommendation.

   On August 27, 1912, the ABA passed a resolution declaring that the
three black lawyers were elected members by virtue of the prior action of
the Executive Committee. However, the resolution went on to advise that
"as it has never been contemplated that colored men were to be members
of this Association," and the election by the Executive Committee "was
by inadvertence," those who recommend a person of the colored race for
membership are directed hereafter to "accompany the recommendation
with a statement of the fact that he is of such race."[62]

   The next day William R. Morris of Minneapolis, one of the three black
lawyers elected, tendered his resignation by telegram as follows:

   I am informed of proceedings of the American Bar Association ratify-
   ing my membership in the Association. I now most respectfully tender
   my unqualified resignation, because of my sincere, respectful and
   entirely unselfish consideration of the best interests of the leading
   organization of lawyers in the land. My action is intended as that of
   a lawyer towards lawyers, for whose success and progress in their
   work of advancement I most earnestly and sincerely pray.

62. *Reports of the American Bar Association,* vol. 37 (1912), p. 13.

In rising to accept the resignation, Joseph H. Merrill of Georgia said:

> I wish to say one word in addition, and I speak to those who with me
> do not wish to have negroes as members of this Association. . . . It
> becomes us in bidding Mr. Morris good-bye to voice our apprecia-
> tion of the exalted sentiments expressed by him in his farewell to
> us.[63]

This action gave rise to a resolution, passed in 1914, that in the future all
applications for membership must state the race and sex of the applicant.[64]

It was not until almost thirty years later, at the ABA annual meeting
in 1943, that the official action of August 27, 1912, requiring the statement
of race and sex to accompany recommendations for membership, was in
effect rescinded by adoption of a resolution that "membership in the
American Bar Association is not dependent upon race, creed or color."

Faced with formidable resistance to blacks by the American Bar Association, black lawyers felt the need for some kind of formal professional
communication and collaboration, as well as the need to join as lawyers
in the struggle to achieve equal justice for blacks in American law. In 1925,
twelve black lawyers from around the nation (eleven men and one woman)
met in Des Moines, Iowa, to organize and incorporate the National Bar
Association (NBA). Although not restricting its membership by race, the
NBA was designed to be, and became, the chief professional association
of black lawyers.[65]

The NBA's president between 1929 and 1931, Raymond Pace Alexander of Philadelphia (who is discussed in Part One of this book), expressed the organization's aims:

> To form a nationwide organization of practicing attorneys of the
> Negro race in an endeavour to strengthen and elevate the Negro
> lawyer in his profession and in his relationship to his people; to
> improve his standing at the bar . . . , and to stress those values that
> would serve to enhance the ethics of his practice and conduct, to
> condemn actions that would have a tendency to lessen respect for the
> lawyer and to create a bond of true fellowship among the colored
> members of the Bar. . . .[66]

63. Ibid., p. 291.
64. *Reports of the American Bar Association,* vol. 39 (1914), pp. 64–65.
65. S. Joe Brown, "Our Origin," *National Bar Journal,* vol. 2 (September 1944), pp.
161–64. See also Genna Rae McNeil, "The National Bar Association, Incorporated" in *Encyclopedia of Black American Voluntary Associations,* to be published in 1983, ed. Tony Martin (Westport,
Conn.: Greenwood Press).
66. Raymond Pace Alexander, "The National Bar Association—Its Aims and Purposes," *National Bar Journal,* vol. 1 (July 1941), pp. 2–3.

The charter emphasized the association's commitment to "protect the civil and political rights of all citizens of the several states of the United States."[67]

In 1925, when the NBA started, there were fewer than one thousand black lawyers in the country, and only one out of eighty-six blacks joined the association that first year. In 1934, when NBA leader and first full-time head of the NAACP legal department Charles Hamilton Houston (who is discussed in Part Two of this book) reported on the status of Negroes in the profession, he found 1,230 black lawyers, or 0.7 percent of the total lawyer population, which was then listed as approximately 160,000.[68] By 1945 the NBA's longtime secretary, Sadie T. M. Alexander, a pioneer black lawyer in Philadelphia (who is also discussed later in this book) reported that nearly 25 percent of the black lawyers in America were dues-paying members of the NBA.[69] In 1981 the NBA estimated that there were 12,000 black lawyers, of whom about 8,000 belonged to the NBA. From an American Bar Foundation estimate of a total of 535,000 lawyers in the United States in 1980, it appears that black lawyers comprise a little more than 2.2 percent of the American lawyer population.

Before the NBA was started, local black associations had been formed, such as the Cook County Bar Association of Illinois and the John M. Harlan Law Club of Ohio. These became NBA affiliates, and other affiliates were organized in thirty cities, including most of those cities covered in Chapter 9 of this book.[70] Annual NBA conventions have been held, and have been the focus of the organization's efforts, for fifty-six years.

After the ABA explicitly opened its membership to blacks in 1943, and then in the middle and late 1950s and 1960s welcomed black members, the NBA entered a new era. Revius O. Ortique, Jr., a former NBA president and successful practicing attorney in New Orleans who became a judge of the Civil District Court for Orleans Parish, wrote bluntly in *Judicature* in 1970: "Should a legal organization that is predominantly black seriously consider dissolution when an older, well-established, prestigious legal organization that is predominantly white welcomes the blacks and makes a sincere and meaningful effort to absorb them?"[71] His answer was an emphatic: "No—not yet." He stressed the change that had come to pass in the American Bar Association:

67. Articles of Incorporation, in Brown, "Our Origin," p. 163; McNeil, "National Bar Association," p. 4.
68. Charles Hamilton Houston, "The Need for Negro Lawyers," *Journal of Negro Education*, vol. 4 (1935), p. 49.
69. Report of Sadie T. M. Alexander, quoted in McNeil, "National Bar Association," p. 5.
70. McNeil, "National Bar Association," p. 6.
71. Revius O. Ortique, Jr., "The National Bar Association—Not Just an Option," *Judicature*, vol. 53, no. 9 (1970), p. 390.

Let there be no mistake—the American Bar Association, with its current enlightened leadership, does now unequivocally support all of the [NBA] goals. The last ten years, at least, have seen a metamorphosis in ABA unparalleled in the history of traditional professional organizations. We have been fortunate to be part of that metamorphosis. We do not suspect their motives nor their efforts to support the objectives of NBA. The last three presidents of the ABA have, through word and deed, made this unmistakably clear.[72]

Revius Ortique affirmed the long-declared aim of the NBA to "work itself out of existence," but urged black lawyers to continue working together in the NBA until equal justice was at last achieved in America. Ortique joined the 1970 president of the NBA, William E. Peterson, in calling on black lawyers to rededicate themselves to the proposition that they still "have a unique responsibility in making America's words America's deeds, for black as well as white Americans."[73]

In actuality, the elimination of formal admission barriers to the American Bar Association did not quickly bring about any substantial involvement of black lawyers in the programs of the ABA. The relatively few black lawyers practicing during the 1940s and 1950s were occupied with the difficult task of establishing themselves in their local communities. Further, as just noted, there were both local black groups and the National Bar Association, which were far more receptive to black involvement than was the ABA. Finally there was the financial deterrent of dues. Hence, few black lawyers became ABA members, and there were no blacks in the ABA's governing body, the House of Delegates, or in the leadership of the sections and the standing or special committees.

Greater involvement of black lawyers in the organized bar during the 1960s is linked to the greater involvement of the organized bar in civil rights. The major impetus for this may be traced to June 1963, when, as the civil rights movement was beginning to arouse the nation's conscience, Alabama Governor George Wallace threatened to stand at the door of the University of Alabama and defy a federal court order to desegregate the university. Outraged at this open defiance of the law, Bernard G. Segal of Philadelphia (later to become President of the ABA) marshaled a group of forty-six lawyers from all over the nation, including leaders of the organized bar and a number of prominent black attorneys, to issue a public condemnation of Governor Wallace and to call upon him to comply with the federal court injunction. Shortly thereafter, at Segal's instigation, President John F. Kennedy, on June 21, 1963, convened a White House Confer-

72. Ibid., pp. 390–91.
73. Ibid., p. 392.

ence on Civil Rights attended by 244 lawyers from all parts of the country, including a substantial number of black lawyers. At that conference President Kennedy stressed the leadership role that lawyers should play in advancing the cause of equal rights for all citizens and in supporting the pending civil rights legislation. The President asked Harrison Tweed of New York and Bernard G. Segal to co-chair a special committee for these purposes. Known as the Lawyers' Committee for Civil Rights Under Law, it has played a significant role in lobbying for passage of the Civil Rights Act of 1964 and advancing the cause of civil rights in the nation. It still operates on a national scale.

Among the first activities of the Lawyers' Committee was the opening of an office in Mississippi to recruit nationwide volunteer lawyers to handle the multitude of civil rights cases arising in local areas that were receiving no attention at all. At the time there were only three black lawyers in Mississippi. Segal and two members of the committee met in New Orleans with the officers, board members, and past presidents of the Mississippi State Bar, who did not oppose the opening of the office in Jackson, Mississippi. Indeed, the president of the Mississippi State Bar appointed a member to serve as liaison with the Lawyers' Committee in its work in Mississippi.

As originally formed, the Lawyers' Committee included the president and eight past presidents of the ABA, the president and a past president of the National Bar Association, two former attorneys general of the United States, the attorneys general of several states, the deans of fifteen law schools, and the presidents or past presidents of over half the state bar associations. Two members of the Executive Committee of fifteen lawyers were black—William T. Coleman, Jr., of Philadelphia and William R. Ming, Jr., of Chicago. The Board of Directors included the following black members: Samuel R. Pierce, Jr., James M. Nabrit, Jr., Robert E. Lillard and Arthur P. Shores. The number of black members of the Lawyers' Committee has expanded over the years, and black lawyers continue to be active in its leadership and its local branches in various major cities across the nation. The Executive Director, William Robinson, is a black lawyer.

Although the Lawyers' Committee is not an official organization of the ABA, it was understood from the outset that the committee would have the support of the ABA. The ABA promptly formed its own special committee to address the nation's civil rights problems. In 1963 the ABA committee issued a report calling upon the organized bar at national, state, and local levels to become involved in civil rights efforts and to support and actively cooperate with the Lawyers' Committee.

At the 1963 annual meeting of the ABA in Chicago, another important event took place. A group of ABA members, headed by Jefferson B. Fordham (then Dean of the University of Pennsylvania Law School), determined to form a section on individual rights that would serve to promote a sense of responsibility on the part of lawyers to recognize and, through the organized bar, to enforce individual rights under the rule of law. Finally, at the 1966 annual meeting of the ABA in Montreal, the formation of the Section on Individual Rights and Responsibilities was approved by the ABA House of Delegates. It was to prove highly attractive to black lawyers, providing for the first time, as it did, an opportunity for their meaningful involvement and leadership. Among the early leaders of that section were three prominent black lawyers—William T. Coleman, Jr., of Philadelphia; Samuel R. Pierce, Jr., of New York; and Cecil F. Poole of San Francisco (each of whom is discussed in the portion of this book relating specifically to the primary city of his activity). During his continuing affiliation with the Section on Individual Rights, Poole became, in successive years beginning with 1969, the first black vice-chairman, chairman-elect, chairman, or section delegate of an ABA section.

The relationship between the ABA and the National Bar Association also began to develop and grow. In 1970, for example, the National Bar Association asked the Section on Individual Rights to co-sponsor a national conference to train lawyers in litigation relating to equal opportunities in employment. Since then there have been a number of mutual endeavors.

During the late 1960s and the 1970s, black lawyers became more involved in the ABA, particularly as a result of the efforts of a number of ABA presidents who resolved to achieve this result. A black lawyer, William S. Thompson, became Chairman of the ABA Committee on World Peace Through Law, and other black lawyers have become members of section councils and Association committees. The student division of the ABA has also sent black delegates to the House of Delegates.

One of the most prominent areas of black involvement is the ABA Standing Committee on Federal Judiciary, an important and prestigious committee since, at the instance of the President and through the Attorney General and his staff, it investigates and reports on the qualifications of persons under consideration for nomination to the federal judiciary, and also, at the request of the Senate Judiciary Committee, reports the ABA ratings on all such persons who are actually nominated. There presently are two black members on that committee, William T. Coleman, Jr. and Stuart J. Dunnings, Jr. of Lansing, Michigan, who at the time of his appointment to the committee was a vice-president of the National Bar Association.

These are important breakthroughs, but the number and the involvement of black lawyers in the ABA are still at far too low a level.

The collaboration of black and white lawyers for the advancement of civil rights did not, of course, commence with the ABA developments of recent decades. White lawyers played prominent parts in the founding and early development of the NAACP, in collaboration with W. E. B. Du Bois and, later, Walter White. The first president of the NAACP, in 1910, was a leading white Boston lawyer, Moorfield Storey, who as a young man had been secretary to Senator Charles Sumner during the most controversial years of Reconstruction. Moorfield Storey was also the first attorney to appear for the NAACP in the United States Supreme Court, and for many years he was the organization's chief attorney while continuing his Boston practice. Storey wrote the first NAACP brief in the Supreme Court in *Guinn v. United States,*[74] the 1915 case to declare Oklahoma's "grandfather clause" a violation of black citizens' right to vote. In 1927 Moorfield Storey, in his eighty-second year, argued for the last time in the Supreme Court on behalf of the NAACP in the case of *Nixon v. Herndon,*[75] which established the right of black citizens to vote in a party primary.[76]

Just as Moorfield Storey worked with black colleagues in all the NAACP's five appearances in the Supreme Court through 1927, in a later generation the NAACP Legal Defense and Educational Fund benefited from the effective teamwork of Thurgood Marshall and Jack Greenberg, a young white lawyer who joined Marshall's staff in 1949. Created in 1940 as a tax-exempt legal arm of the NAACP, the Legal Defense Fund has played the leading role in most major civil rights cases during four decades. Its black attorneys, such as Robert Carter and Franklin Williams in its first years and James M. Nabrit, III, in the last decade, have been outstanding. And its dedicated and skilled Director-Counsel Jack Greenberg, who took charge of the Fund in 1961 when Marshall left to become a United States circuit court judge, has carried on the tradition of full racial integration in the struggle for civil rights that was established so early and well by Storey and Marshall.

Another example of effective interracial legal teamwork, developed through participation in Legal Defense Fund cases, was the collaboration of William T. Coleman, Jr., and Louis H. Pollak. As practicing attorneys in New York in the early 1950s, they worked regularly with Thurgood Marshall and Robert Carter, especially on *Brown v. Board of Education* and the school desegregation litigation that followed. Pollak's participation continued through his deanships at Yale and the University of Pennsylvania law schools, until he became a United States district court judge in Philadelphia in 1978. Coleman continues his active work with the fund as Chairman of its board.[77]

74. 238 U.S. 347 (1915).
75. 273 U.S. 536 (1927).
76. Richard Kluger, *Simple Justice* (New York: Vintage Books, 1977), pp. 96, 98, 104, 109, 114, 118, 122, 125, 131.
77. Ibid., pp. 292–93, 321, 399, 439, 531–35, 601, 624, 638–39, 642, 722–23, 726, 776.

As late as 1963, Secretary of Labor Willard Wirtz had described the legal profession as the worst segregated group in the whole economy.[78] Whether the situation has changed significantly as a result of the events just recited and especially since the landmark civil rights legislation of 1964 and 1965 is a central question to which this study addresses itself. At least since the White House Conference of June 1963, the organized bar has actively sought to desegregate its membership and accordingly broaden its concern for equal rights for all citizens. At the same time there have been continuing increases in the population of black lawyers—3,260 in 1970 and more than 11,000 in 1980.

It is clear, however, that one must go beyond these committees and statistics and look into more complex questions regarding the nature of legal practice and the quality of professional life for black lawyers. The following chapters are intended to provide an in-depth view, using Philadelphia as a microcosm of the legal community in urban America (Part One). Supplementary data from fifteen representative cities (Part Two) add another dimension to the picture. In most cases, the black members of the profession themselves—judges, law teachers, and practicing lawyers —are the sources for this analysis of their development as a professional group, their present status, and their future prospects.

78. Lawrence White, "The Changing Structure of the Black Legal Community in the United States: Racism and the American Legal Process" (thesis, University of Pennsylvania, 1975), p. 23.

# I

**Blacks in the Law
in Philadelphia:**
An In-Depth Study

# 1

# Historical Background

After Abraham Lincoln signed the Emancipation Proclamation, hope so long suppressed was revived, and blacks, free of bondage yet bewildered by sudden freedom from slavery, began with very cautious optimism to contemplate their long-awaited social, educational, and professional freedom.[1] The Reconstruction period (1867–75) was a time when, with the establishment of law schools by American colleges and universities[2] and of bar examinations rather than sponsorship as the requirement for the practice of law, a career in the legal profession loomed for the first time as a possibility for blacks who desired it.

Blacks who dreamed of becoming lawyers believed that Philadelphia, home of the Quakers who had been so supportive of them during their slavery years, would be a likely place to engage in the practice of law. They were to learn that this dream would take many years to realize. To their surprise and despair, blacks who chose a legal career in Philadelphia faced tremendous obstacles and disappointments well into the twentieth century. Philadelphia did not readily open its doors to welcome them to the legal profession; rather, blacks were systematically barred from practicing law at all. Discouraged and disillusioned, some gave up entirely the idea of becoming a lawyer and entered other fields; some went to other cities in the hope that they would be permitted to practice law there.

A thorough search of all available sources fails to establish when the first black lawyer began to practice in Philadelphia. The *Philadelphia Colored Directory,* one of the best sources for such data could be no more specific than that "Philadelphia got its first black lawyer after the Civil War."[3]

In his book charting black labor in the United States in the nineteenth and the early twentieth centuries, Charles Wesley wrote that, according to

---

1. W. E. B. Du Bois, *The Philadelphia Negro* (New York: Schocken Books, 1967), p. 39.
2. Walter J. Leonard, "Development of the Black Bar," *Annals of the American Academy of Political and Social Science,* vol. 407 (May 1973), p. 136.
3. R. R. Wright, Jr., and Ernest Smith, comps., *Philadelphia Colored Directory,* edition of 1908 (n.p., 1908), Phila., p. 11.

one observer, in the city of Philadelphia there were no professional black gentlemen and very few who were even mechanics between 1850 and 1860.[4] Further, although a careful list of the occupations of blacks in Philadelphia was compiled in 1859, nowhere in the compilation does one find any evidence of the existence of black lawyers.[5]

However, although neither the *Philadelphia Colored Directory* nor Wesley's book has any record of black lawyers admitted to the Philadelphia Bar prior to the Civil War, Theodore Hershberg, director of a project for the study of Philadelphia social history, reports the discovery of the names of two black "lawyers," Henry Johnson and Isaac Parvis, in the city as early as 1850.[6] Two more blacks, James Freeman and Thomas Howard, appeared listed in the same way in 1860. A fifth, John H. Cavenders, is recorded as a "conveyancer" (a term sometimes used for a lawyer) in 1870. Three more black Philadelphia lawyers were in the 1880 census: Jacob Ballad, John D. Lewis, and Howard J. Scott.

None of these names is mentioned in Fleming D. Tucker's 1964 *Directory of the Colored Members of the Philadelphia Bar.* The first black lawyer to appear in the *Directory* is Theophilus J. Minton, admitted in 1887. Aaron Mossell, Jr. became a member of the Philadelphia Bar in 1893. Five more lawyers were admitted before 1900: John S. Durham, John Wesley Parks, and John Adams Sparks, in 1895; M. Luther Nicholas, in 1896; and George W. Mitchell, in 1898.[7] In 1899 W. E. B. Du Bois noted: "There are at present 10 practicing Negro lawyers in the city [Philadelphia]. . . . Two of these are fairly successful practitioners. . . . Three others are with difficulty earning a living at criminal practice in police cases, and the rest are having little or no practice. . . ."[8]

Because so little is known of the early history of the Philadelphia Bar, biographical information is available for only two of these black pioneers, Aaron Mossell, Jr., and John Adams Sparks.

Aaron Mossell was the first black to graduate from the University of Pennsylvania Law School.[9] Born in Hamilton, Ontario, the son of a free black who migrated to Canada to avoid having his children reared in a

4. Charles H. Wesley, *Negro Labor in the United States, 1850–1925* (New York: Vanguard Press, 1927), pp. 30–32.

5. Ibid., pp. 45–46.

6. Philadelphia Social History Project, affiliated with the University of Pennsylvania, operating under grants from the National Institute of Mental Health, the National Science Foundation, and the National Endowment for the Humanities.

7. Fleming D. Tucker, comp., *A Directory of the Colored Members of the Philadelphia Bar, Including a List of the Pioneer Lawyers,* revised to April 1, 1964 (n.p., n.d.); and, *Negro Members of the Philadelphia Bar and Judiciary,* December, 1972 (n.p., n.d.).

8. Du Bois, *Philadelphia Negro,* p. 114.

9. John A. Saunders, *100 Years After Emancipation: History of the Philadelphia Negro, 1787–1963* (Philadelphia: F.R.S. Publishing Co., 1960s [?]), p. 128.

slave state, he returned to Philadelphia after the Emancipation.[10] He entered Lincoln University (situated near) as an undergraduate[11] and then matriculated at the University of Pennsylvania Law School, from which he graduated in 1888.[12] After he was admitted to the Philadelphia Bar on February 18, 1893,[13] he began the practice of law. He and John Wesley Parks later formed a partnership and practiced law together,[14] apparently successfully. Mossell was the father of the distinguished lawyer, Sadie Tanner Mossel Alexander, whose achievements will be noted later.[15]

John Adams Sparks graduated from the University of Pennsylvania Law School in 1893[16] and became a specialist in real estate law.[17] In 1920 he was appointed Assistant City Solicitor and held this office for twenty-four years until his death.[18]

Both John A. Saunders and Fleming D. Tucker record the names of some additional black lawyers admitted to the Philadelphia Bar after Mossell: G. Edward Dickerson, John C. Asbury, William H. Fuller, and Harry W. Bass. According to Saunders's description, "each was a lawyer of the first rank, but each was forced by prejudice, discrimination and bias to engage in pursuits other than law."[19]

The 1910 census reported that there were thirteen black lawyers in Philadelphia.[20] Tucker records an admission of a black lawyer in 1908, then none until 1920, when one was admitted.[21] There seems to be no record of any black being admitted to the Philadelphia Bar during that span of twelve years. From 1920 to 1930 thirteen black lawyers were admitted (twelve males and one female), three between 1930 and 1933, then none at all between 1933 and 1943.[22] This fact has been advanced as significant evidence of the continuing racism in the bar at that time, although the economic conditions of the Depression years also may have been a factor. By 1945 only five more black lawyers had been added to Philadelphia's legal community.[23] The net effect of this abysmal record is that from 1909

10. Conversation with his daughter, Mrs. Sadie T. M. Alexander.
11. Saunders, *100 Years After Emancipation,* p. 128.
12. Information obtained from Registrar, University of Pennsylvania Law School.
13. Tucker, *Directory.*
14. Conversation with Mrs. Alexander.
15. See notes 33–36 of this chapter and the accompanying text.
16. *Philadelphia Inquirer,* November 24, 1944.
17. University of Pennsylvania Archives.
18. City Central Personnel Records, Philadelphia, Pa., February 1, 1920.
19. Saunders, *100 Years After Emancipation,* pp. 128–29.
20. U.S. Bureau of the Census, *Thirteenth Census of the United States, 1910: Occupational Statistics,* vol. 4 (Washington, D.C.: Government Printing Office, 1914), p. 589.
21. Tucker, *Directory.*
22. Ibid.
23. Ibid.

to 1945, a period of thirty-six years, only twenty black lawyers (nineteen males and one female) were admitted to the Philadelphia Bar.

A remarkable number of these twenty lawyers went on to achieve success in the profession and to attain judgeships and other public offices, thereby doing a great deal to enhance the standing of the black lawyer in Philadelphia.

Herbert E. Millen had the distinction of being the first black judge in Philadelphia when he became a judge of the Municipal Court in 1948.[24] Raymond Pace Alexander, husband of Sadie T. M. Alexander, gave up a lucrative law practice in 1958 to become the first black judge on the Court of Common Pleas, the trial court of general jurisdiction.[25] He had also had a distinguished career as Counselor to the Haitian Embassy in Washington from 1947 to 1948, and as Honorary Consul to the Republic of Haiti in Philadelphia from 1948 to 1956. He was also Chief Counsel for the NAACP and was elected and reelected to the Philadelphia City Council in the 1950s.[26] Robert N. C. Nix, Sr. was elected to fill the unexpired term of a Philadelphia Congressman in 1958 and served in the House of Representatives until January 1, 1979.[27] J. Austin Norris, after a successful career as a newspaper publisher in Pittsburgh, returned to the practice of law in Philadelphia and started a law firm that produced its own corps of talented black lawyers, several of whom became judges and high-level public officials. Among these are: A. Leon Higginbotham, Jr., United States Court of Appeals for the Third Circuit; Clifford Scott Green, United States District Court for the Eastern District of Pennsylvania; Robert W. Williams, Jr., Commonwealth Court of Pennsylvania; Doris M. Harris and Harvey N. Schmidt, Court of Common Pleas of Philadelphia; William F. Hall, United States Magistrate; and William H. Brown, III, whose career is discussed later in this chapter. Norris himself later became the first black member of the Board of Revision of Taxes.[28] Robert B. Johnson moved to New Jersey and subsequently became a judge of the Superior Court there.[29] Others of this group who were elevated to the bench in Philadelphia were Theodore O. Spaulding, initially to the Municipal Court, then to the Supe-

24. Mary Mace Spradling, ed., *In Black and White* (Detroit: Gale Research Co., 1980), vol. 2, p. 67.

25. Saunders, *100 Years After Emancipation,* p. 128.

26. W. Augustus Low and Virgil Clift, eds., *Encyclopedia of Black America* (New York: McGraw-Hill, 1981), pp. 97, 500; Harry E. Groves, *Opportunities for Negroes in the Law* (Washington, D.C.: American Association of Law Schools, 1967).

27. Peter M. Bergman, *The Chronological History of the Negro in America* (New York: Harper & Row, 1969), p. 346.

28. Conversation with J. Austin Norris.

29. Tucker, *Directory;* Bob Reichenbach, "A Judge with an Interest in Humanity," *Courier-Post* (Camden, N.J.), March 24, 1974.

rior Court as the first black appellate court judge in Philadelphia, and indeed in Pennsylvania[30]; Herbert R. Cain, Jr.[31] and Thomas M. Reed[32] to the Court of Common Pleas.

This group of twenty black lawyers also included Sadie T. M. Alexander, who achieved three historic firsts: she was the first black woman to receive a Ph.D. degree from the University of Pennsylvania,[33] the first black woman to graduate from the University of Pennsylvania Law School, and the first black woman to be admitted to the Pennsylvania Bar.[34] She was also Secretary of the National Bar Association and the first black woman to be appointed to a presidential commission.[35] The wife of Raymond Pace Alexander, noted earlier as the first black judge of the Court of Common Pleas of Philadelphia, she engaged in an active private practice with him from 1927 to 1959.[36] Other black lawyers admitted to the Philadelphia Bar from 1909 to 1945 were Eugene Washington Rhodes, who was Assistant United States Attorney, President of the National Bar Association, and later publisher of a black newspaper; and Walter A. Gay, Jr., who was also Assistant United States Attorney. Thus, more than half of the twenty became judges or held other government offices.

Of the eighty-eight blacks admitted to the Philadelphia Bar in the next twenty-five years (1945–70), twelve became judges in federal or state courts sitting in Philadelphia: Robert N. C. Nix, Jr., son of Congressman Nix noted above, the first black justice on the Supreme Court of Pennsylvania, who in the 1981 retention election was reelected to an additional ten-year term and who in normal course will become Chief Justice in 1984, the first black chief justice in any state; Robert W. Williams, Jr., who was serving on the Court of Common Pleas at the time of his appointment to the Commonwealth Court; A. Leon Higginbotham, Jr., who, after serving as the first black member of the Federal Trade Commission, was appointed to the United States District Court for the Eastern District of Pennsylvania, and in 1977 was elevated to the United States Court of Appeals for the Third Circuit; Clifford Scott Green and James T. Giles, United States District Court for the Eastern District of Pennsylvania; Matthew W. Bullock, Jr., Curtis C. Carson, Jr., Paul A. Dandridge, Doris M. Harris, Julian F. King,

30. Tucker, *Directory;* Spradling, *In Black and White,* p. 902; *Philadelphia Tribune,* September 23, 1974.

31. Tucker, *Directory; Pennsylvania Manual,* vol. 99 (1968–69), p. 513.

32. Tucker, *Directory;* Low and Clift, *Encyclopedia of Black America,* p. 729.

33. Conversation with Mrs. Alexander.

34. *Verdict,* Philadelphia Trial Lawyers Association, vol. 6, no. 4 (September 1970), p. 3.

35. Saunders, *100 Years After Emancipation,* p. 128.

36. John Calpin, "Alexander's Sanguine Stand," *Philadelphia Magazine,* vol. 47, no. 10 (1957), p. 26; Saunders, *100 Years After Emancipation,* p. 128.

Lawrence Prattis, Juanita Kidd Stout, Calvin T. Wilson, Charles W. Wright, Eugene H. Clarke, Jr., Norman A. Jenkins, Levan Gordon, and John L. Broxton, Court of Common Pleas; Kenneth S. Harris, Ricardo C. Jackson, and Lynwood Blount, Municipal Court.[37]

William T. Coleman, Jr., one of the most successful black lawyers in the country, graduated *summa cum laude* from the University of Pennsylvania in 1941 and received his LL.B. degree from Harvard *magna cum laude* in 1946. He served as law clerk for Judge Herbert F. Goodrich of the United States Court of Appeals for the Third Circuit (1947–48) and for Justice Felix Frankfurter, of the United States Supreme Court (1948–49). He represented the Commonwealth of Pennsylvania in litigation to remove racial restrictions from Girard College and was on the team that worked under Thurgood Marshall in *Brown v. Board of Education.* He also served as Secretary of Transportation during the administration of President Gerald Ford and has since become the ranking partner in the Washington office of one of the two largest Los Angeles law firms. He serves on the boards of directors of such major corporations as International Business Machines, Chase Manhattan Bank, PepsiCo., American Can Company, Pan American World Airways, Inc. and INA Corporation. He is Chairman of the Board of the NAACP Legal Defense and Educational Fund and has served on a large number of federal and state government, as well as civic and public welfare commissions and committees.[38]

William H. Brown, III, recognized as an outstanding lawyer, was Deputy District Attorney for Philadelphia and then served five years on the Equal Employment Opportunity Commission, the last four as Chairman, before becoming a partner in one of Philadelphia's largest law firms. Christopher F. Edley, who had been head of the Division of Law and Government of the Ford Foundation, and then became Director of the United Negro College Fund. Cecil B. Moore (deceased) served on the Philadelphia City Council and was active as a civil rights leader.

Among Philadelphia's black lawyers who occupy important posts in the city government are George Burrell, Deputy Mayor of Philadelphia; Joseph E. Coleman, President of City Council; John Street, Councilman; and Augusta Clark, Councilwoman. Serving in federal government is Edward S. G. Dennis, Chief of the Narcotic and Dangerous Drug Section of the Criminal Division, United States Department of Justice.

Ragan A. Henry has acquired seven radio stations and one television station, which combine to make up Broadcast Enterprises National, Inc.,

37. Saunders, *100 Years After Emancipation,* p. 133, and updating through interviews and official records.

38. Low and Clift, *Encyclopedia of Black America,* p. 278; Raymond Pace Alexander, "Tardy Honors Catch Up with His Honor," *Christian Science Monitor,* October 1, 1970, p. 5.

the only minority enterprise to own majority control of a network-affiliated VHF station. At the same time he is a partner in one of Philadelphia's leading law firms.

Black lawyers are now on the faculties of the three leading Philadelphia-area law schools—two at the University of Pennsylvania, seven at Temple University, and two at Villanova. Carl E. Singley, First Deputy City Solicitor for the City of Philadelphia, is on leave of absence as Associate Dean and Professor of Law at Temple University.

After 1970 the statistics for blacks in the legal profession in Philadelphia vary according to the source; it is difficult to arrive at precise figures because many persons who are qualified to practice may be employed in other occupational categories.[39] In 1974, Charles Mitchell stated that there were at that time approximately 265 black lawyers in the city, the number suggested to him in interviews with Philadelphia black attorneys.[40] That estimate would appear to be high, since for the present study (1978) a figure of 212 was arrived at from lists provided by the National Bar Association and the Barristers Club and from Tucker's *Directory of the Colored Members of the Philadelphia Bar.* Of this number, 19 were judges (17 males, 2 females). While the total of 212 should not be regarded as conclusive, it does appear to be fairly accurate for the year 1978.

Despite the increase in their numbers over the years, the ratio of black lawyers to the black population in Pennsylvania in 1970 was one black lawyer to approximately 7,600 black persons.[41] However, since the 1980 Philadelphia population was 1,751,780 with the black segment comprising 638,878 (37.1%),[42] and since there were approximately 400 black lawyers as of November 1981,[43] there would be approximately one black lawyer to 1,597 black Philadelphians. This is an estimate, not verifiable until the results of the 1980 census are published.

The difficulties that blacks have faced both in gaining access to the legal profession and in advancing within it have been noted in the Introduction. In Philadelphia this situation improved significantly in 1952, when efforts were made to break down racial barriers that existed in the legal profession. Bernard G. Segal, who became Chancellor of the Philadel-

39. John P. Davis, ed., *The American Negro Reference Book* (Englewood Cliffs, N.J.: Prentice-Hall, 1966), pp. 582–83.

40. Charles L. Mitchell, "The Black 'Philadelphia Lawyer,' " *Villanova Law Review,* vol. 20, nos. 2 and 3 (1974–75), p. 372.

41. "Report of the Philadelphia Bar Association Special Committee on Pennsylvania Bar Admission Procedures—Racial Discrimination of the Pennsylvania Bar Examinations," *Temple Law Quarterly,* vol. 44, no. 2 (Winter 1971), p. 164.

42. Advance Reports on the 1980 census by the U.S. Bureau of the Census.

43. Information supplied by the Barristers Association of Philadelphia, generally referred to as the Barristers Club.

phia Bar Association in January 1952 on the occasion of its 150th anniversary, instituted in his inaugural address an affirmative-action program to urge lawyers from minority groups to participate in association activities. Segal invited all lawyers, regardless of race, religion, or national origin, to advise him of the committees on which they would like to serve, noting their first, second, and third choices; he assured particularly those from minority groups of appointment to a committee, even if this necessitated enlarging the membership of some committees.[44]

In 1970 Judge Raymond Pace Alexander, noted above, published an article in the *Christian Science Monitor* pointing out that this action of the Philadelphia Bar Association in the early 1950s triggered an opening of the gates to black lawyers by bar associations elsewhere as well:

> America and the American bar have made great, and in some instances rapid, strides to correct their sins of omission and commission during the twentieth century.
>
> The Philadelphia Bar Association has been the leader of all American bar associations in this respect. But it took men of leadership and vigorous determination to reach this goal. Men of such quality became the leaders of our bar association beginning in the early 1950s. Before that date, I must frankly say our association failed to grasp such meaning.
>
> The present president of the American Bar Association, the Hon. Bernard G. Segal, was the first of our chancellors to realize this responsibility of the lawyers. It was then, for the first time, Negro lawyers in Philadelphia began to attend the meetings and gained membership in more than a token way, on all of the bar committees.[45]

These changes are well documented by the results of the present study of the individual black lawyers from every age-group who practice in Philadelphia today.

## The Conduct of the Study

In order to understand the background and attitudes of black lawyers in Philadelphia today, the author prepared a nine-page questionnaire concerning each respondent's family background, pre-law and law school education, career motivations, bar examinations, employment history, membership in professional organizations, self-evaluation, and opinions on relevant subjects (see Appendix 1). The questionnaire was reviewed by

44. Conversation with Bernard G. Segal.
45. Alexander, "Tardy Honors," p. 11; and to the same effect, idem, "Blacks and the Law," *Verdict* (Philadelphia Trial Lawyers Association), vol. 6, no. 4 (1970), p. 5.

Dr. Renée C. Fox (then Chairman of the Sociology Department), Dr. Digby Baltzell (then Graduate Group Chairman of the Sociology Department), and Judge A. Leon Higginbotham, Jr. (Adjunct Professor), all of the University of Pennsylvania, as well as by members of the Barristers Club. In early 1978 questionnaires were sent, in two mailings one month apart, to 212 black members of the Philadelphia Bar. Their names and addresses were compiled from lists of the Barristers Club and of the National Bar Association as well as from two directories prepared and distributed by Fleming D. Tucker.[46]

To the 212 questionnaires sent out, 141 replies were received. Two persons responded that they did not care to answer the questions, six reported having moved to other cities, four questionnaires were returned marked "Unknown," and fifty-nine were not returned at all. Thus approximately 66.5 percent of the 212 addressees returned completed questionnaires. While most of those responding answered all questions, a fair number appeared reluctant to confront some of the subjects covered.

In order to supplement the questionnaires, the author conducted and, with their approval, taped interviews with fifteen lawyers and judges. Significant portions of the interviews have been incorporated into this book.

In order to discover how various age-groups of black Philadelphia lawyers compare with each other, the subjects were divided into three "cohorts" according to dates of birth: 1890–1920, 1921–1937, and 1938–1954. These will be respectively referred to as the oldest or first, middle or second, and youngest or third cohort. The 141 returned questionnaires were fed into a computer keyed to note the differences among responses from the three age-groups. Of the oldest cohort, between fifty-seven and eighty-seven years of age at the time they answered the questionnaire, there were eighteen respondents, fifteen males and three females. In the middle cohort, which ranged between forty and fifty-six years of age, there were thirty respondents, twenty-nine males and one female. Of the youngest group, then twenty-three to thirty-nine years of age, there were ninety-three respondents (seventy-one males and twenty-two females). Thus there emerges not only a general profile of the black lawyers practicing in Philadelphia today but also a broad view of the changes that have taken place over the years as well as the changes that black lawyers envision for their future.

---

46. Tucker, *Directory;* and *Negro Members of the Philadelphia Bar and Judiciary.*

# 2

# Family Influences

The family is the foundation of every child's rearing, not simply because it provides for basic needs during the formative years but also because the family experience tends to be reflected in the self-image and life choices of each individual. The black attorneys in our study were therefore questioned about their upbringing in order to isolate those factors that may have contributed to their choice of the law as a profession.

## Birthplace

Blacks migrated in large numbers from the South to the North between 1910 and 1930. This movement dropped sharply during the 1930s, the decade most marked by the Great Depression, then increased again over the next two decades.[1] Such migration was influenced by two sets of factors: those pushing people out and those pulling people in. Among the "push" factors were the deterioration of agriculture and the continuation of injustice, discrimination, and segregation in the South. Pulling people to the North were the needs of industrial labor occasioned by the wars in Europe, which cut off the usual supply of such labor through immigration. Between 1960 and 1970 the black population in central United States cities increased by 2.6 million persons; by 1970, some 3.2 million of the 13 million blacks over five years of age born in the South were living in other parts of the country.[2]

This nationwide trend, together with the statistically established fact that blacks with greater educational attainment are more likely to migrate than those with less education, may explain the fact that many black lawyers who are currently practicing in Philadelphia had their origins in a wide variety of places other than this city. Although the southern states were the birthplaces of the majority of the oldest cohort, northern states

1. John P. Davis, ed., *The American Negro Reference Book* (Englewood Cliffs, N.J.: Prentice-Hall, 1966), pp. 109–11.
2. Harry A. Ploski and Warren Marr, eds., *The Negro Almanac,* 3d ed. (New York: Bellwether Publishing Co., 1976), pp. 368, 374.

and countries outside the United States were the birthplaces of the middle and the youngest cohorts. Thus, the backgrounds vary, the cultural interests differ, and the educational attainments are unequal.

Only six (35.2%) of the seventeen oldest respondents were born in Pennsylvania (one did not respond to this question). The others, and their parents and grandparents, had their origins in fourteen other states, primarily in the South, most frequently in Georgia. The West Indies was also represented.

Twenty (66.7%) of the thirty respondents in the middle cohort were born in Pennsylvania. Pennsylvania, three additional states, and Canada were the birthplaces of their parents and grandparents. Virginia led as the other state of origin in this cohort.

Further evidence of the migration enlargement is seen in the youngest cohort. Only thirty-nine of the ninety-three youngest lawyers were born in Pennsylvania, a reduction to 41.9 percent for this group. Fifty-two came from twenty-three other states as well as from Puerto Rico, England, France, South America, Spain, and the Soviet Union. (See Appendix 2 for birthplaces by region.)

## Siblings

With regard to siblings, the responses were roughly similar in all three groups of black lawyers: they did not belong to large families. Seventy-eight (55.3%) of them had no siblings, and only thirty-seven (26.2%) had one brother or sister. Twenty-one (14.9%) grew up in households that included additional relatives, such as grandparents, aunts, and uncles. Thus, the predominant pattern was that respondents were either the only children of their parents or came from very small families.

## Religion

The religion of respondents apparently had no statistical significance.

According to John P. Davis, "Baptists are by far the largest single group of Negro Christians in the world. . . . They have played a great part in the progress of the Negro in education, in civic leadership and in other ways."[3] Members of the Baptist church do predominate in the three cohorts studied, as in the black population in general, but there is a sprinkling of other religions as well, particularly Methodists and Episcopalians.

Two trends that come into focus in analyzing the questionnaires are one toward Catholicism and another toward no religious affiliation whatever. Davis observed: "The Catholic Church has always been interested in

3. Davis, *American Negro Reference Book*, p. 403.

the conversion of Negroes to that faith. . . . Negro membership has practically tripled in the past twenty-five years."[4] In this study of respondents and their parents and grandparents, Christian Science has consistently attracted the smallest number.

## Education of Parents

According to John P. Davis, "the Negro lawyer of the last two generations [the 1950s and 1960s] is the product of families with high literacy and relatively high occupational status."[5] The parents in the present study, especially in the oldest and youngest cohorts, exhibit a high degree of literacy.

Among the fathers of the sixteen respondents in the oldest cohort who answered the question regarding their parents' education, four (25%) had completed high school; one graduated from college and one from normal school; seven earned graduate or professional degrees, including LL.B., Ph.D., S.T.M., D.D., and B.D.

There was a significant decrease in the percentage of fathers of the second cohort who had completed high school, from 25 percent in the first cohort to 10 percent in the second. Of the fathers of the thirty respondents of this cohort, three completed high school, one completed college, and two earned advanced degrees, one an M.A. and one a J.D. (The explanation for this decrease may be found in the economic and educational climate of that period, particularly the Depression, and should provide a topic for future study.)

Of the ninety respondents in the youngest cohort who replied to this question, nine fathers finished college and twenty-one earned higher degrees—LL.B., J.D., M.D., C.E., or M.A. Twenty-two (22%) completed high school.

Fathers of the youngest and oldest cohorts were the most highly educated.

Eight (50%) of the sixteen mothers of respondents in the oldest cohort completed high school; two completed college and went on to earn graduate degrees, one an M.A. and the other an M.S.W.

Of the mothers of the thirty respondents in the second cohort, nine (30%) completed high school; three others went to college, receiving the B.A. degree; and one continued on to graduate school and earned an M.A.

The mothers of forty-seven (52.2%) of the ninety respondents in the youngest cohort who answered this question at least completed high school. Of the twenty-two others who went to college and earned B.S.,

4. Ibid., p. 409.
5. Ibid., p. 581.

A.A., B.A., B.F.A., and B.Th. degrees, fifteen continued their studies and received advanced degrees—M.A., M.D., M.Ed., M.S., and Ph.D. Two became licensed practical nurses.

The mothers of the lawyers in the second cohort exhibited the same lag in education as did the fathers, while the mothers in the first and third cohorts were more highly educated.


## Occupations of Parents

Since the career aspirations of children are influenced at least partly by the occupations and occupational status of their parents, an investigation into the occupations of respondents' parents was made. As might be expected, the parents of respondents of all three cohorts had a higher occupational status than their contemporaries in the black population as a whole.

In 1890 the first United States census on the occupations of blacks disclosed that almost 90 percent were in agriculture or domestic and personal service, compared with 60 percent of native white workers so employed. Early in the twentieth century, however, a large number of blacks moved into industrial occupations. By 1940, on a national scale, only 20 percent of whites were still in agriculture or domestic and personal service, compared with 55 percent of blacks. Many more whites moved into skilled and white-collar occupations, resulting in a still wider occupational gap in 1940.[6]

World War II was the turning point, as white civilian workers went into the armed forces. During their absence blacks had an opportunity to gain valuable training experience on a front far wider than before. The economy was growing and black involvement was growing with it. But despite their gains, blacks were not to achieve proportional representation. A computed projection indicated that if representation were to increase at only the 1940–60 rate, it would not be until the year 2490 that proportional representation would be attained; even in that period blacks in each occupational group were concentrated in lower-paying and lower-prestige occupations.[7]

In 1960, throughout the country, 11.4 percent of the black population was in the professional category, compared with 31 percent of the white population. During the 1960s, white consciousness of the problems faced by minorities began to develop and racial barriers began to break down. This new awareness was responsible, in significant measure, for the opening of higher-level government jobs to blacks and the emergence of black

6. Leonard Broom and Norval D. Glenn, *Transformation of the Negro American* (New York: Harper & Row, 1965), p. 107.

7. Ibid., pp. 107–11.

lawyers into fields previously denied them. According to a 1966 Labor Department bulletin,

> faster entry . . . into professional, sales, clerical, and crafts jobs has been accompanied by greater differentiation within these broad occupation groups. Thus, the professional and technical group of oc-cupations traditionally followed by educated Negro men, such as clergymen, doctors, and teachers, is now expanded by other profes-sionals in callings such as dentists, [and] lawyers.[8]

In his 1934 study of 503 black professionals, Carter G. Woodson concluded that in most cases they were of humble parentage.[9] Twenty-five years later, G. Franklin Edwards studied the black professional class as of 1959 and commented: "Over a period of time those who enter professional occupations came increasingly from fathers in the upper occupational groups—professional, proprietor and clerical." His respondents had a larger percentage of fathers in the white-collar category than in the blue-collar category.[10]

In the current study, ten (58.8%) of the seventeen fathers of the oldest cohort were in the professional-managerial category; others were in agri-culture and in service jobs. There were no laborers in this category.

The effects of the Depression are apparent in the occupations of fathers of the second cohort (born between 1921 and 1937). In this cohort four fathers were deceased and three respondents did not answer the occupation question. Of the twenty-three respondents who answered this question, eight (34.7%) of the fathers were in the professional-managerial category. Two were in the clerical category, three in factory work, one in the armed forces. Five were laborers, and four were in service jobs (not domestic). None was in agriculture.

Twenty-nine (33.3%) of the fathers of the eighty-seven of the youn-gest cohort who responded were in the professional-managerial category, thirteen were in factory work, ten were laborers, eight were in crafts, seven were employed in some area of service (not domestic), seven were in clerical positions, three were in the armed forces, two were unemployed, one was in sales, and seven were deceased.

In the three cohorts, therefore, more fathers were in professional-

8. Lawrence White, "The Changing Structure of the Black Legal Community in the United States: Racism and the American Legal Process" (paper, University of Pennsylvania, 1975), pp. 32–33 (citing U.S. Department of Labor, "The Negroes in the United States: Their Economic and Social Situation," Bulletin No. 1511, June 1966, p. 28).

9. Carter G. Woodson, *The Negro Professional Man and the Community* (Washington, D.C.: Association for the Study of Negro Life and History, 1934), p. 185.

10. G. Franklin Edwards, *The Negro Professional Class* (Glencoe, Ill.: Free Press, 1959), p. 78.

managerial occupations than in any other category. Only two were unemployed. These data are in accord with Davis's findings.

Of the seventeen mothers of the oldest lawyers, eleven (64.7%) were not employed outside the home. One was in the professional group (a social worker), one was a clerk, and one was a domestic.

There were thirty mothers in the second cohort. Fourteen (46.7%) were not employed, four were professionals, and three were clerks; one was in crafts, two were factory workers, one was a farmer, three were in service jobs (not domestic), one was in domestic service, and one was in farm labor.

Of the ninety respondents to this question in the youngest group, twenty-eight (31.1%) of their mothers were not employed, twenty-two were in the professional-managerial category, and forty were in a variety of other jobs, including one domestic worker and nine office workers.

Thus, the trends of mothers leaving the home for outside employment are obvious. In a 1964 study of black college students in the South, one conclusion was that sons of working mothers are more highly motivated for intellectual achievement than sons of nonworking mothers.[11] In a 1975 study of 441 ghetto-dwelling black mothers questioned about family size, education, income, and aspirations, 73 percent had professional aspirations for their daughters and 65 percent for their sons. Mothers with better educations and larger incomes had higher aspirations for their children.[12]

Of the fifteen lawyers personally interviewed, ten had fathers who were college graduates, including three teachers, one minister, two lawyers, one pharmacist, and one dentist. Five had mothers who were college graduates majoring in education, all of whom became teachers.

The results of the present study concur with the findings of G. Franklin Edwards, who reported that 63 percent of his respondents came from the upper ranks of black society. He concluded that black lawyers were unusually disciplined and stable and were more likely to have white-collar grandparents and parents than any other professional group among blacks.[13]

11. Edgar G. Epps, Irwin Katz, and Leyland J. Axelson, "Relation of Mothers' Employment to Intellectual Performance of Negro College Students," *Social Problems*, vol. 11, no. 4 (Spring 1964), pp. 414, 418.

12. Robert H. Jackson, "Some Aspirations of Lower Class Black Mothers," *Journal of Comparative Family Studies*, vol. 6, no. 2 (Autumn 1975), pp. 175–76.

13. Edwards, *Negro Professional Class*, p. 78.

# 3

# Education and Career Motivation

Professional opportunity is ultimately a reflection of educational opportunity, for few students, whatever their native talents, are in a position to surpass consistently the standards and boundaries of their formal schooling. Since success in education is cumulative, and professional students tend generally to reflect the strength or weakness of their preprofessional preparation, questions concerning the respondents' early schooling and undergraduate education were included in the questionnaire.

## Early Schooling

All the respondents in the oldest category attended public grade school. In the middle age-group, twenty-nine (96.6%) of the thirty respondents went to public grade schools and one went to private school. Seventy-eight (83.8%) of the youngest group attended public grade school; three, private school; and eleven, parochial school.

The oldest group followed the same pattern in high school attendance. There was a slight decrease in public high school enrollment in the middle cohort and a slight trend toward private and parochial school attendance. This was also true of the youngest respondents.

Between 40 percent and 50 percent of each cohort went to grade schools in which 50 percent or more of the student body was black. In high school attendance, however, there was a sharp reduction for each cohort in the number attending predominantly black schools, particularly among the oldest group, where only two went to high schools with populations of 50 percent or more blacks. In the middle and youngest cohorts the numbers were, respectively, seven and twenty-nine.

## Undergraduate Education

The "Negro college," with an all-black student body, was for many years the predominant source of college education for blacks. There were 99 such colleges in the United States in 1900.[1] By 1950 the number had increased

1. John P. Davis, ed., *The American Negro Reference Book* (Englewood Cliffs, N.J.: Prentice-Hall, 1966), pp. 381–82.

to 118, of which 114 were in the South.[2] According to Martin D. Jenkins, only about half were accredited or approved by the associations having jurisdiction in their areas.[3]

In 1835, Oberlin College offered its presidency to Professor Asa Mahan of Lane Seminary. He accepted on condition that Oberlin be integrated, with blacks and whites being admitted on equal terms.[4] The result was that "in 1835, the Trustees [of Oberlin College] established a policy of admitting students 'irrespective of color' and Oberlin came to be the first college to declare its instruction open to all races."[5]

But Oberlin was the rare exception. If blacks wanted higher education, they had to provide it for themselves. Blacks and abolitionists, discouraged by the realization that admission to northern institutions was an unlikely prospect, "concluded that separate colleges for colored people were necessary."[6] As a result, Fisk, Howard, and Hampton came into being. Even later, when northern schools became available, many northern blacks preferred to attend the southern black schools.[7]

It was not until the World War I period that blacks began to apply for admission to northern colleges and universities.[8] Of the 43,821 black graduates between 1926 and 1936, only 6,424 (14.7%) graduated from northern colleges, while 37,397 (85.3%) were alumni of southern black colleges.[9] Nevertheless, Richard Bardolph noted that only six of the leading black lawyers in the 1940s and 1950s went to black colleges.[10] In his study of black lawyers in 1934, Carter G. Woodson found that 27.6 percent had not attended college and 18.2 percent had received legal training either by reading in law offices or serving lawyers as clerks or apprentices.[11]

In the present study of 141 lawyers, fourteen (77.7%) of the oldest cohort went to undergraduate schools in the North; nine (50.0%) of them

2. Ibid., p. 384 (citing Gunnar Myrdal, *An American Dilemma* [New York: Harper & Row, 1944], p. 947).

3. Davis, *American Negro Reference Book*, p. 364 (citing Martin D. Jenkins, *Journal of Negro Education*, vol. 18 [Spring 1948], p. 207).

4. Peter M. Bergman, *The Chronological History of the Negro in America* (New York: Harper & Row, 1969), p. 148.

5. Maurice W. Britts, *Blacks on White College Campuses* (Minneapolis: Challenge Productions, 1975), p. 2.

6. Ibid., p. 3.

7. Ibid., p. 4.

8. Ibid., p. 5.

9. Ibid. (citing Charles S. Johnson, *The Negro College Graduate* [Chapel Hill, N.C.: University of North Carolina Press, 1938], p. 20).

10. Richard Bardolph, *The Negro Vanguard* (Westport, Conn.: Negro University Press, 1959), p. 321.

11. Carter G. Woodson, *The Negro Professional Man and the Community* (Washington, D.C.: Association for the Study of Negro Life and History, 1934), pp. 187–88.

having been born in the North. Nineteen (63.3%) of the middle cohort went to college in the North; seventeen (56.6%) of them were born in the North. Sixty-six (70.9%) of the youngest group went to college in the North; forty-nine (52.6%) of them were born were in the North.

Of the fifty-two undergraduate colleges attended by the respondents, those of Howard, Lincoln, and Temple Universities each attracted approximately 12 percent of them. No other institutions attended by the respondents had such large percentages. Seventy-five (54.3%) of the sample attended nonblack colleges, broken down as follows: oldest cohort, nine; middle cohort, seventeen; youngest cohort, fifty-three (see Appendix 3).

There was a sex variation in the modes of tuition payments. The three most common methods of meeting tuition costs in the sample were (1) by scholarship, (2) by compensation from employment, and (3) by family funds. A higher percentage of females received family assistance.

There was an increasing probability of family funding as the education of the respondents' fathers increased, ranging from 33 percent of the fathers who completed elementary school to 77 percent of those who completed graduate or professional school. This may be a reflection of the father's income or of his attitude toward education or both. Family financing was most apparent where the mother also had a higher level of education. Funds were most forthcoming where one or both of the parents were in the professional-managerial category.

The drive to attract blacks into higher education really got under way in the 1960s. In January 1964, Robert F. Goheen, then President of Princeton University, said that "the competition among colleges and universities for able Negro students was much more intense than the traditional competition for football players."[12] Scholarship programs for blacks were initiated in a majority of the colleges attended by the respondents in this study (see Appendix 4).

Occupation and income of parents appear to have had no bearing upon the awarding of scholarships. Of the sixty-nine respondents in the sample who received some form of scholarship, forty-five (65.2%) had fathers who were employed and twenty-four (34.8%) had fathers who were unemployed. The same situation existed regarding employment of mothers. If a scholarship was based on need, it did not appear in the responses to the questionnaires. The largest percentage of scholarships was awarded to respondents who were living at home with both parents, either one or both of whom were engaged in a professional occupation. Four (22.2%) of the oldest cohort, eleven (36.6%) of the middle cohort, and forty-nine (52.6%) of the youngest cohort received some form of scholarship. None of the females of the oldest cohort, one female of the middle

12. Davis, *American Negro Reference Book*, p. 388.

cohort, and eleven of the youngest received scholarships. While the respondents did not specify the dollar amount of scholarships, eighty-five (61.6%) replied that they supplemented scholarship funds with their personal funds, as from savings accounts or earnings from employment undertaken in order to make such payments.

Another source of tuition payment was through loans or grants. Only one of the oldest cohort used this method. Three of the middle group did so, but a high percentage (48.0%) of the youngest cohort received tuition loans. Those whose mothers or fathers were in the professional-managerial category constituted the lowest percentage of students utilizing this mode of payment. For parents in the professional-managerial field, the percentage of applicants was 12.5 percent; for parents in other occupations, the percentage was 40.0 percent. There was no sex variation.

Twenty (14.5%) of the sample received veterans' benefits for tuition payments. The largest group utilizing such benefits, twelve respondents, were born between 1921 and 1937. One of the oldest cohort and seven of the youngest also replied that they paid tuition in this way.

Responses to the question of residence in undergraduate schools followed an expected pattern, with on-campus residence significantly on the increase over the years. Five (27.7%) of the oldest, eleven (36.6%) of the middle, and forty-five (50%) of the youngest cohort lived on campus during their undergraduate years. The highest percentage of those who resided off-campus lived at home with their parents. Again, it was the advent of civil rights legislation in the 1960s that brought the largest upsurge in on-campus residence, particularly in integrated housing.

One hundred one (72%) of all respondents earned B.A. degrees: fourteen (77.7%) in the oldest cohort, nineteen (63.3%) in the middle cohort, and sixty-seven (72.0%) in the youngest cohort. The middle group had the highest percentage of holders of B.S. degrees. Why this occurred is not clear; the heightened emphasis on science and technology following World War II may have been a factor.

## Blacks in Integrated Colleges

Even with the admission of more blacks to white colleges, the problem of social integration still inhibits many blacks. Maurice Britts observed that while the number of blacks attending integrated colleges seems to be increasing, "the predominantly Negro colleges enroll the bulk of the Black college students. The main reason seems to be the social aspect of college life, which the Black student can fully participate in at Negro colleges."[13]

Questioned about friendships with whites, forty-five respondents in

13. Britts, *Blacks on White College Campuses*, p. 14.

this study answered that this question was not applicable because they attended schools that had no white students. However, the majority of respondents attended integrated colleges. Where there was a racial mix, six of the oldest cohort had no white friends, while eleven had such friends but with minimal reciprocal visiting. (This response raises the question of the subjective analysis distinguishing friends from acquaintances.) Sixteen of the second cohort reported having white "friends" with an increase in reciprocal visiting. Sixty-eight of the youngest group said that they had formed friendships with white students, had visited with each other while students, and had continued such friendships after they graduated from college.

In the course of personal interviews, several interviewees of the middle cohort voiced their opinions of social life at predominantly white colleges in the North. While there was agreement that academically the schools were "okay," sentiments regarding social life varied from "tolerable" to "intolerable."

A male judge being interviewed recalled that in the 1940s a black college student in a white college was in a limited situation because 85 percent of the student body belonged to fraternities that did not accept blacks. The small number of black students were therefore socially isolated from the rest of the student body.

A female judge said that she was not involved in social life at school. Her ambition was to become a lawyer, and she directed her energies to that end. She believes that blacks who attended colleges and law schools in the 1930s, 1940s, and 1950s would concur with the observation that "social behavior" was not a predominant factor; they were "going to school to learn, not for social life."

A male judge who was in undergraduate school in the late 1940s said that the three blacks in his junior class formed their own political party, and although several parties were in the running, they came in second in the school elections. This experience, unique for that time, promoted a number of good relationships, some developing into ongoing friendships.

Another jurist commented that his undergraduate years were good years. A number of his white classmates became and still are among his best friends. Nevertheless, there were evidences of segregation. For example, he traveled with a sports team but was not allowed to stay in a hotel with his white teammates. Furthermore, blacks were not admitted to fraternities or invited to parties given by whites. He purposely disregarded these disturbing evidences of racism and devoted himself to his studies.

Writing of black students in eastern colleges, Barbara Lewisohn cited comments of blacks who attended college between 1925 and 1939. One remarked that in 1928, no matter how accepted a black was academically, the situation of being one of only three or four in a school became too much. In his institution there were five suicides among black students in six years. Another pointed out the limitations in eating facilities, since many of the restaurants in his college area were off limits to blacks. Lewisohn mentioned specifically Brown, Rutgers, and Dartmouth as institutions where black undergraduates had such experiences during the years in question.[14]

Despite demoralizing incidents and unsettling evidences of racism, the determination of blacks to complete college was strong, according to a 1963 study by Kenneth B. Clark and Lawrence Plotkin. Clark and Plotkin found that black students in integrated colleges had a lower dropout rate than white students or black students attending segregated colleges. They found further that the dropout rate was one-quarter of the national rate; that fewer than 10 percent of the black students who were studied failed to obtain a degree, while approximately 40 percent of the whites did not earn degrees; that financial reasons for dropping out of college led all others; that college grades for these students were average, with 31 percent earning a "B" average or better; that less than 10 percent were graduated with honors; that little more than one percent were elected to Phi Beta Kappa; that there was no relationship between family income and academic success; and that academic success was directly related to parents' occupational level.[15]

## Choosing the Legal Profession

After graduation from college, respondents were faced with choosing a career.

Sixty-seven (47.5%) of the respondents went directly from college to law school. The percentage of those who did not have to work—fifty-nine (42.1%) males and fifteen (10.7%) females—increased in each cohort. Two (11.1%) of the oldest, six (20.0%) of the middle, and sixty-five (69.9%) of the youngest were able to enter law school immediately upon graduation from college. Some respondents entered military service, some became teachers, others obtained jobs at the post office. A few replied that they entered industry, while others said they did odd jobs. Four did not answer the question.

Why, in view of the obstacles confronting blacks, did the respondents ultimately choose the law as a profession? Their reasons, which vary in their broad outlines from one cohort to the next, demonstrate that the

14. Barbara Lewisohn, "Black Students in Eastern Colleges 1895–1940," *The Crisis*, vol. 81, no. 3 (March 1974), p. 86.

15. Davis, *American Negro Reference Book*, pp. 389–90 (citing Kenneth B. Clark and Lawrence Plotkin, *The Negro Student at Integrated Colleges* [New York: National Scholarship Service and Fund for Negro Students, 1963], pp. 7–9).

attitudes of blacks who become lawyers have changed over the years. At the same time, however, they show a wide variety of personal motivations, even within the same age-group.

In recent years there have been important studies involving the dynamics of motivation. Speaking specifically of blacks and the legal profession, Earl L. Carl and Kenneth R. Callahan wrote:

> Motivation . . . means not only that which prompts one to seek a legal education, but it also implies a strong desire to learn with the hope or knowledge that one's effort and determination will be satisfied by the rewards of a profession: social status, respect, the opportunity to render service, as well as the acquisition of some of the comforts and pleasures of life.[16]

G. Franklin Edwards noted in his 1959 study that his respondents saw in the legal profession an opportunity to be of service, primarily in the area of social welfare.[17] This substantiated the 1948 findings of Herbert H. Hartshorn, who compared the scores of black and white lawyers and found that blacks had a higher score on the "Interest-Maturity" scale. They thought of the legal profession primarily in terms of social welfare.[18]

Fifty-seven percent of Edwards's respondents were born in the South. They were motivated strongly by the consideration of service to their families who, because of inadequate legal advice and protection, had lost property, suffered injustices, and repeatedly been denied their civil rights.[19] Edwards's respondents wanted to engage in the legal battles started by such leading black lawyers as Charles Houston, whom Edwards considered the single most outstanding black lawyer of his time.[20] Edwards observed that the lawyers in his survey expressed greater interest in the field of social work and the ministry than did any other group. Some of his interviewees had had previous experience as clergymen or social workers.[21]

On the other hand, in his 1959 study of black lawyers in the vanguard of the 1940s and the 1950s, Richard Bardolph found that very few chose the law in order to fight the race's battles. The primary motivation in his

16. Earl L. Carl and Kenneth R. Callahan, "Negroes and the Law," *Journal of Legal Education*, vol. 17, no. 3 (1964–65), p. 254.
17. G. Franklin Edwards, *The Negro Professional Class* (Glencoe, Ill.: Free Press, 1959), p. 133.
18. Ibid., p. 134 (citing Herbert H. Hartshorn, "Vocational Interest Patterns of Negro Professional Men" (Ph.D. dissertation, University of Minnesota, 1948).
19. Edwards, *Negro Professional Class*, p. 133.
20. See Geraldine R. Segal, *In Any Fight Some Fall* (Rockville, Md.: Mercury Press, 1975), for a biography of Charles H. Houston.
21. Edwards, *Negro Professional Class*, p. 134.

sample was the expectation of financial success. And while all were drawn mainly from the upper stratum of black society, nearly all had to work their way through law school. Bardolph's sample was very small, however, and should not be equated with the findings of Edwards.[22]

Of the fifteen judges and lawyers personally interviewed in the present study, ten said they were motivated primarily by their interest in the law, two simply "drifted" into the law, and three were inspired by such black legal heroes as Charles Houston and Judge Raymond Pace Alexander. One lawyer of the middle cohort went to law school "on a bet with a buddy in Korea." He viewed his acceptance at law school as a means of getting out of the army early, expecting to go to law school for a year, then drop out and go into another field such as journalism. Once he entered Temple Law School, the conditions of blacks at home convinced him that "law was the only chance for me and my family." His mother feared that he "couldn't do it," not referring to his scholastic ability but to the disappointments and frustrations she felt were in store for him. However, he completed law school and has been in practice ever since.

Another interviewee said that he decided to become a lawyer because his parents wanted him to "be something." They did not specify the profession and he chose the law, inspired by Dean Erwin N. Griswold of Harvard Law School and Judge Raymond Pace Alexander of Philadelphia.

Of the ten judges and lawyers interviewed who said they always wanted to be lawyers, only one said he chose the profession in order "to get rights for Negroes." When he entered Yale Law School in 1948, however, he asked where the constitutional law classes were being held and was told, "Boy, you're not ready for that." His response was, "That's just what we want—the Constitution."

Another who always wanted to be a lawyer was attracted to courtroom proceedings from early childhood. At the age of eleven or twelve he would visit courtrooms and listen to arguments and pleadings with an increasing awareness that the legal profession would be his career choice. His father wanted him to be a social worker, his mother urged the ministry, but he knew that the law was the only profession for him.

One of the lawyers who "drifted into the law" said he had planned to study medicine because "it seemed that doctors drove around in nice cars, had money and a good life." But at Bates College he came under the influence of a science professor who urged him not to go into medicine unless he had a gift for it, not to do so merely in order to make more money. Since making money was his goal, he decided to prepare for a business career and entered the Wharton School of Business Administra-

22. Bardolph, *Negro Vanguard*, pp. 321–22.

tion at the University of Pennsylvania. During his years at the Wharton School, he met a leading black lawyer who persuaded him to study law. He applied to Harvard Law School and was accepted.

An outstanding member of the judiciary said that when he was contemplating a career, his lawyer-father gave him no other choice than the law. He has never regretted this pressure or his own final decision.

A leading female judge said that she could give no specific reason for having studied law but that she had decided to do so when she was in junior high school. It may have come about by the process of elimination. She had no hero in the law, but she did have an unusual father. Although he earned only $3,800 a year, he saw to it that his three children went to college. She could have become a teacher, but this career did not appeal to her. She wanted a profession that would offer more challenge. When she chose the law she was considered "some sort of kook." Women, and all the more black women, did not go into the law in those pre–civil rights days. She knew only two black women in the law. Her friends ridiculed her, wondering what she was trying to prove by enrolling in law school. Then, after she showed that she could become not only a lawyer but also a judge, some of the same women sent their daughters to her for career advice.

An analysis of responses to the question of motivation in the mailed questionnaires revealed that frequently a combination of motives directed the respondents toward a legal career. Ninety-three of the respondents said that "interest in the law" was their primary motivation. Sixty-one said that they were motivated by a desire for justice for minorities. Approximately forty-seven said that economic benefits and family encouragement influenced them in their decision. Only thirty-two were inspired by black lawyers to pursue a legal career. The least inspiration came from white lawyers; only nine noted this influence. A rather surprising disclosure was that while ninety-three were motivated by interest in the law, only thirty-one felt that they had an aptitude for the law.

A sex-variation analysis showed that more females than males felt that they had an aptitude for the profession; also more females were inspired by black lawyers and more were encouraged by their families to become lawyers. Fewer women were motivated by the desire to achieve justice for minorities than by the economic benefits of the profession. Their "interest in the law" as a motivating factor (82%) was even greater than that of the men (66%).

Thus the three cohorts were in agreement in two areas of motivation. All said that their interest in the law was their primary motivation, and all agreed that white lawyers provided the minimal motivation. The members of the oldest cohort were motivated by the successes of black lawyers, but this motivation decreased with the other two cohorts. There was a sharp difference in the motivation of justice for minorities. Nine (50.0%) of the oldest and forty-seven (50.0%) of the youngest said that this was a strong motivating factor, while only five (16.7%) of the middle cohort gave this reason.

Strong family encouragement came where one or both parents were professionals. Among all three cohorts the family member most responsible for encouragement was the father. However, mothers who were homemakers, and not otherwise employed, as well as mothers who were in the professional-managerial category, played strong roles in encouraging their children to enter the law.

# 4

# Blacks in the Law Schools

## Philadelphia Law Schools

Minority students educated in law schools in large cities practice primarily in the city in which they attended law school. Thus, the impact of CLEO and the other forces discussed above on the number of black Philadelphia lawyers may be seen in the black enrollment trends (see Table 3, below) at the three local Philadelphia law schools: University of Pennsylvania Law School,[1] Temple University Law School,[2] and Villanova Law School.[3]

The Philadelphia law schools, like law schools nationally, show a dramatic increase in black enrollments since the late 1960s, from a total of 31 in the 1968–69 academic year to highs of 185 in the 1977–78 and 1978–79 years. However, it was in the 1979–80 academic year, when the black enrollment dropped from 185 to 146, that the national decrease in black enrollments became apparent in Philadelphia's law schools as well. Since that time there has been an increase to 165.

The most dramatic increase at Villanova occurred between the academic years 1968–69, when there were eight black law students, and 1971–72, when there were twenty-four. Between 1976 and 1982, the next schools years for which statistics on black enrollment exist, the numbers dropped from sixteen to eleven, rose to eighteen, dropped to fifteen, then rose to twenty-three. The causes of the fluctuation are unclear.

Black law school enrollment at the University of Pennsylvania conformed more closely to general national trends, going from ten (1.8% of total enrollment) to seventy-seven (12.6%) in the ten-year period from 1967–68 to 1977–78. However, the school years from 1977–78 through

1. Statistics for 1968–78 supplied by Mrs. Christine Jackson, Registrar; 1979–80 statistics supplied by Dean Morris Arnold, Law School of the University of Pennsylvania; 1981–82 statistics supplied by Rae DiBlasi, Assistant to the Dean; and all statistics were reviewed by Ernie R. Gonzalves. These figures take on added significance when it is realized that from 1955 to 1969 the University of Pennsylvania graduated only 12 of a total of 17 blacks who were enrolled during that period. "Report of the Philadelphia Bar Association Special Committee on Pennsylvania Bar Admission Procedures—Racial Discrimination of Pennsylvania Bar Examinations," *Temple Law Quarterly*, vol. 44, no. 2 (Winter 1971), p. 182.

2. Statistics supplied by Dean Peter Liacouras, Temple University School of Law.

3. Statistics supplied by J. Miriam McFadden, Registrar.

Table 3
**Black Enrollment in Philadelphia Area Law Schools**

| Year | University of Pennsylvania | Temple University | Villanova University | Total |
|------|------|------|------|------|
| 1967–68 | 10 | 3 | NA | NA |
| 1968–69 | 13 | 11 | 8 | 31 |
| 1969–70 | 18 | 21 | 6 | 42 |
| 1970–71 | 31 | 28 | 16 | 62 |
| 1971–72 | 39 | 47 | 24 | 99 |
| 1972–73 | 38 | 65* | 23 | 125 |
| 1973–74 | 47 | 51 | 24† | 124† |
| 1974–75 | 47 | 57 | 28† | 137† |
| 1975–76 | 54 | 64 | 22† | 141† |
| 1976–77 | 69 | 88 | 16 | 170 |
| 1977–78 | 77 | 97 | 11 | 185 |
| 1978–79 | 70 | 104 | 11 | 185 |
| 1979–80 | 51 | 77 | 18 | 146 |
| 1980–81 | 40 | 100 | 15 | 155 |
| 1981–82 | 38 | 104 | 23 | 165 |

*The first year in which the Special Admissions program was in operation.
†Before 1973 the only group considered "minority" at Villanova were blacks. From 1973 through 1975 other nonwhite ethnic groups were also considered minorities, but the statistics were not broken down.

1981–82, inclusive, saw a disproportionate decrease in black enrollment, from seventy-seven to thirty-eight (6.1%)black students.

The increase in the number of black students at the Temple University School of Law was even more dramatic. This was due to a combination of causes. Significant is the fact that, as a state-affiliated institution, Temple has much lower tuition rates. Another factor may be that Temple maintains the only night law school in the area, thus enabling students to pursue their law studies even though they must work during the day. The primary reason, however, is that Temple recruits diligently in black institutions, and in historically white ones with substantial numbers of black students, and publicizes widely its objective of increasing its enrollment of black students. In the 1981–82 academic year at Temple, blacks comprised 8.8 percent of the total law school enrollment, whereas at the University of Pennsylvania Law School the percentage had dropped from 11.0 percent in 1978–79 to 6.1 percent (38 out of 628) in 1981–82. At Villanova, while only 3.5 percent of the law school enrollment in the 1981–82 year was black (23 out of 649), this was 68.6 percent higher than the percentage in the 1980–81 year.

Most striking is the increase in the numbers and proportion of black women students in all three schools during the period analyzed. The rise in the proportion of females in the black student population at the University of Pennsylvania Law School during these years has been especially dramatic. Black women, who constituted only 20 percent of the ten black students in 1967–68, comprised 30.8 percent of its thirty-nine black students in 1971–72 and 63.2 percent of its thirty-eight black students in 1981–82.

At Temple there were only three black law students in 1967–68, all males. By the 1971–72 academic year, women comprised 19.1 percent of Temple's forty-seven black students; by the 1981–82 year, 59.6 percent of the 104 black students were women.

Villanova at first lagged significantly behind the other two schools in increasing its percentage of black women, but recently it has made progress in equalizing the representation of the sexes. For the 1968–69 academic year there were eight black men and no black women at Villanova; in 1971–72 only two of twenty-four black students were women; but by 1981–82 twelve (52.2%) of Villanova's twenty-three black students were women.

At the University of Pennsylvania Law School (see Table 4, below), black male enrollment peaked in 1976–77; black female enrollment peaked two years later. During the 1967–80 period the proportion of black women to black men rose from 20.0 percent in 1967–68 to 70.0 percent in 1980–81, but dropping in 1981–82 to 63.2 percent. Since 1978 the majority of black students have been women.

There are two black assistant professors on the faculty, one male and one female (see Appendix 18).

Temple University School of Law (see Table 5, below) has had a gradually increasing percentage of blacks in its total law school enrollment, going from 0.5 percent in 1967–68 to 8.8 percent in 1981–82. The peak year for black students at Temple University, in actual numbers as well as percentages, was 1978. This number decreased substantially in 1979 but moved back up in 1980 and 1981. While the number of black males decreased, there has been a dramatic increase in the number and percentages of black women to total black enrollment at the law school, from 18.2 percent in 1968–69 to 59.6 percent in 1981–82.

Temple University School of Law has a substantial black faculty: three professors, five part-time lecturers, and one administrator (see Appendix 18).

In 1970 the first black female entered Villanova University School of Law (see Table 6, below). The percentage of black law students was small; in 1967 it was one percent. By 1981 it had increased to 3.5%. In the 1981–82 academic year the number of black women doubled since 1980 from six to

Table 4
**Black Enrollment at University of Pennsylvania Law School**

| | Total Enrollment | Black Students | % Black to Total | Black Male | % Black Male to Total Black | Black Female | % Black Female to Total Black |
|---|---|---|---|---|---|---|---|
| 1967–68 | 547 | 10 | 1.8 | 8 | 80.0 | 2 | 20.0 |
| 1968–69 | 510 | 13 | 2.5 | 9 | 69.2 | 4 | 30.8 |
| 1969–70 | 508 | 18 | 3.5 | 12 | 66.7 | 6 | 33.3 |
| 1970–71 | 582 | 31 | 5.3 | 23 | 74.2 | 8 | 25.8 |
| 1971–72 | 643 | 39 | 6.1 | 27 | 69.2 | 12 | 30.8 |
| 1972–73 | 625 | 38 | 6.1 | 24 | 63.2 | 14 | 36.8 |
| 1973–74 | 615 | 47 | 7.6 | 31 | 66.0 | 16 | 34.0 |
| 1974–75 | 594 | 47 | 7.9 | 34 | 72.3 | 13 | 27.7 |
| 1975–76 | 588 | 54 | 9.2 | 37 | 68.5 | 17 | 31.5 |
| 1976–77 | 600 | 69 | 11.5 | 39 | 56.5 | 30 | 43.5 |
| 1977–78 | 613 | 77 | 12.6 | 38 | 49.4 | 39 | 50.6 |
| 1978–79 | 635 | 70 | 11.0 | 25 | 35.7 | 45 | 64.3 |
| 1979–80 | 637 | 51* | 8.0 | 17 | 33.3 | 34 | 66.7 |
| 1980–81 | 650 | 40 | 6.2 | 12 | 30.0 | 28 | 70.0 |
| 1981–82 | 628 | 38 | 6.1 | 14 | 36.8 | 24 | 63.2 |

*"Minority Students at the University of Pennsylvania Law School," Report as of 1979-80, states that out of a total enrollment of 637, there were 52 (51 on table) blacks, 25 Asians, and 26 Hispanics. Information taken from brochure produced by minority students at University of Pennsylvania Law School: "Our Continued Presence."

Table 5
**Black Enrollment at Temple University School of Law**

| | Total Enrollment | Black Students | % Black to Total | Black Male | % Black Male to Total Black | Black Female | % Black Female to Total Black |
|---|---|---|---|---|---|---|---|
| 1967–68 | 504 | 3 | 0.5 | 1 | 33.3 | 2 | 66.7 |
| 1968–69 | 575 | 11 | 1.9 | 9 | 81.8 | 2 | 18.2 |
| 1969–70 | 677 | 21 | 3.1 | 17 | 80.9 | 4 | 19.1 |
| 1970–71 | 804 | 28 | 3.4 | 22 | 78.5 | 6 | 21.5 |
| 1971–72 | 942 | 47 | 4.9 | 38 | 80.8 | 9 | 19.2 |
| 1972–73 | 1,148 | 65 | 5.6 | 50 | 76.9 | 15 | 23.9 |
| 1973–74 | 1,181 | 51 | 4.3 | 38 | 74.5 | 13 | 25.5 |
| 1974–75 | 1,180 | 57 | 4.8 | 42 | 73.6 | 15 | 26.4 |
| 1975–76 | 1,151 | 64 | 5.6 | 37 | 57.8 | 27 | 42.2 |
| 1976–77 | 1,115 | 88 | 7.9 | 50 | 56.8 | 38 | 43.2 |
| 1977–78 | 1,145 | 97 | 8.5 | 54 | 55.7 | 43 | 44.3 |
| 1978–79 | 1,128 | 104 | 9.2 | 58 | 55.8 | 46 | 44.2 |
| 1979–80 | 1,088 | 77 | 7.1 | 39 | 50.6 | 38 | 49.4 |
| 1980–81 | 1,188 | 100 | 8.4 | 44 | 44.0 | 56 | 56.0 |
| 1981–82 | 1,185 | 104 | 8.8 | 42 | 40.4 | 62 | 59.6 |

Table 6
**Black Enrollment at Villanova University School of Law**

| | Total Enrollment | Black Students | % Black to Total | Black Male | % Black Male to Total Black | Black Female | % Black Female to Total Black |
|---|---|---|---|---|---|---|---|
| 1967–68 | 414 | 4 | 1.0 | 4 | 100 | | |
| 1968–69 | 411 | 8 | 1.9 | 8 | 100 | | |
| 1969–70 | 433 | 6 | 1.4 | 6 | 100 | | |
| 1970–71 | 477 | 16 | 3.3 | 15 | 93.8 | 1 | 6.2 |
| 1971–72 | 605 | 24 | 4.0 | 22 | 91.7 | 2 | 8.3 |
| 1972–73 | 625 | 23 | 3.7 | 21 | 91.3 | 2 | 8.7 |
| 1973–74 | 662 | 24 | 3.6 | | | | |
| 1974–75 | 649 | 28 | 4.3 | | | | |
| 1975–76 | 632 | 22 | 3.6 | 13 | 59.1 | 9 | 40.9 |
| 1976–77 | 637 | 16 | 2.5 | 9 | 56.3 | 7 | 43.8 |
| 1977–78 | 638 | 11 | 1.7 | 4 | 36.4 | 7 | 63.6 |
| 1978–79 | 636 | 11 | 1.7 | 8 | 72.7 | 3 | 27.2 |
| 1979–80 | 667 | 18 | 2.7 | 12 | 66.7 | 6 | 33.3 |
| 1980–81 | 637 | 15 | 2.4 | 9 | 60.0 | 6 | 40.0 |
| 1981–82 | 649 | 23 | 3.5 | 11 | 47.8 | 12 | 52.2 |

NOTE: From 1973 through 1975 other ethnic groups were considered minorities, but statistics do not show the breakdown.

twelve. Although the number and percentages remained small, there was an upsurge in black student enrollment, both male and female, in 1981.

Blacks on the faculty consist of a judge who is a part-time lecturer, a full-time professor, and an assistant professor who also serves as librarian (see Appendix 18).

## Legal Education of Respondents

### Law School Attended

Although enrollment statistics of Philadelphia law schools provide a good indicator of local trends, black lawyers now practicing in Philadelphia have attended a large number of law schools outside Philadelphia. Respondents in the present survey attended twenty-eight different law schools (see Appendix 6), of which three were predominantly black—Howard University, North Carolina Central, and Robert Terrell (an evening school that operated until 1957).[4] Of these, Howard, Temple, and the University of

4. Harold R. Washington, "History and Role of Black Law Schools," *Howard Law Journal*, vol. 18, no. 2 (1974), p. 396.

Pennsylvania had the highest enrollment of black law students. Four (24%) of the oldest cohort went to Howard (all males); two (12%) to Temple (one male, one female); and four (24%) to the University of Pennsylvania (three males, one female). The middle cohort had a substantial representation at Temple, where there were seventeen (57%) (all males); six (20%) attended Howard (all males); and three (10%) matriculated at the University of Pennsylvania (two males, one female). The youngest cohort showed a sharp decrease in proportionate attendance at Temple— seventeen (19%) (all males)—while the attendance at Pennsylvania rose to eighteen (20%) (fourteen males, four females); there was a slight increase at Howard—sixteen (18%) (twelve males, four females).

In addition to these law schools, the oldest and the middle cohorts were each represented at five other law schools. For the youngest, there was an increase of twenty-two additional law schools.

## Financing Law School Tuition

A law school education is an expensive proposition—at a minimum, three years of rising tuition as well as the ordinary living expenses. Financing this professional training represents a significant monetary burden upon the individual black student involved, upon his family, upon the various funding agencies that have sought to encourage minority enrollment in law school, or upon some combination of all three.

Of the forty respondents' fathers who were in the professional-managerial category, twenty-seven (68%) paid tuition for their children at college but only seventeen (43%) paid law school tuition. Of the ninety-two families of the entire parent population, including those with professional-managerial heads, thirty families (34%) paid for or contributed to their children's law-school tuition.

Opportunities for black students to attend law school have increased over the years, and the number of respondents attending law school during the day rather than at night has increased from 71 percent for the oldest cohort to 97 percent for the youngest. Among the members of the youngest cohort, family contributions to tuition dropped sharply, but funds from employment and scholarships replaced a large proportion of family funding. Sixty-one percent of the respondents—sixty-five of the men and twenty of the women—stated that they had had scholarships in varying amounts. In terms of the three cohorts, the recipients of scholarships were as follows: five (27%) of the oldest cohort (one male to Pennsylvania, one male to Howard, one male to Harvard, and one male and one female to Temple); nine (30%) of the middle cohort (one male and one female to Pennsylvania, three males to Howard, one male to Harvard, and three males to Temple); and forty-four (47.3%) of the youngest cohort (fourteen to Pennsylvania, eleven males and three females; thirteen to Howard, ten males and three females, twelve to Temple, ten males and two females; and five to Yale, four males and one female. (See Appendix 7 for a complete chart of scholarships, showing law schools.)

In the course of the personal interviews, lawyers told of their experiences with scholarships. One, a member of the oldest cohort and a *cum laude* graduate of the College of the University of Pennsylvania, paid his first term's tuition at Harvard Law School. Following his examinations, he received a refund of this tuition plus a full scholarship.

Another lawyer interviewed, who was also a member of the oldest cohort, said that he was offered $750 to attend the University of Tennessee Law School in 1933. He also was approached by a representative of the Office of Admissions at Yale Law School, who asked him how much he needed for support. He replied that his wife would keep her job as a secretary, and he therefore could manage if he received approximately $300 each term. Yale responded by giving him $450 each term.

Another means of meeting tuition payments came into existence in the early 1960s: the loan or grant plan whereby the student could borrow from federally funded student aid programs and begin repayment after he or she completed law school. Approximately 8,300 undergraduate and graduate institutions have taken part in this program.[5] The program was not in existence when the oldest cohort went to law school, and only two of the middle cohort entered law school when it was available. By the time the youngest cohort was applying for law school admission, the loan or grant program was fully operative in law schools throughout the country. In the sample studied, sixty-three of the youngest cohort paid their tuition by this method.

The use of veterans' benefits diminished with the generations. Altogether, twenty-five of the respondents availed themselves of this method of payment for law school tuition—seven of the oldest cohort, eight of the middle, and ten of the youngest.

The number of male students who worked while at law school was 16 percent greater than in the case of women students. This percentage increased with each cohort. Six of the oldest cohort, eighteen of the middle, and sixty of the youngest cohort had some employment while at law school. They listed teaching, post office work, law office employment, and "odd jobs" as types of work in which they engaged.

Approximately 30 percent of each cohort were married when they entered law school, but the movement away from their parents' homes to

5. *New York Times,* December 4, 1977, p. 65.

residences of their own was not restricted to married students. Thus, twenty of the unmarried respondents in the youngest cohort lived in their own quarters, nine of them lived in an integrated dormitory, and nine lived in apartments with roommates. In this cohort there was a great deal of mobility. Nineteen reported that they changed residences frequently— living with their parents, living with friends, or living alone. Sometimes they resided with black friends, other times with white friends.

## Social Life at Law School

In spite of its academic and financial rigors, there is some time for socializing in law school, and the social patterns among law students to a certain extent anticipate their relationships with other legal professionals after graduation.

Thirteen of the oldest cohort replied that they had white friends while at law school, and nine said that these friendships had continued after graduation. This may seem a large percentage (77%) for the oldest cohort, since they attended law school prior to the push for integration stimulated by the civil rights movement. However, since only one attended an all-black law school (Robert Terrell) and four attended Howard, which was predominantly but not entirely black, it is understandable that with so relatively large a proportion attending white schools, friendships with white students developed. Twenty-four of the middle cohort stated that they had formed such friendships, and twenty-one said they had retained such friendships. Seventy-five of the youngest cohort reported friendships with white students, but only fifty-four said that after graduation from law school they had remained friends. A possible explanation for the cessation of friendships with white persons is that the widening areas of opportunities for the graduates in the youngest cohort led them in so many different directions that they seldom saw each other. Another explanation, gleaned from interviews, is that younger black lawyers feel the need to become more cohesive, to close ranks, and to present a more united front.

In the course of interviews a member of the oldest cohort said that every black student who went to law school in those days was under the "handicap of work," that is, work for pay outside school. The black students had to be at work four to five hours daily and were fatigued, he said, while other students had a head start when it came to studying. Although there were good relationships, there was not much time for socializing or developing friendships.

Another of the oldest cohort responded in his interview that he enjoyed the Yale community, that after admission one becomes part of the Yale Law School family. There were only three black students there when he attended in 1917. Since then his daughter has also graduated from Yale

Law School. A judge in the oldest cohort advised that while everyone at Yale was friendly, he had not entered into the social life of the university or of the law school. Another lawyer in the same cohort recalled that his years at Harvard Law School provided pleasant experiences, although social activities were limited for blacks and for Jews.

A lawyer in the middle cohort answered in his interview that he had had no social problems at Harvard Law School and maintained good relations with roommates. However, he married after his first year and subsequently lived with his wife off campus.

A member of the youngest cohort, also a graduate of Harvard Law School, said that he and other blacks at Harvard had felt that race was not significant in relations with white students, but he added that black-white social interaction was nevertheless minimal.

Among all the black lawyers surveyed, a frequent response to questions concerning extracurricular activities or social life at law school was "no time." However, sixty-six of the respondents stated that they engaged in social activities of their own while at law school, that is, with other blacks. The Black American Law Students' Association (BALSA) attracted a large number of the youngest cohort.

## Academic Honors in Law School

Law schools confer a variety of honors upon students who perform particularly well. The most widely conferred and publicly recognized of these honors is election to an editorship on the school's law review, the journal that offers commentary on general legal issues and recent cases decided by the courts. Of the 138 answers to the question about election to an editorship on the law review, fourteen respondents were editors on their respective law review staffs. In this group were eleven males (three in the oldest cohort, five in the middle, and three in the youngest) and three females (one in the oldest and two in the youngest cohort). Two, one a male in the middle cohort and the other a female in the youngest cohort, were elected members of the Order of the Coif, an honorary fraternity for both men and women that corresponds to Phi Beta Kappa in the liberal arts undergraduate school, recognizing "pre-eminent scholarship in the law."[6]

6. *Encyclopedia of Associations,* 11th ed. (Detroit: Gale Research Co., 1977), vol. 1, p. 1151. As of 1977 only 56 law schools had chapters of the Order of the Coif.

# 5

---

# Bar Examinations and Admissions

In 1903 the Supreme Court of Pennsylvania established the State Board of Law Examiners, redesignated by the court in 1977 as the Pennsylvania Board of Law Examiners, and formalized the bar examinations as one of the general requirements for admission to the Pennsylvania Bar.[1]

Although there have been changes in some provisions, the general requirements for admission to the Pennsylvania Bar have not been materially altered since 1903 insofar as the objectives of the present study are concerned. In addition to good character and a connection with Pennsylvania, the requisites are (1) receipt of an undergraduate degree from an accredited college or university or of an education that, in the opinion of the board, is the equivalent of an undergraduate college or university education; (2) receipt of an earned Bachelor of Laws or Juris Doctor degree from an accredited law school; and (3) passing one of the bar examinations given by the board.[2] (An "accredited" law school is one accredited by the American Bar Association,[3] which has published detailed "Standards and Rules of Procedure for the Approval of Law Schools."[4]) Special rules[5] permitting admission on motion rather than by taking the bar examination apply in the case of an attorney who is a member in good standing of the bar of a reciprocal state and has practiced law outside Pennsylvania for five years;[6] of the 141 respondents, only

---

1. Order of the Supreme Court of Pennsylvania, In Re Pennsylvania Bar Admission Rules, issued June 6, 1977, 471 Pa. lxxxvii (1977).

2. Ibid., p. lxxxii, Rule 203.

3. Ibid., p. lxxix, Rule 102.

4. Approval of Law Schools, American Bar Association Standards and Rules of Procedure, as Amended, 1979, pamphlet published by the American Bar Association and again on December 17, 1981.

5. 471 Pa. lxxxiii, Rule 204. Rule 204 was amended on November 11, 1978. See Order of the Supreme Court of Pennsylvania, In Re Pennsylvania Bar Admission Rules, Amendments, 480 Pa. xxix (1978), Rule 204, and Order of the Supreme Court of Pennsylvania, In Re Amendment of Rules 203, 204, and 205 of the Pennsylvania Bar Admission Rules, 494 Pa. lvii (1981), Rule 204.

6. A reciprocal state is a state having a reciprocal agreement or arrangement with the Commonwealth of Pennsylvania concerning admission to the bar; 471 Pa. pp. lxxix–lxxx,

three were admitted in this manner, two in the first cohort and one in the second.

One hundred and nineteen (84.3%) of the respondents did not answer the request for comments about the bar examination. The twenty-two who did respond provided the widest possible range of answers. Of the three in the first cohort who did so, one simply said, "No comments"; another replied that the questions were "fair"; and the third stated that she could recall only one question she could not answer at all but had been told by Attorney General of Pennsylvania Francis Shunk Brown that she had finished first that year.

Of the eight lawyers in the second cohort who responded, two labeled the examination "fair," one as "no problem," one as "rough," another as "difficult," and still another as "Ouija Board." One stated that he had passed the examination on the first attempt but could not remember much about the questions. The eighth commented in more detail: "The Pennsylvania Bar exam until recently had its own reputation for the apparent difficulty it presented to the black examinees. I failed to pass upon taking it immediately after graduation in 1956. After two years in the army, I took the exam again within two months of discharge from the army and passed with points to spare."

The most responses, and the widest variation, came from the bar members in the youngest cohort. Four responded favorably: one, "not difficult"; another "a breeze"; and two that they "took the examination only once." On the other hand, one reported that he had taken the examination four times and another that he had failed once and passed on his second try. Three were strong in their statements that the bar examinations were discriminatory, were a means of prejudicially excluding blacks, and were otherwise unfair; and two used profane expressions to convey their negative opinions.

A number of black lawyers interviewed charged that there was discrimination, racism, and bias in bar examinations. Some even claimed that they were so designed that whites would pass and blacks would fail. Several pointed out that no black had been admitted to the Pennsylvania Bar for a ten-year period between 1933 and 1943.[7] Some attributed this situation to the racism and bias of a longtime former secretary of the Board

---

Rule 102. As rule 204 presently provides, after admission in a reciprocal state the attorney must have practiced law in that state or other reciprocal states outside Pennsylvania, or engaged full-time in the teaching of law at an accredited law school, for at least five of the seven years immediately preceding application for admission to the Pennsylvania Bar. 494 Pa. lviii, Rule 204.

7. This fact is substantiated in Fleming D. Tucker, *A Directory of the Colored Members of the Philadelphia Bar, Including a List of the Pioneer Lawyers,* revised to April 1, 1964 (n.p., n.d.); and *Negro Members of the Philadelphia Bar and Judiciary,* December 1972 (n.p., n.d.).

of Law Examiners, who, they said, made no secret of her feelings about blacks and particularly her bias against those who came from Howard. One such lawyer told of his experience with this secretary in the early 1950s. He was confident of passing the examination and indeed believed that he had done so. But he failed. When he questioned the secretary, she replied that not one student from Howard University Law School had passed in the last eight years, and she had not expected that he would be the exception. He told her that she was probably right but that he would like to have another chance anyway. He had his second chance and passed. He concluded, "They [blacks] just failed wholesale."

A female lawyer, replying to a question about bar examinations in Pennsylvania, stated that when pressure was applied, the number of blacks who passed increased, although their qualifications were no better than those who previously had failed. "They came," she said, "from the same law schools, the same socioeconomic group, with the same credentials."

Litigation based on allegations of discrimination against blacks in bar examinations spanned the country in the 1970s (see Introduction). However, these problems have existed for many years. In Philadelphia, as early as 1953, Chancellor of the Philadelphia Bar Association Bernard G. Segal, who had been conducting a campaign to involve minority lawyers in bar association affairs, appointed a special committee to investigate alleged discrimination in the grading of bar examinations in Philadelphia County by the State Board of Law Examiners. His appointees were two white lawyers—the late Abraham L. Freedman, City Solicitor of Philadelphia, later a judge of the United States District Court for the Eastern District of Pennsylvania, and still later a judge of the United States Court of Appeals for the Third Circuit; and G. Ruhland Rebmann, Jr., a prominent lawyer who at the time of his appointment was serving as Chairman of the Philadelphia County Board of Law Examiners, the members of which were appointed by the judges of the Philadelphia Courts of Common Pleas— and a black lawyer, the late Theodore O. Spaulding, who a few months later became a judge of the Municipal Court of Philadelphia and after that a judge of the Superior Court of Pennsylvania. Appointed as chairman was the late William H. Hastie, a judge, later Chief Judge, of the United States Court of Appeals for the Third Circuit. By the time it filed a report on July 7, 1954, the committee consisted of two black judges and two white lawyers and had become known as the Hastie Committee. In its report to Chancellor C. Brewster Rhoads, who succeeded Segal, the committee noted:

[an] extraordinary high percentage of failures of Negro candidates from Philadelphia County on recent Bar examinations. . . . From July 1950 to the end of 1952, thirty Negro candidates from Philadelphia

County took a total of 43 examinations, some individuals being examined two or more times. Only six candidates passed, three of them with very high grades. . . .

The report went on to state that a "high percentage of Negro failures continued [in 1953, but] the January 1954 examination was taken by eleven Negro candidates, six of whom passed."[8]

The Hastie Committee, with the full cooperation of the State Board of Law Examiners, very carefully investigated all of the board's procedures and concluded: "It is only in a final procedure, applicable only to those papers which after grading and regrading are not passing but very close to passing, that we find that the candidate is identified." At this stage, the committee continued, all that can happen is a raising, not a lowering, of the grade, but nevertheless,

> the individual record which comes before the board at this final recommendation of borderline failure cases does identify the candidate by name [and where the candidate went to school] . . . [so that] he is identified in a number of ways which may or may not suggest his race. However, we are advised that certain items, including the identification card which bears the candidate's photograph, are not in the record which the Board examines.[9]

After referring to assurances that the committee had received that "when this final evaluation results in a passing grade for any paper, all marginal papers which theretofore had the same or a higher grade are also regarded as passing" and stating "such procedure is an appropriate means of preventing any discriminatory advantage from accruing to any candidate," the report concluded: "We have no reason to believe that any member of the Board of Law Examiners would be reluctant to give a candidate the full benefit of this discretionary re-evaluation because of any aspect of this personal identification." Citing no evidence of racial bias, the committee nevertheless stated:

> The use of a photograph as a device for facilitating racial discrimination is so familiar in so many fields, and therefore is so generally

8. "Report of the Philadelphia Bar Association Special Committee on Pennsylvania Bar Admission Procedures—Racial Discrimination of Pennsylvania Bar Examinations," *Temple Law Quarterly*, vol. 44, no. 2 (Winter 1971), pp. 165, 166. A later Philadelphia Bar Association Committee—the Special Committee on Bar Admission Procedures—whose reports are discussed herein, commented, "Nor did perceptive observers overlook the 'coincidence' that it was only in the January 1954 Bar Examination, while the 'Hastie Committee' was investigating the alleged discrimination in grading, that Blacks as a group ever fared as well as non-Blacks." Ibid., p. 179.

9. Ibid., pp. 165–66.

suspect, that it would seem to be sound policy, wherever practicable, to use some other device for the [purpose] of ensuring that the person who takes an examination is the eligible candidate.[10]

The report of the special committee was submitted to Chancellor Rhoads, and the minutes of the Board of Governors meeting for October 1954 reflect that Rhoads stated: "The Committee has made a complete investigation and reports that there were no discriminatory practices." The full text of the report is appended to the minutes of the board.[11]

Although there were indications following the committee's report that changes would be made to eliminate any appearance or possibility of bias in accordance with the recommendations of the Hastie Committee, no significant alterations were made in the procedure of the State Board of Law Examiners or in the character or the content of the bar examination.

The bar examination covered fourteen different fields of the law and consisted of twenty-four essay-style questions. Each question required a candidate to consider a case, define the significant issues, and discuss them meaningfully. A candidate had to have an average score of 70 in order to pass.[12] These procedures continued to be attacked for being both intentionally and unintentionally prejudicial to blacks and other minority candidates.

On June 23, 1970, Chancellor of the Philadelphia Bar Association Robert M. Landis appointed a second Special Committee on Pennsylvania Bar Admission Procedures "to investigate the claims of possible discrimination against Black law students in these procedures."[13] The committee consisted of Paul A. Dandridge, a black judge of the Municipal Court of Philadelphia, currently Judge of the Family Court Division of the Court of Common Pleas of Philadelphia; Clifford Scott Green, a black judge of the Family Court Division of the Court of Common Pleas of Philadelphia, currently Judge of the United States District Court for the Eastern District of Pennsylvania; Ricardo C. Jackson, a black member of the Philadelphia Bar, currently a judge of the Trial Division of the Court of Common Pleas of Philadelphia; W. Bourne Ruthrauff, a white member of the Phildelphia Bar, and, as Chairman of the committee, Peter J. Liacouras, a white professor of law and subsequently Dean at the Temple University Law School and now the President of Temple University. Thus there were on the

10. Ibid., p. 166.

11. Ibid.

12. Donald R. Very, "Pennsylvania's New Bar Examination—Save the Essay-style Bar Examination," *Pennsylvania Bar Association Quarterly*, vol. 44, no. 4 (1973), p. 541. See also Robert G. Bernreuter, "Pennsylvania's New Bar Examination—A Report on the Pennsylvania Bar Examination," ibid., p. 533.

13. "Report of the Philadelphia Bar Association Special Committee," p. 159.

committee three blacks, two of them judges and one of them a lawyer, and two whites, one of them a law professor and the other a lawyer.[14]

The committee filed an extremely comprehensive report on December 19, 1970. It spans 109 pages in the *Temple Law Quarterly*[15] and abounds in statistics primarily intended to show the relatively small proportion of black candidates who passed the examination in addition to the unfavorable relation between these results and those in various other states. The committee made a study of the "pass" rates in bar examinations of graduates of Howard University Law School during the period from 1965 to 1970 in the District of Columbia and seven states including Pennsylvania. This study revealed that in Pennsylvania the pass rate for blacks was only 11.4 percent as against 77.9 percent for all persons taking the examination; the rates in New York were 70.0 percent for blacks and 71.0 percent for whites. The next lowest percentage was in Maryland, where it was 32.2 percent, the pass rate for all who took the examination being 44.0 percent.[16]

The situation in Pennsylvania prompted the following public statement by Dean Paul Miller of the Howard Law School:

> For years we at Howard have cautioned our students considering law practice in Pennsylvania to think about it again. We have told them what we know. Blacks are not welcome in Pennsylvania, and the Bar examination is the State Board's way of making sure that the number of Black lawyers in that state remains small.[17]

An interesting set of statistics compiled by the committee relates to the comparative pass rates of black and of white graduates of the law schools of Temple University, the University of Pennsylvania, and Villanova University during the period from January 1955 to July 1970. Whereas 80.2 percent of all graduates and 53.8 percent of black graduates of the University of Pennsylvania Law School passed the bar examination in Pennsylvania, the corresponding figures for Temple are 65.1 percent and 38.3 percent, and for Villanova, 75.5 percent and 50.0 percent (see Appendix 9). The committee also isolated statistics for the last five and one-half years of this fifteen-year period. Although the passing percentages for the three law schools in the Philadelphia area (85.6% Pennsylvania graduates,

14. Ibid., p. 141.

15. Ibid., pp. 149–258; a summary of the report and recommendations appears on pp. 141–53, a summary table of contents on p. 153, and a detailed table of contents on pp. 154–58.

16. Ibid., pp. 177–78. For more details see Appendices 8 and 9. Appendix 8 gives the complete results in the District of Columbia and the seven states studied, together with a statement showing the basis for estimates in some of the states and in the District of Columbia.

17. Ibid., pp. 179–80.

83.2% Temple graduates, and 81.7% Villanova graduates) remained in the same order, the rank order of black graduates who passed significantly changed, with Temple taking the lead (70.0% Temple graduates, 57.1% Pennsylvania graduates, and 50.0% Villanova graduates).

In summary, the Special Committee first pointed out that it could not examine individual answer booklets since they are systematically destroyed but that it did conduct "a thorough and comprehensive investigation of the entire Bar examination processes."[18] In concluding that certain practices "raise the strongest presumption that Blacks are indeed discriminated against under procedures used by the State Board of Law Examiners," the committee cited the following evidences:

1. The State Board of Law Examiners has access to and makes use of personal data that can reveal the race of the candidate.
2. A photograph of every candidate, together with his signature, his preceptor's signature, and his file number is in the custody of the board.
3. At the time of the examination, each candidate's examination number, which is assigned alphabetically (except for repeaters) is displayed prominently on his desk.
4. Master lists bearing each candidate's name and number are in the examination rooms on the desk of each chief proctor.
5. In the July 1969 examination a majority of black candidates, all of them repeaters, were seated consecutively on the same row.[19]

Next the Special Committee cited statistical evidence that while 98 percent of those taking the bar examination eventually pass, only 70 percent of blacks do so, and they are the only identifiable group "weeded out" by the bar examination. The committee concluded that these results, "coupled with staff authoritarianism, and the Blacks' reasonable perceptions that they were being singled out for special treatment, places unreasonable and undue pressure on Black candidates."[20]

The committee found further support for its conclusions in the failures of the State Board "to take any affirmative action to alter this gross racial imbalance notwithstanding the facts that . . . no Black was admitted to the Bar for a 10-year period (1933–1943)." The committee also cited the Hastie Committee report of 1953–54 and noted that "there were only 130 Black lawyers out of nearly one million Black persons in Pennsylvania, while there were in excess of 12,300 non-Black lawyers out of a non-Black population of 10.4 million in Pennsylvania." The Special Committee con-

18. Ibid., p. 149.
19. Ibid.
20. Ibid., p. 150.

cluded that Pennsylvania ranked near the bottom of industrial states on the ratio of black lawyers to black population.[21]

Reviewing the bar examination generally, the committee determined that it "fails to meet the legitimate expectations of the public, the legal profession, and candidates without regard to race, but particularly Blacks."[22] It therefore recommended that (1) those candidates who have failed past bar examinations should be admitted by motion since the bar examination as developed and administered is invalid and discriminatory; and (2) that "if some form of additional bar examination is deemed necessary," the examination "meet the objections of discrimination, invalidity, and lack of review detailed in this report." Chancellor of the Philadelphia Bar Association John R. McConnell, at the request of the Editor-in-chief of the *Temple Law Quarterly,* Alan S. Fellheimer, wrote a foreword that appears as the first item in the issue containing the "Report of the Philadelphia Bar Association's Special Committee."[23]

McConnell stated that on January 7, 1971, the Board of Governors of the Philadelphia Bar Association had unanimously resolved that the chancellor should enter into immediate discussions and negotiations with the State Board of Law Examiners to eliminate any possibility of racial discrimination in connection with bar procedures. McConnell then referred to a second resolution adopted by the board of governors on January 21, 1971, commending the action of the Board of Law Examiners in effecting the following changes in the type of examination and in procedures:

1. That commencing in 1972, the Bar examination in substantial part will be composed of an examination prepared by a committee of law school faculty members from various parts of the United States, will be a multiple choice examination, and will be marked electronically by an independent testing service in Princeton, New Jersey; and

2. That by reason of the time required to prepare the above system of conducting the examination, it will not be possible to effectuate it in 1971 and that therefore the 1971 examinations will be conducted under the following conditions:

a. The examinees' numbers will be determined by lot;

b. The examinees will, as far as possible, be seated as they choose;

c. There will be only one copy of the list of numbers and names and that list, upon its completion, will be replaced in a locked vault where it will remain until all examination marks have been finalized;

d. Every paper will be reread by a marker who will read the entire paper;

21. Ibid., pp. 149–50.
22. Ibid., p. 152.
23. Ibid., p. 143.

e. All photographs of each examinee will be returned to him immediately upon the conclusion of the examination;

f. The papers will be marked by the same markers and examiners as heretofore less only those, if any, unable to perform their duties by reason of illness. . . .[24]

The speed with which the Special Committee acted augured well for its new leadership. On May 15, 1970, Roy Wilkinson, Judge of the Commonwealth Court of Pennsylvania and a member of the State Board of Law Examiners since January 5, 1959, had been appointed its chairman. Wilkinson was hailed by the Special Committee for his "keen interest in reforming anachronistic practices."[25] However, invited by the *Temple Law Quarterly* to comment on the charges made in the committee's report, Judge Wilkinson stated "categorically, unequivocally and emphatically, . . . such accusations [i.e., "that the Board devises questions, administers the examination, marks the papers or determines who passes in a manner calculated to discriminate against any applicant, black or white, or any law school"] are utterly without basis in fact." He chided the committee for publicizing the report "in the press, on the air, and on TV prior to bringing it to the appointing authority." He resented "unfounded charges of discrimination against individual Board members," remarking that "it will only polarize those most concerned."[26] Judge Wilkinson noted that the examiners had been concerned with the failures among black applicants and had searched for "specific causes." Called upon by the State Board for advice, an expert in education and psychology, and the Educational Testing Service as well, concluded that the board's existing procedures and the questions in the examination were adequate for the essay type. They expressed a preference for a multiple-choice bar examination but recognized that it would take several years and a great deal of money to develop one.

However, a committee of the Board of Governors of the National Conference of Bar Examiners, having received a very substantial grant from the American Bar Endowment, retained the National Conference and Joseph Covington, a former dean of the University of Missouri Columbia School of Law, to make an in-depth study of bar examinations. After several months of researching the problem, and with the assistance of five committees consisting of nationally known law professors and bar examiners, they developed a multiple-choice examination. As a result, Pennsylvania, together with eighteen other states, adopted a multiple-choice examination now known as the MBE, or Multistate Bar Examination.

24. Ibid., p. 144.
25. Ibid., p. 184.
26. Ibid., pp. 146, 148.

There would be one day of essay questions and one day of multiple-choice questions. The chairman of the investigatory committee stated that he would "urge that passing either day will be sufficient for admission."[27]

Considerable experimentation with the essay examination continued, both in content and in grading. A practice was instituted whereby the essay questions, along with the tentative model answers and the proposed point allocations, were considered by the examiners who prepared the questions, the other members of the State Board of Law Examiners, and representatives of each of the law schools located in Pennsylvania. Representatives of Howard University were also invited to join the meetings, did so for a short time, but soon ceased to attend.

Because the MBE was an experiment, no one was quite sure how applicants would perform, and initially the passing grade was set extremely low. As a result, in February 1972 over 98 percent of those taking the bar examination passed. In July 1972 a rule was initiated that an applicant could pass by achieving the minimum score on the MBE portion alone. When in July 1974 the State Board also adopted a method of combining the MBE and the essay scores, as recommended by the Educational Testing Service and the National Conference of Bar Examiners, there was another experimental period in grading. Numerous applicants scoring no better than a 50 on the essay part of the examination, not in itself a passing grade, were being admitted because of the score achieved in the MBE. While most states do not allow the applicants to pass the bar examination on the basis of the MBE alone, Pennsylvania does so, and also gives applicants the alternative of a combination score, so that a good grade on either portion will lower the requisite grade on the other.[28] In February 1975 the Board of Law Examiners established a passing grade that it believed adequately tested an applicant's competence to practice law. In 1978 it still stated that it had no present plan to raise this grade any further, although it was the lowest passing grade in any state using the MBE. This grade was modestly raised in July 1980.

In 1976 a new challenge was made to the bar examinations in Pennsylvania. A class-action lawsuit, *Delgado et al. v. McTighe et al.*, was instituted in the United States District Court sitting in Philadelphia on behalf of black and Puerto Rican applicants who had taken the Pennsylvania examination one or more times and had failed to pass while receiving grades equal to or higher than the passing grades in earlier years.[29] The plaintiff

27. Ibid., p. 148.
28. Joseph Covington, "The Multistate Bar Examination—1976," *The Bar Examiner*, vol. 45, no. 3 (1976), p. 72.
29. Affidavit of Desmond J. McTighe, *Delgado et al. v. Desmond J. McTighe et al.*, No. 76-1206 (E.D. Pa. December 1, 1977) (Broderick, J.), filed February 2, 1977.

in *Delgado*[30] complained that the Pennsylvania Board of Law Examiners' administration of the bar examination violated the Fourteenth Amendment to the Constitution of the United States, Title VII of the Civil Rights Act of 1964,[31] and the Civil Rights Acts of 1870 and 1871.[32]

The plaintiffs did not initially allege that the board engaged in intentional discrimination but asserted that the examination is not reasonably related to the aim of distinguishing between qualified and unqualified applicants to the bar, and that in arbitrarily setting and in successively raising the passing grade on the examination as a whole, the Board discriminated against black and Puerto Rican examinees because those examinees have been affected disproportionately.[33]

The defendants argued that under a decision of the Supreme Court of the United States in *Washington v. Davis*[34] (handed down a month and a half after plaintiffs filed their lawsuit), the existence of a disparate racial impact alone could not establish a *prima facie* case of discrimination constituting a constitutional violation. Rather, proof of intentional discrimination is required. Accordingly, defendants filed a motion to dismiss the plaintiffs' complaint.[35]

Plaintiffs thereupon voluntarily amended their complaint, adding the claim that the State Board knew that if there was a slight increase in the passing grade, a disproportionately large percentage of black and Puerto Rican applicants would fail the examination and that the board thus intended to accomplish this result. They also alleged that the methods of grading employed by the board and the points at which the passing grade had been set since 1972 were "inadequately designed to distinguish between qualified and unqualified entry-level lawyers" and that there was no justification reasonably related to the aim of so distinguishing that would support the board's decision to raise the passing grade.[36] Plaintiffs in other states have not succeeded in establishing such claims (see Introduction).

On December 1, 1977, Judge Raymond Broderick dismissed the case insofar as it charged violations of Title VII of the Civil Rights Act of 1964 and of the Civil Rights Acts of 1870 and 1871. The case was tried on the remaining issue of intentional discrimination and arbitrariness of the board's decision in the summer of 1981; and on August 10, 1981, Judge

30. *Delgado v. McTighe,* esp. Complaint, par. 12.
31. 42 U.S.C. § 2000(e) et seq.
32. Ibid., §§ 1981, 1983.
33. Complaint, pars. 12–13, *Delgado v. McTighe.*
34. 426 U.S. 229 (1976).
35. *Delgado v. McTighe,* No. 76-1206, Slip Op. at 7 (E.D. Pa. December 1, 1977) (order granting defendants' motion to dismiss complaint).
36. Amended Complaint, pars. 12–16, *Delgado v. McTighe.*

Broderick determined these issues in favor of the defendants, holding that their decision to raise the passing grade had been based on their desire to require applicants for the Pennsylvania Bar to demonstrate greater competence prior to their admission.[37]

37. *Delgado v. McTighe,* Slip Op. at 5, 20.

# 6

# Employment of Black Lawyers

As might be expected, the employment histories of the black attorneys in the three different age-groups surveyed are extremely varied. They also reveal significant changes over the years in the ways in which the legal profession has welcomed new black members and recognized their accomplishments.

There is almost a nine-year difference in the mean ages at which the oldest and the youngest cohorts were admitted to the Philadelphia Bar. The mean age for the oldest group was 36, for the middle group, 33, and for the youngest, 27.5. These findings, particularly as to the youngest cohort, may be interpreted in several ways. Because of the climate of the times and the emphasis placed on attracting minority students to the study of law by offering financial incentives, fewer blacks had to postpone entering law school in order to earn tuition money. Loans, grants, and scholarships that became generally available in 1959 were utilized to pay partial or full tuition, depending upon the scholastic ability and the financial circumstances of the minority students. Respondents' answers make clear that the incentive to pursue a career in the law came much earlier for the youngest cohort by virtue of the drive by law firms to offer positions to minority students when they are in their final year of law school and, in the case of the more promising students, summer employment at the end of their second year as well. These incentives resulted in such students making every effort to do well at law school and to complete their bar examinations successfully in order to embark upon their chosen careers.

The practice of soliciting law students to join law firms is relatively recent. It was not until the early 1960s that "scouting" the law schools began, and before long this became standard procedure, at least for the larger law firms. Members of firms travel from coast to coast to woo the "cream" of graduating classes with invitations to visit their offices. The search for black students is particularly intense since the demand is so vastly greater than the supply. Many lawyers have criticized the elaborate lengths to which some firms go to attract law students, entertaining them and their spouses with expensive luncheons and dinners, paying all their expenses to visit the law firms and meet the lawyers there, and offering them starting salaries equal to the earnings of the oldest cohort after forty years as practicing attorneys. Accordingly, job offers to black students began to pour in, increasing from 41 percent upon law school graduation for the oldest cohort to 88 percent for the youngest, as may be seen in Tables 7 and 8. (For an in-depth study of the types of employment offers according to cohorts, see Appendix 10.)

As the times and circumstances changed, a different occupational picture developed. Offers from white sole practitioners, from law firms and corporations, and from federal and state governments, which were unknown to the oldest cohort, became routine for the youngest cohort. Offers from black practitioners and black firms, which were the major employers of the oldest cohort, decreased proportionately in the youngest cohort, while white law firms and corporations vied for the services of the outstanding black law school graduates.

The increase in offers from the federal government was the most significant, moving from 0 percent for the oldest cohort to 23 percent for the middle and 45 percent for the youngest. Awakened by the temper of the times and political considerations, the federal government publicized the fact that the welcome mat was out for blacks in government positions and thus became the largest employer of the middle and the

Table 7
**Employment Offers upon Graduation**

|  | Cohort 1<br>17 respondents | Cohort 2<br>30 respondents | Cohort 3<br>93 respondents |
|---|---|---|---|
| No offers | 10 (59%) | 17 (57%) | 11 (12%) |
| Offers | 7 (41%) | 13 (43%) | 82 (88%) |

Table 8
**Employment Offers According to Sex**

|  | Cohort 1 | | Cohort 2 | | Cohort 3 | |
|---|---|---|---|---|---|---|
|  | M | F | M | F | M | F |
| No offers | 9 | 1 | 17 | 0 | 8 | 3 |
| 1 offer | 4 | 1 | 5 | 1 | 30 | 7 |
| 2 offers | 0 | 1 | 5 | 0 | 17 | 8 |
| 3 offers | 1 | 0 | 0 | 0 | 9 | 3 |
| 4 offers | 0 | 0 | 1 | 0 | 3 | 0 |
| 5 offers | 0 | 0 | 1 | 0 | 1 | 1 |
| 6 offers | 0 | 0 | 0 | 0 | 2 | 0 |
| 7 offers | 0 | 0 | 0 | 0 | 1 | 0 |

youngest cohorts. White firms came second as would-be employers. It was a day long overdue for the black lawyer.

But what happened to the black lawyers in Philadelphia who received no offers from major firms? For the oldest cohort, the choices were limited. They could apply to black sole practitioners and black firms if they wanted to enter private practice.[1] If they preferred government service, they could seek a post in the District Attorney's Office, where black lawyers had held positions from the early years of the twentieth century. They could join a friend or associate in a partnership or a space-sharing arrangement.

The alternative chosen by two members of the oldest cohort was to become sole practitioners, lawyers who conduct their own practice and do not share space with others.[2] (The topic of sole practitioners will be dealt with more fully later in this chapter.) Of the eight who had previously received no offers and who did not become sole practitioners, two went with black firms, two went with black sole practitioners, one entered city government, one formed a partnership with a friend, one went with the public school system, and one gave no information.

With the opening of opportunities, those of the middle cohort who had received no offers of jobs on graduation had new avenues of approach in the search for employers. Of the seventeen who had received no offers, seven became sole practitioners; seven took posts with government (three city, one state, and three federal); one went with a black sole practitioner; and one with a white firm. One respondent gave no information other than that he received no offers. For the younger members of the middle cohort, the scene changed with the advent of new employers; here again, federal and state and city governments and white firms.

As stated above, white firms were not in evidence as employers of blacks when the older members of the second cohort came to the bar. The change in this situation was triggered by the civil-rights movement. One older member of the second cohort told of his experience in seeking a job in Philadelphia. Armed with credentials from Harvard Law School, including his *magna cum laude* citation, he said that he scouted every Philadelphia law firm after passing the bar examinations in 1947. He received no offer from any of them. Philadelphia was his home and that was where he wanted to practice. But, he continued, he was black and unwelcome in the city touted for its "brotherly love." He then left for New York, where five white law firms offered him positions. He accepted one and stayed with

---

1. Private practice is defined as "lawyers practicing their profession who are either members of a partnership, personally own a practice, or who are employed by such lawyers." Daniel J. Cantor & Co., "Negro Lawyers in the United States, 1966: An Economic Study," a project of Howard University School of Law in cooperation with the National Bar Association, October 1966,.

2. Ibid., p. iv.

that firm for five years. In the meantime, he stated, Bernard G. Segal had become Chancellor of the Philadelphia Bar Association and was dedicated to eliminating the racist situation that had theretofore existed. Blacks were becoming visible in the legal community, and cracks were beginning to appear in the hitherto white united front. The District Attorney of Philadelphia, Richardson Dilworth, who later became Mayor, invited the interviewee to join his firm in Philadelphia. He accepted and thus, in 1952, became the first black attorney in Philadelphia to enter a white firm. He commented that he is delighted with the situation as it is at present.

At the District Attorney's Office black lawyers have been projected into as many situations as possible, some say in order to make them visible in court proceedings. One respondent, who is now a judge, advised in his interview that when he went into the District Attorney's Office in 1952, so far as was known, no black lawyer had ever tried a case in the Court of Quarter Sessions in City Hall. One or two had argued in the Magistrate's Court and in the old Coroner's Court, "but they had never seen a black lawyer try [in the Court of Quarter Sessions] and you could feel the tension." He recalled that when he became an assistant district attorney and appeared before one of the old judges, he stood in the area reserved for the district attorney or a member of his staff, a customary procedure. He continued to stand after everyone else in the courtroom had been seated. Whispers circulated through the room wondering where the assistant district attorney or his representative was. He still remembers the disbelief on the faces of those assembled in the courtroom when he introduced himself as the assistant district attorney. "Today no one would bat an eye or think twice about the district attorney having a black assistant," he mused.

Currently, qualified members of the youngest cohort are sought after and welcomed, not refused and rebuffed, by the leading Philadelphia firms. All except four of the eleven who said that they had received no offers upon graduation are practicing their profession. Of the four, one reported being unemployed, one entered the army, and two gave no other information. Of the seven others, one joined a corporation and four entered government—two city, one state, one federal—and two joined their fathers in the practice of law.

One respondent, who described himself as "atypical," went to law school at night and, upon graduation in 1950, took a position with the federal government, where he remained for twenty-three years. Upon retirement from his federal post he decided that he wanted to practice law. He applied himself to this goal and in 1975, at the age of sixty-seven, became a sole practitioner specializing in immigration law.

Black women in the law did not become highly visible in Philadelphia until the youngest cohort arrived on the scene. Twenty-three of the twenty-six female lawyers who responded to the questionnaires belong to the youngest group. Whereas only one woman of the oldest cohort received an offer (to join the District Attorney's Office) and one of the middle cohort (to join a black firm), sixteen of the youngest group received the following offers and accepted them:

| | |
|---|---|
| White firm | 1 |
| Corporation | 2 |
| Federal government | 6 |
| State government | 3 (1 a law clerk) |
| City government | 4 (1 a law clerk) |

One woman who received an offer from the city government was also solicited by the federal government and a law school, but she preferred to accept the position of assistant district attorney. Another who was offered a position by a black sole practitioner chose to accept an offer from a corporation. One was unemployed at the time of the survey, and two who had not received any offers did ultimately obtain positions, one with the city and the other in private practice.

Asked about their first employers (see Table 9), twenty-six of the 141 respondents declined to reply. The following figures and statements therefore apply to 115 respondents—13 of the oldest category, 24 of the middle, and 78 of the youngest.

Black sole practitioners, black firms, and the city were the major first employers of the oldest cohort. The alternatives were to set up one's own practice or to enter a business. However, in the relatively early legal careers of the youngest members of the middle cohort, black lawyers and the city ceased to be the major first employers. Initially, the federal government opened its doors to black lawyers. Second in new sources of employment were white firms, followed by mixed firms and by corporations.

Table 9
**Number and Percentages of Those Listed as First Employers**

| First Employers | Cohort 1 | Cohort 2 | Cohort 3 |
|---|---|---|---|
| White firms | 0 | 2 (6.7%) | 13 (14.0%) |
| Mixed firms | 0 | 1 (3.3%) | 1 (1.1%) |
| Corporations | 0 | 1 (3.3%) | 8 (8.6%) |
| Federal government | 0 | 6 (20.0%) | 20 (21.5%) |
| State government | 0 | 1 (3.3%) | 11 (11.8%) |
| City government | 2 (11.1%) | 1 (3.3%) | 15 (16.1%) |
| Other (business, etc.) | 3 (16.7%) | 2 (6.7%) | 4 (4.3%) |
| Black sole practitioners | 4 (22.2%) | 4 (13.3%) | 5 (5.4%) |
| Black firms | 4 (22.2%) | 3 (10.0%) | 0 |

For the youngest cohort, the federal government continued its lead, and white firms more than doubled their number as first employers. Corporations and the state government forged ahead, and the city government, particularly the district attorney, reappeared as a major employer. Black sole practitioners did not attract the newcomers to an appreciable extent, and black firms did not attract them at all.

When one embarks upon a career, regardless of its nature, there is usually a certain degree of trepidation. When the additional factor of racial difference adds its burden to the psychological load the newcomer already carries, the weight can be heavy indeed. This must have been particularly true for those pioneering black lawyers who entered white firms and corporations, or embarked on careers in government, when those employers first opened their doors to black lawyers. At best, there was uncertainty on both sides as to how the situation would develop. For the middle cohort, this was surely a trial period, since they and their employers were breaking new ground in testing the professional association and its concomitant social relationship. It was a period when biases on both sides had to be exorcised, aired, or camouflaged. Complex interrelationships varied with the size of firms, corporations, and government departments. For some the experience worked out well; for others it was stressful and disillusioning.

In their interviews black lawyers and judges expressed concern for the marginal member of the bar who enters a white firm. "Unless he is top rank he may be lost and become disheartened," one black judge observed. A black lawyer said he suspects that white firms are taking in blacks for "showcase" purposes, while a female black judge, recounting her experiences before ascending to the bench, commented:

> The average black lawyer entering a white firm should have no more problems than I had. What you lack in native ability can be made up with hard work. Many brilliant lawyers have been flashes. Some are so brilliant and success comes to them so easily, they are not prepared for failure. If a mediocre black lawyer enters a white firm, he may not get advances but he'll get something he can take when he leaves. I never would be wasting time. While he is working me, I'd be working him too.

She believes that hard work is the answer and attributes much of her success to the zeal instilled by her hardworking father, who impressed all his children with the "work ethic." Though a *magna cum laude* undergraduate student at Howard University, she was only an average student at the University of Pennsylvania Law School. But being "average" did not deter her from becoming a successful advocate and then ascending to the bench as one of two female judges on the Philadelphia bench at the time.

Echoing similar sentiments, another black judge added that very few black lawyers today have to worry about making a living. The question facing the young black today is whether to go into a white firm or to go into a practice more identified with the black community. White law firms must make concessions to the black lawyers, he said, or blacks will refuse to join them.

"If black lawyers could acquire sufficient expertise by association with white firms, they might be able to form good black firms," stated another black jurist respondent.

Another black jurist observed that the paucity of black law firms is due to the lack of black-owned businesses, adding that a problem in the Philadelphia area is that there is no one competent to advise blacks in the field of business when they are seeking to form some economic power base.

A black jurist, viewing the situation from a different angle, pointed out that a number of young black lawyers object to the "large-firm syndrome," lest they be pigeonholed without the possibility of promotion. He said that others may prefer that role, not wanting too much responsibility. He proposed some sort of testing to determine psychologically how well an individual is equipped for the practice of law.

One black lawyer said that he has been encouraging young black law school graduates to make associations with other black graduates and to form firms with a diversified practice, thus negating the criticism that "they [black law firms] all do the same type of work." Apparently more black lawyers are heeding the suggestion to become more cohesive and form their own firms. Although black firms were the first employers of 29 percent of the first cohort, 13 percent of the second cohort, and 0 percent of the youngest cohort, now 28 percent of the lawyers in the first cohort, 21 percent in the second, and 33 percent of the youngest group are in black law firms.

In response to the question whether they are still with their first employer, fourteen of the oldest cohort stated that they had changed positions for "other opportunities." None of the oldest and middle cohorts gave "dissatisfaction" as a reason. This reason was to appear later among the youngest when blacks entered white firms. Nineteen of the middle cohort left their first position for "other opportunities," "private practice," or "opened own office." As one would expect, since they have been at the bar for a relatively short time, fifty-three of the youngest cohort are still with their first employer. Seven, all of whom had served clerkships with judges, then joined law firms. Eight who had left their original employers gave as reasons that they were "dissatisfied and uncomfortable in white firms" and that "the pay was inadequate." Of these, several said they wished to enter practice on their own or with other black lawyers.

Inasmuch as one of the purposes of this study is to point out in what respects the three cohorts are alike and how they differ, it is interesting to note how the employment picture has changed with the years. Perhaps the most striking change has come with the resurgence of black firms as noted above.

Another development worthy of consideration is the appearance of black judges, both state and federal, a phenomenon unknown to the oldest cohort and making its first appearance with the second cohort. The youngest group, because its members have been at the bar so few years, has few judges as yet, but it is likely that in the near future there will be a decided upsurge in this area.

A significant change in employment opportunities came with the introduction of the public interest law firm, a creation of the 1970s with meager beginnings in the late 1960s.[3] The purpose of this type of practice is to represent the interests of the community at large in issues of broad public interest. The majority of these firms were formed to institute litigation in the courts or before administrative boards and agencies.[4] In August 1975 the American Bar Association approved a resolution defining public-interest law as legal service provided without fee, or at a substantially reduced fee, which falls into one or more of the following areas: poverty law, civil-rights law, public-rights law, charitable organization representation, and administration of justice.[5] (Public-interest law does not include representing individual clients in such matters as disputes with their landlords, repossession of household items, or domestic disputes like divorce. These constitute the practice of poverty law and are usually handled by legal-aid societies, neighborhood legal services, and, in more recent years, by a growing but still very small number of private law firms and sole practitioners without fee. Most recently government financing, as by the Legal Services Corporation, has become the dominant factor.) Many public-interest law groups have boards composed of citizens from a variety of callings, though each has a legal staff. Some have broad areas of operation and others are restricted to specific ones, such as problems of the mentally ill, children, the environment, and regulation of television and radio.

Justice Thurgood Marshall has pointed out that the major problem of public-interest law is funding, even though the lawyers con-

3. For a discussion of public-interest law firms and their origins and purposes, see "The New Public Interest Lawyers," *Yale Law Journal,* vol. 79, no. 6 (May 1970), p. 1068; *Public Interest Law: Five Years Later,* published by the Ford Foundation and the American Bar Association Special Committee on Public Interest Practice (1976).

4. See Guidelines Formulated by the Internal Revenue Service, Rev. Proc. 71-39, 1971–72, C.B. 575–76.

5. *Public Interest Law: Five Years Later,* pp. 9, 45.

cerned usually accept substantially lower salaries than they could earn in law firms.[6] Since 1970 the Ford Foundation has provided by far the largest foundation support and funded a substantial number of public-interest law firms. However, having provided the seeding and sustaining funds for more than a decade, the Ford Foundation has largely left the field. Other foundations are continuing to provide funds, and law firms in larger cities are contributing support as well. A very recent development with respect to public-interest firms concentrating on environmental problems, and some in the other fields as well, is that they are becoming self-supporting. Government support has also been forthcoming. Nevertheless, Justice Marshall observed in 1975, funding continues to be the major obstacle to the growth and development of such firms and to assurance that they will become a permanent part of our legal landscape.[7]

Public-interest law firms, unknown to the first cohort, have one member in the second cohort and five in the youngest group. However, since this is a recent development and since the largest number of lawyers attracted by public-interest law firms are the younger ones, the prospect is that the number of black lawyers joining such firms will increase substantially in the years ahead. The lower salaries offered lawyers in public-interest law will almost certainly deter most of the higher-ranking recent graduates and the more successful, more competent lawyers from accepting these positions.

Another development has been the sharp decrease in the percentage of sole practitioners. In the first cohort there were five (27.7%); in the second, nine (30.0%); and in the third, a drop to seventeen (18.3%).

How the types of present employers of black lawyers vary with the cohorts is evident in Table 10, below. The reason for the discrepancy between the numbers in Table 10 and the number of respondents is that a few of the respondents had part-time employment for more than one employer; for example, a sole practitioner working part-time in the District Attorney's Office.

Table 10 does demonstrate, however, that the state has shown a decline as employer while the federal government, having declined for the second cohort, has increased for the youngest group. Corporations and white firms have shown a steady, although slight, increase.

Of the 139 respondents, only one in the middle cohort was a member of the federal judiciary.[8] The percentage of respondents in the state judiciary increases as the cohort gets older.

6. Ibid., pp. 6–7 (foreword by Justice Thurgood Marshall).
7. Ibid., p. 7.
8. One of the youngest cohort became a federal judge in 1980.

Table 10
**Numbers and Percentages of Present Employers**

|  | Cohort 1 | Cohort 2 | Cohort 3 |
|---|---|---|---|
| White sole practitioner | 0 | 0 | 1 (1.1%) |
| Black sole practitioner | 0 | 0 | 0 |
| State government | 0 | 3 (10.0%) | 5 (5.4%) |
| Public-interest firm | 0 | 1 (3.3%) | 5 (5.4%) |
| Federal judiciary | 0 | 1 (3.3%) | 0 |
| Corporation | 1 (5.6%) | 2 (6.7%) | 12 (12.9%) |
| Law school | 1 (5.6%) | 1 (3.3%) | 2 (2.2%) |
| White firm* | 2 (11.1%) | 1 (3.3%) | 13 (14.0%) |
| City government | 2 (11.1%) | 1 (3.3%) | 9 (9.7%) |
| Federal government | 3 (16.7%) | 2 (6.7%) | 14 (15.1%) |
| State judiciary | 4 (22.2%) | 4 (13.3%) | 0 |
| Sole practitioner | 5 (27.7%) | 9 (30.0%) | 16 (17.2%) |
| Black firm | 5 (27.7%) | 6 (20.0%) | 31 (33.3%) |

*Of those firms, in the youngest cohort, all but one had 50 or more lawyers; in recent years, 1 to 4 black lawyers (1% to 4% of the total) joined their respective firms. The one exception is a 16-lawyer firm of whom 3, or 19% are black. In the first cohort, these were small firms —1 of 5 and the other of 6 lawyers, each having one black lawyer. In the middle cohort, the one white firm had 110 lawyers of whom 4, or 4%, including the respondent, were black. All had come to the firm within the past few years.

Forty-one respondents were, or are currently, in private law firms. Table 11 shows the division according to cohorts.

At the time of the study, graduates of the University of Pennsylvania Law School and of Howard University Law School were equally represented—nine from each school—in the law firms of Philadelphia. There

Table 11
**Affiliations with Private Law Firms**

|  | Cohort 1 | Cohort 2 | Cohort 3 |
|---|---|---|---|
| Black firms with 1–10 members | 1 | 2 | 9 |
| Other firms with 1–10 members | 3 | 1 | 8 |
| Other firms with 11–30 members | 0 | 1 | 2 |
| Other firms with 31–50 members | 0 | 1 | 1 |
| Other firms with 51–70 members | 0 | 0 | 5 |
| Other firms with 71–90 members | 0 | 0 | 4 |
| Other firms with 91–115 members | 0 | 1 | 2 |

These figures pertain to when questionnaires were returned (1978) and apply only to those who answered questionnaires, approximately 70%.

were six Temple graduates, four from Yale, and one or two lawyers each from Harvard, Villanova, Columbia, Virginia, Rutgers, Michigan, University of California, and Robert Terrell.

Also, at the time of the study, four of the first cohort were members of law firms. Two were "Of counsel"[9] in small law firms, both integrated. In the other small firms, one was a partner in an all-black firm, the other was an associate in a firm in which there are whites and blacks. No blacks of the first cohort were in firms of more than ten members.

Of the second cohort, there were six practicing in private law firms. One was a partner in an all-black firm, one a partner in a firm of whites and blacks, and one an associate in an all-black firm. Three were partners in large firms, which until recent years were all white.

The fact that 75 percent of the third cohort were employed in private law firms is proof of the advances in this direction in recent years. Nine were in all-black firms, eight of them partners (including one female) and one an associate. Fourteen were in formerly all-white firms, four as partners, and ten as associates (including two females).

## Areas of Practice

As expected, the survey discloses that lawyers with more years at the bar have greater variety in their practice. All the significant tables show a decreasing percentage of "yes" answers to practice categories as the year of admission becomes more recent. Few of the oldest cohort claim a specialty. Their largest areas of practice are domestic relations, criminal law, estates and trusts, followed closely by personal injury and real estate law, with some in the field of civil rights. Fifteen (83.3%) of the lawyers in this cohort said their practice includes domestic relations. Fourteen (77.8%) practice criminal law and estates and trusts, while twelve (66.7%) said they represent clients in personal injury cases. Sixty-one percent have some real estate practice. Litigation and civil-rights cases are a small part of their practice. The fields in which they have minimal practice are research and corporation law. No member of the oldest cohort said that he or she represents employers in labor work; two have represented unions; one has engaged in tax law.

Lawyers of the middle cohort have had roughly the same percentage of work in criminal law, personal injury, and real-estate law as the oldest cohort. However, they have had more work in litigation, employer representation, and tax and corporation law and less work in domestic relations

---

9. Ordinarily the term "of counsel" applies to a retired partner who continues to come into the office on a reduced-time basis. He or she often draws a pension and is compensated for any work that may be taken on for the firm.

and estates and trust law. Approximately the same percentage of lawyers in the two older cohorts (47%) engaged in civil-rights practice.

Personal injury, criminal law, domestic relations, estates and trusts, and real-estate law, in which so large a percentage of lawyers in the first and second cohorts engage, are reduced sharply for the youngest cohort. Approximately the same percentages of first cohort lawyers have clients in litigation and corporation work as those in the second cohort. But more members of the youngest cohort, pro rata, practice tax law, do research and brief-writing, and have certain other types of practice such as those involving military, maritime, immigration, and entertainment law. However, the percentage of younger lawyers is sharply lower in the civil-rights field. For example, 70 percent of the practitioners of the oldest cohort admitted to the bar between 1926 and 1949 practice civil-rights law, compared with 42 percent of those admitted between 1950 and 1967, and 32 percent of those admitted in 1968 or later. With the youngest cohort, other specialities have begun to emerge.

## Sole Practitioner

In contrast to the lawyer who is a member of a firm is the lawyer who is in practice by himself or herself, known as the sole, or solo, practitioner.

Jerome E. Carlin, studying the Chicago lawyer in the early 1960s, concentrated on the sole practitioner. He noted that "the individual practitioner is frequently a dissatisfied, disappointed, resentful, angry man . . ." who makes "the least money . . . with the most restricted type of practice."[10] "Most individual practitioners in the metropolitan bar are men of fairly high ambition who haven't made it. . . . [They enjoy] little freedom in choice of clients, type of work, or conditions of practice."[11]

Jack Ladinsky writes that there is a wide division between solo and firm lawyers by "social origin," "education," and "work history."[12] He notes that solo lawyers are most likely to stem from some minority, ethnic, or religious group. The firm lawyer, he points out, generally comes from the upper middle class and possesses the dominant prestige attributes of this community. His study reveals that whereas only 14.0 percent of the solo practitioners come from nationally known law schools, 72.9 percent of lawyers in firms come from such schools.[13] Ladinsky also notes that solo

10. Jerome E. Carlin, *Lawyers on Their Own* (New Brunswick, N.J.: Rutgers University Press, 1961), pp. 168, 172.

11. Ibid., pp. 200, 206.

12. Jack Ladinsky, "Careers of Lawyers, Law Practice and Legal Institutions," *American Sociological Review*, vol. 5, no. 1 (February 1963), pp. 47–54.

13. Ibid., pp. 48–49.

lawyers are confined to "dirty work," such as criminal practice, collections, personal injury, divorce work, and title searching. He adds a remark by David Riesman that "big firms are insulated from intellectual slums such as the above."[14]

In the Daniel J. Cantor study of 1966, the investigators reported that in the United States the majority of black private practitioners practice alone, while some share offices. This study suggests the following reasons for black lack of participation in partnerships: (1) lack of understanding of arrangements that would make such partnerships feasible; (2) a high desire for personal independence; and (3) lack of importance of partnership as an economic incentive. Black law firms, it finds, do not attract institutional clients.[15]

In *The Lawyers,* Martin P. Mayer observes that historically most black lawyers in the United States have practiced alone. "In the past," he points out, "Negro lawyers . . . have found few chances to build or participate in the partnerships which are the source of substantial incomes in the law: of the graduates of the Howard University Law School who are in private practice five-sixths are solo practitioners."[16]

In their study of professionalization, Howard M. Vollmer and Donald L. Mills commented that "Negroes and those of second generation immigrant background may make a precarious livelihood as their own employers."[17]

Turning to the 1978 Philadelphia survey, we find that twenty-five males and five females are sole practitioners (14.1%)—five (27.7%) in the first cohort, nine in the second (30.0%), and a drop to seventeen (18.2%) in the third. In comparing these sole practitioners with non–sole practitioners, we find very little difference in background and education. One difference, however, appears to be that the sole practitioners entered the bar at a later age. In the matter of motivation, too, there was a difference. Not one of the sole practitioners said that the motivation for becoming a lawyer was to achieve justice for minorities.

The respondents who became sole practitioners were not flooded with offers of jobs. Of those who reported that they were sole practitioners, only seventeen said that they had received job offers while at law school. No offer came from a white sole practitioner. There was only one offer from a white firm and one from a black firm. The federal government offered jobs to seven, followed by the city government and business with

14. Ibid., p. 50.
15. Cantor & Co., "Negro Lawyers in the United States," pp. 13, 14.
16. Martin P. Mayer, *The Lawyers* (New York: Harper & Row, 1966, 1967), pp. 97–98.
17. Howard M. Vollmer and Donald L. Mills, *Professionalization* (Englewood Cliffs, N.J.: Prentice-Hall, 1966), p. 303.

six offers from each. There were five from the state government and five from black sole practitioners.

The sole practitioners did not seek jobs to the extent that the other lawyers did. Several factors may be responsible for this. Sole practitioners, particularly in the first and the second cohorts, may have decided when they chose their careers that they preferred to practice alone, especially since the other choices for these cohorts were limited. White firms and the state and federal governments did not appear as prospective employers until the later years of the middle cohort. As far as the youngest cohort is concerned, the picture is different. Only one started as a sole practitioner, but as time went on sixteen more joined this group. Reasons for this are speculative, but from personal interviews and written comments on questionnaires, the impression emerges of disenchantment with original employers or with the type of practice offered or with the restrictive aspects of group association. One does not get the impression, suggested by Carlin, of the "angry, hurt, resentful man."[18]

In general, the practice of the sole practitioner varied from that of other lawyers, particularly in domestic relations, in which 83 percent of the sole practitioners were engaged, in contrast to 54 percent of the other lawyers. Ninety percent of the sole practitioners had some criminal law practice, while 50 percent of other lawyers engaged in this type of practice. Fifty-three percent of the sole practitioners had estates and trusts work, compared to 34 percent of the other lawyers. No sole practitioner represented employers in labor-relations matters, while 13 percent of the lawyers in the firms had clients in this category. A larger proportion, 73 percent, of sole practitioners stated that they had some civil-rights practice, compared to 61 percent of the firm lawyers who made this assertion.

Sole practitioners in the oldest cohort have the following distribution. All reported criminal law and domestic relations practice. In addition, three (60%) reported civil-rights, real-estate, and estates and trusts practice and two (40%), personal-injury cases. In addition, one in each of the foregoing groups engages in litigation, union representation, and research and brief-writing.

Predominant percentages of sole practitioners of the middle cohort reported practicing criminal law (100%), domestic relations (90%), real estate and estates and trusts (each 70%), personal injury (60%), and litigation (60%). Far fewer engaged in the areas of civil rights (30%), research and briefs (30%), and labor and corporation law (20% each).

The predominant number of the sole practitioners of the youngest group reported practice in the fields of criminal law, domestic relations, and personal injury law. A smaller percentage than in the middle cohort

18. Carlin, *Lawyers on Their Own*, p. 168.

work in the areas of real estate, litigation, and estates and trusts, but a larger percentage practice corporation law. Civil rights and tax law engage the efforts of the fewest lawyers in the youngest cohort.

In all other areas of practice, approximately the same percentages apply to the sole practitioner as to the lawyer in a firm.

## Specialization

It is difficult to draw any general conclusion as to what factors determine the specialty of a young lawyer. In some firms he or she is given a choice, but even this is dependent on whether an additional lawyer can be used in the particular field. In other firms the specialty of a given lawyer is largely determined by a committee or a designated lawyer who necessarily takes into account the particular needs of the firm at the moment. The probable aptitude of the lawyer is also a factor in this decision. One firm in Philadelphia insists that each new associate rotate through at least four departments before determining the specialty of his or her choice. Then, if it is at all possible, the associate is permitted to choose a specialty.

As to sole practitioners, while occasionally one may embark upon a specialty of choice, this, as previously indicated, is probably largely a matter of chance. Many times the kinds of cases that determine a lawyer's specialty do not come until later in his or her career.

Is there any correlation between type of law school attended and type of practice lawyers are assigned to? In an examination of this question, it appears that graduates of leading law schools are less likely to be involved in criminal law, plaintiffs' personal-injury work, and domestic-relations fields. These findings apply to those lawyers who are in firms, not sole practitioners, and the reason is that few large law firms handle these types of matters. No such difference exists insofar as the fields of general litigation, real estate, and estates and trusts are concerned. Regardless of the schools attended or whether in law firms or as sole practitioners, it would appear that black lawyers are still not customarily assigned to practice in the labor field, and, curiously, this applies to tax law as well.

A jurist of the middle cohort mentioned during an interview the "glaring deficiency in labor law" for the black practitioner. He noted that some blacks who have had access to work for labor unions have done well, adding that "as the Negro begins to exert muscle in the labor movement, he has seized or assumed leadership roles in some unions."

To summarize, the black lawyers have the largest practice in criminal law, personal injury, and domestic relations and the least in labor and tax law. The sole practitioner, as opposed to the firm lawyer, has an even more restrictive practice unless he is fortunate or talented enough to become a specialist.

## Income

Because of the sensitive nature of the topic of income, this study, like many others, refrained from asking specific questions on this subject either in questionnaires or interviews.

The Cantor economic study provides some general information that gives an overall impression of the situation as it existed in 1966 throughout the United States. Cantor found that the typical income of black lawyers in private practice was lower than the income of those employed by the government, law schools, and corporations. In the Pennsylvania study he found that the earnings of black lawyers were well behind the average earnings among lawyers in general.[19]

Black lawyers outside of private practice reported incomes similar to those of other lawyers.[20] Black sole practitioners, according to Cantor, had lower incomes than those associated with others.[21] As with other groups of lawyers, there is a definite relationship between net income and number of lawyers in the law firm. It is well recognized that lawyers in the law firms generally have the largest earnings. Writing for the *Michigan Law Review,* Harry T. Edwards observed: "Diversity of practice is . . . related to size of the law firm. Lawyers in the larger firms are at the top of the status ladder; individual practitioners and small-firm lawyers are the lowest group. . . . Large-firm lawyers have the highest average incomes."[22]

In our 1978 survey, all three cohorts agreed that black lawyers have lower incomes than white lawyers, except in the larger firms, where there is no difference in the distribution of income.

Thirty-nine of the forty-one respondents in private firms replied to the question regarding the establishment of income in the firm by fixed formula. Twenty-one said there was no fixed formula. Of this group, nineteen said they were satisfied with the method employed in distributing the firm's income. Thirty-three of those in private firms said their practice had developed as they had anticipated. No one in the oldest cohort expressed displeasure with the progress of his or her career. Complaints emerged from lawyers in the middle cohort who resented their restriction as a practical matter to certain areas of practice and, in some cases, their inability to attract major white business clients. Cantor cites a statement made by an interviewee in this regard: "There is a direct relationship between the racial composition of clients and income from law practice."[23]

19. Cantor & Co., "Negro Lawyers in the United States," pp. 37, 38.
20. Ibid.
21. Ibid., p. 42; *Villanova Law Review,* vol. 20, nos. 2 and 3 (1974–75), p. 385.
22. Harry T. Edwards, "A New Role for the Black Graduate—A Reality or an Illusion?" *Michigan Law Review,* vol. 69 (1971), p. 1407.
23. Cantor & Co., "Negro Lawyers in the United States," p. 55.

The youngest cohort echoed the complaints of the middle group, adding the difficult problems of fee collection, the high cost of operation, and the reluctance of white clients to accept young black lawyers, particularly young black female lawyers. Black lawyers generally find too few substantial clients and too many poor ones.

## Members of the Judiciary

Philadelphia has been far from a leader in the appointment or election of black judges. The first black judge in Washington, D.C., assumed his duties in 1909; the first black to sit on a federal court (a territorial district court in the Virgin Islands) was appointed in 1937; and a black woman judge was appointed in New York in 1939.[24] Not until 1948 was Philadelphia's first black judge, Herbert E. Millen, appointed to the Municipal Court of Philadelphia.[25] One year later William H. Hastie was appointed Judge of the United States Court of Appeals for the Third Circuit, which sits in Philadelphia, thus becoming the first black to serve on a federal court on which judges have lifetime tenure.[26] In 1969 he became Chief Judge of that court, the first black to hold that position on any United States circuit or district court. Hastie held many important posts before his appointment to the bench. In 1932 he was appointed Assistant Solicitor in the Department of the Interior, and in 1940 he became Civilian Aide to Secretary of War Henry L. Stimson. He resigned that post in protest over continued segregation of training facilities in the air force and the army. In 1937, only six years after his admission to the bar, he was appointed judge of a territorial court, the District Court of the Virgin Islands, and thus became the first black to sit on any federal court. Nine years later he became Governor of the Virgin Islands, the first of his race to attain so high a position in the executive branch of the government.[27]

Judge Hastie became not only a towering figure in the law but also one of the most highly regarded jurists of his generation by blacks and whites alike. His stature in his adopted home is evidenced by the fact that in 1974

24. M. Sammy Miller, "Robert H. Terrell: First Black D.C. Municipal Court Judge," *The Crisis*, vol. 83, no. 6 (June–July 1976), pp. 209–10; Peter M. Bergman, *The Chronological History of the Negro in America* (New York: Harper & Row, 1969), pp. 480–85.

25. Mary Mace Spradling, ed., *In Black and White* (Detroit: Gale Research Co., 1980), vol. 2, p. 67.

26. Marjorie Hunter, "Kennedy Counters Negro Criticism on Judgeships," *New York Times*, October 6, 1963, p. 75.

27. Peter M. Bergman, *The Chronological History of the Negro in America* (New York: Harper & Row, 1969), pp. 458, 480, 490, 501, 513, 521. See also Robert C. Weaver, "William Henry Hastie, 1904–1976," *The Crisis*, vol. 83, no. 8 (October 1976), p. 268.

he was the recipient of the highly prestigious Philadelphia Award, the first jurist to be so honored.[28]

The next first for blacks on the bench in Philadelphia, as previously noted,[29] came in 1958, when Raymond Pace Alexander was appointed Judge of the Court of Common Pleas.

The first black judge to be appointed to the United States District court for the Eastern District of Pennsylvania, which sits in Philadelphia, was Judge A. Leon Higginbotham, Jr., appointed in 1964 and elevated in 1977 to the United States Court of Appeals. When Judge Higginbotham was under consideration for the Court of Appeals, the American Bar Association's Standing Committee on Federal Judiciary, which investigates and reports to the Attorney General of the United States on the qualifications of all persons under consideration for appointment by the President to a federal court, accorded Judge Higginbotham its highest rating, "Exceptionally Well Qualified."[30] Like Judge Hastie, Judge Higginbotham has brought great pride to the black bench and bar and at the same time has won the affection and the esteem of the bar and the citizenry at large. By virtue of appointment to important committees, commissions, and boards by Presidents, Chief Justices, and Congresses of the United States and by presidents of the American Bar Association, he exerts widespread influence. He is also an author of note.

Robert N. C. Nix, Jr., son of the veteran and highly regarded Congressman Robert N. C. Nix, also a lawyer, became the first black justice of the Supreme Court of Pennsylvania when he was appointed in 1972, serving as Judge of the Court of Common Pleas of Philadelphia. Before the age of fifty he had already held positions of leadership in and served as a member of the boards of directors of leading civic, charitable, and educational organizations in the community. He also was the recipient of the First Pennsylvania Award in 1971.[31] He too is an inspiration for the black lawyers of Pennsylvania and for black aspirants to careers in the law.

Since Judge Millen's appointment in 1948, black judges have ascended to the bench in increasing numbers, so that of the 130 judges sitting in Philadelphia at federal, state, or local levels, twenty-four (18.5%) are black. The representation is presented in Table 12, below.

28. Francis M. Lordan, "Hastie Wins Philadelphia Award," *Philadelphia Inquirer,* January 26, 1979.

29. See Chapter 1, note 26, and accompanying text.

30. ABA Informational Reports to the House of Delegates, 1978 Mid-Year Meeting, New Orleans, La., February 13–15, 1978, Report of Standing Committee on Federal Judiciary, Item No. 38, p. 2 (to be published in volume 102 of *Reports of the American Bar Association*).

31. Mary Reincke and Nancy Lichterman, eds., *The American Bench: Judges of the Nation,* 2nd ed. (Minneapolis: Reginal Bishop Forster & Assoc., 1979), pp. 1701–2; Conversation with Juanita Copeland, Secretary to Justice Nix.

Table 12
**Black Representation Among Judges in Philadelphia**

| Court | No. Judges | No. Black Judges | % Black Judges |
|---|---|---|---|
| United States Court of Appeals for the Third Circuit | 4 | 1 | 25.0 |
| United States District Court for Eastern District of Pennsylvania | 16 | 2 | 12.5 |
| Supreme Court of Pennsylvania | 2 | 1 | 50.0 |
| Superior Court of Pennsylvania | 3 | 0 | 0 |
| Commonwealth Court of Pennsylvania | 2 | 1 | 50.0 |
| Court of Common Pleas of Philadelphia | 81 | 16 | 19.8 |
| Municipal Court | 22 | 3 | 13.6 |
| Total | 130 | 24 | 18.5 |

Federal judges as of April 1982, 527 F. Supp. X-XI; State and local judges as of November 1981.

The question has arisen as to whether bias operates in decisions by judges who have themselves been targets of bias and discrimination. Do they lean toward the black defendant? Are they overly sympathetic to blacks? William Stevens of the *New York Times* observes:

> Black judges are making particular efforts to apply the law more evenly. . . . [They] demonstrate heightened sensitivity to the rights and sensibilities of the accused. . . . [Many have a tendency] to be lenient with first offenders and those who commit victimless crimes, but tougher on crimes of violence. . . . [While] there are probably as many differences among them as there are among white judges . . . [they do have in common] a strong identification with the poor and powerless and a strong urge to reform administration in the interest of the poor.[32]

On the other hand, at a December 1968 meeting of the National Conference of Black Lawyers and Law Students in Chicago, a jurist voiced his

32. William K. Stevens, "Black Judges Becoming a Force in U.S. Justice," *New York Times*, February 19, 1974, p. 18.

concern that a black judge may be unduly severe on black defendants in an effort to avoid bias.[33]

Thus it would appear that, at least for the black judges interviewed, the transition from practicing lawyer to judge was very similar to the experience of white lawyers when they became judges. Those judges who were active trial lawyers find it emotionally difficult. One observed, "After being in the ring and throwing the punches, it's pretty hard to rest and stay out of it. . . . But one must exercise restraint." Another remarked that he was fortunate in having had some instruction in order to change roles from lawyer to judge. Without this, he would have had great difficulty in making the adjustment.

Another topic discussed with the black judges was the "complexion" of the jury. One jurist commented that where there is a black defendant and a black victim, the ratio of "complexion" of the jury does not matter; in the case of a black defendant and a white victim, unless there is an indication of a racial motive, a problem usually does not exist. The instance where a problem arises is where the victim is a white woman and the defendant a black male, and there are overtones of sex, even rape. In such situations there is a need to have a sufficient number of blacks on the jury to ensure against deliberation based on prejudices instead of on the facts of the case. With a sufficient number of blacks just as concerned as whites about such issues, it is not a matter of one being white and one being black. According to this judge, members of the jury who are aware of their tendency to think in terms of black and white make a greater effort to be fair. This resembles the situation of a black judge in the judicial system; it is his presence as well as what he himself does to bring about fairness that makes his colleagues aware of their own responsibility to be fair and just. Thus, in a sense, black judges have become the conscience of their respective courts.

33. This meeting took place in December 1968. Should black judges be disqualified from adjudicating cases involving claims of racial discrimination? For a superb analysis of the argument and a thoroughly convincing argument against disqualification, see *Commonwealth of Pennsylvania and Raymond Williams et al. v. Local Union 542 International Union of Operating Engineers, et al.*, 338 F. Supp. 155 (1974). Portions of this opinion have been reprinted in Gilbert Ware, *From the Black Bar* (New York: G. P. Putnam's Sons, 1976), pp. 61–72.

# 7

## Bar Associations and Other Professional Organizations

Bar associations afford lawyers the opportunity to get together to exchange views on matters concerning their profession, to discuss the instrumentalities of justice, and to plan projects in the public interest. Concomitant with these activities is the social aspect of good fellowship.

The associations of greatest relevance (not in the order of relative importance) to the blacks in the legal profession in Philadelphia are the Philadelphia Bar Association, the Barristers Club, the National Bar Association, the Pennsylvania Bar Association, and the American Bar Association.

One hundred nineteen (87.5%) of 136 respondents said they belong to the Philadelphia Bar Association. This association was the first to be organized in the United States, having celebrated its 175th anniversary in December 1977. Seventy-eight of the youngest cohort belong, but of this group only thirty-eight said they have found membership helpful.

There has been a steady increase in membership in the Philadelphia Bar Association, the Pennsylvania Bar Association, the National Bar Association, and the Federal Bar Association in the two older cohorts. Only the American Bar Association, which had its 100th anniversary in August 1978, shows an upward trend in the youngest cohort. The percentage of membership in the Barristers Club was the same for all three cohorts.

In a 1963 study of black lawyers in the Philadelphia Bar Association, questionnaires (not nearly so expansive as the one in connection with the present study) were sent by this author to every black member of the bar. The survey concentrated on eighty-two lawyers admitted to practice from 1920 to 1962; forty-five replied. Of this group, thirty-six (80%) belonged to the Philadelphia Bar Association. The main attraction of this membership, according to the respondents, was the privilege of using the association's law library. Seven were on the association's Civil Rights, American Citizenship, Criminal Justice, and Law Enforcement Committees. Of the nine who did not belong, eight said that the cost of membership was the deterrent. Only one mentioned the possibility of discriminatory treatment as a reason for not joining. One can see by the figures above how the enrollment picture has changed. In the 1978 survey, comments regarding the advantages of membership ranged as follows: "contacts," "referrals of business," "keeping informed and current as to developments in law," "exchange of ideas," "articles and study courses on practical areas of law," "health insurance," "help to reduce barriers in practice," "good exposure with white collegues," and "continued awareness of the struggle and need for more minority lawyers."

A jurist in the middle cohort recalled during his interview that in the past the Philadelphia Bar Association was not attuned to the problems of black lawyers, though in recent years there has been a change. Moreover, it was at one time a purely professional organization that did not provide for the needs of young lawyers. In this judge's view, the establishment of a Young Lawyers' Section of the association discouraged the participation of young lawyers in the inner workings, by segregating them from the rest of the association. He commented that it would be better to have an age-integrated association to enable young lawyers to have rapport with the older practitioners and derive from them the benefit of their experience.

This jurist also observed that a class system formerly existed in the Philadelphia Bar Association and was reflected in the membership of its various committees. In 1951, for instance, there was only one black lawyer on an association committee. In 1952, there was a dynamic change as to association. (See Historical Background.) In recent years, too, there have been efforts to remedy the situation generally. There was a sharp distinction, this jurist said, between the large prestigious firms unwilling to relinquish power in the association, and the sole practitioner or member of smaller firms. But, he added, there have been steps in the right direction, albeit slow-moving.

Another jurist in the oldest cohort observed in his interview that membership in bar associations is helpful to black lawyers in promoting their careers, but he criticized blacks for not utilizing such associations to the fullest extent. He believes that black lawyers could become a vital force to exert pressure and to prick the conscience of the association. He added that his comment applies primarily to the Philadelphia Bar Association and not to the National Bar Association.

A lawyer of the oldest cohort, admitted to the bar in 1929, said in his interview that he did not find membership in the Philadelphia Bar Association particularly helpful: "You belong because everybody belongs. They have a library." He qualified his remarks by stating that as executive director of a civic organization, and therefore not a private practitioner, he does not require the fraternal, professional, and educational advantages of membership.

The Pennsylvania Bar Association, operating on a statewide scale, as its name indicates, attracted fewer black members of the bar than the

Philadelphia Bar Association: fifteen (83.3%) of the oldest cohort, twenty (66.6%) of the middle cohort, and sixty-two (66.6%) of the youngest.

A lawyer of the middle cohort who is not in private practice said that although he belongs to the Philadelphia and the Pennsylvania Bar Associations, he too does not feel that he derives much benefit from his membership in either. However, he believes that as a general rule membership is a potential help to black lawyers, observing that in 1963, or thereabouts, the Pennsylvania Bar Association passed a resolution regarding racial discrimination in the hiring practices of law firms, urging the integration of such firms. He subsequently has seen many new young black lawyers become associated with large, formerly all-white law firms.

Next to the Philadelphia Bar Association, the Barristers Club, the local affiliate of the National Bar Association, attracted the highest membership, 113, of whom fourteen (77.7%) were of the oldest cohort, twenty-three (76.6%) of the middle cohort, and seventy-six (81.7%) of the youngest cohort.

The National Bar Association, the black counterpart of the American Bar Association, consists of "members of the Bench and Bar, primarily Negro; with increasing white membership."[1] Founded in Des Moines, Iowa in 1925,[2] its purpose is "to stimulate interest in the study of Law; to assist in the development of judicial reforms; to sponsor and support educational institutes for the practicing bar; to promote fellowship among the members of the Bench and Bar."[3] The membership of the respondents in the NBA is as follows: nine of the oldest cohort, fourteen of the middle cohort, and forty-four of the youngest cohort.

The American Bar Association was established in 1878, with five objectives stated in its original constitution: to advance the science of jurisprudence; "to promote the administration of justice"; "to promote uniformity of legislation throughout the union"; "to uphold the honor of the profession"; and "to encourage cordial intercourse among the members of the American Bar."[4] Yet despite these lofty objectives, it was not until 1943 that it adopted a resolution that "membership in the American Bar Association is not dependent upon race, creed or color" (see Introduction).[5] In February 1982, the ABA had 292,000 members, and while there is no record of how many of these are black, it is apparent that the number has

1. *Encyclopedia of Associations,* 11th ed. (Detroit: Gale Research Co., 1977), vol. 1, p. 311.

2. Edward P. Toles, *History of the National Bar Association—Fifty Years of Progress for Black Lawyers,* souvenir booklet distributed at the annual meeting of the National Bar Association, Chicago, 1974, p. 24.

3. *Encyclopedia of Associations,* p. 311.

4. Edson R. Sunderland, *History of the American Bar Association and Its Work* (n.p., 1953), pp. 3, 17.

5. *Reports of the American Bar Association,* vol. 68 (1943), pp. 109, 110.

increased in recent years.[6] This is reflected in their appearance as members of important committess of the association, as exemplified by the appointment of Charles Z. Smith, Associate Dean of the University of Washington School of Law, as the first black member of the Standing Committee on Federal Judiciary,[7] which investigates and reports to the Attorney General of the United States on the qualifications of all persons under consideration for appointment to the federal courts. As is developed in Chapter 10, the committee now has two black members.

The youngest cohort has the largest proportion of members in the ABA (fifty-six [60.2%] of the ninety-three respondents), the middle has the next largest (thirteen [43.3%] of thirty respondents), and the oldest has the lowest percentage (six [35.3%] of seventeen respondents).

The Federal Bar Association, founded in 1920, is a professional society of attorneys employed by the federal government as legislators, lawyers, judges, or members of quasi-judicial boards and commissions. It also includes those who have had previous government legal experience.[8] Since current or past federal government service of the types described are required for membership in this association, the number of respondents who belong is understandably the lowest of any of the bar associations considered. The membership is as follows: five of the oldest cohort, seven of the middle, and eighteen of the youngest cohort. Its immediate past president, J. Clay Smith, Jr., of Washington, D.C., is black, and is now its ABA House of Delegates representative.

While the organizations discussed have attracted the largest membership, fifty-eight (41.1%) of the respondents also belong to other organizations and bar associations, some memberships being by invitation only (see Appendix 11). William T. Coleman, Jr., while still practicing in Philadelphia, was elected to the prestigious governing body, the Council, of the American Law Institute and was also elected a Fellow of the professionally prestigious American College of Trial Lawyers. Most of the twenty-five respondents who said that they were members of other state bars merely replied "yes" to the question, without specifying the state.

While both black sole practitioners and lawyers in firms have high rates of membership in the Philadelphia Bar Association and in the Barristers Club, there is a slightly lower tendency for sole practitioners to join the national associations. For example, there is a 40 percent membership of sole practitioners in the ABA, in contrast to a 58 percent

---

6. *Encyclopedia of Associations,* 15th ed. (Detroit: Gale Research Co., 1980), vol. 1, p. 317.

7. John P. Mackenzie, "Black Added to ABA Judiciary Unit," *Washington Post,* October 19, 1976, p. A-2.

8. *Encyclopedia of Associations,* 11th ed., p. 306.

membership by other lawyers. One reason may be that the specialty sections of the ABA have publications and from time to time supply data that are most helpful to lawyers specializing in those areas, and, as noted, lawyers in firms specialize to a greater extent than do sole practitioners.

In the case of the NBA, one-third of the sole practitioners and one-half of the other lawyers belong to that organization. Membership in the FBA is the same for sole practitioners as for other lawyers.

All in all, less than half of the respondents who belong to professional organizations—only sixteen sole practitioners and forty-five other lawyers—said they considered them helpful.

Only eighteen of the respondents gave reasons for not joining bar associations. A typical response was, "Waste of time, energy, and patience." Other comments were: "Membership fees too high"; "not beneficial economically, personally"; "too big, white, and they are not potential clients."

Taking a positive view, one lawyer who was admitted to the bar in 1929 (oldest cohort) stated in his interview that membership in bar organizations is important for the socialization of young lawyers in that it provides them with an appreciation of the dignity of the profession. He believes that the young "get inspiration from rubbing elbows with the best lawyers and receive the vision of what they can aspire to."

A female jurist of the middle cohort noted in her interview that the meaning of membership in bar associations has changed. Years ago blacks were merely tolerated, not accepted or encouraged, and understandably felt that they were wasting time and effort. Now, however, not only can the young lawyer get something from membership but there also is the reciprocal benefit of what he or she can give the organization. "Now when you speak up with a point of view in support of a program, you're listened to."

During the course of interviews, other jurists of the same age-group supported the view that "people can change things from the inside, not the outside. . . . It is important to get into organizations . . . to become involved in committees . . . to help with decision-making processes and influence legislation on public policy." One jurist succinctly stated what is probably the most compelling argument for joining professional organizations in recent years: "Now you have a voice."

The loudest dissent came from a lawyer of the middle cohort who said he belongs to no bar associations because "they are not worth a damn—too discriminatory."

Comments on this subject came largely from middle cohort respondents. The youngest group had very little to say. Cantor, in his national survey, found that "[a] number of lawyers interviewed have refused, as a matter of personal pride, to join racially integrated Bar associations that were formerly not open to them."[9]

Generally, however, there still was a lack of wholehearted enthusiasm and a general feeling among black lawyers that bar associations have not yet reached their full potential in making membership a meaningful experience, especially for the younger blacks in the legal profession. Nevertheless, the consensus among black judges and lawyers was that membership in professional organizations has some benefits to offer.

9. Daniel J. Cantor & Co., "Negro Lawyers in the United States, 1966: An Economic Study," a project of Howard University School of Law in Cooperation with the National Bar Association, October 1966, p. 31.

# 8

# Self-Perceptions, Evaluations, and Predictions

Although it is impossible to analyze black lawyers' opinions of themselves statistically, their personal impressions are important not only for understanding the present situation but also for projecting the future of blacks in the legal profession.

## On the Status of Black Lawyers

Only 74 (52.5%) of the 141 respondents (6 in the first cohort, 21 in the second, and 47 in the third) replied to the question of the status of black lawyers in Philadelphia. Moreover, the question was interpreted in a variety of ways, such as referring to income, to regard by the black or white communities or both, to access to opportunities, to types of practice, or to a combination of two or more of these.

From the variety of interpretations, however, a picture emerges that clearly delineates how black lawyers of each cohort see themselves, and, with few exceptions, it is as second-class citizens given second-class opportunities in an environment where justice may be blind but definitely not color-blind and where white lawyers have a decided edge in every respect over black lawyers.

Members of all cohorts, with the exception of those few black lawyers who are in large white firms or in government positions, noted that black lawyers have lower incomes than white lawyers. In fact, income appears to be the dominant factor in the respondents' determination of status. Their comments confirm a 1967 study of occupations of black Americans, in which Leonard Broom and Norval Glenn report that "as long as he [the Negro] evaluates his economic status in relation to other Negroes, he may be fairly well satisfied, but when he begins to judge his status in relation to whites, he ranks himself lower and is less satisfied."[1]

While one would have expected the status of the black lawyer to increase with access to important government positions, corporations, and

1. Leonard Broom and Norval D. Glenn, *Transformation of the Negro American* (New York: Harper & Row, 1965), p. 107.

large white firms, the percentage of the youngest cohort who rated their prestige lower than that of the white lawyer was triple the percentage of those in the oldest cohort expressing the same opinion.

Of the six members of the oldest cohort who responded to the question of status, two considered the status of the black lawyer "as good as the white lawyer," and the other four described it as inferior, both economically and socially. One of them commented that "with few exceptions both the bar and the bench consider the black lawyer inferior." Another said, "There is substantial discrimination in the structure, making it difficult to root out." Still another remarked, "Bad, except for a few socially conscious lads."

Twenty-one (70%) of the middle cohort discussed the question of status, providing detailed explanations of the reasons for the inferior status of black lawyers. As reasons for the disparity in income, they cited most frequently the lack of opportunities for blacks to "develop substantial, economically viable clients"; restriction of the black lawyer to the "types of practice for which he or she is engaged, particularly criminal law"; and "the failure of the black community to patronize its own." They also noted that black lawyers "do not obtain anywhere near the percentage of black clients [we should]," that "appointments [of black lawyers] to decision-making bodies are far below par," and that they receive "practically no recognition by the corporate community or other large retainer-type clients."

Socially, black lawyers of the middle group feel they are beneath the white lawyer. They generally are not members of clubs to which white lawyers and judges belong, although the membership rolls are beginning to be opened to blacks. The representation of black lawyers on municipal boards, commissions, and elected legal positions (for example, district attorney and city solicitor) is disproportionately low in comparison with whites. This contributes to their lower self-esteem and belief in their inferior status.

In general, the responses of the middle cohort were predominantly negative but tempered by some degree of optimism for the future. Their dissatisfaction over income disparity was somewhat mitigated by the increase in the number of black judges and recruitment of blacks in greater numbers by white law firms and law schools. The situation, though still disturbing to them, was seen as substantially better than it had been.

Forty-seven (50.5%) of the youngest group voiced their opinions on status. Six who had no comment said that they had not been members of the bar long enough to make a judgment. Those who responded, with few exceptions, felt that while the situation was improving, blacks still were not on a par with white lawyers in terms of income, opportunities, and recognition. They also pointed out that despite their qualifications, they do not receive appointments from white judges commensurate with those given to white lawyers: "Extremely talented black lawyers who don't know anyone are not able to get positions in which they might maximize their talents." Some stated that blacks do not get enough judgeships. Others complained that they often are "shunned by blacks." They stated that businessmen and other members of the black community are still hesitant to use the services of black lawyers, for they believe "that the black client and/or lawyer will not fare as well as the white client and/or lawyer." If the lawyer is black, "[judges or juries] are more apt to [render] diminished judgments in civil trials." Several commented that black lawyers were "still locked into criminal law and struggling with general practice . . . for survival rather than choice."

"Racism places a second class or inferior stigma on black attorneys," one respondent summarized, while another commented, "The situation of the black lawyer corresponds with society in general."

A significant development in the experience of the younger black lawyer is the effect that Community Legal Services and similar organizations, largely supported by government appropriations, foundation grants, and private contributions, have had and increasingly will have on private practice. Since the black practitioners in private practice feel that they are "outside the mainstream of Philadelphia big law practice" and "retainer clients are almost nonexistent," they fear that groups like Community Legal Services will deprive them of potential fee-generating business. "Black lawyers have a long way to go," explained one, "i.e., the law and justice seem to be money and whom you know."

A few of the youngest cohort responded positively to the question of status, noting that "today the black lawyer has the advantage in the job market." One noted that "the situation is better in Philadelphia than in Virginia since the disparities are in areas of practice and type of client rather than in treatment from judges and bar associations." The number of black judges sitting in Philadelphia—twenty-four (18.5%) on federal, state, and local courts of general jurisdiction—while still not substantial, nevertheless impresses some of the youngest lawyers and also lends support for the increasing respect accorded black lawyers by whites. All in all, the situation was characterized by them as inferior to white lawyers but "improving."

## On Client Attitudes

Most of the respondents in this study also viewed the attitude of their clients toward black lawyers as "improving." This was the consensus of the oldest cohort, even to the extent that six out of sixteen who responded found that clients were "favorable" toward them. Several of those who said the attitude of clients was improving qualified their statement by saying that blacks still thought whites were more effective and clients still took important cases to white lawyers.

Twenty-three (76.7%) of the middle cohort replied to this question. Their responses ranged from "improving" to "good," although "not 100 percent acceptance of black lawyers." Public-interest lawyers in this group said that their clients were skeptical, believing that they could get better results from white lawyers. Government lawyers stated that their clients "doubt that black lawyers have equal opportunity to bring about just results in a white-dominated community." Consequently their clients are "not too trusting." Even in the black community, many noted, there is a lack of confidence in black lawyers that militates against blacks achieving just results for their own people. Black lawyers in the middle cohort hope that confidence in them will improve with the increasing number of black officials.

Among the seventy-three (78.5%) of the youngest group who responded, the consensus is that in large firms generally there is no problem, that "professionalism" is the important consideration, and that clients want quality representation and are therefore "color-blind." However, those in small firms observed that the racial handicap still exists, although there is some improvement. Federal and state government lawyers of the youngest cohort also noted that their clients are apprehensive and lack confidence, especially when important cases are involved. Those lawyers who are employed by corporations had a range of reactions, from "skeptical" to "good." The black female lawyer in a corporation was described as especially vulnerable because clients still seemed to "prefer white males."

Those young lawyers who were in city government, particularly in the District Attorney's Office, had generally favorable reactions from their superiors and associates. Though some sole practitioners had the same evaluation, most of them found client attitudes toward them to be "poor"; clients tend to be suspicious and critical of them; "they act as though they can pay less, later, and get quicker service."

## On Emerging Trends

Many of the respondents welcomed the opportunity to comment not only on their own experiences but also on trends that they have noticed in the legal profession, and their views may suggest future developments.

Asked whether they thought that young black lawyers would establish their own firms in the future, ninety-nine (84.6%) of the 117 respondents predicted that they would. Expressing this opinion were fourteen (77.7%) of the oldest cohort, seventeen (56.6%) of the middle, and sixty-eight (72.4%) of the youngest. Of the 112 who replied to the question of whether they thought that black lawyers in the future would join white firms, twelve members of the oldest cohort (66.6%) made this prediction. As the cohorts grew younger, the percentage of those with this opinion decreased, with twenty-one (70.0%) in the middle and fifty-three (56.9%) in the youngest cohort. As to whether black lawyers would join black firms, there was a difference in thinking. While eleven (61.1%) of the oldest cohort thought this would occur, only fifteen (50.0%) of the middle cohort agreed. The youngest group, with fifty-seven (61.3%), was in accord with the oldest group.

While thirty-eight failed to predict the future of the sole practitioner, the responses of 103 indicated the trend away from practicing alone. Only eight of the oldest cohort believed that the sole practitioner had a role in the future, five in the middle cohort, and thirty-two in the youngest were of this opinion.

Sole practitioners of the oldest cohort envisioned a decline in their solo practice because lawyers are increasingly absorbed by white, and to a greater extent black, firms. They too see a dramatic upsurge in the establishment of black firms.

Sole practitioners of the middle cohort could not follow the same thinking pattern, while the youngest envisioned an even greater development and establishment of black firms with an accompanying decline in solo practice.

The fourteen (77.7%) respondents of the oldest cohort, both firm lawyers and sole practitioners, were overwhelmingly optimistic about the future. They visualized improvement for black lawyers "as skill, reputation for integrity, and marketing techniques are more fully developed." They expressed the view that black lawyers will enter or establish black firms in increasing numbers and that there will be a decrease in the number of those who will join white firms.

Twenty (71.4%) of the twenty-eight respondents in the middle cohort were also optimistic about the future. They foresaw an increase in black firms "to insure the black population as a whole a more sound economic base, personal identification, and respect both among peers and in this society." However, in contrast to the expectations of the oldest cohort, they believe that along with the increase in black firms, more black lawyers will join white firms and many others will use their background in law to enter government and private business. In order to dispel the charge that in black firms "all do the same work," they saw "an emphasis on specialization in order to develop firms with a diversification of practice." Some of the respondents of this cohort decried lack of black involvement in politics and business and expressed the belief that this situation must and will change. Certainly the election of a black president of the Philadelphia City Council, Joseph E. Coleman, a member of the bar, must be encouraging. "The future augurs well for those who want to work," said one respondent. Another declared enthusiastically that he saw ahead "a bright, bright, sunny day."

Only three of the middle cohort viewed the future pessimistically, suggesting that resistance by white lawyers to equality for blacks will deter progress. Two did not respond.

A jurist of the middle cohort, pondering the future of blacks in the law in this city, said he believes that for the bright young lawyer there is a bright future; for the mediocre student who does not meet the standard of a well-established white office, there is hope in a government position. Give young lawyers the opportunity even if they do not succeed, he urged; his argument was that exposure is important. "In my generation they didn't have the opportunity. Today's black lawyer is burgeoning. There are more blacks in law schools today than there were blacks practicing five years ago all over the country."

Several members of the middle cohort commented about the black lawyer's changing role in commitment to causes. One lawyer in practice for twenty years remarked that lawyers of today are very bright but not so committed as the young men of his generation who went to work for the ACLU and the NAACP—men like Supreme Court Justice Thurgood Marshall and Chief Judge Spottswood Robinson of the United States Court of Appeals for the D.C. Circuit. "Economic opportunity came along and removed them from civil-rights litigation," he said. But today many of them are giving as much service to their people in different ways from those who came along earlier— there are, for examples, the Public Defender, Community Legal Services, and the Public Interest Law Center sponsored by the Philadelphia Bar Association. Another remarked that black lawyers have changed, not in direction but in the instrumentalities they utilize. According to some, black lawyers no longer are necessarily regarded as leaders of the civil rights movement to the extent they once were. It was pointed out, however, that although their "style is different," they still harbor a deep concern. There is of course still strong motivation, although there is less inclination to pursue civil rights through association with private firms or through government programs. Another attorney remarked that every big law firm should contribute either lawyers or funds for poverty law. This view is shared and implemented by a growing number of large law firms.

One jurist commented that the major difference between the old and the new crop of black lawyers is access to large white firms. "When these youngsters come out they are not concerned with getting into large firms, although they are given all sorts of inducements."

Economic motivation among black lawyers has varied with the economic climate of the nation. Those who came to the bar in the 1930s "looked for the opportunity to earn substantial amounts of money with very little thought of service to society except in terms of serving society well." As the years passed, social consciousness increased, causing black lawyers to have wider concerns for the nation at large.

One anonymous respondent said: "The black lawyer formerly became aware of the community through cases in which he was involved and which happened to touch on a problem. But today's lawyer feels that he must become involved in more than a tangential way in the affairs of the community." In this respect—concern with public responsibility—today's black lawyers differ from their predecessors of twenty years ago.

As evidence of their interest in public affairs, one need only look to the extent of their involvement in voluntary public service. Now black lawyers serve on the boards of banks, colleges, hospitals, art museums, and charities and on boards concerned with government employment policy and environmental quality. They are amassing such an exhaustive array of outside interests that an older lawyer was tempted to comment that many lawyers are "spreading themselves too thin" and "are overdoing outside interests to the point where they don't have time to be good lawyers."

The optimism expressed in the oldest and middle cohorts was not so pervasive in the youngest group. Twenty-two (23.7%) failed to respond to the question about the future, and seventy-one (76.3%) offered a variety of views and concerns on several fronts. Their comments, accompanied by suggestions, range along a continuum from "bleak" to "improving" to "good," even "excellent."

Those who foresaw the future as "bleak" anticipated a continuation of individual and institutional racism, limiting blacks to specific areas of practice: "Certain areas will always remain white, e.g., large corporation tax problems." One predicted that there will be "selective absorption of 'safe' blacks in the system, while the others will continue to struggle as sole practitioners." Some thought that the growth of law clinics would deprive them of potential clients and threaten their source of livelihood. Others suggested that although the number of black lawyers will increase, they will have little input in power or policy-making roles in Philadelphia. One respondent remarked that "things are so bad they can only go up."

Those young lawyers who see the situation as improving believe that with more black lawyers passing the bar they will begin to "organize to effect basic changes in their image." The lawyers who view the situation as good note that "many traditionally closed doors are now open." There are more opportunities today, and the future will see an ever-increasing number of black lawyers as well as better professional opportunities, but "only as a result of superior effort, not as the product of affirmative action, a phenomenon of the past."

While the increasing number of lawyers may work a hardship on some, it will provide black professionals with a stronger voice, for they may involve themselves in larger numbers and more deeply in politics and government.

Another positive factor is that as the number of black judges increases so does the recognition accorded the black bar.

Some expressed the opinion that private practice may see a decline while more blacks go into government service "where greater opportunities exist, where the political climate is favorable, and the cost of living less."

Many young lawyers believe that the female lawyer will have better access to positions in white organizations. She will be "in the power position in the future," one stated. This book will not present an in-depth study of the black female lawyer in Philadelphia, primarily because of the paucity of numbers. However, black female lawyers in Philadelphia have made up in quality for what they have lacked in quantity. One is Sadie Tanner Mossell Alexander, a distinguished graduate of the University of Pennsylvania Law School who has been in the forefront of legal excellence in this city for more than fifty years. Two outstanding female judges also grace the bench, both as members of the Court of Common Pleas of Philadelphia: Juanita Kidd Stout in the Trial Division and Doris May Harris in the Family Court Division.

## On Practicing in Philadelphia: A Summary

Those blacks who are in the law in Philadelphia today are in a situation far removed from that experienced by their predecessors through the generations who aspired to the practice of law and found themselves unable first to enter, then to cope with, a profession from which they were systematically barred.

Fortitude and dedication made it possible for Philadelphia's pioneer black lawyers to overcome the obstacles and achieve the position where today law firms, both black and white, are vying for talented male and female graduates of law schools to join them, where positions in city, state, and federal governments await them, and where corporations seek them.

But how did the respondents themselves view Philadelphia as a workplace for black lawyers? Their opinions varied with their experience and age.

Fourteen of the oldest cohort stated with an unqualified "yes" that Philadelphia is a satisfactory city for blacks who wish to practice law. One replied that it was satisfactory "as American cities go." Two noted improvement but did not feel that it was as yet "satisfactory."

The middle cohort was less enthusiastic, although of the twenty-eight who responded, twenty-one considered Philadelphia conditions satisfactory. Three gave a qualified "yes" with no further explanation, one said it was "all right but not outstanding," and another noted that Philadelphia "fails to provide business opportunities for blacks." Two replied without explanation that Philadelphia is "unsatisfactory."

When we review the responses of the youngest cohort we find a sharp decrease in the number of black lawyers who expressed satisfaction with conditions in Philadelphia. In this cohort only forty (45.9%) of the eighty-seven who replied to the question gave an unqualified "yes," and one gave a qualified "yes," noting that there were good opportunities for career development but that burgeoning numbers of lawyers may prove to be an obstacle to rapid growth. One replied that it was "a satisfactory place in which to make a living, but progress will be a little slower than in smaller cities, where there is greater cohesiveness among blacks."

Thirty-three (37.9%) said it was "not satisfactory," for reasons such as "Philadelphia lacks major black business foundation," there are "too many black lawyers," and "more must be done to upgrade blacks in general." Some emphasized the lack of unity plus "lack of community support." Only one mentioned the racist aspect of practice in the city, noting the "cliquish exclusionary bar." Several pointed to the fact that blacks lack "political involvement." Charles L. Mitchell, in his "Comment" in the *Villanova Law Review*,[2] cited a statement by John Hadley Strange that "Negroes have not made . . . significant gains in political power or in the rewards and benefits they receive from the local political system." One respondent commented that Philadelphia does not provide "satisfactory progress for blacks as a whole, needless to say in a profession where they make up only one percent of the total lawyers."

Thus, the majority of the members of the oldest cohort, remembering the past, expressed satisfaction with the present situation in Philadelphia as they noted the progress that has been made along the way. The majority of the members of the middle cohort were less enthusiastic, less satisfied, and less optimistic but not dissatisfied; they had more mixed feelings. The majority of the youngest members who were not in large flourishing firms were the most disenchanted with the slow pace of progress for blacks in the law in Philadelphia.

The road from exclusion to acceptance has been rocky indeed. The oldest lawyers remembered well the ostracism and rebuffs they experienced. Those in the middle age-group saw doors open and opportunities so long denied appear, particularly for the younger members of the middle group. The youngest lawyers, while not satisfied with the areas of

2. Charles L. Mitchell, "The Black 'Philadelphia Lawyer,' " *Villanova Law Review*, vol. 20, nos. 2 and 3 (1974–75), p. 396 (citing John Hadley Strange, "The Negro and Philadelphia Politics," in *Urban Government*, ed. E. Banfield [New York: Free Press, 1969], p. 408).

practice to which so many of them believed themselves "locked in," are surrounded by opportunities commensurate with their talents.

While the situation in Philadelphia is far from ideal, the clear consensus is that it is "improving."

# Blacks in the Law Across the Nation:
## An Overview

# 9

# A Survey of Fifteen Cities

Part One of this book presents a detailed account and evaluation of the development, employment patterns, and status of black lawyers and judges in the city of Philadelphia. Part Two takes up the question of whether the Philadelphia study reflects the situation of black lawyers and judges across the country. It also surveys the situation with regard to black teachers in law school.

In order to view the Philadelphia study in a national context, in April 1980 a supplementary survey was instituted, focusing on the fifteen additional cities in the United States that had two or more law firms of ninety or more lawyers each: Atlanta, Boston, Chicago, Cleveland, Columbus, Detroit, Houston, Los Angeles, Milwaukee, Minneapolis, New York, Pittsburgh, Richmond, San Francisco, and Washington, D.C. With reasonable diversity in size and location, these cities represent a cross-section of urban America, the milieu in which legal practice is most developed and vigorous. Thus, information on the situation of black lawyers in these cities should provide meaningful comparisons for the Philadelphia story and broaden our perspective on the overall progress and achievements of blacks in the American legal profession.

As already discussed in the Introduction and in Part One of this book, blacks who have passed state bar examinations have a variety of career choices open to them in the legal profession: they may go into private practice, enter government service, accept a position in the law department of a corporation, fill an academic post, or serve on the judiciary. It was not feasible within the scope of this study to conduct the extensive original surveys on the numbers and percentages of black lawyers in each of these areas of activity. The primary focus of this chapter therefore has been on gathering statistics in each of the cities regarding the number of black lawyers, both partners and associates, in large and medium-size, predominantly white, law firms. (Partners are "part owners" of the firm and receive a percentage of the profits generated by the firm as a whole. Associates are employees of the firm who are compensated by a fixed salary, often supplemented by a year-end bonus; with occasional exceptions, they have come to the firm directly from law school or after up to two years as law clerks to a judge or in other government legal positions; in time, usually seven, increasingly eight, years, those who in the opinion of the partners qualify may be elected partners.) Information on the inroads that blacks have made into these firms will provide an overview of the extent to which the most successful element of the legal profession in this country is becoming integrated. Data on black representation in the judiciary also have been gathered and offer an added dimension to the assessment. Black representation on the bench and in the predominantly white firms are two important indexes to the progress that blacks have made in the legal profession as a whole.

To evaluate the status of black lawyers in the major integrated firms, questionnaires requesting the number of partners and associates, subdivided into male and female, and the number of black lawyers in each group, were mailed in April 1980 to the 107 law firms of 90 or more lawyers (referred to hereafter as "large firms") in the fifteen cities.[1] Seventy percent of these firms returned completed questionnaires, and subsequently the data were procured concerning the remainder. Similar statistics were secured for 218 law firms of more than 25 but less than 90 lawyers in the same fifteen cities (hereafter "medium-size firms"). The data concerning the medium-size firms, as well as those concerning a small number of the large firms, were derived from university law school admission and law placement services.

The overall results of these investigations, including comparisons with Philadelphia situations, are discussed below in individual sections on each of the fifteen additional cities. Tables 13 and 14 provide a summary view of the findings and afford a comparative view of all the cities vis-à-vis one another. Since the 1980 survey changes in the number of black lawyers in the firms have of course occurred. Where such later information has been obtained, reference to it is made in the individual city sections.

The findings show that, in general, the large firms have a somewhat better record of recruiting black lawyers into their ranks; but there are still very few black associates in both categories of firms, and even fewer partners. However, the fact that all the firms have a larger number of black associates than partners may provide hope for black partners in the future.

Although the statistics vary from city to city, it is clear that black lawyers in Philadelphia and elsewhere in the United States have not made the inroads into the leading firms of the legal community that were envi-

---

1. One hundred of these firms had been listed in the *National Law Journal,* October 1, 1979, p. 28.

Table 13
**Black Representation in Large Law Firms in Sixteen Cities (1980)**

|  | %<br>Partners | %<br>Associates |
|---|---|---|
| Atlanta | 0 | 1.8 |
| Boston | 0.6 | 1.6 |
| Chicago | 0.3 | 2.2 |
| Cleveland | 0.8 | 2.1 |
| Columbus | 0 | 4.5 |
| Detroit | 0 | 7.3 |
| District of Columbia | 1.1 | 3.5 |
| Houston | 0 | 1.6 |
| Los Angeles | 0.8 | 3.0 |
| Milwaukee | 0.7 | 2.4 |
| Minneapolis | 0 | 1.6 |
| New York | 0.1 | 2.2 |
| Philadelphia | 0.8 | 3.9 |
| Pittsburgh | 0.4 | 0.8 |
| Richmond | 0 | 2.1 |
| San Francisco | 0.2 | 2.4 |

Table 14
**Black Representation in Medium-size Law Firms in Sixteen Cities (1980)**

|  | %<br>Partners | %<br>Associates |
|---|---|---|
| Atlanta | 0.4 | 4.1 |
| Boston | 0.2 | 1.6 |
| Chicago | 0.1 | 1.7 |
| Cleveland | 0.7 | 3.2 |
| Columbus | 0 | 5.6 |
| Detroit | 1.0 | 6.0 |
| District of Columbia | 0.8 | 2.9 |
| Houston | 0 | 1.7 |
| Los Angeles | 0.7 | 2.8 |
| Milwaukee | 0 | 0 |
| Minneapolis | 0 | 0 |
| New York | 0.2 | 1.4 |
| Philadelphia | 0.3 | 1.9 |
| Pittsburgh | 0 | 0 |
| Richmond | 0 | 1.2 |
| San Francisco | 0 | 1.2 |

sioned in the late 1960s and early 1970s. The 1980 survey of the law firms (Tables 13 and 14) showed three cities—Milwaukee, Minneapolis, and Pittsburgh—with no black partners or associates in their medium-size firms, and four more—Columbus, Houston, Richmond, and San Francisco —with black associates but no black partners. Though large firms in all the cities represented had some black associates, six cities—Atlanta, Columbus, Detroit, Houston, Minneapolis, and Richmond—had no black partners in their large firms. Philadelphia's position in this statistical profile is slightly above average for the medium-size firms and stronger for the large firms. But, obviously, all the percentages, including those for Philadelphia, are extremely low.

Black representation on the judiciary (state, local and federal) in the cities studied is more varied—highest in Washington, 28.6 percent, and lowest in Minneapolis, 2.5 percent, compared to 18.5 percent in Philadelphia. Table 15 (below) brings together data on local, state, and federal judgeships (as of November 1981–82) for an overview of black representation on the bench in Philadelphia and the fifteen additional cities. These data have been assembled in cooperation with the National Center for State Courts through its Executive Director, Edward B. McConnell, and the Center's staff. Many milestones for blacks in the judiciary are noted in the city sections below, and the topic in general is discussed more broadly in Chapter 10.

Statistics regarding black representation in law firms and on the bench are all the more realistic and valid when judged relative to the size of the black population of each city and the proportion of blacks to the total population. This information is provided in Table 16 (below).

The population figures are important underpinnings for the stories of black involvement in the sixteen legal communities under consideration. In addition to the population data and the statistics that have been gleaned through the questionnaires, from publications, and from government agencies, information on significant developments and milestones for blacks in the law has been provided by judges, law faculty, and lawyers within each of the fifteen cities being compared with Philadelphia. These source persons have provided for inclusion here events and individuals that are reflective of the developments and trends for black lawyers in many areas of their communities, not exclusively in integrated private practice.

What follows is thus a blend of statistical data and social history, sometimes oral history. A section on each of the cities reviews the entry of blacks into its legal community and evaluates their status as practitioners today. Each section may also include significant information about (though not a complete picture of) the representation of blacks in various branches of the judiciary, noting particularly their movement up from the

Table 15
State and Local and U.S. Court of Appeals and District Judges in Sixteen Cities (1981-82)

| | State & Local | | | Federal | | | Total | | |
|---|---|---|---|---|---|---|---|---|---|
| | State & Local Judges | No. Black Judges | % Black Judges | U.S. Court of Appeals & District Judges | No. Black Judges | % Black Judges | State & Local and U.S. Court of Appeals & District Judges | No. Black Judges | % Black Judges |
| Atlanta | 50 | 11 | 22.0 | 13 | 2 | 15.4 | 63 | 13 | 20.6 |
| Boston | 76 | 9 | 11.8 | 11 | 1 | 9.0 | 87 | 10 | 11.5 |
| Chicago | 407 | 34 | 8.4 | 20 | 1 | 5.0 | 427 | 35 | 8.2 |
| Cleveland | 63 | 10 | 15.9 | 7 | 1 | 14.3 | 70 | 11 | 15.7 |
| Columbus | 42 | 2 | 4.8 | 3 | 1 | 33.3 | 45 | 3 | 6.7 |
| Detroit | 100 | 25 | 25.0 | 12 | 3 | 25.0 | 112 | 28 | 25.0 |
| Houston | 104 | 9 | 8.7 | 10 | 1 | 10.0 | 114 | 10 | 8.8 |
| Los Angeles | 280 | 29 | 10.4 | 19 | 2 | 10.5 | 299 | 31 | 10.4 |
| Milwaukee | 40 | 2 | 5.0 | 4 | 0 | 0 | 44 | 2 | 4.5 |
| Minneapolis | 37 | 1 | 2.7 | 3 | 0 | 0 | 40 | 1 | 2.5 |
| New York | 442 | 47 | 10.6 | 39 | 6 | 15.4 | 481 | 53 | 11.0 |
| Philadelphia | 110 | 21 | 19.1 | 20 | 3 | 15.0 | 130 | 24 | 18.5 |
| Pittsburgh | 49 | 5 | 10.2 | 9 | 1 | 11.1 | 58 | 6 | 10.3 |
| Richmond | 24 | 2 | 8.3 | 3 | 0 | 0 | 27 | 2 | 7.4 |
| San Francisco | 69 | 4 | 5.8 | 15 | 2 | 13.3 | 84 | 6 | 7.1 |
| Washington, D.C. | 53 | 15 | 28.3 | 24 | 7 | 29.2 | 77 | 22 | 28.6 |

Note: Federal judges as of April 1982, 527 F. Supp. VII–XXV; State and local judges as of November 1981. For these detailed statistics, but including U.S. bankruptcy judges and magistrates, see Appendix 12.

Table 16
**Black Proportion of Population in Sixteen Cities in 1980**

| City | Total Population* | Black Population | % Black |
|------|------------------|------------------|---------|
| Atlanta | 430,864 | 282,912 | 65.7 |
| Boston | 599,092 | 126,229 | 21.1 |
| Chicago | 3,447,133 | 1,197,000 | 34.7 |
| Cleveland | 591,594 | 251,347 | 42.5 |
| Columbus | 569,522 | 124,880 | 21.9 |
| Detroit | 1,232,309 | 758,939 | 61.6 |
| Houston | 1,697,310 | 440,257 | 25.9 |
| Los Angeles | 3,782,752 | 505,208 | 13.4 |
| Milwaukee | 642,323 | 146,940 | 22.9 |
| Minneapolis | 375,635 | 28,433 | 7.6 |
| New York | 8,476,987 | 1,784,124 | 21.0 |
| Philadelphia | 1,751,780 | 638,878 | 36.5 |
| Pittsburgh | 423,938 | 101,813 | 24.0 |
| Richmond | 221,424 | 112,357 | 50.7 |
| San Francisco | 762,347 | 86,414 | 11.3 |
| Washington, D.C. | 655,303 | 448,229 | 68.4 |

*White, Hispanic, black, and other.
SOURCE: *New York Times,* April 16, 1980, and *1980 Census,* Advance Reports.

lower courts. While the information for each of these fifteen cities, taken alphabetically, is limited in scope compared with the Philadelphia study, each section does provide a general view of the status of the black lawyers and judges of the city and of how their situation compares with Philadelphia.

While recorded facts are sparse, through research and principally interviews, with a great deal of cooperation from both black and white judges and lawyers, it has been possible in many instances to list and tell something about numerous "firsts" for black lawyers in the fifteen cities —the first black lawyer in the city, the first one to practice in the courts; the first black to be appointed a judge, the first to sit in an appellate court; the first local prosecuting attorney, the first United States Attorney; the first to be elected to the state legislature, the first to the Congress of the United States; and other categories as well.

The material covered in each of the cities is quite specific, dealing with details in the forward movement of blacks in the law largely through the progress of individuals. Broader comparisons and conclusions will be drawn in Chapter 10.

# Atlanta

Atlanta, Georgia, generally considered the South's most progressive city, has been described as the "hub of academia for the Negro world"[2] because of the Atlanta University system, a complex of black academic institutions established by the Freedmen's Bureau after the Civil War.[3] The complex includes Morehouse, Spelman, Clark, and Morris Brown Colleges, Morehouse Medical College, and Gammon Theological Seminary. Atlanta is also the home of a leading black-owned bank, Citizens Trust Company, of the black-owned Mutual Savings and Loan Association and Atlanta Life Insurance Company, and of the black newspaper, the *Atlanta Daily World.* [4] It is the only city in the country to have elected two black mayors (Maynard Jackson and Andrew Young).

Atlanta has also been fertile ground for the development of blacks in the legal profession. Despite the small beginnings in the nineteenth century, a solid foundation was established during the second half of the twentieth century for blacks who desired to pursue a legal career.

The only black lawyer known to have been a resident of Atlanta before 1900 was Aaron A. Bradley, who had been admitted to the Massachusetts Bar in 1856. After moving to Georgia, Bradley did not practice law but served twice in the Georgia state legislature.[5] The first black lawyers to practice law in Georgia were Henry Lincoln Johnson of Augusta and Peyton Allen of Atlanta. By 1910, the year the NAACP was founded, there were approximately eighteen black lawyers in the state.[6] This was not an inconsiderable number, for of the 114,000 lawyers in the country at that time, only 795 (0.69%) were black.[7]

During the 1920s there came on the scene in the Atlanta area two black lawyers from whom a rich lineage of black practicing lawyers can be traced: Thomas James Henry, Jr. (1891–1977), and Austin T. Walden (1885–1965).

Thomas James Henry, Jr., a native of Atlanta, attended Clark University in Atlanta and Brooklyn School of Law, and he is believed to have

2. Russell L. Adams, *Great Negroes Past and Present* (Chicago: Afro-American Publishing Co., 1969), p. 114.
3. Mabel Morsbach, *The Negro in American Life* (New York: Harcourt Brace and World, 1966), p. 108.
4. Adams, *Great Negroes,* p. 77.
5. Gilbert Ware, "A Word to and About Black Lawyers," *The Crisis,* vol. 85, no. 7 (August–September 1978), p. 247.
6. U.S. Bureau of the Census, *1910 Census,* vol. 4 (Washington, D.C.: Government Printing Office, 1914), table 7, p. 450.
7. August Meier and Elliot Rudwick, "Attorneys Black and White: A Case Study of Race Relations Within the NAACP," *Journal of American History,* vol. 62, no. 4 (March 1976), p. 915.

started practicing law after military service during World War I. It is said that he devoted himself to developing special expertise in title and real estate law because of a severe hearing impairment sustained as a result of constant exposure to subfreezing temperatures during the war. Henry became the first black to practice with a title company in Atlanta. He was also a founder of Mutual Federal Savings and Loan Association of Atlanta and served as its General Counsel from 1925 until 1973. In his lifetime Henry received many honors, including recognition in 1976 by the Georgia Conference of Black Lawyers. At the time of his death in 1977, at the age of ninety-six, he was Georgia's oldest black attorney.

Austin T. Walden was born the son of slaves in rural Fort Valley, Georgia. By 1907 he had managed to earn an A.B. degree at Atlanta University, and in 1911 he obtained his law degree from the University of Michigan Law School. He subsequently had a military career as a commissioned officer and a trial judge advocate. Throughout his legal career Walden continued his remarkable achievements and became known as the "dean" of Atlanta's black lawyers. He figured prominently in the struggles and accomplishments of the city of Atlanta and was associated with many civic and religious organizations. In 1964 Walden was appointed by Mayor Ivan Allen to the Municipal Court of Atlanta, thereby making him the first black judge in the South since Reconstruction. After his death in 1965, the Georgia State Senate paid tribute to him in a resolution acknowledging his "distinguished career." He was lauded by both blacks and whites for his ability to provide guidance that ultimately led to legal change felt not only within the organized bar but throughout the Atlanta community.

The next era in the history of black attorneys in Atlanta began in 1948, when ten of them met and organized themselves as the Gate City Bar Association. Atlanta was thought to be "the Gate City of the South for black people," symbolizing "the opening and beginning of opportunity and progressiveness in the areas of education, business, and the professions."[8]

Those ten attorneys—Thomas J. Henry, Jr., Austin T. Walden, S. S. Robinson, Mrs. R. Pruden Herndon, T. W. Holmes, R. E. Thomas, Jr., E. E. Moore, Jr., James E. Salter, Charles M. Clayton, and E. S. D'Antignoc —formed the nucleus of the organization that later spearheaded the legal aspects of the civil-rights movement and progress toward political power of blacks in the Atlanta area. Henry and Walden were the association's first two presidents.

R. E. Thomas, Jr. was elected the third president of the Gate City Bar on October 4, 1954. Thomas received his undergraduate training at Atlanta University and Morehouse College and his legal training at the University

---

8. Stanley Foster, "The First Thirty Years—The History of the Gate City Bar Association," *Nexus,* vol. 1, no.1 (1979), n.p.

of Michigan Law School. During World War II he served in the Pacific Theater of Operations and received the Soldier's Medal for Action. Admitted to the Georgia Bar in 1947, Thomas became active in the civil rights movement. He later served as Pro Hoc Judge of the Municipal Court.

Samuel B. Wright, Jr. was born in 1913 in Forsyth, Georgia, where he spent his early years. He graduated *magna cum laude* from Morris Brown College in 1934, and, after service in the army, he entered Howard University Law School, receiving his degree in June 1949. In May 1956 Wright was elected President of the Gate City Bar Association. In his inaugural address he spoke for the majority of the members on the much debated issue of disbanding or of merging into the Atlanta Bar Association. Pointing out that "some organizations can be integrated and some—by their nature—cannot," Wright affirmed the Gate City Bar's unique function in the community, "one that cannot (by its very nature) be completely filled by the Atlanta Bar Association, the Lawyer's Club, or the Women's Bar Association." While he expressed hope that the Gate City Bar Association's members would become affiliated with those groups, he stressed that it would remain a separate and distinct association that "concerned itself with the unique needs of black lawyers and the black community."[9] This point of view has motivated associations of black lawyers in many cities throughout the country.

Rachael Pruden Herndon, elected President of the Gate City Bar Association on September 5, 1958, was the first woman to hold that office. A teacher and legal secretary who read law in the office of Austin T. Walden, Herndon was admitted to the bar in 1943. She was the first black woman from the South to be admitted to practice before the United States Supreme Court. In 1965 she was appointed by Mayor Sam Massell as Judge Pro Hoc of the Atlanta Municipal Court. She died in 1979.

Donald L. Hollowell became President of the Gate City Bar Association on June 6, 1960. Extolled as an outstanding legal scholar and preeminent trial lawyer, he was associated with almost every major civil rights and civil liberties case in Georgia and was personal attorney to Martin Luther King, Jr. In 1966 President Lyndon B. Johnson appointed Hollowell to his post as General Counsel for the Southeast Region of the Equal Employment Opportunity Commission.

The list of lawyers trained by Hollowell is evidence of his profound influence in Atlanta and across the country. A sampling includes Howard Moore, defender of Angela Davis; United States District Court Judge Horace T. Ward; Fulton County State Court Judge William Alexander; Urban League President Vernon Jordan; Democratic National Committee executive Ben Brown; and Peter Rindskopf.

It was not until the *Brown v. Board of Education* decision in 1954 that the

9. Minutes of the Gate City Bar Association, May 7, 1956, p. 6.

black lawyer in Atlanta had the freedom to function effectively as a profes-sional. Before then, as Atlanta attorney Stanley Foster recounted in a recent article, association with white lawyers was inconceivable, and until 1962 blacks were excluded from membership in both the Atlanta and the Georgia Bar Associations. "The judicial machinery," Foster observed, "mirrored the private practices of the local and state bar associations."

> No black faces could be counted among the judges, law enforcement officers, and various other court personnel who constituted the dis-pensers of justice. Of course, it must be noted that within the physical confines of the court building black practitioners and their clients drank from separate water fountains, used separate lavatory facilities, and lunched at H. L. Green's or at establishments on Auburn Avenue, because the lunchroom within the courthouse was reserved for "whites only."[10]

It was in the same year as the *Brown v. Board of Education* decision that the first legal challenge to segregation of public facilities in Atlanta, *Holmes v. City of Atlanta,*[11] was successfully brought by R. E. Thomas, Jr., S. S. Robinson, and E. E. Moore, Jr., all black attorneys. Following this litigation, the great majority of civil-rights cases in the area were handled by black attorneys, which had a threefold economic result: (1) more black attorneys were employed, often gaining fees for successful challenges; (2) the litiga-tion was often complex, giving black attorneys invaluable expertise and experience; (3) the black community was given an opportunity to see the abilities of the black attorneys and thereby develop a trust that would yield both political and economic gains for them.

Another result of the *Brown* decision, which would be realized years later, was increased opportunities for blacks to gain a legal education. In 1950, when Horace T. Ward, the first black to seek admission to the University of Georgia School of Law, was turned down, he filed a suit against that university in the United States District Court. The suit was dismissed. He applied to and was accepted by the Northwestern School of Law, from which he graduated in 1959. Following his admission to the bar in 1960, he practiced law as an associate with Donald L. Hollowell for three years, and one of his first actions was to join in litigating a suit against the University of Georgia, *Holmes v. Danner,*[12] which resulted in the first black being admitted to that institution. The integration of the law schools of the University of Georgia, Emory University, and Mercer University finally provided black law students with a "choice" of accredited schools within their own state.

10. Foster, "The First Thirty Years, p. 2.
11. 222 F.2d 382, *reversed* 350 U.S. 879 (1955).
12. 191 *F. Supp.* 394 (D.C. M.D. Ga. 1961).

In the late 1960s and the 1970s black lawyers in Atlanta, no longer excluded from white law schools and professional associations, continued to make important breakthroughs. In 1962 Leroy R. Johnson became a state senator.[13] In 1969, at the height of the civil-rights movement, Prentis Q. Yancey and John L. Kennedy, both native sons of Atlanta, became the first blacks to enter white law firms in that city. Yancey, a graduate of Emory University School of Law, subsequently became a partner in the firm. Kennedy, a graduate of Harvard Law School, left in 1971 to start his own firm of Kennedy, Sampson and Edwards.

The first black woman—the first woman and the first black— to serve as a city attorney for Atlanta is Marva Jones-Brooks. She is one of only two black city attorneys in the nation. Isabel Gates Webster, First Assistant City Attorney, is the first woman to serve as an assistant city attorney in Atlanta. A 1953 graduate of Boston University Law School, she came to the Georgia Bar in June 1958 and has been involved in major litigation in the area of employment discrimination. While President Jimmy Carter was still Governor of Georgia, he appointed her the first black to the State Personnel Board. She received the 1981 Outstanding Woman Award from the Georgia Federation of Business Women.[14]

Admitted to the Georgia Bar in 1965, Maynard H. Jackson, Jr. served as attorney for the Emory Community Legal Services Center from 1967 to 1969. In 1970 he founded Georgia's first and largest black firm—Jackson, Patterson, Parks and Franklin. In 1974 he became Mayor of Atlanta,[15] the first black to hold that office, and was reelected by a landslide in 1978.[16] Over the years he has gained national recognition for his activities in the public interest in causes ranging from civil rights to gun control.

It was in the 1970s that blacks first gained representation on the state and federal courts in Atlanta. When Romae Turner Powell was appointed a judge of the Juvenile Court of Fulton County in 1973,[17] she became the first black to sit on a state court of record in Georgia.

Horace T. Ward, noted above, practiced with the firm of Hollowell, Ward, Moore and Alexander and its successors until 1969, when he was appointed Deputy City Attorney in the Law Department of Atlanta. In 1974 he was appointed to the Fulton County State Court, and three years later he was elevated to the Superior Court, the court of general jurisdiction.[18] In 1979 Ward became the first black federal judge in Georgia when

13. *Who's Who in America, 1968–69,* vol. 35, p. 1138.

14. Information furnished by Flora Devine, Atlanta attorney.

15. *Who's Who in America, 1980–81,* vol. 1, p. 1684; Newsletter, National Conference of Artists, vol. 2, no. 1 (April 1980), p. 1.

16. Newsletter, *National Conference of Artists,* vol. 2, no. 1 (April 1980), p. 1.

17. Mary Reincke and Nancy Lichterman, *The American Bench: Judges of the Nation,* 2nd ed. (Minneapolis: Reginald Bishop Forster & Assoc., 1979), p. 532.

18. Ibid., p. 540; *National Bar Bulletin,* vol. 9, no. 3 (March 1977), p. 1.

President Carter appointed him to the United States District Court for the Northern District of Georgia.

Another black lawyer, Isaac Jenrette, a former police officer who became Assistant District Attorney, was appointed to fill the vacancy thus created on the Superior Court in 1980. The first black elected (1981) to the Superior Court was Clarence Cooper, who also had served as Assistant District Attorney (1968–76).[19]

In percentages of black judgeships on federal, state, and local courts, Atlanta in 1981–82 outranked New York, Chicago, Los Angeles, and Philadelphia and nine of the other cities—all but Detroit and Washington D.C. (see Table 15). However, while this very significant progress has been made, none of the black judges in Atlanta is as yet on the Supreme Court or on the Court of Appeals (intermediate appellate court), and only two are on the Superior Court (trial court of general jurisdiction). In Philadelphia a black justice sits on the Pennsylvania Supreme Court; a black judge is on each of the other state appellate courts (Superior Court and Commonwealth Court); and fifteen black judges (18.51%) sit on its trial court of general jurisdiction (Court of Common Pleas). While the first federal court judge in Atlanta was sworn in on December 6, 1979, on the District Court, the first federal court judge in Philadelphia (and first also in the country) was appointed in 1949 to the Court of Appeals for the Third Circuit (and the first to the District Court in 1964.) These differences are reminders of the advantages that black lawyers have had in the northern cities, where they were beginning to enter the legal profession even while blacks in the South were still slaves.

The comparative statistics for Atlanta and Philadelphia are as follows:

|  | Atlanta | Philadelphia |
|---|---|---|
| State & Local Judges | 50 | 110 |
| Black Judges | 11 (22.0%)[20] | 21 (19.1%) |
| U.S. Court of Appeals & District Judges | 13 | 20 |
| Black Judges | 2 (15.4%) | 3 (15.0%) |
| Total Judges | 63 | 130 |
| Total Black Judges | 13 (20.6%) | 24 (18.5%)[21] |

Federal judges as of April 1982, 527 F. Supp. XXIII–XXV, X–XI; State and local judges as of November 1981.

19. Information supplied by Flora Devine, Atlanta attorney.

20. Two of these judges (Municipal Court) are part-time.

21. For detailed statistics on black and white judges in all cities surveyed, including U.S. bankruptcy judges and magistrates, see Appendix 12.

Our 1980 survey of Atlanta's large and medium-size law firms showed that blacks continued to enter the predominantly white firms during the 1970s. In Atlanta the large firms have lagged behind the medium-size firms in their engaging of black lawyers. In both categories Philadelphia has been ahead, even though blacks comprise 65.7 percent of the population of Atlanta, compared to 36.5 percent of the population of Philadelphia.

| Large Firms* | Total Lawyers | Black Lawyers | Total Partners | Black Partners | Total Associates | Black Associates |
|---|---|---|---|---|---|---|
| Atlanta | 432 | 4 (0.9%) | 212 | 0* | 220 | 4 (1.8%) |
| Philadelphia | 1,094 | 26 (2.4%) | 531 | 4 (0.8%) | 563 | 22 (3.9%) |
| Medium-size Firms* | | | | | | |
| Atlanta | 620 | 15 (2.0%) | 278 | 1 (0.3%) | 342 | 14 (4.1%) |
| Philadelphia | 550 | 6 (1.1%) | 228 | 1 (0.4%) | 262 | 5 (1.9%)[22] |

*According to the 1980 survey conducted by the author. Since then at least one black has achieved partnership in a large firm, according to local sources.

The Atlanta Bar Association has 3,800 registered members and estimates some 6,000 attorneys in the nine-county metropolitan area. The Gate City Bar Association has approximately 300 members. One association official estimates a 10 to 1 ratio of white lawyers to black in Atlanta, which would mean approximately 380 black lawyers in Atlanta.[23] In Atlanta, blacks comprise 65.7 percent of the total population (see Table 16). For blacks on law school faculties, see Appendix 18.

# Boston

It is generally accepted that until almost the middle of the nineteenth century there were no black lawyers in the United States and that the first black lawyer was associated with Boston, Massachusetts. Macon B. Allen, who was admitted to the bar in Maine in 1844, soon moved to Boston, and was admitted to the bar of Suffolk County in 1845, and is most authoritatively cited as the first.[24] After the Civil War, Allen moved to Charleston, South Carolina, was admitted to the bar there, and in February 1873 was

22. For detailed statistics on black and white lawyers in all cities surveyed, see Appendices 13 and 14

23. Information supplied by Flora Devine, Atlanta attorney.

24. Derrick A. Bell, Jr., "Black Students in White Law Schools: The Ordeal and the Opportunity," *Toledo Law Review*, vols. 539, 540, no. 5 (1970); Walter J. Leonard, "Development of the Black Bar," *Annals of the American Academy of Political and Social Science*, vol. 407 (May 1973), p. 136; idem, *Black Lawyers* (Boston: Senna & Shih, 1977), p. 49.

elected by the legislature to the position of Judge of the Inferior Court of Charleston County.[25]

Robert Morris, Jr., the second black lawyer in Massachusetts, was admitted to the bar of Suffolk County in 1846 or 1847.[26] Morris is said to have been appointed a magistrate by Governor George N. Briggs in about 1850, which would make him the first black to have held a judicial post in the United States.[27] Robert Morris participated in a landmark case when in 1849, along with Charles Sumner, he appeared before the Supreme Judicial Court of Massachusetts to argue the historic *Roberts v. City of Boston.*[28] The *Roberts* case was an action seeking damages in behalf of five-year-old Sarah Roberts, a black child who was excluded from a public school that was nearer her home than the black school to which she had been assigned. The action was ultimately unsuccessful, and Chief Justice Lemuel Shaw's opinion for the court was cited by the United States Supreme Court in 1896 in support of the "separate but equal" doctrine announced in *Plessy v. Ferguson.*[29] Nevertheless, Morris's effort in *Roberts* represents an early attempt at the desegregation result finally achieved in *Brown v. Board of Education* in 1954.[30]

Later in the nineteenth century, George Lewis Ruffin achieved in Boston two important milestones for blacks in the legal profession. A native of Richmond, Ruffin's mother brought him to Boston in 1853 because of the Virginia statute prohibiting the teaching of reading and writing to blacks. He attended public school in Boston and later read law in the offices of Jewell and Gaston while earning his living as a barber. In 1869, at age thirty-five, he graduated from Harvard Law School, having completed an eighteen-month course for former law apprentices.[31] One authority lists Ruffin as the "first negro to graduate from any law school in the country."[32] After practicing law successfully for thirteen years, engaging actively in Republican politics, and serving in the Massachusetts legislature and the Boston Common Council (the latter from a black ward), in 1883 he was appointed a judge on the Charlestown Municipal Court[33] and thus became the first black in the North to hold a judicial position higher than magistrate.

25. Charles B. Contee, "Macon B. Allen: 'First' Black in the Legal Profession," *The Crisis,* vol. 83, no. 2 (February 1976), p. 68.

26. Peter M. Bergman, *The Negro in America* (New York: Harper & Row, 1969), p. 187.

27. Beverly Blair Cook, "Black Representation in the Third Branch," *Black Law Journal,* vol. 1, nos. 2 and 3 (1971), p. 260, n. 1.

28. 59 Mass. (5 Cush.) 198 (1849).

29. 163 U.S. 537, 544 (1896); Bergman, *The Negro in America,* p. 192.

30. 347 U.S. 483 (1954).

31. Leonard, *Black Lawyers,* p. 109; Ware, "A Word to and About Black Lawyers," p. 247.

32. Ware, "A Word to and About Black Lawyers," p. 247.

33. Leonard, *Black Lawyers,* p. 110; Charles Sumner Brown, "The Genesis of the Negro Lawyer in New England," *Negro History Bulletin,* vol. 22, no. 2 (1958), p. 173.

John Swett Rock, who opened his dental practice in Philadelphia in 1850 and subsequently attended medical school and practiced medicine, moved to Boston in 1857 and embarked upon a career in the law. It is not clear how he learned law, but in 1861 he was admitted to practice "in all of the courts of the State of Massachusetts" and was appointed a justice of the peace in Boston. On February 1, 1865, he became the first black to be admitted to practice before the United States Supreme Court.[34]

Edwin Garrison Walker was admitted to the Suffolk County Bar in 1861.[35] In 1866 he and another black, Charles Lewis Mitchell, were elected to the Massachusetts House of Representatives, thereby becoming the first blacks to sit in the legislature of any state.[36] Frequently appointed by the court to represent indigent defendants in criminal cases, Walker became a leading member of the criminal bar. As a politician, he was an early advocate of women's suffrage. Originally a Republican, he became disillusioned by his party's failure to deliver on its promises to blacks, and in 1867 he transferred his allegiance to the Democrats. Walker was nominated three times for a judgeship in the Charlestown Municipal Court by Governor (and former Civil War General) Benjamin F. Butler, but the Republican-controlled Governor's Council refused to confirm his appointment on each occasion.[37] The appointment finally went to George Ruffin, a Republican.

William H. Lewis, admitted to the Suffolk County Bar in 1885,[38] became the first black to hold the post of Assistant Attorney General of the United States upon his appointment by President William Howard Taft in 1911.[39] He had served since 1907 as an Assistant United States Attorney and as Chief of the Naturalization Bureau for New England.[40] Having been refused service in a Harvard Square barber shop when he was a student at the Harvard Law School (from which he graduated with honors), Lewis throughout his career—as municipal legislator, state legislator, and highly effective courtroom advocate—dedicated himself to improving the lot of his people.[41]

In 1911 William Lewis and Butler R. Wilson, both of Boston, and William R. Morris of Minnesota were recommended for membership in

---

34. Clarence G. Contee, "The Supreme Court's First Black Member," *Howard University Yearbook,* 1976, pp. 82–85.

35. Leonard, *Black Lawyers,* p. 113.

36. John Daniels, *In Freedom's Birthplace: A Study of Boston Negroes,* reprint ed. (New York: Negro Universities Press, 1968), pp. 99–100.

37. Leonard, *Black Lawyers,* p. 113; Brown, "Genesis of the Negro Lawyer," p. 173.

38. Commonwealth of Massachusetts, Supreme Judicial Court, County of Suffolk, *Roll of Attorneys,* September 18, 1895.

39. Maynard H. Jackson, "The Black American and the Legal Profession: A Study in Commitment," *Journal of Public Law,* vol. 2, no. 2 (1971), p. 378.

40. Daniels, *In Freedom's Birthplace,* p. 302.

41. Ibid., pp. 95–96, 128.

the American Bar Association by the ABA's Massachusetts and Minnesota councils, respectively. As recounted in the Introduction to this volume, they were admitted by action of the ABA Executive Committee, but when it became known that they were "of the colored race," the committee rescinded its action. After the three were nevertheless elected at the ABA annual meeting, Morris resigned for "the best interests of the leading organization of lawyers in the land." Lewis and Wilson became members.[42]

In the generation of black lawyers that followed the outstanding pioneers of the nineteenth and early twentieth centuries, there seems to have been a smaller number of black practitioners against the backdrop of an extremely small black population in Boston. In the recollection of both black and white lawyers, there were during the 1930s only three black lawyers of note—Bill Lewis, his son Tim Lewis, and Henry E. Quarles.[43] Noted for almost half a century of active and effective private practice, Quarles was honored in 1977 (along with Senator Edward W. Brooke) by the Massachusetts Black Lawyers (a National Bar Association affiliate) as "the person who exemplifies the best in the black lawyer." He was then presented with a proclamation by Governor Michael S. Dukakis declaring March 5, 1977 as "Henry E. Quarles, Sr., Day."[44]

During most of the period covered by Quarles's career, black lawyers in general were holding on with difficulty to their earlier gains in Massachusetts.[45] Edward W. Brooke, who did not come to the bar until 1948, was apparently the next black lawyer of prominence in Boston. Brooke actively engaged in practice and in 1963 became the first black Massachusetts Attorney General, the highest office ever held by a black in Massachusetts.[46] He later became the first black United States Senator since the Reconstruction period[47] when Mississippi's Blanche K. Bruce ended his term in 1881.[48] Brooke served in the Senate from 1967 until 1979 and is currently associated with a white law firm in Washington, D.C.[49]

Early in 1980, NAACP Executive Director Benjamin L. Hooks announced the appointment of Boston attorney Thomas I. Atkins as General Counsel, to assume the position vacated by President Jimmy Carter's appointment of Nathaniel R. Jones to the United States Court of Appeals for

42. *Reports of the American Bar Association,* vol. 37 (1912), pp. 28–30.

43. Information supplied by Daniel R. Coquillette, Boston attorney.

44. *National Bar Bulletin,* vol. 9, no. 5 (May 1977), pp. 109–10.

45. Information supplied by Daniel R. Coquillette, Boston attorney.

46. George Reasons and Sam Patrick, *They Had a Dream* (Los Angeles: Los Angeles Times Syndicate, 1970), vol. 1, p. 19.

47. Russell L. Adams, *Great Negroes Past and Present* (Chicago: Afro-American Publishing Co., 1969), p. 130.

48. Reasons and Patrick, *They Had a Dream,* vol. 1, p. 19.

49. *Who's Who in America 1980–81,* vol. 1, p. 431.

the Sixth Circuit. Atkins, who came to the bar in 1971, had been President of the Boston NAACP branch and had served as Chief Counsel for all of the association's litigation involving school desegregation, trying and arguing cases all over the country.[50] In 1967 Atkins became the first black to be elected to the Boston City Council in a citywide contest, and from 1971 to 1975 he was Secretary for Community Development in the cabinet of Governor Francis Sargent.[51]

Serving as members of the judiciary in Boston are an impressive group of black lawyers who have come to the bench since the 1960s. One of them, Joseph S. Mitchell, graduated from Boston University Law School in 1951 and, after thirteen years of general practice, was appointed Judge of the Superior Court of Massachusetts in 1966.[52] Harry J. Elam, who also graduated from Boston University Law School in 1951, was active as a practicing attorney and as Assistant Attorney General before his appointment in 1971 to the Boston Municipal Court; in 1978 he became Chief Justice. Four years after she graduated from the University of Pennsylvania Law School in 1973, Margaret Burnham was appointed to the Boston Municipal Court.[53] Roderick L. Ireland, who received his J.D. degree from Columbia Law School in 1969 and his LL.M. from Harvard Law School in 1975, was appointed to the Boston Division–Juvenile Court Department in 1977. Ten years after he was admitted to the Massachusetts Bar in 1967,[54] Frederick L. Brown was appointed to the Massachusetts Court of Appeals, which sits in Boston. During the intervening years he conducted a private practice, taught law courses, and was active in such civic groups as the Lawyers Committee for Civil Rights Under Law.

The first black to receive a federal judgeship in Massachusetts was David Sutherland Nelson. On April 2, 1979, Nelson took his seat on the United States District Court for the District of Massachusetts by virtue of appointment by President Jimmy Carter. At that time he was an associate justice on the Superior Court of Massachusetts, having served there from 1973 to 1979. He had previously been Assistant Attorney General of Massachusetts (1971–73) and United States Commissioner (1968–69). His law practice was considerable, predominantly as a litigator in both civil and criminal litigation, and his teaching experience was broad (see below).[55]

The reverse of Judge Nelson's move from the state to the federal judicial system was the appointment of Judge Rudolph F. Pierce from the po-

50. "General Counsel Named," *The Crisis,* vol. 87, no. 6 (June–July 1980), p. 222.
51. Ibid.
52. Reincke and Lichterman, *The American Bench,* p. 934.
53. Ibid., pp. 922, 918; University of Pennsylvania, *Black Law Alumni Directory* (Philadelphia, 1979), p. 9.
54. Reincke and Lichterman, *The American Bench,* p. 928.
55. Ibid., pp. 935–36.

sition of Magistrate in the United States District Court for Massachusetts to the post of Judge of the Superior Court of Massachusetts in Boston.[56]

In 1981–82 Boston had ten black judges—one on the United States District Court, one on the Court of Appeals of Massachusetts, two on the Superior Court, five on the Boston Municipal and District Courts, and one on the Boston Juvenile Court. Overall, as shown in Table 15 and in the chart below, Boston has 11.5 percent black judges, compared to 18.5 percent in Philadelphia.

|  | Boston | Philadelphia |
|---|---|---|
| State & Local Judges | 76 | 110 |
| Black Judges | 9 (11.8%) | 21 (19.1%) |
| U.S. Court of Appeals & District Judges | 11 | 20 |
| Black Judges | 1 (9.0%) | 3 (15.0%) |
| Total Judges | 87 | 130 |
| Total Black Judges | 10 (11.5%) | 24 (18.5%)[57] |

Federal judges as of April 1982, 527 F. Supp. VIII, X–XI; State and local judges as of November 1981.

Two of Boston's black judges are among the members of the judiciary who have been full-time or adjunct faculty at the several law schools in that city. Judge Brown taught at Northeastern and at Boston University, while Judge Nelson's broad teaching experience includes Boston University and ten years on the Harvard faculty (1969–79).

Derrick A. Bell, Jr., originally from Pittsburgh and Dean of the University of Oregon Law School since January 1, 1980, was the first black appointed to the faculty of the Harvard University Law School in 1969 as an associate professor and in 1971 as a professor. Clarence Clyde Ferguson, Jr., who served with the United States Department of State from 1969 to 1975, became a professor of law at Harvard in 1977.[58] Given the role of Harvard Law School as one of the leaders and trendsetters in Boston as well as nationally, these few appointments were especially significant for blacks in the legal profession. (See section on Black Law Teachers in Chapter 10, pp. 207–241.)

An important milestone for Boston's black lawyers was achieved in 1979 when Wayne A. Budd was elected President of the Massachusetts Bar Association, becoming the first black president of any state bar association

56. Ibid., p. 937.

57. For detailed statistics on black and white judges in all cities surveyed, including U.S. bankruptcy judges and magistrates, see Appendix 12.

58. At the outset of the 1981–82 academic year, only 10 out of the 337 law teachers in Boston were black.

in the nation, in a state in which black lawyers comprise less than 2 percent of the profession.[59] At the age of thirty-eight, Budd also was the youngest president of the association that for so many years had been closed to blacks.[60]

Budd's achievement is all the more remarkable in light of the fact that black lawyers did not begin to enter Boston's white firms until the late 1960s. Even by 1980 they had not made large inroads into the upper echelons of private practice, although there were notable achievements by such black lawyers as Charles J. Beard, admitted to the Massachusetts Bar in 1969, Commissioner of the Massachusetts Cable Television Commission (1972–76), a member of the Governor's Nominating Commission (1976), and a partner in one of the largest medium-size firms in Boston; Harry T. Daniels, admitted to the bar in 1971, a member of the Board of Bar Overseers of the Supreme Judicial Court of Massachusetts, and a partner in one of Boston's large firms; Reginald C. Lindsay, admitted to the bar in 1970, a Commissioner of Public Utilities (1975–77), and a partner in one of the medium-size firms; and Richard A. Soden, a partner in a large firm, admitted to the bar in 1970 and a former president (1980) of the Massachusetts Black Lawyers Association.

The representation of black lawyers in Boston's large and medium-size firms is shown in the following chart.

The low percentages are all the more striking when one considers that in 1980 blacks comprised 21 percent of the total population of the city of Boston (see Table 16). The achievements of the outstanding lawyers and judges discussed above constitute numerous significant milestones, but the really meaningful breakthrough for blacks in private practice in Boston still lies ahead. For blacks on law school faculties, see Appendix 18.

| Large Firms* | Total Lawyers | Black Lawyers | Total Partners | Black Partners | Total Associates | Black Associates |
|---|---|---|---|---|---|---|
| Boston | 368 | 4 (1.0%) | 182 | 1 (0.5%) | 186 | 3 (1.6%) |
| Philadelphia | 1,094 | 26 (2.4%) | 531 | 4 (0.8%) | 563 | 22 (3.9%) |
| Medium-size Firms* | | | | | | |
| Boston | 1,015 | 9 (0.8%) | 524 | 1 (0.2%) | 491 | 8 (1.6%) |
| Philadelphia | 550 | 6 (1.1%) | 288 | 1 (0.3%) | 262 | 5 (1.9%)[61] |

*According to the 1980 survey conducted by the author.

59. Calculation based on estimated 211 black lawyers in the state, according to Massachusetts Black Lawyers' Association and Boston BALSA, and 17, 968 active lawyers total, according to the Board of Bar Overseers.

60. *Martindale-Hubbell Law Directory 1981*, vol. 4, p. 35B; *National Law Journal*, August 20, 1979.

61. For detailed statistics on black and white lawyers in all cities surveyed, see Appendices 13 and 14.

## Chicago _____

Although Chicago, Illinois, was founded by a black man from Haiti, Jean Baptiste Pointe de Sable, who settled there in 1772,[62] there were only 323 blacks in Chicago in 1850 and fewer than 1,000 in 1860.[63] After the Civil War, however, the number increased to 3,559 by 1870,[64] and it was during that period that blacks began to enter the legal profession in Chicago.

On April 20, 1869, Lloyd Wheeler became Chicago's first black to be admitted to the Illinois Bar.[65] Twenty-five years later, Ida Platt was Chicago's first black woman to be admitted. On that occasion in 1894, one of the justices of the Supreme Court of Illinois commented, "We have done today what we never did before—admitted a colored woman to the bar. It may now be truly said that persons are admitted to the Illinois Bar without regard to race, sex, or color."[66] By 1896 Chicago had thirty-three black lawyers, the largest number in any city in the country at the time.[67]

One notable example of a black lawyer in Chicago at the turn of the century was Robert S. Abbott, an 1899 Kent Law School graduate who in 1905 started the *Chicago Defender,* a black newspaper. He chose journalism over the law because of his conviction that he could do a better job of defending blacks through the printed word than in the courtroom.[68]

After World War I, the black population in Chicago grew from 44,103 in 1910 to 109,458 in 1920, a 148.2 percent increase. The black population more than doubled between 1920 and 1930, reaching 233,903.[69] During that decade, as the black population of the city reached significant numbers, several important milestones for blacks in the law occurred in Chicago—the graduation of the first black from the prestigious University of Chicago Law School, the election of the first black judge in the North, and the founding of the first national association of black lawyers.

In 1926 Chicago was the site of the formal action of chartering the National Bar Association, which had been organized by a group of twelve

62. Adams, *Great Negroes,* p. 24; see also Margaret Burroughs, "The First Chicagoan, Jean Baptiste Point Du Sable," in *History of the National Bar Association* (souvenir booklet distributed at 1974 national convention in Chicago), p. 44, in which the date given is 1779.

63. E. Franklin Frazier, *The Negro in the United States* (New York: Macmillan Co., 1957), pp. 256–57. The black population of Chicago in 1860 was 955. *1860 Census,* vol. 1, table 3, p. 90.

64. *1870 Census,* vol. 1, table 8, p. 380.

65. Edward B. Toles, "Fifty Years of Progress for Black Lawyers," in *History of the National Bar Association,* p. 23.

66. Ibid., p. 29.

67. Ibid., p. 23.

68. Adams, *Great Negroes,* p. 88.

69. U.S. Bureau of the Census, *1910 Census,* vol. 2, table 2, p. 505; *1920 Census,* vol. 2, table 13, p. 47; *1930 Census,* vol. 3, table 15, p. 628.

black lawyers who met in Des Moines, Iowa, in 1925 under the leadership of George H. Woodson, a Des Moines lawyer, for the purpose of presenting a national organization for what they stated to be the 1,200 black lawyers in the nation[70] (see Introduction).

In 1924 Albert B. George was elected to the Chicago Municipal Court, thus becoming the first black judge elected in the North.[71] (George Lewis Ruffin, discussed in the Boston section, was the first black judge appointed in the North in 1883.)

The graduation of Earl B. Dickerson from the University of Chicago Law School in 1920 marked not only a first for blacks but also the beginning of the long career of one of Chicago's most outstanding black lawyers. Born in Canton, Mississippi, in 1891, Dickerson came to Chicago at age fifteen, entered law school in 1915, left for two years during World War I to become one of the first black lieutenants in the United States Army, and returned to graduate in 1920. Widely recognized for his legal ability, both in and out of the courtroom, he fought numerous civil rights cases and argued his most celebrated one, *Hansberry v. Lee,*[72] before the Supreme Court of the United States in 1940. This was a landmark decision that eliminated the use of racial restrictive covenants in the Hyde Park Kenwood community of Chicago. Dickerson served as General Counsel and President of the Supreme Life Insurance Company of America, the second largest black-owned insurance company in the country. In his many civic activities, he was one of the founders of the American Legion, President of the National Bar Association, President of the Chicago Urban League, and an appointee of President Franklin D. Roosevelt to the first Fair Employment Practices Commission. At ninety years of age, he continued to go to his law office and to be regarded with affection and esteem.[73]

During the numerous decades of Dickerson's career the black population of Chicago grew steadily, beginning with an influx of 60,000 after World War II, so that blacks comprised 13.8 percent of the total population in 1950, 33.3 percent in 1970, and 39.9 percent in 1980. The city's population dropped from 3,369,357 in 1970 to 3,005,072 in 1980, whereas in the same period the black population increased from 1,102,620 to 1,197,000.[74]

70. Toles, "Fifty Years of Progress," pp. 23–24.

71. Ibid., p. 35.

72. 311 U.S. 32 (1940).

73. Karen Gardner, "Earl B. Dickerson at 88," *University of Chicago Law School Record,* Spring 1980.

74. In 1950 the black population of Chicago was 492,635 and the total population was 3,611,580 (*1950 Census,* vol. 2, pt. 13, table 53, pp. 13–208). In 1970 the black population was 1,102,620 (*1970 Census,* vol. 1, pt. 15, table 23, pp. 15–103) and the total population was 3,369,357 (Advance Reports, PCH80-V-15, Illinois, table 2, p. 46 [issued March 1981]). In 1980 the black population was 1,197,700 and the total population was 3,005,072 (ibid.).

The black legal community grew concurrently. The best estimate of Judge Edward B. Toles, who is discussed below, is that the number of black lawyers in Chicago in 1981 was between 600 and 700. Judge Toles advises that in 1981 the black Cook County Bar Association had 586 active members out of a total of approximately 820 black lawyers in the Chicago metropolitan area.[75]

As their numbers grew, black lawyers in Chicago made outstanding achievements in law and public life. In 1934 Arthur W. Mitchell became the first black Democratic lawyer elected to Congress. He served four terms as a member of the Illinois delegation to the House of Representatives.[76]

Also influential in the political arena at that time was William L. Dawson, a black lawyer who was a member of the Chicago City Council. Campaigning on the platform "A white man cannot adequately represent black people," Dawson amassed a strong organization under Democratic aegis in 1939 and succeeded in having well-qualified black men and women appointed to important posts in Chicago. He was elected to Congress in 1942 and in 1949 became the first black chairman of a major House committee, the House Committee on Government Operations.[77]

In 1952 Charles E. Lomax became the first black lawyer appointed to the staff of the Chief Counsel of the Internal Revenue Service. He was later assigned as trial attorney on the staff of the Regional Counsel for Chicago, where he served until 1975, except for four years as Assistant United States Attorney for the Northern District of Illinois. In 1975 he joined a leading large white Chicago firm as a partner.[78]

Another black lawyer who had a varied career in Chicago and also achieved national recognition was William R. Ming, Jr. Ming attended the University of Chicago Law School, served as a member of the first Board of Editors of the *University of Chicago Law Review,* was elected to the Order of the Coif, and graduated *cum laude* in 1933. He then entered the general practice of law with Earl B. Dickerson and William E. King. In 1937 he accepted an appointment as a professor at Howard University Law School. He left that position in 1941, first to serve as Assistant General Counsel in the Office of Price Administration in Washington and then to accept a commission in the Judge Advocate General's Department in 1942. In 1949 he became Special Assistant Attorney General of Illinois, acting as General Counsel of the Illinois Commerce Commission. When he was appointed a professor at the University of Chicago Law School in 1947, Ming became the first full-time black faculty member at

75. Conversations with Judge Toles.
76. Toles, "Fifty Years of Progress," p. 36.
77. Ibid.
78. Resumé of Charles E. Lomax.

a predominantly white American law school.[79] He remained at the University of Chicago until 1950.[80] During Ming's career in the private practice of law, he participated in numerous civil-rights cases of the period, being perhaps best remembered in that capacity as one of the plaintiffs' attorneys in *Brown v. Board of Education.* He published several articles in legal periodicals and was one of the co-authors of *Discrimination and the Law,* published by the University of Chicago Press. Ming served as one of the most active and useful members of the Executive Committee of the Lawyers' Committee for Civil Rights Under Law, organized at the instance of President John F. Kennedy during the White House Conference for Lawyers on Civil Rights.[81]

Another black lawyer from Chicago who has been outstanding in the legal teaching field and in contributions to public-interest law is Henry W. McGee, Jr., Professor of Law at the University of California School of Law in Los Angeles. McGee won academic honors at Northwestern University by maintaining a straight-A average and subsequently was the first black to be elected Editor-in-Chief of the *De Paul University Law Review.* He has served as a professor of law at Columbia University School of Law and at Ohio State University College of Law and is responsible for the organization and funding of thirty-five legal service agencies in six states.[82]

While it is not possible to include all blacks in the legal profession who have gained prominence in Chicago, mention should be made of two women who achieved significant firsts. Edith Spurlock Sampson was born in Pittsburgh, moved to Chicago, and in 1927 became the first black woman to receive a Master of Laws degree from Loyola University.[83] She practiced law in Chicago for thirty-five years and was nominated by the Democratic Party in 1962 to serve an unexpired term on the Municipal Court. In 1964 she was elected Associate Judge of the Cook County Circuit Court.[84]

Arnette Hubbard, President of the National Bar Association for 1981–

---

79. Kellis E. Parker and Betty J. Stebman, "Legal Education for Blacks," *Annals of the American Academy of Political and Social Science,* vol. 407 (May 1973), p. 152; biographical sketch of William R. Ming on file at the University of Chicago Law School.

80. Letter from University of Chicago Law School Dean Gerhard Casper, September 9, 1981.

81. Biographical sketch from the University of Chicago files; "Rites Tuesday for Civil Rights Lawyer Ming," *Chicago Sun Times,* July 3, 1973; "William Ming Jr. Rites Set," *Chicago Daily News,* July 3, 1973.

82. Kenneth L. Collins, "Attorneys Around the Country," *Black Law Journal,* vol. 1, no. 1 (1971), pp. 42–43.

83. *Negro Women in the Judiciary,* Alpha Kappa Alpha Sorority Heritage Series 1 (Chicago, 1968), p. 15.

84. Reasons and Patrick, *They Had a Dream,* vol. 1, p. 48.

82, became in 1979 the first black woman delegate to serve in the House of Delegates of the American Bar Association.[85]

Turning to the judiciary, there are two black judges on the United States District Court for the Northern District of Illinois, which sits in Chicago. On August 30, 1971, President John F. Kennedy appointed the first of these, James Benton Parsons, who thereby became the first black United States district judge in the country's history.[86] Less than one month later, Kennedy appointed Wade H. McCree, Jr. to the United States District Court for the Eastern District of Michigan[87] (see section on Detroit). Parsons became Chief Judge on April 16, 1975. He previously had been Assistant Corporation Counsel of the City of Chicago (1949–51), Assistant United States Attorney for the Northern District of Illinois (1951–60), and Judge of the Superior Court of Cook County (1960–61).[88]

The other black district court judge sitting in Chicago is George Neves Leighton, who was appointed by President Gerald Ford on February 4, 1976. Leighton was a practicing lawyer for eighteen years following his graduation from Harvard Law School in 1946. From 1954 to 1964 he was in partnership with other black lawyers, one of them William Ming. Leighton subsequently served as Master in Chancery, Circuit Court of Cook County (1960–64), as judge of the Circuit Court of Cook County (1964–69), and as justice of the Illinois Appellate Court, First District, Chicago (1969–76).[89]

Edward B. Toles, a United States bankruptcy judge in the Northern District of Illinois since 1969, has also earned high praise and awards for his extracurricular activities, including his excellent writings as historian and data source for significant developments nationally in all phases of the black legal profession. Born in Columbus, Georgia, he attended college and law school in Illinois, began the general practice of law in Chicago in 1936, and held several posts in government service prior to his judicial appointment.[90]

In an overall view of Chicago's judiciary, 35 (8.2%) of Chicago's 427 federal, state, and local judges are black. This places Chicago eleventh among the sixteen cities in this study. Chicago's 8.4 percent compares with 18.5 percent in Philadelphia, 20.6 percent in Atlanta, 25.0 percent in Detroit, and 28.6 percent in Washington. On the other hand, it is not very far from the 11.0 percent of New York and the 10.4 percent of Los Angeles. (See the following chart and Table 15.)

85. *National Bar Bulletin*, vol. 11, no. 9 (September 1979), p. 3.
86. Cook, "Black Representation," p. 269.
87. *Who's Who in America 1980–81*, vol. 2, p. 2219.
88. Ibid., p. 2567.
89. Ibid., vol. 1, p. 1991.
90. Ibid., vol. 2, p. 3305.

|  | Chicago | Philadelphia |
|---|---|---|
| State & Local Judges | 407 | 110 |
| Black Judges | 34 (8.4%) | 21 (19.1%) |
| U.S. Court of Appeals | | |
| & District Judges | 20 | 20 |
| Black Judges | 1 (5.0%) | 3 (15.0%) |
| Total Judges | 427 | 130 |
| Total Black Judges | 35 (8.2%) | 24 (18.5%)[91] |

Federal judges as of April 1982, 527 F. Supp. XVII, X–XI; State and local judges as of November 1981.

In Chicago's top law firms black representation is low. An article in the *Chicago Sun Times* in 1975 reported that a survey of "17 of the most prestigious law firms in the city showed that out of more than 1,300 lawyers . . . only 14 (1%) were black . . . [and] only 1 had achieved the status of partner."[92]

Our 1980 study reveals twenty-two (1.3%) black lawyers in Chicago's large firms and nineteen (0.9%) in its medium-size firms. Comparing Chicago with Philadelphia, we find that Philadelphia has higher percentages of both black partners and black associates in its large and medium-size firms, but the differences are comparatively small.

| Large Firms* | Total Lawyers | Black Lawyers | Total Partners | Black Partners | Total Associates | Black Associates |
|---|---|---|---|---|---|---|
| Chicago | 1,691 | 22 (1.3%) | 812 | 2 (0.2%) | 879 | 20 (2.2%) |
| Philadelphia | 1,094 | 26 (2.4%) | 531 | 4 (0.8%) | 563 | 22 (3.9%) |
| Medium-size Firms* | | | | | | |
| Chicago | 2,050 | 19 (0.9%) | 1,000 | 1 (0.1%) | 1,050 | 18 (1.7%) |
| Philadelphia | 550 | 6 (1.1%) | 288 | 1 (0.3%) | 262 | 5 (1.9%)[93] |

*According to the 1980 survey conducted by the author.

Marion S. Goldman's study of the black legal community in Chicago, made under the auspices of the American Bar Foundation and completed in 1972, found, similar to the present Philadelphia study, that until the late 1960s blacks in the legal profession had faced discrimination by the metro-

91. For detailed statistics on black and white judges in all cities surveyed, including U.S bankruptcy judges and magistrates, see Appendix 12.

92. John T. Baker, "Black Lawyers and Corporate and Commercial Practice: Some Unfinished Business of the Civil Rights Movement," *Howard Law Journal,* vol. 18 (1975), p. 687, n. 10.

93. For detailed statistics on black and white lawyers for all cities surveyed, see Appendices 13 and 14.

politan bar as well as lack of recognition by white colleagues. In 1968 some opportunities did start opening up for black lawyers.

The turmoil of 1968 produced one basic difference between the lawyers in the Goldman study and those in the present study: a certain degree of militance in the Chicago black lawyers. In 1968, when Chicago was the scene of violent riots and mass arrests of blacks, the situation in Philadelphia did not reach such extremes. While no studies have come to light examining the direct effects of those turbulent times on the attitudes of black lawyers, Goldman observed that "in recent years, black attorneys have begun to ignore the expectations of their white colleagues and have increasingly come to identify themselves with black activists."[94] Similarly, some of the black lawyers interviewed in Philadelphia foresaw an increase in black firms and a decrease in the number that would join white firms. It remains to be seen whether joining and achieving partnership in successful, predominantly white firms will be an important goal and substantial result for black lawyers in the 1980s in Chicago, Philadelphia, and other American cities.[95] For blacks on law school faculties, see Appendix 18.

# Cleveland

The most noteworthy black lawyer in nineteenth-century Cleveland was John Patterson Green, who moved there from North Carolina in 1845 after the abolition of slavery. Green was educated in Cleveland's public schools, studied law at the Ohio Union Law School in Cleveland, and was admitted to the Ohio Bar in 1871. From 1873 to 1882 Green was the first black justice of the peace in Cleveland. In 1882 he was elected a member of the Ohio General Assembly, and four years later was elected to the Senate, where he served until 1891. During the years when Cleveland's black population was very small (only 84,504 by 1940), Green was such an illustrious citizen that on April 4, 1937, the city officially celebrated his ninety-second birthday as "John P. Green Day." In 1940, after almost seventy years at the bar, Green was fatally injured by an automobile. His funeral service was overflowing with judges, city officials, and lawyers who sounded his praises.[96]

Charles W. Chestnutt, a black native of Cleveland, also earned recognition as a lawyer in that city during the nineteenth and early twentieth century. He studied law while he was employed as a stenographer in the

94. Marion S. Goldman, *A Portrait of the Black Attorney in Chicago* (Chicago: American Bar Foundation, 1972), p. 50.

95. For more on this subject, see Chapter 8.

96. Thomas J. Brady, *The First Hundred Years: A History of the Cleveland Bar Association, 1873–1973* (Cleveland, 1973), p. 44; Fitzhugh Lee Styles, *Negroes and the Law* (Boston: Christopher Publishing Co., 1973), p. 141; *The Plain Dealer* (Cleveland), September 6, 1940.

law office of Judge Samuel Williamson and managed to rank first among those who were admitted to the Ohio Bar in 1887. In addition to practicing law, he operated a court reporting business and devoted his interests primarily to writing for leading periodicals, including the *Atlantic Monthly.* Eventually he gained prominence as a novelist.[97]

In the middle of the twentieth century, particularly beginning in the 1950s, there was a notable increase in both the black population of Cleveland (151,755 in 1950) and in the number of black lawyers who entered the Ohio Bar. Blacks not only broadened their legal practice but also obtained a significant number of judgeships and roles in government and politics.

In 1942 Perry B. Jackson, a *magna cum laude* graduate of Western Reserve University, became the first black to serve as a judge in Ohio when, upon recommendation of the Cleveland Bar Association, he was appointed to the Cleveland Municipal Court. Jackson had previously served as a State Representative, as Special Counsel for the state Attorney General, as a member of City Council, as Police Prosecutor, and as Secretary to the Director of Public Utilities.[98] He later became a judge of the Court of Common Pleas.[99] At eighty-five, Judge Jackson, the oldest jurist sitting in Cleveland, still works forty hours a week as a visiting judge for the Cuyahoga County Common Pleas Court system.[100]

Another outstanding black jurist who rendered notable service to Cleveland was Charles W. White. After serving for fifteen years as a member of the Cleveland Metropolitan Housing Authority, White was appointed to the Court of Common Pleas in 1955, on recommendation of the Cleveland Bar Association. In 1966 he was elevated to the Eighth District Court of Appeals, of which he became the first black Chief Justice in 1970, the year of his death. At that time he received many tributes for his thirty-seven years of effective and dedicated service to the city.[101]

On December 24, 1959, Theodore M. Williams became the second black lawyer to be named to the Cleveland Municipal Court.[102] A native of Cleveland, he had combined his law practice with public service, having been Assistant Police Prosecutor for the city (1941–47), Assistant County Prosecutor (1948–52), and a member of the Cleveland City Council from 1952 until his appointment as a judge.[103] In 1974, when the position of Administrative Judge of the Municipal Court was created by the Ohio

97. Brady, *The First Hundred Years*, p. 17.
98. *The Cleveland Press*, January 28, 1971.
99. Brady, *First Hundred Years*, p. 48.
100. *The Plain Dealer*, June 23, 1979.
101. *The Cleveland Press*, May 1, 1969; August 21, 1970; December 11, 1971.
102. Ibid., December 24, 1959; *Cleveland News*, December 24, 1959.
103. *The Plain Dealer*, September 26, 1974.

Supreme Court, Williams was unanimously elected by his fellow judges.[104] He retired at age seventy after sixteen years on the Municipal Court bench.[105]

After five years of government service as Police Prosecutor and then as First Assistant Prosecutor, Paul D. White served as a judge of the Cleveland Municipal Court from 1964 to 1967. In 1967 he was appointed Director of the Department of Law for the city. In 1968 he returned to private practice, joining a large Cleveland law firm as its first black associate. He was elected its first black partner in 1971.[106]

Another black Municipal Court judge, Frederick M. Coleman, worked two decades as a mail carrier before he could finance his legal education. He became a member of the Ohio Bar in 1953 at the age of thirty-five and was in private practice for fourteen years before he became a judge on the Cleveland Municipal Court. In 1970 he was appointed United States Attorney for the Northern District of Ohio, and seven years later became a judge of the Common Pleas Court.[107]

The first black to be elected Chief Justice of the Cleveland Municipal Court was Augustus G. Parker in 1965. During his thirty-four prior years of practice he devoted a great deal of time to public service, including fourteen years as a member of the Cleveland City Council (1940–50 and 1957–61) and almost two years as vice-chairman of the Ohio Industrial Commission.[108]

Lloyd O. Brown has been a judge on three courts. After serving as Assistant Attorney General for Ohio (1958–59) and as Cleveland Assistant City Prosecutor (1959–67), he was elected to the Cleveland Municipal Court in 1967. He retained that seat until 1971, when he became the second black appointed Associate Justice on the Ohio Supreme Court, where he served until 1972. (The first black on that court, Robert M. Duncan, subsequently became a federal judge and will be discussed later in the section on Columbus.) Brown currently is a judge of the Court of Common Pleas.[109]

When appointed in 1968, Lillian Burke was the first black woman on the Cleveland Municipal Court, and the same year she was elected to that court. Admitted to the Ohio Bar in 1951, she also had been the first female assistant attorney general of Ohio and the first female vice-chairperson of the Ohio Industrial Commission. In December 1980 she became the first black woman to be Administrative Judge of the Cleveland Municipal

104. Ibid., October 28, 1974.

105. *The Cleveland Press*, November 25, 1975.

106. *Who's Who in American Law*, 2d ed. (Chicago: Marquis Who's Who, 1979), p. 968.

107. Ibid., p. 447; *The Cleveland Press*, January 17, 1975; *The Plain Dealer*, January 17, 1975.

108. The Cleveland Press Candidates' Questionnaire, 1965 (obtainable from *The Cleveland Press*).

109. Reincke and Lichterman, *The American Bench*, p. 1513.

Court by appointment and, on December 29, 1980, she was elected to that position.[110]

In the 1970s two other female black lawyers, Jean Murrell Capers and Sarah J. Harper, were appointed and then elected to judgeships on the Cleveland Municipal Court. Capers was previously in government service. While in private practice she worked for the law firm of noted black attorneys Norman S. Minor and Merle McCurdy and served five terms in the City Council. Harper was previously a prosecutor in the Department of Law of Cleveland (1968–69), and in 1969 she became Assistant Director of the department.[111]

A significant milestone for blacks in the Cleveland judiciary was achieved in June 1980, when George W. White became, by appointment of President Carter, the first black judge of the United States District Court for the Northern District of Ohio, which sits in Cleveland. Admitted to the Ohio Bar in 1956, White practiced law as a sole practitioner for twelve years, was elected to the City Council in 1963, and then reelected in 1965. First elected in 1968 to fill an unexpired two-year term as Judge of the Common Pleas Court, he then was elected to two six-year terms, the second unexpired when he moved to the federal district court.[112]

The percentages of black representation in the Cleveland judiciary are similar to those in Philadelphia: 15.7 percent overall in Cleveland; 18.5 percent in Philadelphia (see the following chart and Table 15). Philadelphia has a black judge on the United States Court of Appeals for the Third Circuit, which sits in Philadelphia, whereas there is no black judge from Cleveland on the Court of Appeals for the Sixth Circuit, which includes Cleveland but sits in Cincinnati; however, the court in the Sixth Circuit does have a black judge from Detroit, Michigan (Damon J. Keith).

|  | Cleveland | Philadelphia |
|---|---|---|
| State & Local Judges | 63 | 110 |
| Black Judges | 10 (15.9%) | 21 (19.1%) |
| U.S. Court of Appeals |  |  |
| & District Judges | 7 | 20 |
| Black Judges | 1 (14.3%) | 3 (15.0%) |
| Total Judges | 70 | 130 |
| Total Black Judges | 11 (15.7%) | 24 (18.5%)[113] |

Federal judges as of April 1982, 527 F. Supp. XVI, X–XI; State and local judges as of November 1981.

110. *The Cleveland Press,* December 31, 1980; information obtained from Hilbert Black.
111. Reincke and Lichterman, *The American Bench,* pp. 1514, 1529.
112. *The Cleveland Press,* May 23, 1980; March 28, 1980.
113. For detailed statistics on black and white judges in all cities surveyed, including U.S. bankruptcy judges and magistrates, see Appendix 12.

At the beginning of the 1960s the involvement of Cleveland's black lawyers in government service and political life became increasingly extensive. In 1960 Merle McCurdy, a black who was generally reputed to be the leading criminal lawyer in Cleveland, was appointed Cleveland's first public defender. In 1961 he achieved a highly significant milestone when he became the first black in the nation to receive appointment as United States Attorney. In 1967 he was appointed to the position of General Counsel to President Lyndon Johnson's National Commission on Civil Disorders. In 1968, the year of his death, he became the first Consumer Counsel for the federal government.[114]

Carl B. Stokes and his brother Louis Stokes, who have made significant contributions to government and politics on a national level as well as in the Cleveland community, have done much to advance the status of the black lawyer.

Admitted to the Ohio Bar in 1957, Carl Stokes[115] conducted an active practice for ten years, during which time he was elected a member of the Ohio House of Representatives. The first black Democrat elected to the Ohio legislature, he served there from 1962 to 1967.[116] In 1967 he was elected Mayor of Cleveland, the first black elected mayor of a predominantly white major American city, and he was reelected in 1969 by double his 1967 margin.[117] In 1970 he was elected president of the National League of Cities, the first black to hold this office in an organization representing more than 14,000 municipal governments in all fifty states.[118]

In 1971 Stokes opted not to run for reelection as Mayor in order, as he expressed it, "to expand my efforts beyond the Cleveland area to assist others, particularly the locked-in minority groups, to better understand their role in politics and government." After lecturing in pursuit of this goal in twelve states and twenty-three cities, he joined New York City's WNBC-TV News as a commentator and urban affairs editor, receiving an Emmy Award from the National Academy of Television Arts and Sciences for "outstanding individual craft in feature reporting."[119] After returning to Cleveland late in 1980, in March 1981 he started the firm of Stokes and Green, the Cleveland office of a Youngstown firm that has the largest labor law practice in the state.

Louis Stokes is a practicing lawyer who trained in the criminal law

114. Hilbert Black, Assistant Metropolitan Editor, *The Cleveland Press,* as a result of interviews and other research by him.

115. *Who's Who in America 1980–81,* vol. 2, p. 3187.

116. NBC News Biographical Information, New York City, June 1979.

117. Joan Martin Burke, *Civil Rights,* 2nd ed. (New York: Bowker & Co., 1974), pp. 110–11.

118. NBC News Biographical Information, June 1979.

119. Ibid.

field under Norman S. Minor for fourteen years. Elected to the House of Representatives in 1968, he became the first black Congressman from Ohio. He was reelected in 1972 and in 1973 was elected Chairman of the Congressional Black Caucus.[120] In his second term of office he was appointed the first black member on the House Appropriations Committee, and in 1980 he was elected Chairman of the House Committee on Standards of Official Conduct, popularly known as the Ethics Committee.[121]

Another of Cleveland's most prominent citizens is John H. Bustamante, a black lawyer who has not only been a distinguished member of the Ohio Bar but has also been extensively involved in Cleveland's business, cultural, and philanthropic activities.[122] Bustamante is presently Chairman of the Board of the First National Bank Association, Cleveland's only minority-owned bank, and is a partner in *Call & Post*, the state's largest black weekly newspaper.[123]

Second only to former Mayor Carl B. Stokes as the most influential black politician in Cleveland's history is Charles V. Carr, who came to Cleveland from Clarksville, Texas, at age fourteen for the "better educational opportunities up North." His legal practice was largely in the fields of criminal law and civil rights. Elected a member of the Cleveland City Council in 1945, he demonstrated considerable political acumen in securing legislation in both fields and became the council's first black majority leader.[124]

The first black to be elected president of the Cleveland City Council (1971) was George L. Forbes, one of Carr's political trainees.[125] While Forbes continued to practice law in his firm, he also was active in politics and pursued business interests.

At the age of thirty-four, Clarence L. James was appointed by Mayor Stokes to become the youngest director of the Department of Law in Cleveland history. Before leaving the post in 1971, James had developed an affirmative-action law that is said to have been used as a model throughout the country.[126] While practicing law, James was active in politics, including Jimmy Carter's presidential campaign.

Upon graduation from law school in 1971, Almeta A. Johnson became an associate in one of Cleveland's well-known larger white law firms. Four years later, not yet twenty-eight years of age, she became the first black woman to serve as chief police prosecutor for the city, having by then been

120. Burke, *Civil Rights*, p. 111.
121. *The Plain Dealer*, December 21, 1980.
122. *Who's Who in America 1980–81*, vol. 1, p. 504.
123. Ibid.; biographical information obtained from Hilbert Black.
124. *The Plain Dealer*, November 5, 1975; *The Cleveland Press*, November 5, 1975.
125. *The Plain Dealer*, November 2, 1975.
126. Ibid., November 2, 1977.

a co-founder and first president of the Black Women Lawyers Association of Greater Cleveland.[127] In 1980 she joined two other black women who were leaving city government service—Patricia A. Blackmon, an assistant Police prosecutor, and Una H. R. Keenon, Chief of the Juvenile Division in the Public Defender's Office—to form the law firm of Johnson, Keenon and Blackmon.[128]

An important achievement for Cleveland's black lawyers occurred in 1977 when, for the first time in its 105-year history, the Bar Association of Greater Cleveland (as it was called from March 1973) elected a black president, Andrew L. Johnson, Jr.[129] Johnson had been admitted to the Ohio Bar in 1960 and conducted an active practice.[130]

In addition to these many milestones in judgeships and other public service, black lawyers in Cleveland have begun to make some inroads into the traditionally white areas of private practice. Our 1980 survey of Cleveland's large and medium-size firms, as compared with those of Philadelphia, reveals the following picture:

| Large Firms* | Total Lawyers | Black Lawyers | Total Partners | Black Partners | Total Associates | Black Associates |
|---|---|---|---|---|---|---|
| Cleveland | 536 | 8 (1.5%) | 246 | 2 (0.8%) | 290 | 6 (2.1%) |
| Philadelphia | 1,094 | 26 (2.4%) | 531 | 4 (0.8%) | 563 | 22 (3.9%) |
| Medium-size Firms* | | | | | | |
| Cleveland | 584 | 12 (2.1%) | 268 | 2 (0.7%) | 316 | 10 (3.2%) |
| Philadelphia | 550 | 6 (1.1%) | 288 | 1 (0.3%) | 262 | 5 (1.9%)[131] |

*According to the 1980 survey conducted by the author.

While the numbers and percentages of blacks in the large firms remain small, the greater percentages of partners and associates in the medium-size firms reflect an encouraging situation for black lawyers in Cleveland today. Ronald B. Adrine, President of the Norman S. Minor Bar Association (formed several years ago by black lawyers), observes a trend toward broader participation of blacks in all areas of legal practice.[132] Adrine notes that black lawyers are becoming involved in such specialized areas as land

127. *Who's Who in American Law,* p. 447; *The Cleveland Press,* January 17, 1975; *The Plain Dealer,* January 17, 1975.

128. *The Cleveland Press,* March 3, 1980.

129. Ibid., May 17, 1978.

130. *Martindale-Hubbell 1981,* vol. 5, p. 859B; *The Plain Dealer,* May 24, 1977.

131. For detailed statistics on black and white lawyers in all cities surveyed, see Appendices 13 and 14.

132. Adrine's observations were supplied through Thomas J. Brady, Executive Director, Bar Association of Greater Cleveland.

development work, entertainment and sports law, and communications law. He also sees a trend toward positions as in-house counsel for corporations in lieu of private practice.

According to Adrine, there are approximately 350 black lawyers in Greater Cleveland in 1981. Taking the 5,383 total lawyers in the Martindale-Hubbell data bank for Cleveland, which inevitably is somewhat lower than the actual number, black lawyers would now constitute more than 6.5 percent of the profession in that city. In 1980 blacks constituted 42.5 percent of the total population of Cleveland (see Table 16). For blacks on law school faculties, see Appendix 18.

# Columbus

One of the earliest pioneers among black lawyers in Columbus, Ohio, was Wilbur King, who practiced in the first half of the twentieth century. King was an early member of the Robert B. Elliott Law Club, an organization created in 1932 by black attorneys in Columbus as a forum for sharing common problems and goals. King is said to have been recognized by both bar and bench as an outstanding lawyer. He had a private practice in Columbus and at one time held the position of Assistant County Prosecutor.[133]

D. J. Murray and L. A. Ransom, alumni of Ohio State University College of Law in the classes of 1922 and 1927, respectively, are two early black graduates who attained significant recognition in the years ahead. Despite the fact that he was blind, Murray managed to complete his studies, pass the Ohio bar examination, and establish a law practice in Wilberforce, Ohio. Ransom entered law school without a college degree and graduated as one of the top five of his class. As an attorney in Columbus, Ransom shared an office with Wilbur King and Ray Hughes. Ransom later became Professor of Law, and eventually Dean, at Howard University Law School in Washington, D.C.[134]

Ray Hughes, an outstanding trial lawyer who was privately tutored in the law, served as Assistant Prosecuting Attorney in Columbus for ten years from 1921 to 1931. Like King and Ransom, Hughes was not a member of a law firm. Black attorneys were not in firms at that time, although they did often share office space.[135]

David D. White, a resident of Columbus since 1903, graduated from the Columbus College of Law (later the Capital Law School) in 1931. He

133. Information supplied by Paul R. Gingher, John W. E. Bowen, David D. White, and Mike Flowers, Recording Secretary of the Robert B. Elliott Club.
134. Ohio State University College of Law "Pioneers" Booklet.
135. Information supplied by David D. White.

conducted a full-time general practice of law for over thirty years and also served by appointment in state and city government posts. White was on the Board of Governors of the Columbus Bar Association from 1970 to 1976. Remaining active in civic and political affairs, he became a senior partner in the newly formed, predominantly black firm of Bell, White, Stein, Lehman and Ross (now Bell, White and Ross).[136]

The first black woman to graduate from Ohio State University College of Law in Columbus was Eva Crosby, who received her degree in 1936. After practicing law for ten years in Oberlin, teaching school there, and rearing a family, she came to Columbus in 1963 and set up a law office. When her husband died in 1966, she took over his funeral business. While continuing to practice law, she also runs a real estate business.[137]

After receiving his college and law degrees from North Carolina University, Ralph Frazier worked for a North Carolina corporation for a brief time. He then came to Columbus and served as Senior Vice-President and General Counsel of the Huntington National Bank.[138]

William H. Brook, admitted to the Ohio Bar in 1938, was the first black to fill the position of Municipal Court Judge in Columbus when he was appointed to fill an unexpired term in 1963. After his defeat in the next election, he left the bench and became Director of the Public Utilities Commission of Ohio in Columbus (1964–71). From 1972 until 1977 he was Assistant City Attorney, and since then has been a sole practitioner in Columbus.[139]

In 1953 Edward Cox, a graduate of Ohio State University College of Law, was the first black to be appointed to the position of Chief Counsel to the City Attorney.[140]

In 1975 John Francis, a later law graduate of Ohio State, was the first black to be appointed City Attorney, though he was defeated for election to that post in 1977.

When Robert M. Duncan received his J.D. degree from Ohio State University College of Law in 1952, he also had the honor of being the first black to be elected class president at that school. This distinction of being "first" followed him throughout his career. After three years in the general practice of law in Columbus, he entered the Attorney General's Office as Assistant Attorney General of Ohio and served in that position for eight years. In 1966 he was appointed a judge of the Franklin County Municipal

136. Idem.
137. Information supplied by Eva Crosby; *Martindale-Hubbell 1981*, vol. 5, p. 864.
138. Data from associate of Ralph Frazier.
139. Information supplied by William H. Brook.
140. Information supplied by John W. E. Bowen.

Court and subsequently became the first black to be elected to that position. In 1969 he was appointed Justice of the Supreme Court of Ohio, the first black in that position as well. In the 1969 election he was elected to that post, but while on the bench he received a presidential appointment to the United States Military Court of Appeals and was promoted to Chief Judge of that court in 1974. His latest appointment, also in 1974, was as Judge of the United States District Court for the Southern District of Ohio, again a "first," the first black to serve on a United States District Court in Ohio.[141]

In 1955 James A. Pearson achieved recognition by becoming the first black referee in Probate Court, a position in which he served until 1961. In 1969 he became a judge of the Municipal Court. He has been a member of the Board of Governors of the Columbus Bar Association since 1978.[142]

The first black to become a partner in a firm of white lawyers in Columbus was John W. E. Bowen, elected a partner on June 1, 1971. He received his legal education at Ohio State University College of Law and was admitted to the Ohio Bar in 1953. His has been a varied career. He served as Assistant City Attorney, taught law at Ohio State University College of Law, and was a member of the Ohio State Senate.[143]

Another first in the judiciary is Grady L. Pettigrew, who in 1977 became the first black United States Bankruptcy Court Judge of the United States District Court for the Southern District of Ohio. At Ohio State University College of Law, from which he graduated in 1971, he was the first black National Moot Court finalist and a member of the 1970 moot court team that captured first place in the national competition and received the award for the best brief. Judge Pettigrew is also an adjunct law professor at Capital University Law School.[144]

All in all, as shown in the following chart, black representation in the federal judiciary in Columbus has been more impressive than in state and local judgeships. One of three United States Court of Appeals and District Court judges sitting in Columbus (33.3%) is black, as compared to three of twenty (15.0%) in Philadelphia, one of whom is on the Court of Appeals for the Third Circuit. However, when state and local judges are added, the percentage in Columbus falls to 6.7 percent, substantially below Philadelphia (see Table 15).

141. Resumé of Robert M. Duncan; information supplied by David D. White and John W. E. Bowen.

142. Information supplied by Judge James A. Pearson and John W. E. Bowen; Reincke and Lichterman, *The American Bench,* p. 1554.

143. *Martindale-Hubbell 1981,* vol. 5, p. 3092B.

144. Information supplied by John W. E. Bowen and a member of Judge Pettigrew's staff.

|  | Columbus | Philadelphia |
|---|---|---|
| State & Local Judges | 42 | 110 |
| Black Judges | 2 (4.8%) | 22 (19.0%) |
| U.S. Court of Appeals |  |  |
| & District Judges | 3 | 20 |
| Black Judges | 1 (33.3%) | 3 (15.0%) |
| Total Judges | 45 | 130 |
| Total Black Judges | 3 (6.7%) | 24 (18.5%)[145] |

Federal judges as of April 1982, 527 F. Supp. XVI, X–XI; State and local judges as of November 1981.

The first known black faculty member of the Ohio State University College of Law is Warner Lawson, who served as an assistant professor during the academic years 1971 to 1974. He then transferred to Howard University in Washington, D.C., where he became an associate professor.[146]

Linda G. Howard joined the faculty of Ohio State University College of Law in 1975 and subsequently became its first black Associate Professor. She was admitted to the Virginia Bar in 1973 and for the year 1973–74 was Special Assistant to the Chief Counsel of Urban Mass Transportation in Washington, D.C. The following year she served as Legislative Assistant to United States Senator Lloyd Bentsen.[147]

Not until 1971 did a black lawyer in Columbus, John W. E. Bowen, as noted above, become a partner in a white firm. A decade later (1980) our survey of the large and medium-size firms reveals that there still were no black partners in either category. There were five black associates in the large firms and one in the medium-size, as the following chart shows, but since then the situation has changed, as stated below in the footnote to the chart (see following page).

According to Ben Espy, President of the Robert B. Elliott Law Club, in 1980 there were 170 black attorneys practicing in Columbus.[148] They constituted 5 percent of the total of 3,262 lawyers in the Martindale-Hubbell data bank for Columbus. Blacks constitute 21.9 percent of the total population of Columbus (see Table 16). For blacks on law school faculties, see Appendix 18.

145. For detailed statistics on black and white judges in all cities surveyed, including U.S. bankruptcy judges and magistrates, see Appendix 12.

146. Black American Law Students Association; information supplied by Linda G. Howard.

147. Information supplied by Linda G. Howard; *1978–1979 Directory of Minority Law Faculty Members* (Washington, D.C.: Association of American Law Schools, 1979), p. 32.

148. Above information supplied by Vicki W. Linville, attorney in Columbus, who conducted the interviews.

| Large Firms* | Total Lawyers | Black Lawyers | Total Partners | Black Partners | Total Associates | Black Associates |
|---|---|---|---|---|---|---|
| Columbus | 223 | 5 (2.0%) | 111 | 0 | 112 | 5 (4.5%)* |
| Philadelphia | 1,094 | 26 (2.4%) | 531 | 4 (0.8%) | 563 | 22 (3.9%) |
| Medium-size Firms* | | | | | | |
| Columbus | 42 | 1 (2.0%) | 24 | 0 | 18 | 1 (5.6%)* |
| Philadelphia | 550 | 6 (1.1%) | 288 | 1 (0.3%) | 262 | 5 (1.9%)[149] |

*According to the 1980 survey conducted by the author. Reports indicate that since that time there are two additional black associates in the large firms and two in the medium-size firms.

# Detroit

In 1885 the *Evening Journal* printed an article entitled "Well-Off in the World / Detroit Colored Citizens of Prominence and Wealth." The only lawyer on the list was Thomas R. Crisup, credited in the *Michigan Manual of Freedmen's Progress* (1915), with being the first black attorney to practice before the Detroit courts, having started in "the early eighties."[150]

Another black attorney, and a contemporary of Crisup, was D. Augustus Straker, who in 1842, at the age of twenty-five, came to South Carolina from Barbados to continue his legal education and pursue the practice of law in the United States. Finding his teaching and law practice unremunerative in South Carolina, he moved to Detroit, where he continued to practice law. There he became an authority on the South, publishing books and pamphlets on the subject. In 1890 he achieved distinction when he secured public accommodations for blacks in Michigan. In 1892 and 1894 Straker, a staunch Republican in a strong Democratic community, was elected to the office of Wayne County Circuit Court Commissioner.[151]

William W. Ferguson, a close friend of Straker, was a practicing lawyer who went on to become the first black elected to the Michigan legislature (1893–94). By his own account, in 1868 he was "the first colored boy to sell newspapers on the streets of Detroit and also one of the first to enter the Detroit public schools."[152]

Robert J. Willis, who was admitted to the Michigan Bar in 1893 and

149. For detailed statistics on black and white lawyers in all cities surveyed, see Appendices 13 and 14.

150. Letter from Otis M. Smith, Vice-President and General Counsel for General Motors, containing material from David A. Collins on the early history of the black bar in Detroit, December 23, 1980.

151. M. Sammy Miller, "David Straker and Other Reconstruction Jurists," *The Crisis*, vol. 81, no. 9 (November 1974), p. 316.

152. Letter from Otis M. Smith.

practiced primarily in criminal law, was the first to urge that black motor-men be employed on streetcars and that blacks be employed in the post office and fire departments.[153] Willis M. Graves, a 1921 graduate of How-ard Law School, and Francis Dent, who came to the bar during World War I following graduation from Amherst College and Howard Law School and military service, brought the question of the enforceability of racially restrictive covenants before the United States Supreme Court in *Sites v. McGhee,* a companion case to *Shelley v. Kramer.* [154]

In 1905 the first prominent black law firm in Detroit was formed by Robert C. Barnes and Walter H. Stowers.[155] But the number of black lawyers in Detroit, and the size of the black population in general, re-mained very small until after World War I.

It was not until the period between the two world wars, when the black population increased significantly, that systematic growth and meaningful success began to occur in the black legal community. In the 1920s and 1930s there were between fifty and one hundred black lawyers in Detroit, and about twenty of them practiced in two moderately suc-cessful black firms. One firm was Lewis, Roulette and Brown (Joseph Brown being the brother of the influential Pittsburgh lawyer, Homer S. Brown). The other was Loomis, Jones, Piper and Colden, which repre-sented most of the black business interests. In August 1950 Charles W. Jones became the first black appointed to a court of record in the state, but despite the excitement aroused by his appointment, he was defeated in the primary that fall. In 1954 he was named to the Wayne County Circuit Court.

After World War II, when the boom in automobile production brought about another influx of blacks and other minorities to Detroit in search of job opportunities, many black lawyers followed the migration. They saw in Detroit a ready clientele that needed to be serviced, and over the ensuing years the lawyers prospered as their clientele grew and pros-pered. Gradually they assumed positions of authority in the community, participated in politics, and obtained government posts, so that at the outset of the 1980s Detroit has a black mayor, a black majority in City Council, and a significant number of black judges.[156]

The first politically active black attorney in Detroit to depart from affiliation with the Republican Party was Harold E. Bledsoe, who worked in the presidential campaigns of Al Smith and Franklin Roosevelt and in

153. Ibid.
154. 334 U.S. 1 (1948).
155. Letter from Otis M. Smith.
156. Information furnished by Dennis Davenport.

the gubernatorial campaigns of several Michigan Democrats. Thus Bledsoe earned appointments to state office by three Democratic governors—William A. Comstock, Frank Murphy, and Pat VanWaggoner.[157]

Several prominent black attorneys practiced in their earlier years with Bledsoe. These included his daughter, Geraldine Bledsoe Ford, now a judge on Detroit's Recorder Court (which is essentially a municipal court); his son, William Bledsoe, now attorney for the city of Highland Park; Julian Abele Cook, Jr., who later became a United States district court judge; and Wade H. McCree, Jr.

When McCree was named to the United States District Court for the Eastern District of Michigan, which sits in Detroit (September 1961), he became the second black United States district court judge in the nation's history; the first (James Benton Parsons, United States District Court for the Northern District of Illinois) was appointed one month earlier. At the time of his appointment he was a judge of the Circuit Court in Detroit, to which he had been appointed in 1954 at the age of thirty-four, when he was a practicing lawyer in Detroit. In 1966 he was elevated to the United States Court of Appeals for the Sixth Circuit, which sits in Detroit. In 1977 he resigned, after twenty-three years as a judge, to accept appointment as Solicitor General of the United States, the second black to serve in that office; the first was Thurgood Marshall. Upon the conclusion of his term as Solicitor General in June 1981, McCree, one of the most highly esteemed figures in the legal profession, accepted a professorship at the University of Michigan Law School. Twenty-four colleges and universities have bestowed honorary degrees upon him.[158]

John Conyers, Jr. and Hobart Taylor, Jr. are two black lawyers from Michigan who went to Washington, D.C., in the 1960s to serve in the federal government. Conyers has been in the House of Representatives since January 3, 1965, never having been defeated for election.[159] After a year's law clerkship with the Supreme Court of Michigan, Taylor divided his time until 1964 between private practice (beginning in Harold Bledsoe's office) and Detroit municipal and Wayne County government posts; perhaps most important were his ten years (1951–61) as Detroit Corporation Counsel. He went to Washington in 1964, where he achieved recognition in several government posts, including Special Assistant to Vice-President Lyndon Johnson (1963) and Associate Counsel to President Johnson (1964–65), after which he combined public activities with private practice

157. Letter from Otis M. Smith.

158. *Who's Who Among Black Americans 1977–78*, 2d ed. (Northbrook, Ill: Who's Who Among Black Americans, 1978), p. 601; *Who's Who in America 1980–81*, vol. 2, p. 2219.

159. *U.S. Congress & Administrative News*, February 2, 1979, p. 7.

in Washington. He also served on the boards of directors of several of the nation's leading corporations—Eastern Airlines, Aetna Life and Casualty Co., Great Atlantic & Pacific Tea Co., Westinghouse Electric Corporation, Burroughs Corporation, and Standard Oil Company of Ohio. In 1980 he became "of Counsel" to one of the country's largest law firms.[160] Taylor died in April 1981.

One of the most prominent black lawyers in Detroit and nationally is Otis M. Smith, Vice-President and General Counsel of General Motors, the second largest corporation in the United States. Smith began his practice of law in the Flint office of Dudley Mallory, the second black graduate of the University of Michigan Law School. Smith's standing in Flint was such that the Chamber of Commerce named him the outstanding young man of the year in 1955. This brought him to the attention of Governor G. Mennen Williams, who appointed him Chairman of the Public Service Commission and soon after that Auditor General of the state. After his subsequent election to that office, he was appointed to the Supreme Court of Michigan in 1961, becoming the first black supreme court justice in any state since Reconstruction days. Smith serves on university, hospital, civic, and government boards and commissions and is similarly active in civil-rights organizations. In 1967 he joined the legal staff of General Motors, and, after rising through various posts, became General Counsel in 1977.[161]

As a successful practicing lawyer, Damon J. Keith was also an active leader in civic affairs. Among his public activities, he served as President of the Detroit Housing Commission (1958–67), Chairman of the Michigan Civil Rights Commission (1964–67), and Commissioner of the State Bar of Michigan (1960–67). In 1967 President Johnson appointed him to the United States District Court for the Eastern District of Michigan, where he served until 1977, from 1975 to 1977 as Chief Judge. In 1975 he received the distinction of election by the judges of the Sixth Circuit as their official representative at the Judicial Conference of the United States. In 1977 President Jimmy Carter appointed him a judge of the United States Court of Appeals for the Sixth Circuit, an appointment that was widely acclaimed.[162]

President Carter appointed two more blacks to the United States District Court for the Eastern District of Michigan. The first was Julian Abele Cook, Jr. in 1978. Prior to his appointment, Cook had divided his time between private practice in Pontiac, Michigan, primarily in law firms,

160. *The Afro American,* week of February 6–10, 1979.
161. Beverly Blair Cook, "Black Representation in the Third Branch," *Black Law Journal,* vol. 1, nos. 2 and 3 (1971), p. 260, n. 1.
162. *Who's in America 1980–81,* vol. 1, p. 1976.

and public office, the latter including Special Assistant Attorney General for Michigan (1968–78) and Chairman of the Michigan Civil Rights Commission (1968–71). As a judge on the District Court for the Eastern District of Michigan, he presides in Detroit.[163]

Immediately after her admission to the bar, Anna Diggs-Taylor became an attorney in the United States Department of Labor (1957–60), following which she alternated between private practice, always in a law firm, and public office, including Assistant Prosecutor of Wayne County (1961–62), Assistant United States Attorney (1966), and Assistant Corporation Counsel for the city of Detroit (1976–79).[164] She was appointed a District Court judge in 1979.

The percentage of black judges sitting in the United States Court of Appeals and District Court in Detroit (25.0%) and on state and local courts (25.0%) are the second highest among the sixteen cities in this study, just behind Washington with 29.2 percent and 28.3 percent, respectively (see Table 15). The detailed comparison of the statistics on black judges in Philadelphia with those of Detroit is set forth in the following chart. It also should be noted that whereas no black judge in Detroit now sits on the Michigan Supreme Court or the intermediate appellate court, a black justice in Philadelphia is on the Supreme Court of Pennsylvania, and a black judge is on each of Pennsylvania's two intermediate appellate courts, the Commonwealth Court and the Superior Court. Hence, while Detroit leads in numbers, Philadelphia has judges on higher-ranking courts. As to federal judges, both cities have a black judge on the Court of Appeals and two black judges on the District Court.

|  | Houston | Philadelphia |
|---|---|---|
| State & Local Judges | 104 | 110 |
|   Black Judges | 9 (8.7%) | 21 (19.1%) |
| U.S. Court of Appeals |  |  |
| & District Judges | 10 | 20 |
|   Black Judges | 1 (0.1%) | 3 (15.0%) |
| Total Judges | 114 | 130 |
|   Total Black Judges | 10 (8.8%) | 24 (18.5%)[189] |

Federal Judges as of April 1982 (527 F. Supp. XIII–XV, X–XI; State and local judges as of November 1981.

163. Ibid., p. 700.

164. *Who's Who Among Black Americans 1977–78*, p. 869.

165. For detailed statistics on black and white judges in all cities surveyed, including U.S. bankruptcy judges and magistrates, see Appendix 12.

Black lawyers in Detroit are developing a growing community, some 500 in 1981 (425 members of the Wolverine Bar Association). With 5,872 listed members of the Detroit bar, they comprise approximately 8.5 percent of the total population of lawyers in the city. The percentage of black lawyers, like the percentage of blacks in the total population (61.6%), is high in relation to other cities (see Table 16). Although many black lawyers are in government work, the black legal community still consists mainly of sole practitioners or partners with a basically black clientele.

One highly unusual firm, now Lewis, White, Clay & Graves, an integrated small firm that was started in 1973 and is headed by three black lawyers—David Baker Lewis of Michigan Law School, David T. White of Harvard, and Eric L. Clay of Yale. This firm is believed to be the first, and perhaps the only black firm in the nation to work in the municipal bond area, initially in conjunction with the city's three largest firms.

David Lewis represents the third generation of his family to have graduated from Michigan Law School. His grandfather, Oscar W. Baker, Sr. (deceased) was the school's first black graduate in 1902; Oscar W. Baker, Jr. graduated in 1935, and his brother James in 1951. Their firm, now Baker, Baker and Selby, still maintains a thriving quality practice in Bay City, Michigan.

In comparing Detroit's law firms with those of Philadelphia, the survey found that while Detroit had no black partners in its large firms at the time of the survey in 1980, it has the highest percentage of black partners in its medium-size firms and a larger, although still far from adequate, percentage of black associates in both its large and medium-size firms.

| Large Firms* | Total Lawyers | Black Lawyers | Total Partners | Black Partners | Total Associates | Black Associates |
|---|---|---|---|---|---|---|
| Detroit | 212 | 8 (3.8%) | 103 | 0* | 109 | 8 (7.3%) |
| Philadelphia | 1,094 | 26 (2.4%) | 531 | 4 (0.8%) | 563 | 22 (3.9%) |
| Medium-size Firms* | | | | | | |
| Detroit | 368 | 10 (2.7%) | 206 | 2 (1.0%) | 162 | 8 (5.0%) |
| Philadelphia | 550 | 6 (1.1%) | 288 | 1 (0.3%) | 262 | 5 (1.9%)[166] |

*According to the 1980 survey conducted by the author. Since the survey was concluded, two blacks are known to have become partners in large Detroit firms.

For blacks on law school faculties, see Appendix 18.

166. For detailed statistics on black and white lawyers in all cities surveyed, see Appendices 13 and 14.

# Houston _____

After the Civil War, freed blacks were better off in Texas than in other states in the South because they were far removed from the battle centers and undisturbed by the "federal invasion." In a mostly rural population, Texas blacks were able to raise good crops, received fair payment for their labors, and in general enjoyed tolerable economic conditions.[167] Yet of all the southern states in this vast farming area except North Carolina, Texas had the smallest number of blacks in its state legislature, and none was a lawyer.[168]

At the turn of the century, Wilford M. Smith was one of the first, and very few, black lawyers to practice in the state of Texas. In 1900 he argued the case of *Seth Carter v. State of Texas*[169] in the United States Supreme Court and was successful in securing the reversal of the Texas Court of Criminal Appeals in its refusal to order the quashing of the indictment on the ground that systematic and arbitrary exclusion of Negroes from grand juries solely on the basis of race or color denied the defendant equal protection of the law under the Fourteenth Amendment. This was the same argument successfully made in the Scottsboro case *(Norris v. Alabama)* in 1935.[170]

In nearby Waco, Texas, in 1919, R. D. Evans tried the first case to prevent the Democratic Party from forbidding blacks to vote in the primary. He also carried the first white primary case to the United States Supreme Court, but the attempt was mooted since the party primary was held before the case could be argued.[171]

This type of civil rights activity was continued in the 1930s in Houston by such black lawyers as Carter Wesley, W. J. Durham, W. M. C. Dickson, and M. W. Plummer.

Wesley and Durham were close associates of Thurgood Marshall and very active in the civil-rights movement. Carter Wesley was further noted as editor, publisher, and owner of the newspaper, *Afro-American*, which for two decades was the only black newspaper in Texas. In 1932 he joined with J. Alston Atkins in researching the law pertaining to white democratic primaries.[172] Durham, who served as counsel for the NAACP, was known in Texas as one of the best prepared trial lawyers in the state.[173]

167. J. Mason Brewer, *Negro Legislators of Texas* (Dallas: Mathas Publishing Co., 1935), p. 9.

168. Bergman, *The Negro in America*, p. 265; Brewer, *Negro Legislators*, p. 116.

169. 177 U.S. 442 (1900).

170. 294 U.S. 558 (1935). Styles, *Negroes and the Law*, p. 16.

171. Ibid., p. 22; *Love v. Griffith*, 266 U.S. 32 (1924).

172. Charles H. Houston, "The Need for Negro Lawyers," *Journal of Negro Education*, vol. 4, no. 1 (January 1935), p. 52.

173. Information supplied by Aloysious M. Wickliff, Sr., Houston lawyer.

M. W. Plummer became the first black prosecutor's investigator in the South when he was appointed to the District Attorney's Office in Houston in 1953. He himself was the plaintiff in the civil rights case of *Plummer v. Derringer,* a case that challenged the exclusion of blacks from the then segregated cafeteria facilities at the Harris County Courthouse. Plummer describes his fellow attorney, W. M. C. Dickson, a Harvard law graduate, as "a brillant and astute lawyer" who was also extremely active in the civil-rights movement.[174]

Until 1950 no blacks graduated from law school in Texas. Texas Southern University (originally the University of Texas Law School, then part of Texas State University for Negroes) was created in 1947 largely because of a suit filed by a black letter carrier, Herman M. Sweatt, who was refused admission to the University of Texas on racial grounds. Sweatt's case was successfully argued in the District Court of Travis County and eventually before the United States Supreme Court by the Chief Legal Counsel for the NAACP, Thurgood Marshall.[175] Before the case reached the high court, the law school of Texas State University for Negroes was created under the "separate but equal" doctrine set forth by the Court in *Plessy v. Ferguson.*[176] In 1951 the words "for Negroes" were dropped and the school was renamed Texas Southern University. The school weathered attempts in the 1960s to phase it out, when the College Coordinating Board decided there was no need for two integrated, state-supported schools. In 1976 the School of Law at Texas Southern University was formally designated as the Thurgood Marshall School of Law.[177] Most of Houston's black lawyers have graduated from Texas Southern.[178]

Henry E. Doyle was the first black graduate of Texas Southern University School of Law in 1950, and he engaged in the general practice of law for twenty-seven years. In *Texas v. Johnnie Lee Morris,* his most famous case, Doyle was associated with fellow blacks W. J. Durham and Thomas Dent in the defense of a young black man who had been accused of killing a white Houston bus driver. Doyle was appointed to Houston Municipal Court No. 6 in 1977. On December 1, 1978, he was appointed Associate Justice of the First Court of Civil Appeals of Texas, the highest judgeship ever held by a black in Texas. In November 1980 he was elected to a four-year term.[179]

As the civil rights movement burgeoned in the 1950s and 1960s,

174. Idem.
175. See *Sweatt v. Painter,* 229 U.S. 629 (1949).
176. 163 U.S. 537 (1896).
177. Texas Southern University, "The Thurgood Marshall School of Law," pamphlet.
178. Vonciel Jones, " 'Born a Black Bastard . . .': The Education and Origin of Houston's Black Lawyers" (Master's thesis, Rice University, 1976), p. 70.
179. Information and resumé supplied by Judge Henry E. Doyle.

Doyle, Francis Williams, and Weldon Berry were leaders in the struggle. Williams was instrumental in developing poverty programs in Houston, and in 1940 he was counsel in the case that ultimately desegregated the Houston public schools.[180] For twenty-five years Berry was lead counsel in a desegregation case against the Houston Independent School District. On June 17, 1981, the case was settled and United States District Judge Robert O'Connor found that the school district had legally become integrated.[181]

Aloysius M. Wickliff, Sr., another prominent black Houston attorney who began practicing law in the 1950s, received his B.S. degree in political science from American University and his LL.B. degree from Catholic University, becoming its second black law graduate. In September 1955 he was employed as an associate professor of law at Texas Southern University, where he taught for three years; he is presently engaged in private practice with emphasis on business transactions and ventures. Wickliff is a co-founder and past president of the Houston Lawyers Association, an association formed in 1953 to provide the means of personal and professional interchange among black lawyers. He also was campaign manager for Barbara Jordan, who in 1972 became the first black Congresswoman from Texas.[182]

Barbara Jordan, a 1959 graduate of Boston University Law School, served as a member, and for a time as President Pro Tem, of the Texas Senate before her election to the House of Representatives in the 93rd through the 95th Congresses. During that period she was a member of the House Committee on the Judiciary and played an active role in the Watergate investigation. She has won national recognition as one of the most influential women in the country, devoting much of her time to public causes and civil rights.[183]

In 1961 Carl Walker, Jr. became the first black in the South to be appointed an assistant United States attorney. He was a general practitioner in a black law firm in Houston until his appointment. On June 7, 1968, he was elevated to Executive Assistant United States Attorney, a position he held until November 3, 1980, when he was named United States Attorney for the Southern District of Texas by all nine United States district judges who make up the Southern District of Texas.[184]

The first black to serve as a judge in the state of Texas was Harrell Tillman, who was appointed to the Municipal Court in 1964. He served

180. Idem.
181. Information supplied by A. Martin Wickliff, Jr., Houston lawyer.
182. Idem.
183. *Who's Who in America 1980–81*, vol. 1, p. 1748.
184. Ibid.

in that capacity until 1968 and presently is engaged in the private practice of law with emphasis on international transactions.[185]

In 1976 Alice Bonner was appointed a Municipal Court judge, thereby becoming the first black woman judge in Houston. She was recently defeated in her bid for reelection as a state district court judge.

Calvin Botley became the first and still the only black United States magistrate in Texas in 1979, and only the second in the United States Court of Appeals for the Fifth Circuit.[186]

Andrew Jefferson was appointed a judge of the Court of Domestic Relations No. 2, Harris County, Texas, in 1970. When in 1974 he was appointed a state district court judge, he thus became the first black district judge in Texas. He resigned that judgeship in 1975 to return to the private practice of law and now serves as President of Jefferson, Sherman and Mims. While on the bench, Jefferson was voted by the members of the Houston Bar Association as the most competent judge in Harris County.[187]

In 1979 Veronica Morgan Price, a graduate of Texas Southern University's Thurgood Marshall School of Law, was appointed Juvenile Court Referee for all the juvenile courts of Harris County. She was the first black attorney to hold this important position.[188]

On May 11, 1979, President Carter appointed Gabrielle K. McDonald to the United States District Court for the Southern District of Texas, thereby making her the first and only black federal judge in Houston. After spending four years at three different undergraduate schools, working full-time and attending part-time because of financial pressures, McDonald entered and graduated from Howard University Law School without having had the resources to enable her to receive an undergraduate degree. After serving two years as a staff attorney at the NAACP Legal Defense and Educational Fund, she formed a partnership for the practice of law with her husband and also taught part-time at the Texas Southern University Thurgood Marshall School of Law until she became a judge.

As seen in the following chart and in Table 15, there are only 10 black judges out of a total of 114 judges sitting in Houston, despite the welcome "firsts" attained by the black judges mentioned above. Philadelphia's percentage of black state and local judges far exceeds Houston's, as does its percentage of the total of state, local, and federal judges.

A decade after the first black judge was appointed in Texas in 1964,

185. Information supplied by Aloysius M. Wickliff, Sr.
186. Information supplied by A. Martin Wickliff, Jr. and public records.
187. Information supplied by Judge Doyle.
188. Information supplied by Wickliff, Sr.

|  | Houston | Philadelphia |
|---|---|---|
| State & Local Judges | 104 | 110 |
| Black Judges | 9 (8.7%) | 21 (19.1%) |
| U.S. Court of Appeals |  |  |
| & District Judges | 10 | 20 |
| Black Judges | 1 (0.1%) | 3 (15.0%) |
| Total Judges | 114 | 130 |
| Total Black Judges | 10 (8.8%) | 24 (18.5%)[189] |

Federal Judges as of April 1982 (527 F. Supp. XIII–XV, X–XI; State and local judges as of November 1981.

Rufus Cormier and James C. Plummer became the first black lawyers to be hired by one of Houston's largest law firms. In 1975 A. Martin Wickliff, Jr., son of Aloysius M. Wickliff, Sr., was the first black to be hired by another leading law firm, of which he became a partner in 1981. Other large firms began to retain one or two black lawyers as associates over the next few years.[190] Although two blacks (Cormier and Wickliff) have been made partners in large Houston firms since our survey was conducted in 1980, even the altered statistics reflect a very low representation of black lawyers in these upper ranks of the profession.

| Large Firms* | Total Lawyers | Black Lawyers | Total Partners | Black Partners | Total Associates | Black Associates |
|---|---|---|---|---|---|---|
| Houston | 1,045 | 10 (1.0%) | 424 | 0* | 621 | 10 (1.6%) |
| Philadelphia | 1,094 | 26 (2.4%) | 531 | 4 (0.8%) | 563 | 22 (3.9%) |
| Medium-Size Firms* |  |  |  |  |  |  |
| Houston | 729 | 7 (1.0%) | 301 | 0 | 428 | 7 (1.6%) |
| Philadelphia | 550 | 6 (1.1%) | 288 | 1 (0.3%) | 262 | 5 (1.9%)[191] |

*According to the 1980 survey conducted by the author. Since then two additional blacks are reported to have become partners in large firms.

The 300 black lawyers in Houston comprise 3.5 percent of the total 8,373 lawyers on record in the Martindale-Hubbell data bank for that city. As a group, the 440,257 blacks in Houston comprise 25.9 percent of the total population of that city (see Table 16). For blacks on law school faculties, see Appendix 18.

189. For detailed statistics on black and white judges in all cities surveyed, including U.S. bankruptcy judges and magistrates, see Appendix 12.
190. Information supplied by A. Martin Wickliff, Jr., Houston lawyer.
191. For detailed statistics on black and white lawyers in all cities surveyed, see Appendices 13 and 14.

# Los Angeles

Before 1940 in Los Angeles, when the black population was insignificant in number, a few remarkable blacks earned recognition in the field of law. As early as 1880, Robert Charles O'Hara Benjamin, known as the only Negro lawyer on the Pacific Coast at the time, became also the first black attorney to practice in the courts of California. He later was the first black city editor of the Los Angeles *Daily Sun* and apparently the first black in the nation to hold so prominent a position on any white newspaper.[192] In the early 1900s, Charles Darden became the first black to argue before the Supreme Court of California.[193] Sidney Dones, born in Texas in 1887, overcame poverty to build his own real estate business in Los Angeles and eventually became a lawyer after six years of reading law.[194]

In 1931 Henry Claude Hudson was the first black to receive a degree from Loyola Law School in Los Angeles, but he never actually practiced law.[195] Son of a freed slave, Hudson grew up in Alexandria, Louisiana, where racism was rampant. He moved to Indian Territory and, while working there in 1910, decided to enroll in the dental school of Howard University. There he became involved with a group of blacks and whites who organized the Niagara Movement on the Canadian side of Niagara Falls, since no hotel in the country would give the group meeting space. The name Niagara Movement was later changed to the National Association for the Advancement of Colored People. Hudson practiced dentistry in Shreveport, but was threatened by the Ku Klux Klan because of his active role in the NAACP. Realizing the precariousness of his position, he decided to move to Los Angeles, where he became president of the NAACP, a position he held for ten years. At that time blacks in Los Angeles were segregated in restaurants, theaters, and at beaches, and Hudson played an active role in removing beach segregation. His involvement in the battle for civil rights continued throughout his lifetime.

In his late nineties, Hudson reminisced about an occasion in the 1970s when he was guest of honor at the Biltmore Hotel. When the toastmaster introduced him and told of his efforts to bring peace to the community, everyone stood and applauded. When the ovation had quieted, he told of his coming to that hotel many years ago and not being permitted to enter. "I said, 'This shows how far you have come.' I suggested that they all stand and give themselves a hand."[196]

192. Delilah L. Beasley, *The Negro Trail Blazers of California,* reprint ed. (New York: Negro Universities Press, 1969), pp. 195–96.
193. Ibid., pp. 198–99.
194. Ibid., p. 205.
195. Comments of Judge David Williams.
196. Arnold Peyser, "Citizen Claude," *The Crisis,* vol. 87, no. 8 (October 1980), p. 296.

Progress began in the 1930s when a number of black lawyers began to serve in important government posts. Notable among them were Ivan J. Johnson III, who in 1937 became the first black United States Attorney in Los Angeles.[197] Also in the 1930s, Leon Whittaker became the first black in the District Attorney's Office.[198] Pauli Murray is believed to be the first black woman to serve in the California State Attorney General's Office when she was appointed in the 1940s.[199]

The turning point for blacks and black lawyers in Los Angeles followed World War II. The black population swelled from 38,894 in 1930 to 63,744 in 1940,[200] becoming the third largest in an American city. According to E. Franklin Frazier, one-third of all blacks in the United States were in Los Angeles.[201] The climate for black lawyers improved steadily, and by 1952 blacks and other minorities were for the first time granted membership in the Los Angeles Bar Association. Just a few years later, in 1956, the association held a plebiscite asking lawyers' preference among candidates for contested judicial offices. David W. Williams, a black candidate for the Superior Court, who subsequently became a United States district court judge, received more votes than any candidate had ever received before, indeed more than any candidate thereafter received in the plebiscites held during at least the next twelve years.

Samuel L. Williams's career has been important for blacks in Los Angeles, and especially for black lawyers. His public recognition began when he served as Deputy Attorney General of California (1962–65). In 1974 he became Chairman of the State Bar of California Committee of Bar Examiners after serving as a member for three years.[202] A partner in one of Los Angeles' large white law firms, in 1977 he became the first black to be elected president of the Los Angeles County Bar Association.[203] The association had indeed come full circle.

In October 1981 Williams became the first black president of the State Bar of California, another highly significant step forward for the black bar of the nation.[204] Elected president of the bar association of the most populous state in the nation, Williams is also only the second black president of any state bar association; Wayne A. Budd was president of the Massachusetts Bar Association in 1979.

197. Comments of Loren Miller, Jr., April 4, 1981; comments of Judge Williams.

198. Ibid.

199. Comments of Judge Williams and Estella Wheatly Dooley, May 7, 1981.

200. U.S. Bureau of the Census, *1930 Census*, table 12, p. 248; *1940 Census*, table 5, p. 132.

201. Frazier, *The Negro in the United States*, p. 269.

202. *Martindale-Hubbell 1981*, vol. 2, p. 1152B.

203. *100 Years: The Los Angeles County Association* (Los Angeles: County Bar Association, 1979), p. 38.

204. *Bar Leader*, July–August 1981, p. 29.

The career of Los Angeles Mayor Tom Bradley has also been an inspiration and an aid to black lawyers in that city. Bradley served on the Los Angeles Police Force for twenty-one years, during which time he obtained his law degree from Southwestern University School of Law in 1956. He practiced law from 1961 until he became a member of the Los Angeles City Council in 1963. When he was elected Mayor in 1973, it was a momentous milestone for blacks.[205]

Turning to the judiciary, we find that Edwin L. Jefferson's appointment to the Municipal Court in 1941 made him the first black judge to have served not only in Los Angeles but anywhere in the state of California.[206] In 1965 Earl C. Broady was the second black to be appointed to the Superior Court in Los Angeles.[207]

In 1969 David W. Williams became the first black judge of the United States District Court for the Central District of California. Williams had been a sole practitioner from the date of his admission to the California Bar in 1937 for eight years, then had practiced for an additional eight years in partnership with another lawyer conducting a successful, primarily civil, practice until 1955. In that year, he was appointed to the Los Angeles Municipal Court, being elected to full six-year terms in 1956 and 1962. He was appointed to the Superior Court in 1962 and elected to a full six-year term in 1963. He has been extremely active and effective in civic causes, including those in the civil-rights area.[208]

Loren Miller, whose father had been born a slave, practiced law for more than twenty-five years in Los Angeles and appeared before the United States Supreme Court in a number of important cases involving discrimination in housing. A vice-president of the NAACP, he was for a time publisher of the *California Eagle,* a Los Angeles black newspaper. Widely respected as a practicing attorney, he was appointed a judge of the Los Angeles Municipal Court in 1955. Miller was the author of the book *The Petitioners: The Story of the Supreme Court of the United States and the Negro,* published in 1966.

Admitted to the bar in 1954, Billy G. Mills did not start to practice law until 1957. In 1963 he was elected a member of the Los Angeles City Council, where he served for eleven years, three of them as President Pro Tem. He ended his service in the council upon his appointment as a judge of the Superior Court of California in Los Angeles County in 1974.

In February 1980 Terry J. Hatter became the second black judge of the United States District Court for the Central District of California.

205. Comments of Judge Miller.
206. Comments of Judge Williams, confirmed by Judge Thomas Griffiths, May 21, 1981.
207. Idem.
208. Ibid.

Hatter's career began after his admission to the Illinois bar in 1960. He then spent a year as an adjudicator with the United States Veterans Administration and another year divided between private practice and serving as Assistant Public Defender in Cook County, after which he moved to San Francisco, where he was immediately appointed Assistant United States Attorney in the Northern District of California. After four years in this post, he went from a year directing a neighborhood legal assistance program, to three years directing a center on law and poverty, to three years teaching at Loyola University Law School in Los Angeles, and then a year on varied assignments as Executive Assistant to the mayor of Los Angeles. In 1977 he was named to the California Superior Court, where he served until his appointment as a federal judge on February 1, 1980.

A highly meaningful development for Los Angeles's black lawyers, as well as other lawyers and indeed citizens all over the state of California, was the appointment in 1977 of Wiley W. Manuel as an associate justice of the Supreme Court of California. He had practiced law in Oakland, California, and had been a judge of the Superior Court of Alameda County prior to his appointment. As a Supreme Court justice, he served in San Francisco from 1977 until his death in 1981.[209]

The first black woman to be appointed to the bench in California was Vaino Hassan Spencer in 1961, when she became a judge of the Los Angeles Municipal Court. Spencer served until 1976, when she was appointed to the Superior Court of California.[210] Later she was elevated to the Court of Appeals for the Second Appellate District, on which she serves as Presiding Justice of Division One.[211]

Appointed to the United States District Court for the Central District of California, Consuelo Bland Marshall became the first black woman appointed to any of the three United States district courts in California. Following her admission to the bar in 1962, she had been employed as Deputy City Attorney for five years and thereafter was in private practice with a small law firm for three years, a commissioner for the Juvenile Court of the Los Angeles Superior Court for five years, and then a judge of the Inglewood Municipal Court for less than a year. In July 1977 she became a judge of the Criminal Division of the Los Angeles Superior Court, where she served until she assumed her duties as a United States district judge in 1980.[212]

209. *National Bar Bulletin,* vol. 9, no. 3 (March 1977), p. 1.
210. *California Courts and Judges Handbook,* 3d ed. rev. (San Francisco: Law Book Services Co., 1979), pp. 305–6; Reincke and Lichterman, *The American Bench,* p. 296.
211. Information supplied by Leonard S. Janofsky, Los Angeles attorney and past president of the American Bar Association.
212. Information supplied by Judge Marshall's secretary.

Female black lawyers in California also have been active in government. In 1966 one of them, Yvonne Braithwaite Burke, became the first black lawyer elected to the California Assembly. She later won Congressional office and then became the first black to hold the position of Los Angeles County Supervisor, until she was defeated for reelection in 1980.[213]

Lola McAlpin-Grant achieved a first in the field of legal education in Los Angeles when in 1970 she became the first black woman to hold the position of Assistant Dean of Loyola Law School. She also serves as Adjunct Professor.[214]

According to McAlpin-Grant, the past decade has seen an upsurge in the number of black lawyers in Los Angeles as the result of broadened minority admissions by the major law schools of California. The number of black lawyers in Los Angeles–Long Beach (the Standard Metropolitan Statistical Area for the Census) has increased from 297 in 1970 to 600 in 1980, the number in Los Angeles proper being 400. All three of these figures are approximations. The State Bar of California, with the concurrence of the Los Angeles County Bar Association, estimates that there are 26,400 lawyers in Los Angeles County and 18,000 in the city of Los Angeles. Thus black lawyers in Los Angeles in 1980–81 comprised 2.2 percent of the lawyers in the city. In 1980 blacks comprised 13.4 percent of the total population of Los Angeles (see Table 16).

In McAlpin-Grant's evaluation, black lawyers in the past decade have been able to find significant placements in Los Angeles, including positions as associates although not as partners in major firms. She notes, however, that two blacks have now become partners in Los Angeles's large firms.

Our survey confirms these observations and shows that Los Angeles and Philadelphia have identical percentages of black partners in their large firms (0.8%). While Philadelphia has a slightly higher percentage of black associates in its large firms (3.9%) than Los Angeles (3.0%), Los Angeles has a higher percentage of black associates in its medium-size firms (2.8%) than Philadelphia (1.9%). It is interesting to note that William T. Coleman, Jr., the former Secretary of the United States Department of Transportation who spent most of his outstanding legal career in Philadelphia, is now a partner in one of Los Angeles's two largest law firms, heading its Washington, D.C., office.

As to judges in all categories, Los Angeles has smaller percentages of black judges than Philadelphia (see the following chart and Table 15). Representation in the judiciary remains a matter of concern to black lawyers in Los Angeles.

213. Information from resumé.
214. Statement of Dean Lola McAlpin-Grant.

|  | Los Angeles | Philadelphia |
|---|---|---|
| State and Local Judges | 280 | 110 |
| Black Judges | 29 (10.4%) | 21 (19.1) |
| U.S. Court of Appeals | | |
| & District Judges | 19 | 20 |
| Black Judges | 2 (10.5%) | 3 (15.0) |
| Total Judges | 299 | 130 |
| Total Black Judges | 31 (10.4%) | 24 (18.5%)[215] |

Federal judges as of April 1982, 527 F. Supp. XX–XXI, X–XI; State and local judges as of November 1981.

| Large Firms* | Total Lawyers | Black Lawyers | Total Partners | Black Partners | Total Associates | Black Associates |
|---|---|---|---|---|---|---|
| Los Angeles | 716 | 16 (2.0%) | 250 | 2 (0.8%) | 466 | 14 (3.0%) |
| Philadelphia | 1,094 | 26 (2.4%) | 531 | 4 (0.8%) | 563 | 22 (3.9%) |
| Medium-Size Firms* | | | | | | |
| Los Angeles | 1,444 | 26 (1.0%) | 682 | 5 (0.7%) | 762 | 21 (2.8%) |
| Philadelphia | 550 | 6 (1.1%) | 288 | 1 (0.3%) | 262 | 5 (1.9%)[216] |

*According to the 1980 survey conducted by the author.

Speaking in 1977, Carl E. Jones, President of the black lawyers' Langston Law Club of Los Angeles, said that "until Governor Jerry Brown was elected, minority appointments were ridiculously low. Brown has made a number of minority appointments to the bench, both men and women, but we are still left with an under-representation."[217] For blacks on law school faculties, see Appendix 18.

# Milwaukee

Until the 1960s the black population of Wisconsin was so small that little is known of black history in the state. The number of blacks grew slowly, from 1,000 in 1850 to 21,910 a century later.[218] By 1970 there were 128,000

215. For detailed statistics on black and white judges in all cities surveyed, including U.S. bankruptcy judges and magistrates, see Appendix 12.
216. For detailed statistics on black and white lawyers in all cities surveyed, see Appendices 13 and 14.
217. *National Bar Bulletin,* vol. 9, no. 3 (March 1977), p. 5.
218. *1950 Census,* vol. 2, p. 49, table 53, pp. 49–136.

blacks in Wisconsin, and more than four-fifths of this number were concentrated in Milwaukee.[219]

William T. Green was the first black graduate of the University of Wisconsin Law School (1892), the first black lawyer to practice in Milwaukee, and for nearly twenty years the only black lawyer practicing in the courts of Milwaukee County.[220] Following his admission to the bar, Green joined the law firm of J. J. Stover in Milwaukee, later the firm of Bell, Brazee and Stover. In 1893 he began an independent practice in which he engaged until his death in 1911. During his career he defended three-quarters of the cases involving blacks in the Milwaukee district, municipal, and civil courts.[221] In addition to his legal practice, Green was active in political and social causes involving blacks. His most significant political accomplishment was his successful effort to secure passage of the Wisconsin Civil Rights Law in 1895. This measure, of which Green is the acknowledged author, outlawed racial discrimination in restaurants and other public places.[222]

James W. Dorsey succeeded Green as the leading black attorney in Milwaukee until his death in 1966. The first black to graduate from the University of Montana in 1922, he received his law degree from that school in 1927. Dorsey chose to settle in Milwaukee after attempts to set up practice in Des Moines, Iowa, and St. Paul, Minnesota, failed because of their small black populations. He selected Milwaukee because he had heard that Milwaukee "was friendly to Negroes" and had only one practicing black attorney.[223] At that time there were between 5,000 and 7,000 blacks in the city and between ten and fifteen black lawyers.[224] Dorsey became a well-known figure in Milwaukee's black and white communities, and his clientele included many whites as well as blacks because of his ability and personality.[225] He was Milwaukee's first black candidate nominated for a city office and its first black court commissioner. Dorsey was active in human rights organizations and received numerous honors and awards.[226] Another black attorney, Andrew Reneau, proved to be a skillful

219. U.S. Department of Commerce, Bureau of the Census, *Historical Statistics of the United States, Colonial Times to 1970* (Washington, D.C.: Government Printing Office, 1975), vol. 1, p. 37.

220. "First Negro Lawyer from UW Successful," *Milwaukee Journal,* November 6, 1967.

221. Harry H. Anderson, introductory note to "Negroes in Milwaukee" by William T. Green, *Milwaukee Sentinel,* October 16, 1895, reprinted in *The Negro in Milwaukee: A Historical Survey,* published by the Milwaukee County Historical Society (1968), p. 5.

222. Ibid.

223. "James Dorsey Traveled Far, Found Success in Milwaukee," *Milwaukee Journal,* May 11, 1966.

224. Letter from Edward S. Kerstein, Milwaukee lawyer, received August 21, 1981.

225. Ibid.

226. "James Dorsey Traveled Far"; "James W. Dorsey," *Milwaukee Journal,* May 13, 1966; "Negro History Makers in Milwaukee," *Echo,* February 1967.

courtroom practitioner during Dorsey's lifetime. He also had white as well as black clients.

In 1948 Theodore W. Coggs began his career as a well-known criminal defense attorney in Milwaukee. He served as President of the National Bar Association in 1963. Coggs is also a former president of the Wisconsin Conference of the NAACP and a former consultant to the federal government's Office of Economic Opportunity.[227] Another black lawyer who has been in government is Terrence L. Pitts, a longtime member of the Milwaukee County Board of Supervisors.[228]

Lloyd A. Barbee, a black attorney who served many years in the Wisconsin legislature, has had a distinguished law career in Milwaukee. He filed and successfully prosecuted a civil desegregation action against the Milwaukee School Board that resulted in the integration of black and white pupils in the Milwaukee public elementary and high schools in the 1970s.[229]

Vel R. Phillips became the first black judge in Wisconsin when she was appointed by Governor Patrick Lucey in 1971 to the Juvenile Court of Milwaukee County.[230] She was born and reared in Milwaukee, attended Howard University, returned to the University of Wisconsin Law School, and graduated in 1951. She was the first black woman to be elected to the Milwaukee Common Council and the first black to serve on the Democratic National Committee. In 1972 she was defeated for election as a Juvenile Court judge. However, in 1978 she was elected Secretary of State in Wisconsin.[231]

Clarence R. Parrish was appointed a circuit judge of the Milwaukee County Court system in 1980 and was elected in 1981 to a six-year term. He is a 1949 graduate of the St. John's University Law School of New York and received a master's degree in law from the University of Wisconsin Law School in 1952. Parrish practiced law from 1952 until 1980, when he became a judge.

On graduation from Marquette University Law School and admission to practice in Wisconsin, both in 1967, Harold B. Jackson, Jr., began his legal practice with the Milwaukee County District Attorney's Office, remaining there until 1973. In that year, he was appointed a judge of the Wisconsin Circuit Court, having then been elected to a term that expired in December 1981.

As shown in the following chart and in Table 15, in 1981 there were two blacks holding judgeships in Milwaukee—two in the state and local

227. "Negro Leader T. W. Coggs Dies," *Milwaukee Sentinel,* June 13, 1968.
228. Letter to John Kluwin, Milwaukee lawyer, from Edward S. Kerstein, August 20, 1981.
229. Telephone conversation with Edward S. Kerstein, November 10, 1981.
230. "Vel Phillips Named Children's Judge," *Milwaukee Journal,* August 3, 1971.
231. "Vel Phillips Wins Nod for Secretary of State," *Milwaukee Journal,* September 13, 1978.

|                                                      | Milwaukee | Philadelphia |
|------------------------------------------------------|-----------|--------------|
| State & Local Judges                                 | 40        | 110          |
| Black Judges                                         | 2 (5%)    | 21 (19.1%)   |
| U.S. Court of Appeals<br>& District Judges           | 4         | 20           |
| Black Judges                                         | 0         | 3 (15.0%)    |
| Total Judges                                         | 44        | 130          |
| Total Black Judges                                   | 2 (4.5%)  | 24 (18.5%)[232] |

Federal judges as of April 1982, 527 F. Supp. XVIII, X–XI; State and local judges as of November 1981.

| Large Firms* | Total Lawyers | Black Lawyers | Total Partners | Black Partners | Total Associates | Black Associates |
|--------------|---------------|---------------|----------------|----------------|------------------|------------------|
| Milwaukee    | 277           | 4 (1.4%)      | 153            | 1 (0.7%)       | 124              | 3 (2.4%)         |
| Philadelphia | 1,094         | 26 (2.4%)     | 531            | 4 (0.8%)       | 563              | 22 (3.9%)        |
| Medium-size Firms* |         |               |                |                |                  |                  |
| Milwaukee    | 116           | 0             | 60             | 0              | 56               | 0                |
| Philadelphia | 550           | 6 (1.1%)      | 288            | 1 (0.3%)       | 262              | 5 (1.9%)[233]    |

*According to the 1980 survey conducted by the author.

category and no federal, constituting 4.5 percent of the 44 judges sitting in the city. In Philadelphia, by comparison, blacks occupy 24 out of 130 (18.5%) of the judgeships. The current survey of Milwaukee's law firms revealed that out of 153 partners in Milwaukee's large firms there was only one black, and in its medium-size firms there was no black partner. Of 124 associates in the large firms, three were black, but there were no black associates in the medium-size firms.

In both categories of firms, Philadelphia has a slightly higher percentage of both black partners and black associates, which would be expected in light of Philadelphia's larger black population (see Table 16). Blacks comprise only 22.9 percent of the 1980 population of Milwaukee and 36.5 percent in Philadelphia. However, the figures for both cities are low relative to their proportions of black population.

It is estimated that there are between 3,200 and 3,300 practicing attorneys in Milwaukee (3,042 in the Martindale-Hubbell data bank). Of these, only 75 to 100, approximately 2 or 3 percent, are black.[234] For blacks on law school faculties, see Appendix 18.

232. For detailed statistics on black and white judges in all cities surveyed, including U.S. bankruptcy judges and magistrates, see Appendix 12.
233. For detailed statistics on black and white lawyers in all cities surveyed, see Appendices 13 and 14.
234. Letter from Edward S. Kerstein.

# Minneapolis _____

For a century the black population of Minnesota grew very slowly and remained small—100 in 1870, 35,000 in 1970.[235] In 1974 it was reported that only 1.8 percent of Minnesota's total population was "nonwhite."[236] Although the Twin Cities of Minneapolis–St. Paul contain many different ethnic groups, less than 1 percent were black in 1970, even though approximately 90 percent of Minnesota's black population was concentrated in that area.[237] According to the 1970 census, all 23 of Minnesota's black lawyers were found in the Twin Cities area, where they comprised 0.7 percent of the 3,094 lawyers in those two cities. These 23 black lawyers constituted 0.5 percent of the state's total of 4,454 lawyers.[238]

Of the approximately 12,000 licensed lawyers in the State of Minnesota in 1980,[239] there were 56 black lawyers, all of them in the Twin Cities area.[240] Thus, the percentage of black lawyers had not increased since the 1970 census.

The first black lawyer of prominence in Minneapolis was William R. Morris. In 1911 Morris was one of the three black lawyers (along with William H. Lewis and Butler R. Wilson of Boston) recommended to the Executive Committee of the American Bar Association for membership in the association. All three were elected by the committee,[241] which did not know their race. When the fact that they were black was discovered, the Executive Committee revoked its vote. When the three were finally elected at the annual meeting, the Bar Association passed a resolution requiring statements of race to accompany future recommendations. William Morris, acting alone, immediately resigned his membership giving as his reason "the best interests of the leading organization of lawyers in the land." (See Introduction for a more detailed account.)

In the 1920s the best-known black Minnesota lawyer was W. T. Francis. Francis held numerous state and local positions in St. Paul until 1927, when he was appointed United States Ambassador to Liberia. He died there of yellow fever two years later.

From the time of William Morris, no other black lawyer of prominence appeared on the Minneapolis scene until L. Howard Bennett. A 1950 graduate of the University of Chicago Law School, Bennett became a

235. *Historical Statistics of the United States,* vol. 1, p. 30.

236. Burke, *Civil Rights,* p. 156.

237. *The New Encyclopedia Britannica* (Chicago: William Benton, 1974), vol. 12, p. 258.

238. U.S. Bureau of the Census, *Characteristics of the Population,* vol. 1, pt. 5, Minnesota (1973), table 171, pp. 25–631, 25–651.

239. Information obtained from the Clerk of the Minnesota Supreme Court, St. Paul, Minnesota.

240. Information supplied by Marvin R. Anderson, Minnesota Minority Lawyers Association, Minneapolis, Minnesota.

241. *Reports of the American Bar Association,* vol. 37 (1912), pp. 11–16.

municipal court judge. He later served in Washington, D.C., as Deputy Secretary of Defense for Civil Rights (1968–71). In 1974 he entered private practice in Washington, D.C.[242]

The sole black currently on the bench in Minneapolis is William S. Posten, a 1959 graduate of William Mitchell College of Law, who won high praise for his performance during ten years as a government trial lawyer before he became a judge on the Hennepin County Municipal Court. Posten is now a judge on Minnesota's District Court for the Fourth Circuit. Over the years he also has been involved in many civil rights and other civic causes in Minneapolis.[243]

Given the small black population of Minneapolis, it is not surprising that only one of its thirty-seven state and local judges (2.7%) and none of the three federal judges is black. Altogether, blacks constitute 2.5 percent of the bench in Minneapolis out of a total of forty judges.

The current survey found no black partners in either the large or

|  | Minneapolis | Philadelphia |
|---|---|---|
| State & Local Judges | 37 | 110 |
| Black Judges | 1 (2.7%) | 21 (19.1%) |
| U.S. Court of Appeals & District Judges | 3 | 20 |
| Black Judges | 0 | 3 (15.0%) |
| Total Judges | 40 | 130 |
| Total Black Judges | 1 (2.5%) | 24 (18.5%)[244] |

Federal judges as of April 1982, 527 F. Supp. XIX, X–XI; State and local judges as of November 1981.

| Large Firms* | Total Lawyers | Black Lawyers | Total Partners | Black Partners | Total Associates | Black Associates |
|---|---|---|---|---|---|---|
| Minneapolis | 272 | 2 (0.7%) | 145 | 0 | 127 | 2 (1.6%) |
| Philadelphia | 1,094 | 26 (2.4%) | 531 | 4 (0.8%) | 563 | 22 (3.9%) |
| Medium-size Firms* | | | | | | |
| Minneapolis | 184 | 0 | 101 | 0 | 83 | 0 |
| Philadelphia | 550 | 6 (1.1%) | 288 | 1 (0.3%) | 262 | 5 (1.9%)[245] |

*According to the 1980 survey conducted by the author.

242. Burke, *Civil Rights,* p. 10.
243. Reincke and Lichterman, *The American Bench,* 1st ed., p. 953.
244. For detailed statistics on black and white judges in all cities surveyed, including U.S. bankruptcy judges and magistrates, see Appendix 12.
245. For detailed statistics on black and white lawyers in all cities surveyed, see Appendices 13 and 14.

medium-size law firms of Minneapolis. Two of 127 associates in the large firms were black, and there were no black associates in the medium-size firms.

Philadelphia has a higher percentage of both black partners and black associates in its large and medium-size firms. One would expect this, or an even greater, differential in light of Philadelphia's much larger black population. Blacks constitute 36.5 percent of the total population of Philadelphia and only 7.6 percent of the population of Minneapolis. The best estimate the author has been able to obtain is that whereas there are approximately fifty-two black lawyers in the Twin Cities, there are only approximately eighteen in Minneapolis, one reason for so substantial a difference being the state offices in St. Paul, a source of employment for black lawyers. The Martindale-Hubbell data bank contains the names of 3,968 lawyers for Minneapolis in 1981, necessarily an incomplete figure. However, on the basis of this figure, black lawyers would constitute 0.45 percent of the total. The actual percentage is undoubtedly a little higher. For blacks on law school faculties, see Appendix 18.

# New York City

Although before 1850 there already were 15,000 free blacks in New York City, only four of them were lawyers, nine were physicians, and the rest were employed in trades and in service jobs.[246]

George Boyer Vashon (1824–78), the first black graduate of Oberlin College, was also the first black lawyer in the state of New York.[247] From that time on, New York City was the home of many noted black leaders, especially in the legal profession. By 1969, it had become the site of the largest black-owned business establishment of its kind in the United States, the United Mutual Life Insurance Company, and also of the Carver Federal Savings and Loan Association and the Freedom National Bank.[248]

Among the first black lawyers to achieve a public post in New York was Edward Austin Johnson, an 1891 graduate of Shaw University Law School who became the first black to hold a seat in the Assembly of the New York State Legislature. Later dean of this law school, Johnson introduced in the state assembly its Civil Rights Act of 1917 providing equal opportunity to blacks in that state.[249]

246. James E. Allen, *The Negro in New York* (Hicksville, N.Y.: Exposition Press, 1964), p. 21.

247. Joan R. Sherman, *Invisible Poets* (Urbana, Ill.: University of Illinois Press, 1974), pp. 53–54.

248. Adams, *Great Negroes*, p. 77.

249. Ibid., pp. 73, 74.

Born on the Caribbean Island of Montserrat in 1889, Thomas Benjamin Dyett came to New York City at the age of seventeen and was admitted to the New York Bar in 1922. Five years later he began a ten-year term as Assistant District Attorney and continued to be offered and to accept public posts such as membership in the New York Constitutional Convention (1938) and Commissioner of Correction of the State of New York (1940–46) and of the New York City Department of Correction, followed two years later by his appointment to the Civil Service Commission of the City of New York. Active in the organized bar, he was one of the founders of the Harlem Bar Association, and in 1947 he became the first black to be appointed to the Committee on Character and Fitness of the Association of the Bar of the City of New York. Throughout his career Dyett was exemplary in sponsoring and counseling young people, white and black, for legal careers, and he dedicated himself to advancing the status of black Americans socially, economically, and politically. A highly successful practicing lawyer, he saw early that, as paraphrased by New York City lawyer Hope R. Stevens,[250] "the general practice of the law could best be conducted within the firm structure—and . . . individual practice was no longer efficient." In accordance with his conviction, he established the firm of Dyett, Hall and Patterson. In the ensuing years his partners and many of his associates went on to fill posts on the Court of Appeals (Harold A. Stevens), the state Supreme Court (Franklin W. Morton), the Civil Court and later the Supreme Court (Fritz Alexander and Amos S. Bowman), the Criminal Court (the late Kenneth Phipps), as a United States ambassador (Franklin Hall Williams), and as a member of the state legislature (David Dinkins, former Assemblyman).[251]

Born in 1896 and admitted to the bar in 1920, Alan L. Dingle is still going to his office. He has sometimes been referred to as the dean of the black bar of Manhattan.

Two black judges were appointed to the Municipal Court on the same day in 1931. First in order was James S. Watson, who served on the court until his death in 1952. Born in Jamaica, British West Indies, he was admitted to the New York Bar in 1914. Subsequently he was a member of the law firm of House, Gressman and Vorhaus, served as chief of the Tax Contract Division of the Department of Corporations, and also was Special Assistant Corporation Counsel for the City of New York (1922–30).

The second appointment went to Charles E. Toney, who was admitted to the bar in 1905 and practiced actively for the next twenty-six years,

---

250. Hope R. Stevens in *Thomas Benjamin Dyett* (New York: New York City Bar Association, 1971), pp. 20, 22.
251. Ibid., p. 22.

until his appointment. He also served on the Municipal Court until his death in 1951.

In 1966 James L. Watson, son of Judge James S. Watson, received a lifetime appointment by President Lyndon B. Johnson as judge of the United States Customs Court (now the United States Court of International Trade), on which he still serves. Admitted to the bar in 1951, he had been Judge of the Civil Court of the City of New York (1963–66) and New York State Senator from the 21st Senatorial District (1954–63).[252]

Born in Jamaica, British West Indies, in 1904, Stanley Gilbert MacPherson came to New York to attend City College of New York and St. John's University Law School. In 1934 he was appointed Deputy Collector for the Internal Revenue Second District, New York, and was entrusted with the most important tax case in the history of the office to that date, a suit against the Associated Gas and Electric Corporation involving forty million dollars in default payments. He returned to private practice in 1944.[253]

In 1939 Jane Matilda Bolin became the first black woman judge in New York City when she was appointed by Mayor Fiorello La Guardia to the Domestic Relations Court of New York City.[254] The next black appointment to the same court was in 1942, when Hubert T. Delany relinquished his post as Tax Commissioner of New York City, in which he had served since 1934, to accept the judicial post. From 1933 to 1941 he had practiced as a member of the law firm of Mintzer, Toqarelli and Delany, after serving six years as Assistant United States Attorney for the Southern District of New York.

The temper of the times affecting stories of the time, even for brilliant black graduates of colleges and law schools, was revealed in the experience of Francis E. Rivers, who was a Phi Beta Kappa graduate from Yale University in 1915. After applying to clerk in over sixty New York firms and being unable to secure employment, he finally found employment in New Haven, Connecticut, where he worked for two years. He subsequently served in the army in France as a second lieutenant. After he graduated from Columbia University Law School in 1922 and was promptly admitted to the bar, he ran into the same obstacles. But soon after taking a job with the Post Office, he was offered a position as associate in the firm of Goldstein and Goldstein, where he remained for two years before opting to go into practice by himself. Five years later, in 1929, he was elected to the Assembly of the New York State Legislature. In 1938 he was appointed

252. Reincke and Lichterman, *The American Bench,* 2nd ed., p. 48.

253. *Who's Who in Harlem* (New York: Magazine and Periodical Printing and Publishing Co., 1950), p. 22.

254. Bergman, *The Negro in America,* p. 485.

an assistant district attorney, and he remained in that post until 1943, when he was elected the first black judge of the City Court of New York. During his entire legal career he had been an activist in civil-rights affairs. In 1963 he retired from the bench to become President of the NAACP Legal Defense and Educational Fund, where he served until he died in 1975.[255]

An unusual experience in New York in the 1940s was the admission to the bar of Cora Walker Bailey, who at the age of twenty-three, while working as a junior accountant, passed the bar examination and became the youngest black ever to have been admitted to practice law in New York State.[256]

Harold A. Stevens was admitted to the New York Bar in 1938 (to the Massachusetts Bar two years earlier) and was in a partnership with another black lawyer for four years before joining in partnership with Thomas B. Dyett, as noted above. In 1947 he was elected a member of the New York State Assembly and served there until 1951, when he became a judge of the Court of General Sessions of New York City. In 1955 he became a justice of the New York Supreme Court and in 1958 a justice of the Appellate Division, assuming the office of Presiding Judge of that court in 1969, the first black to hold the post. In 1974 he was appointed the first black judge of the New York State Court of Appeals but was not subsequently elected to the post and returned to service on the Appellate Division of the Supreme Court before his retirement. During his career Stevens had served as counsel for or as an active member of many important government, civic, charitable, and civil rights groups.[257]

Franklin Hall Williams was admitted to the New York Bar in 1945, joining the national office of the NAACP as Assistant Special Counsel in that year, then going to California after four years to serve for an additional five as the West Coast Regional Director. While in California he became Assistant Attorney General of that state for two years, after which he joined the Peace Corps in various capacities for two years and then served as United States Representative to the Economic and Social Council of the United Nations. From 1965 to 1968 he was United States Ambassador to Ghana. Williams is a practicing lawyer who also serves on the Board of Directors of the Chemical Bank of New York, Consolidated Edison, Inc., Borden, Inc., and of other leading national business concerns. Currently he is President of the Phelps Stokes Fund, which does a great deal of work in furtherance of the interests of young black people. He is also a television and radio commentator for Westinghouse Broadcasting Company.[258]

255. *National Bar Bulletin*, vol. 11, no. 1 (January 1979); research assistance provided by the Anocostia Neighborhood Museum, Washington, D.C.

256. *Who's Who in Harlem*, p. 30.

257. *Who's Who in American Law 1977*, p. 525.

258. *Who's Who in America 1980–81*, vol. 2, p. 3530.

Herbert B. Evans was elected a justice of the State Supreme Court in 1972, and then was appointed to the Appellate Division by the governor. On March 1, 1979, the Chief Judge of the Court of Appeals appointed him Chief Administrative Judge of the Courts, which involves the major responsibility of administering the courts of New York State.

John T. Patterson, a black lawyer who decided to forego the practice of law and enter the brokerage business in 1953, helped to organize the first black-owned and operated brokerage firm in the Wall Street area and in 1955 established the first New York branch office of FIF Investing Associates.[259]

Thurgood Marshall began his legal career in the early 1930s with the NAACP in Baltimore, his native city, and from the time he went to New York to join the NAACP national legal staff in 1936, the center of his activities was New York City. Moving from NAACP Chief Legal Officer (1936–38) to Director-Counsel of the NAACP Legal Defense and Educational Fund (1940–61), Marshall argued critical civil-rights cases all over the country, including the famous *Brown v. Board of Education* case before the United States Supreme Court in 1954. In 1961 he was appointed the first black on the United States Court of Appeals for the Second Circuit. He resigned in 1965 to become Solicitor General of the United States, the first black to hold the post. On August 30, 1967, he was appointed the first black justice of the United States Supreme Court.[260] Thurgood Marshall has truly been an inspiration as he has continually broken new ground for other blacks, performing his critical roles ably and with distinction.

Constance Baker Motley's legal career consisted primarily of trying cases and arguing appeals for the NAACP Legal Defense and Educational Fund. During one period the fund was victorious in nine out of ten civil-rights cases that she, as its Associate Counsel, had argued in the United States Supreme Court.[261] In 1964 she became the first black to serve in the New York State Senate, and in 1965 accepted appointment as Manhattan Borough President. When she was appointed to the United States District Court for the Southern District of New York in 1966, she became the first black female federal judge in the country. She is scheduled to become Chief Judge of the court on August 13, 1982.[262]

In the 1970s three black lawyers and one City Court judge were appointed to United States district courts sitting in New York City.

The first was Lawrence W. Pierce, who was born in Philadelphia and

259. Harry E. Groves, *Opportunities for Negroes in Law,* (Published for the Association of American Law Schools, 1967).

260. *Who's Who in America 1980–81,* vol. 2, p. 2158.

261. National Bar Association 50th Annual Conference Program, 1975, p. 20; *Who's Who in America 1980–81,* vol. 2, p. 2388.

262. Bergman, *The Negro in America,* pp. 588, 593, 599; Burke, *Civil Rights,* p. 87.

educated in that city through his undergraduate career. He then attended Fordham University Law School in New York City and remained in the city to practice law, starting his career with the Legal Aid Society (1952–54). He went on to become Assistant District Attorney of Kings County (1954–61) and practiced civil law for the last five of these years, after which he served successively as Deputy Police Commissioner of New York City (1961–63), Director of the New York State Division for Youth (1963–66), and Chairman of the New York State Narcotic Addiction Control Commission (1966–70). Over the years, he engaged actively in civic, civil-rights, and professional extra curricular activities.[263] At the time of his appointment to the United States District Court for the Southern District of New York on May 20, 1971, he was Visiting Professor of Criminal Justice at the State University of New York in Albany. On September 8, 1981, President Ronald Reagan sent to the United States Senate the nomination of Judge Pierce to the United States Court of Appeals for the Second Circuit. He was unanimously confirmed November 18, 1981.

Robert L. Carter, who became a federal judge in 1972, was admitted to the New York Bar in 1945. From February 3, 1945, to December 1, 1968, a period of almost twenty-four years, he served with dedication and effectiveness, first as Assistant Special Counsel for the NAACP and Senior Assistant Counsel for its Legal Defense and Educational Fund, and then as General Counsel for the NAACP. In 1969 he became a partner in the firm of Poletti, Friedin, Prashker, Feldman and Gartner and practiced with them until he was appointed Judge of the United States District Court for the Southern District of New York on July 25, 1972. Throughout his career he was active not only in civil-rights issues but also in other civic causes and in the work of the organized bar.[264]

Henry Bramwell, another black federal judge, spent his first five years at the bar as a single practitioner (1948–53) and was then appointed Assistant United States Attorney for the Eastern District of New York (1953–61). He then returned to private practice, alternating it with other public involvements. In 1969 he became a judge of the New York City Civil Court, Brooklyn, where he served until his appointment in January 1975 to the United States District Court for the Eastern District of New York, which sits in Brooklyn.[265]

The fourth black judge appointed to a United States district court sitting in New York City is Mary Johnson Lowe, appointed on June 27, 1978, to the United States District Court for the Southern District of New York. She had previously served, by appointment of Mayor John Lindsay,

263. *Who's Who in America 1980–81*, vol. 2, p. 2635.
264. Ibid., vol. 1, p. 565.
265. Ibid., p. 394.

as a judge of the Criminal Court of New York City (1971–73); by appointment of the justices of the Appellate Division of the Supreme Court, as an acting justice of the Supreme Court of the State of New York (1973–74); as a justice of the Bronx County Supreme Court (1975–76); and, from January 1978, as a justice of the Supreme Court of the State of New York by virtue of her election to the office two months before. She had engaged in private practice primarily in the field of criminal law for sixteen years (1955–71), half of them as a sole practitioner and half with one or more partners.[266]

A highly regarded black practicing lawyer in New York City is Hope R. Stevens. Born in Tortola, British Virgin Islands, in 1905, he was admitted to the New York Bar in 1937 and started his practice in Harlem. After forty-four years, he still insists that the professional corporation he heads—Stevens, Hinds, Jackson and White—retain its offices in Harlem, although the firm's practice is citywide and international as well, representing the governments of Granada and Ethiopia. Steven's interests have gone beyond the law and civil rights into the area of business. After fifteen years as part-time Executive Vice-President of the United Mutual Life Insurance Company, the only insurance company in the state of New York owned and run by blacks, he became in 1955 its full-time president. He then returned to the practice of law and later was one of the organizers of the Carver Federal Savings and Loan Association, the first institution of its kind organized by black people, which today has four branches in New York City with assets in excess of eighty million dollars. For five years ending in 1980, Stevens served as the co-chairperson of the National Conference of Black Lawyers of the United States and Canada.[267]

Having won numerous awards for his service in the United States Army during the Korean conflict, Charles B. Rangel became an assistant United States attorney the year after his admission to the bar (1961–62), held other government posts, then was elected a state assemblyman (1966–70), and has been a member of the United States House of Representatives since 1971.

Admitted to the New York bar in 1962, Barbara M. Watson immediately went into government service in New York City, moving for a period of four years from one municipal post to another, until in 1966 she became Deputy Administrator, and in 1968 Administrator, of the Bureau of Security and Consular Affairs in the Department of State in Washington, the first female and the first black to hold such a high-level position in the State Department. She remained in the post until 1974, then practiced law

266. Ibid., vol. 2, p. 2075.
267. Information supplied by Hope R. Stevens.

briefly, and in 1977 was appointed Assistant Secretary of State. She has been the recipient of many awards and now resides in Washington.[268]

Basil A. Paterson has excelled in combining the practice of law with holding government office and political involvements as well. Admitted to the New York Bar in 1952, in 1956 he became a partner in the law firm of Paterson, Michael, Jones and Cherot and continued there for more than two decades. In 1965 he became a delegate to the New York State Senate, where he served until 1970. In 1972 he became the first black vice-chairman of the Democratic National Committee; he held that post for the next six years, serving also as a delegate to both intervening Democratic National Conventions. In 1978, upon leaving his law firm, he assumed the office of Deputy Mayor for Labor Relations of the City of New York and of Secretary of State of New York the following year.[269]

When Paul Peyton Gibson, Jr. was appointed Deputy Mayor of New York by Mayor Abraham Beame in 1974, he thereby became the first black to hold that office.[270]

In 1979 Franklin A. Thomas was appointed to fill the vacancy left by the resignation of McGeorge Bundy from the presidency of the Ford Foundation.[271] Admitted to the New York State Bar in 1964, he was appointed Assistant United States Attorney for the Southern District of New York in that very year and one year later, Deputy Police Commissioner of New York City in charge of legal matters. In 1967 he became Chief Executive Officer of the Bedford-Stuyvesant Restoration Corporation, and he served with great effectiveness in that capacity until 1977. Thomas is a member of the Board of Trustees of Columbia University and of the boards of directors of such leading national business corporations as Citicorp/Citibank, CBS, Inc., Aluminum Company of America, and Cummins Engine.[272]

Following his admission to the New York Bar in 1949, Samuel Riley Pierce, Jr. began his varied legal career as Assistant District Attorney for the County of New York and, after four years, became Assistant United States Attorney for the Southern District of New York. He went on to be the first black to serve as Assistant to the Undersecretary of Labor, and two years later became Associate Counsel of the Judiciary Subcommittee on Antitrust in the United States House of Representatives. He then practiced law in a prominent white law firm, served for two years as Judge of the New York Court of General Sessions but was not elected, and in 1970

268. Burke, *Civil Rights*, p. 117.
269. *Who's Who in America 1980–81*, vol. 2, pp. 2571–72; Burke, *Civil Rights*, pp. 95–96.
270. Burke, *Civil Rights*, pp. 51–52.
271. *The Afro-American*, week of February 6–10, 1979.
272. *Who's Who in America 1980–81*, vol. 2, p. 3276.

became General Counsel to the United States Treasury Department in Washington, D.C. He has served on a large number of government boards and commissions and since 1964 has become a member of the boards of directors of leading national concerns, including Prudential Insurance Company, U.S. Industries, Inc., International Paper Company, General Electric Company, First National Boston Corporation, and First National Bank of Boston. His courtroom ability and experience are attested to by his election as a Fellow of the American College of Trial Lawyers. On December 22, 1980, President Reagan announced Pierce's appointment as Secretary of Housing and Urban Development (HUD).[273]

A 1962 *cum laude* graduate of the University of Michigan Law School, Amalya Lyle Kearse started her law practice that year as an associate in one of New York's largest law firms. When she became a partner in 1969, she was hailed as the first black and the first female partner in any of New York City's two dozen large law firms.[274] In 1979 she was the first woman elected a Fellow of the American College of Trial Lawyers; and on June 21, 1979, she became the first woman and the second black to be appointed a judge of the United States Court of Appeals for the Second Circuit. Since her appointment, she has been elected a member of the Council of the American Law Institute, the third black and the second woman to serve on that prestigious body.

More than half a century since Thomas Dyett observed that the general practice of the law could best be conducted within the structure of a firm, a trend in that direction now appears to be developing among black lawyers. One example, discussed in the October 1981 issue of *The American Lawyer*, is the young minority law firm of Lake, Bogan, Lenoir, Thompson and Jones, a five-partner, all-black firm that is reported to be moving its quarters to midtown Manhattan in order to accommodate the addition of three associates. Although best known for its work in civil-rights, criminal, and plaintiffs' personal injury cases, according to the article the firm is branching out into other fields, particularly corporate practice.[275]

As early as 1940, E. Franklin Frazier found that New York had the highest concentration of black professionals of any city in the country.[276] This remains so. However, a 1979 study of the city's twenty-three largest law firms reported that black lawyers constituted only 1.3 percent of their total number of lawyers,[277] compared with the 1.4 percent arrived at in our study in 1980 of the New York City firms with ninety or more lawyers.

273. *New York Times,* November 23, 1980, p. A-12; *Who's Who in America 1980–81,* vol. 2, pp. 2635–36.

274. *Who's Who in America 1980–81,* vol. 2, p. 1791.

275. *The American Lawyer,* October 1981, p. 16.

276. Frazier, *The Negro in the United States,* p. 262.

277. *National Law Journal,* July 2, 1979, p. 15.

The best estimate of Hope R. Stevens and the other black lawyers whom he consulted, including officials of black bar associations, is that there are nine hundred black lawyers practicing in New York City. (There are three black lawyers' associations in this city—Bedford-Stuyvesant, Harlem, and Queens, the name of each ending with the words "Lawyers Association.")

In the 1980 study of large and medium-size law firms, Philadelphia emerged with a higher percentage of black partners and associates than New York City, as seen in the following chart. In the comparison with other cities, New York's percentage of blacks in its large firms is low (see Tables 13 and 14).

New York City has 39,491 lawyers according to the office of the State Court Administrator in Albany, approximately double the next largest number in the country (Chicago). With approximately 900 black lawyers in the city, blacks would appear to constitute 2.2 percent of the lawyers in the five boroughs of New York City.

Looking at the judiciary in New York City in 1981, we find that of New York's 481 judges (state, local, and federal), 53 (11%) are black. The

| Large Firms* | Total Lawyers | Black Lawyers | Total Partners | Black Partners | Total Associates | Black Associates |
|---|---|---|---|---|---|---|
| New York | 3,831 | 56 (1.5%) | 1,267 | 1 (0.1%) | 2,564 | 55 (2.1%) |
| Philadelphia | 1,094 | 26 (2.4%) | 531 | 4 (0.8%) | 563 | 22 (3.9%) |
| Medium-size Firms* | | | | | | |
| New York | 4,280 | 40 (0.9%) | 1,565 | 3 (0.2%) | 2,715 | 37 (1.4%) |
| Philadelphia | 550 | 6 (1.1%) | 288 | 1 (0.3%) | 262 | 5 (1.9%)[278] |

*According to the 1980 survey conducted by the author.

| | New York | Philadelphia |
|---|---|---|
| State & Local Judges | 442 | 110 |
| Black Judges | 47 (10.6%) | 21 (19.1%) |
| U.S. Court of Appeals & District Judges | 39 | 20 |
| Black Judges | 6 (15.4%) | 3 (10.5%) |
| Total Judges | 481 | 130 |
| Total Black Judges | 53 (11.0%) | 24 (18.5%)[279] |

Federal judges as of April 1982, 527 F. IX–X, X–XI; State and local judges as of November 1981.

278. For detailed statistics on black and white lawyers in all cities surveyed, see Appendices 13 and 14.

279. For detailed statistics on black and white judges in all cities surveyed, see Appendix 12.

total percentage of black judges in New York is lower than in six of the cities studied—Atlanta, Boston, Cleveland, Detroit, Philadelphia, and Washington, D.C. (see Table 15). The chart on the preceding page gives the comparisons between Philadelphia and New York City.

One should consider, in light of the two charts above, that blacks in 1980 comprised 21 percent of the total population of New York City. For blacks on law school faculties, see Appendix 18.

# Pittsburgh

The earliest known black members of the bar of Pittsburgh, Pennsylvania, were J. Welford Holmes, a native of that city, and William M. Randolph, who came there from New York City and eventually became Pittsburgh's first black assistant city solicitor. Both were admitted to the bar on December 19, 1891.[280] Two other black lawyers in the nineteenth century, and a third right after the turn of the century, were Walter Billows, admitted to the bar on September 17, 1892; William H. Stanton, admitted September 14, 1895; and Frank R. Stewart, admitted September 4, 1902. All five were active and respected practitioners, Stanton being a particularly celebrated and successful trial lawyer, principally in criminal defense work.[281]

Especially noteworthy is the career of Robert L. Vann, a graduate of the University of Pittsburgh Law School who was admitted to the bar on December 18, 1909. The next year he purchased and undertook the operation of the *Pittsburgh Courier,* one of the most widely read black newspapers in the United States, with branches in other leading cities. He also continued to practice law and in 1917 became an assistant city solicitor. In 1924 he was selected as an alternate delegate-at-large to the Republican National Convention and was Publicity Director for Calvin Coolidge's presidential campaign. In 1935 he was appointed to the Committee to Revise the Pennsylvania Constitution. After the Great Depression he switched his allegiance to the Democrats, and President Franklin D. Roosevelt then (1933) appointed him a special assistant to the Attorney General of the United States.[282]

Other early members of the bar included P. J. Clyde Randall, who came from California and was admitted on motion in 1918, and George H. White, admitted in 1919.

Richard F. Jones, who graduated from the University of Pittsburgh

---

280. Official Records of Admission to the Bar, Court of Common Pleas, Allegheny County.

281. Information supplied by a group of Pittsburgh senior lawyers and judges.

282. Ibid.

Law School at the head of his class and became the first black to be inducted into the Order of the Coif in Pittsburgh, was admitted to the Pittsburgh Bar in 1923. Jones practiced law for fifty-one years, first with Homer S. Brown and then with Henry R. Smith, Jr., two black lawyers who left practice to accept judgeships. Judge Cecil F. Poole, a black judge of the United States Court of Appeals for the Ninth Circuit, who was reared in Pittsburgh, cites with pride the fact that his first two years at the bar (1940–42) were spent as an associate in the law firm of Brown and Jones, and particularly that Richard Jones was his preceptor. For eleven years Jones had the distinction of being the first black to serve as an officer of the Pittsburgh Board of Public Education. By then a highly respected member of the Pittsburgh Bar, in 1963 Jones became Chief Counsel of the Allegheny County Sanitary Authority, a post he held until his retirement from active practice in 1974.[283]

During the period when Homer S. Brown was practicing in the firm of Brown and Jones, he served for fifteen years (1935–50) in the State House of Representatives, where he was one of the most influential and respected persons in that chamber. In 1938 he was the first black elected to the Pittsburgh Board of Public Education. Elected in 1950 to the County Court of Allegheny County, he became the first black judge in Pittsburgh; and when he was elevated to the Court of Common Pleas of Allegheny County, he became the first black to occupy a seat on that bench.[284]

Between 1925 and 1930, Thomas E. Barton, Theron B. Hamilton, and Joseph Givens were all admitted to the bar. Barton, an able lawyer, was the main prop of the City Solicitor's Office for many years, serving under four mayors, and became the second black on the Board of Public Education, succeeding Homer S. Brown. Hamilton, with whom Barton was associated, became Special Assistant to the Attorney General of the United States, replacing Robert L. Vann. Givens served as Deputy Attorney General of Pennsylvania after having been an assistant city solicitor.

More recently, Everett E. Utterback, who was the first black to captain a varsity team (track) at the University of Pittsburgh, embarked upon a series of "firsts" for black lawyers in Pittsburgh. In 1953 he became the first black to serve as General Counsel to the Housing Authority; in 1955 he became the first Pittsburgh black admitted to practice before the United States Supreme Court; in 1966 he was appointed the first black trustee of the University of Pittsburgh and today he is its only black emeritus trustee.[285]

On April 7, 1978, Paul A. Simmons was appointed the first black judge

283. Ibid.
284. Ibid.
285. Ibid.

in the United States District Court for the Western District of Pennsylvania, which sits in Pittsburgh. At the time of his appointment he was a judge of the Court of Common Pleas of Washington County, where he had served for five years as the first black Orphans' Court Division Judge in the Commonwealth, having been Presiding Judge. After initial appointment, he was nominated for election by both the Democratic and the Republican parties. He previously had been a widely known trial and appellate practitioner in Washington County, during which time he had served as a member of the Washington County Redevelopment Authority, the Pennsylvania Human Relations Commission, and other government bodies.[286]

Justin M. Johnson practiced in Pittsburgh from the time of his graduation from the University of Chicago Law School in 1962. He immediately joined the partnership consisting of his father Oliver L. Johnson, who had been the first black prosecuting assistant district attorney in Allegheny County, and his brother Livingstone M. Johnson, who was one of two blacks (Harold Randolph, not of Pittsburgh, having been the other) to serve on the Disciplinary Board of the Supreme Court of Pennsylvania, and who was appointed in 1973 to the Court of Common Pleas, where he remained until elected in November 1975 to a full ten-year term. Two years later Justin Johnson became a partner in one of Pittsburgh's leading white law firms, whose fifty-three lawyers included a former justice of the Supreme Court of Pennsylvania (now deceased) and a former mayor of Pittsburgh and former deputy attorney general of the United States. His practice was a varied one, consisting primarily of trial work and corporate representation. He has served as a member for twelve years, six of them as Vice-Chairman, of the Pennsylvania Board of Law Examiners, and until his appointment in 1980 as Judge of the Superior Court of Pennsylvania he served on the Pennsylvania Crime Commission. Johnson was the second black judge to be appointed to the Superior Court; the first, Theodore O. Spaulding, died in 1974 while still on the court.[287]

Several other black lawyers have had an impact in Pittsburgh, though only for a portion of their careers. One of them is Judge Cecil F. Poole, mentioned above, who after his two years of practice in Pittsburgh left that city for brief government service in Washington, D.C., and subsequently a legal and judicial career of distinction in San Francisco[288] (see San Francisco section). Derrick A. Bell, Jr., a native of Pittsburgh and a graduate of the University of Pittsburgh Law School, held positions with the Depart-

286. Ibid.
287. Ibid.
288. Groves, *Opportunities for Negroes in the Law; Who's Who in America 1980–81*, vol. 2, p. 2660.

ment of Health, Education, and Welfare in Washington, D.C., served as director of the California Western Center on Law and Poverty, and taught law at the University of Southern California, before joining the Harvard Law School faculty in 1969.[289] In 1981 he became Dean of the University of Oregon Law School. (See section on Black Law Teachers in Chapter 10, pp. 234ff.)

Ronald Ross Davenport, a Temple Law School graduate who began his career practicing with two outstanding black firms in succession in his native city of Philadelphia, came to Duquesne University School of Law as an assistant professor in 1963, and within seven years rose to full professor (1967) and then Dean (1970) of the school. He is also Chairman and Chief Executive Officer of the Sheridan Broadcasting Company, and from 1973 to 1976 was a member of the Pennsylvania Crime Commission. Currently, he is active on boards involving business and community interests.[290]

Other outstanding black attorneys in Pittsburgh include K. Leroy Irvis, the only black to serve as Speaker, Majority Leader, and Minority Leader of the State House of Representatives; Paul F. Jones, the first black city councilman and worker's compensation referee; Henry R. Smith, Jr., a judge on the Court of Common Pleas of Allegheny County who is the only black serving on the Criminal Procedural Rules Committee of the Pennsylvania Supreme Court; J. Warren Watson, the second black judge elected in Allegheny County and the only black judge presently on the Orphans' Court Division of the Common Pleas Court in the Commonwealth of Pennsylvania, having also been the first black judge assigned to that division in Allegheny County.[291] Watson presently sits as the only black on the State Judicial Inquiry and Review Board, and in 1969 he was the first black in the United States to be honored as Man of the Year by the Disabled American Veterans. Included among the outstanding trial attorneys in both federal and state court are Wendell G. Freeland, a partner of Richard F. Jones until the latter's retirement, and Byrd R. Brown, the son of the late Judge Homer S. Brown and one of the leading trial attorneys in both civil and criminal law for many years. He won high praise for his activities as President of the Pittsburgh branch of the NAACP during the hectic decade of the 1960s. Brown is the senior partner of the largest firm of black lawyers in Western Pennsylvania, Brown and Smith; the firm has five attorneys including Everett Utterback, of Counsel.[292]

289. Kenneth L. Collins, "Attorneys Around the Country, 'Young, Gifted, and Black,' " *Black Law Journal,* vol. 1, no. 1 (1971), p. 40.

290. Ibid., pp. 38–39.

291. Information supplied by group of Pittsburgh senior lawyers and judges.

292. Ibid.

Thomas A. Harper is presently a Common Pleas Court judge and served as the first black member of the Braddock, Pennsylvania, Board of Education. Eric Springer is nationally recognized as an expert in health law and sits on the boards of one of the largest hospitals in the city and one of the major utility corporations in the Pittsburgh area.[293]

Black women also have played a role in Pittsburgh's legal history. The first black female to be appointed a member of the Pennsylvania Public Utility Commission in 1980 was Linda Taliaferro. Verdell Dean was appointed by the Governor to the Pennsylvania Board of Probation and Parole, and Doris A. Smith is solicitor to the Allegheny County Controller and a member of the Pennsylvania Human Relations Commission.[294]

Black attorneys are thus represented in many areas of the legal profession in Pittsburgh. More than half of them work for government or government-funded agencies, many are on the payrolls of corporations, and a large number still are sole practitioners or in practice with other blacks. In Pittsburgh, as in so many other cities, blacks have still not made significant inroads into the white law firms. At the time of our survey (1980), there were but one black partner and two black associates in Pittsburgh's large firms, and none was reported in the medium-size firms, as reflected in the following chart:

| Large Firms* | Total Lawyers | Black Lawyers | Total Partners | Black Partners | Total Associates | Black Associates |
|---|---|---|---|---|---|---|
| Pittsburgh | 497 | 3 (0.6%) | 236 | 1 (0.4%) | 261 | 2* (0.8%) |
| Philadelphia | 1,094 | 26 (2.4%) | 531 | 4 (0.8%) | 563 | 22 (3.9%) |
| Medium-size Firms* | | | | | | |
| Pittsburgh | 145 | 0 | 62 | 0* | 83 | 0* |
| Philadelphia | 550 | 6 (1.0%) | 228 | 1 (0.3%) | 262 | 5 (1.9%)[295] |

*According to the 1980 survey conducted by the author. Since the 1980 survey, the large firms have added two black associates, and the medium firms one black partner and one associate.

Although this picture of the firms is sobering, senior black lawyers and judges in Pittsburgh emphasize that the black legal community has multiplied to more than seven times the number in 1970, when there were only fifteen black lawyers and three black judges then active in the city, all of them male. Blacks were then only slightly more than one-half of 1 percent of the total 2,800 lawyers in Allegheny County.

In April 1981, little more than a decade later, the Homer S. Brown Law

293. Ibid.
294. Ibid.
295. For detailed statistics on black and white lawyers in all cities surveyed, see Appendices 13 and 14.

Association (the local black attorneys' association) counted 110 black lawyers in the county, 24 of them female. As a group they represent 2.4
percent of the 4,500 registered attorneys for the area (4,056 in the Martindale-Hubbell data bank). This is a significant increase but still a small
percentage in a county where blacks constitute roughly 10.5 percent of the
population.[296] The population of Pittsburgh is 24.0 percent black.

The number of black common pleas judges in Pittsburgh in 1981 is a
fairer representation of the black population: four out of thirty-nine. On
the federal district court bench, the one black district judge represents 14.3
percent of the seven district judges in that city. Overall, as shown in the
following chart and in Table 15, blacks have a 10.3 percent representation
in the judiciary in Pittsburgh, lower than Philadelphia's 18.5 percent.
There are also two black magistrates in Pittsburgh.

For blacks on law school faculties, see Appendix 18.

|  | Pittsburgh | Philadelphia |
|---|---|---|
| State & Local Judges | 49 | 110 |
| Black Judges | 5 (10.2%) | 21 (19.1%) |
| U.S. Court of Appeals | | |
| & District Judges | 9 | 20 |
| Black Judges | 1 (11.1%) | 3 (15.0%) |
| Total Judges | 58 | 130 |
| Total Black Judges | 6 (10.3%) | 24 (18.5%)[297] |

Federal judges as of April 1982, 527 F. Supp. X–XI; State and local judges as of November
1981.

# Richmond

George Lewis Ruffin, who is noted as the first black to graduate from an
American law school (Harvard) and later to become the first judge appointed in the North, was born in Richmond, Virginia. His career unfolded
in Boston, however, since his family brought him to that city in 1853
because of the Virginia law forbidding the teaching of reading and writing
to blacks. There appeared to be no future for Ruffin in his hometown.[298]
(See the section on Boston.)

296. "No Room at the Top for Black Lawyers," *Pittsburgh Post-Gazette*, June 22, 1981.
297. For detailed statistics on black and white judges in all cities surveyed, including
U.S. bankruptcy judges and magistrates, see Appendix 12.
298. Leonard, *Black Lawyers*, pp. 49, 285.

On September 13, 1854, John Mercer Langston, a black Richmond lawyer, was admitted to the bar of the Supreme Court of the United States on motion of James A. Garfield, later President of the United States; during the Reconstruction period he was an active practitioner.[299] Langston founded the Howard University Law School in 1869 and was its dean from 1869 to 1876.[300] In 1877 he became Minister-Resident and Consul General of the United States to the government of Haiti, and in 1888 he became the first black man elected to Congress from the state of Virginia.[301]

However, it was not until 1887 that Virginia's black native sons could be admitted to the bar in their own state. On November 30, 1887, Giles B. Jackson, born a slave, became the first black man to be admitted to the practice of law in Virginia. A conservative Republican, Jackson wrote the charters for the first black-owned insurance company and the first black-owned bank in the state of Virginia. In 1901, at the suggestion of Booker T. Washington, Jackson took up the legal fight against Jim Crow laws in Virginia. By 1930, when Jackson had become an acknowledged leader in black fraternal, political, financial, and publishing circles, Richmond was considered an important center of black business activity in the country.[302]

Another of Richmond's earliest black lawyers was Thomas H. Hewing, Sr., who came to the bar in 1900. He was active in civil rights and had a large Richmond clientele for many years. Also involved in civil-rights cases at the beginning of the century was Joseph R. Pollen.[303]

One Richmond lawyer who became a national figure in the representation of black interests is Spottswood William Robinson, III. Starting his career as a member of the faculty of the Howard University Law School, Robinson was admitted to the Virginia Bar in 1943 and practiced law in Richmond with the late Martin H. Martin and Oliver W. Hill, both of whom are discussed below. He continued his teaching, and from 1960 to 1963 he was Dean of Howard Law School. During this period he also served as a member of the United States Commission on Civil Rights. In his practice he represented substantial black business, insurance, and banking clients, but in later years the major portion of his court cases was in the civil rights area. He played a key role in the Prince Edward County (Virginia) school case, one of the five cases decided by the Supreme Court involving the constitutionality of state laws permitting or requiring racial segregation in public schools *(Brown v. Board of Education)*. In 1964 Robinson became the first black federal judge in the District of Columbia, having

299. Styles, *Negroes and the Law,* p. 15.
300. Leonard, *Black Lawyers,* p. 2; Bergman, *The Negro in America,* p. 135.
301. Styles, *Negroes and the Law,* p. 120.
302. *Afro* (magazine section), week of September 18–22, 1973, p. 14.
303. Conversation with Oliver W. Hill.

been nominated by President John F. Kennedy to the United States District Court for the District of Columbia. In 1966 he was elevated to the United States Court of Appeals of the District of Columbia by appointment of President Lyndon B. Johnson. In 1981 he became Chief Judge of that court.[304]

Oliver W. Hill, a black native of Richmond who has conducted his legal career in both Richmond and Washington, has been involved in civil rights activities since the 1930s in Virginia, where he instituted a large number of cases involving the equalization of public school facilities. He was also one of active counsel in *Brown v. Board of Education.* While practicing in Richmond he was a member of the Richmond City Council and of the first President's Committee on Government Contracts Compliance. In 1959 he was selected Lawyer of the Year by the National Bar Association.[305] From 1961 to 1966 Hill served in Washington, D.C., as Assistant to the Assistant Secretary-Commissioner of the Federal Housing Administration, Department of Housing and Urban Development.[306]

Martin H. Martin, who was a partner in the firm of Hill, Martin and Robinson, was formerly an attorney for the United States Department of Justice. He began practice in Richmond in 1943 and was especially active in railroad segregation cases.

One of Oliver Hill's current law partners is Samuel W. Tucker, who at the age of fourteen challenged the Jim Crow laws on an interurban train. This set the pattern for future behavior. He was determined to test and change the law. He became a noted lawyer and in 1974 won the Charles Hamilton Houston Award from the Harvard Law School for his outstanding service for civil rights.[307] Henry Morrison, III, another partner in Hill's firm, has also conducted several landmark cases in the area of affirmative action.

Henry L. Marsh, III, an active practitioner who was one of Hill's partners, is now Mayor of the City of Richmond. He came to the bar in 1961 after receiving his undergraduate degree at Virginia Union University and his law degree at Howard University.[308]

While today there are black mayors in half a dozen cities in Virginia, four blacks in the House of Delegates, and one black in the State Senate,[309] the number of black judges in the state is still very small.

304. *Who's Who in America 1980–81,* vol. 1, p. 420.

305. *Who's Who Among Black Americans 1977–78,* p. 2800.

306. Groves, *Opportunities for Negroes in the Law.*

307. Information obtained from Oliver W. Hill.

308. Letter from R. Harvey Chappell, Jr., January 29, 1981; *Martindale-Hubbell 1981,* vol. 7, p. 159.

309. Megan Rosenfeld, "A Soft-spoken Judge at the Center of Controversy," *Washington Post,* July 20, 1980, p. F-2.

Of the fifteen cities surveyed, Richmond and Minneapolis are the only two in which no federal judge sits. Of Richmond's twenty-four state and local court judges, two are black. When appointed to the Virginia circuit court sitting in Richmond in 1974, James Edward Sheffield became the first black to be appointed to any court of record in Virginia. Sheffield continues to occupy that position[310] and is still the only black circuit court judge in Virginia.[311] After starting his career in the Civil Division of the Department of Justice under Attorney General Robert Kennedy's Honor Program, he spent two years as a full-time assistant professor of law and two years as an adjunct professor of law at Howard Law School. Upon receiving his first teaching appointment, he opened a part-time law office in Richmond, and upon leaving Howard became a full-time sole practitioner, continuing until his appointment to the bench.

In April 1980 President Jimmy Carter nominated Judge Sheffield to the United States District Court for the Eastern District of Virginia, the first black to be so nominated. After a very thorough investigation, the Standing Committee on Federal Judiciary of the American Bar Association reported to the Senate Judiciary Committee that it unanimously found him to be qualified for the post. However, Virginia's Senator Harry F. Byrd, Jr. opposed the nomination on the ground that Sheffield had not been among those proposed by one of the two panels Byrd himself had appointed to make such proposals and was "not the best qualified."[312] The panels had nominated twelve white men. Subsequent charges of income tax violations against him were vigorously denied by Sheffield, who asked that his confirmation hearings before the Senate Judiciary Committee be postponed until he could review FBI and Department of Justice files.[313] The hearings were not rescheduled, and the nomination expired.

The other black judge in Richmond is Willard H. Douglas, Jr., who began serving on the Virginia Juvenile and Domestic Relations District Court on February 1, 1974. He previously had been staff attorney to the United States Commission on Civil Rights (1962–65), had engaged in the private practice of law (1965–69), and had been Assistant Commonwealth's Attorney for Richmond (1969–74).[314]

As the following chart and Table 15 show, the percentage representation of black judges on state and local courts in Philadelphia is more than

310. Donald E. Baker and Glenn Frankel, "A Litany of Mistakes," *Washington Post,* September 21, 1980, p. A-1.

311. Rosenfeld, "A Soft-spoken Judge," p. F-2.

312. Ruth Marcus, "Black Nominee for Bench Runs into New Problems," *National Law Journal,* September 8, 1980, p. 24.

313. Glenn Frankel, "Judge Says He Won't Withdraw as U.S. Nominee," *Washington Post,* September 10, 1980, p. C-1; Marcus, "Black Nominee," p. 3.

314. Reincke and Lichterman, *The American Bench,* 2nd ed., p. 1970.

double that of Richmond. This is apart from the fact that in Philadelphia three of the judges are on appellate courts, including one on the State Supreme Court, and sixteen are on the court of general jurisdiction, whereas in Richmond, one is on a court of general jurisdiction and one on a court of limited jurisdiction. While Richmond has had no black federal judge sit in that city (though, as indicated above, Chief Judge Spottswood Robinson was a Richmond lawyer at the time of his appointments to the U.S. district court and the court of appeals of the District of Columbia), Philadelphia has three (10.34%), one of whom is on the United States Court of Appeals for the Third Circuit.

In the survey of Richmond law firms, there were no black partners in either the large or the medium-size firms. Among associates, a higher percentage of blacks was found in Richmond's medium-size firms than in its large firms. The following chart shows the comparison between Richmond and Philadelphia. In the matter of black partners in large firms, Richmond has none and Philadelphia has four, which, however, constitute

|  | Richmond | Philadelphia |
|---|---|---|
| State & Local Judges | 24 | 110 |
| Black Judges | 2 (8.3%)[315] | 21 (19.1%) |
| U.S. Court of Appeals & District Judges | 3 | 20 |
| Black Judges | 0 | 3 (15.0%) |
| Total Judges | 27 | 130 |
| Total Black Judges | 2 (7.4%) | 24 (18.5%)[316] |

Federal judges as of April 1982, 527 F. Supp. XII–XIII, X–XI; State and local judges as of November 1981.

| Large Firms* | Total Lawyers | Black Lawyers | Total Partners | Black Partners | Total Associates | Black Associates |
|---|---|---|---|---|---|---|
| Richmond | 276 | 3 (1.0%) | 134 | 0 | 142 | 3 (2.1%) |
| Philadelphia | 1,094 | 26 (2.4%) | 531 | 4 (0.8%) | 563 | 22 (3.9%) |
| Medium-size Firms* | | | | | | |
| Richmond | 177 | 1 (0.56%) | 96 | 0 | 81 | 1 (1.2%) |
| Philadelphia | 550 | 6 (1.1%) | 288 | 1 (0.3%) | 262 | 5 (1.9%)[317] |

*According to the 1980 survey conducted by the author.

315. Does not include two "substitute" judges.

316. For detailed statistics on black and white judges in all cities surveyed, including U.S. bankruptcy judges and magistrates, see Appendix 12.

317. For detailed statistics on black and white lawyers in all cities surveyed, see Appendices 13 and 14.

less than one percent of the total partners; but there is a larger difference in the comparative percentages of black associates. In medium-size firms, the two cities are closer to each other in the percentages, both as to partners and as to associates.

Looking back over the past three decades of his career, Oliver Hill believes that the situation for blacks in the law in Richmond has improved steadily, especially since the desegregation decision of *Brown v. Board of Education* (1954) and the passage of civil rights legislation in the 1960s. For one thing, blacks, like most Richmond lawyers, now are able to train at one of the in-state law schools—the University of Virginia, College of William and Mary, Washington & Lee, or the University of Richmond. Hill ascribes the small representation of blacks in the law firms as much to slow change in custom and the short supply of black lawyers as to prejudice. In fact, the number of black lawyers in Richmond is very small, the most liberal estimate being 70 to 75, while there is a total of 1,790 lawyers in the Martindale-Hubbell data bank, which of course is fewer than the actual number. Even taking the higher estimate of black lawyers and the Martindale-Hubbell data bank figure, blacks comprise only 2.7 percent of the lawyers in Richmond today. In 1980 blacks comprised 50.7 percent of the total population of Richmond (see Table 16). For blacks on law school faculties, see Appendix 18.

# San Francisco

Until World War II there were fewer than 5,000 blacks in San Francisco, and they were "lost" among the city's 600,000 residents. In the early 1940s the situation changed dramatically; about 250,000 blacks were drawn to San Francisco, Seattle, and Portland as war workers. In San Francisco many blacks were then crowded into an area evacuated by Japanese in the aftermath of Pearl Harbor. Employers tried to restrict blacks to unskilled and service occupations, and most blacks were employed in shipbuilding and longshoreman's work. Their positions were upgraded as the war went on, however, both because of the manpower shortage and because of the beginning of state action for fair employment practices, forerunner to the creation of a Fair Employment Practice Commission by San Francisco in 1958 and by the state of California in 1959.[318]

In this context it is not surprising that there were only a few outstanding black lawyers in San Francisco's early days; it is remarkable that any could be found at all. Yet in the early 1900s a young black graduate of the University of California Law School named Leonard Richardson suc-

318. Frazier, *The Negro in the United States*, pp. 269–71.

ceeded, in his first case after being admitted to practice, in removing segregated seating in an Oakland movie house.[319] Oscar Hudson, admitted to practice law in 1911 by the Appellate Court of the First District of California, subsequently became the Consul for Liberia at the port of San Francisco. He was the first and only black in San Francisco of that era to hold a membership in any bar association in the state of California.[320] For several decades following that milestone, scarcely a handful of black lawyers appeared in that city. Judge Cecil Poole recalls that when he came to the San Francisco Bar in 1946, there were only four or five other black lawyers in the city. According to an article published in 1973, the Attorney General's Office and the federal courts in San Francisco had no blacks on their respective staffs; the Attorney General's Office had employed only one black lawyer since 1953, and he took the job because there were no other offers despite the fact that he was third in his class and editor of the law review at the University of California. The article goes on to say that in 1973 a few black lawyers were working for all-white firms and were commonly referred to as "house lawyers," meaning that white corporations used them for show purposes to give the appearance of a liberal hiring policy toward minorities. The article states that in San Francisco proper, where blacks constituted 12 percent of the population in 1973, there were fewer than ten black lawyers in private practice.[321] Judge Cecil Poole and other knowledgeable jurists and lawyers in the area are able to name at least twenty-three black lawyers who were practicing in San Francisco at the time, although not all in private practice.

Blacks first entered the judiciary in San Francisco in 1958, when John Bussey was appointed to the Municipal Court, where he served until 1962. He was then appointed to the Superior Court, where he sat until his death in 1969. Prior to ascending the bench, he was a highly regarded lawyer and was also well known for the bar review course he taught to law school graduates.

The second black judge in San Francisco was Joseph P. Kennedy, who was appointed to the Municipal Court in 1963. In 1972 he ran successfully for election to the Superior Court, where he served from 1973 until his death in 1979. Following Judge Kennedy came Raymond J. Reynolds, who, after considerable service as Deputy City Attorney, in 1969 was appointed a judge on the Municipal Court, serving until his retirement in 1979.

In 1977 Judge Wiley W. Manuel of the Superior Court of Alameda County was elevated to the California Supreme Court, thus becoming the

319. Beasley, *Negro Trail Blazers*, p. 190.
320. Ibid., p. 194.
321. Julius Debro, "Black Lawyers in the Bay Area and the Black Community," *Journal of Social and Behavioral Sciences*, vol. 19, nos. 3–4 (Spring–Fall 1973), pp. 20–21.

first black justice on that court in the state's history. In the November 1978 election he was confirmed for a twelve-year term on a "yes" or "no" retention ballot. Manuel had been Order of the Coif and Editor-in-Chief of the law journal at Hastings College of Law. He spent almost twenty-five years in the California Attorney General's Office before his appointment to the court in 1977. He died on January 5, 1981.[322]

In July 1981 Allen E. Broussard was confirmed as a justice of the Supreme Court of California, becoming the second black to have served on that court. He had been appointed to the Oakland Municipal Court in 1964 and then to the Alameda Superior Court in 1975, his entire practice and judicial service having been in Oakland, just across the San Francisco Bay. However, his chambers are now in San Francisco.

Cecil F. Poole was born in Birmingham, Alabama, and reared in Pittsburgh, Pennsylvania, where he practiced during his first two years at the bar (1940–42). After a brief period with the National Labor Relations Board and in the United States Air Force as a trial judge advocate and second lieutenant, he came to San Francisco in 1946 for a year and a half of service in the Regional Office of Price Administration and remained there, becoming one of the city's outstanding black lawyers and judges. He served in the District Attorney's Office for nine years, four as Assistant District Attorney and five as Assistant District Attorney Chief of the Superior Court. After that, he was United States Attorney for the Northern District of California for almost nine years. On leaving that office in 1970, he accepted a post as Regents Professor of Law at the University of California School of Law, Boalt Hall, at Berkeley, but soon concluded that he preferred the practice of law and joined a law firm in San Francisco. Upon his appointment in 1976, he became the first black judge on the United States District Court for the Northern District of California, and in 1979 the second black judge to be appointed to the United States Court of Appeals for the Ninth Circuit (the first—Jerome Farris of Seattle—having been appointed approximately two months before).[323]

On July 9, 1980, Thelton E. Henderson was the second black judge to be appointed to the United States District Court for the Northern District of California. Starting his career in 1962 as an attorney in the Civil Rights Division of the United States Department of Justice in Washington, where he remained for a little over a year, he practiced law for two years and then became Directing Attorney of the East Bayshore Neighborhood Legal Center, an organization providing civil representation for low-income individuals. After approximately two years, he left to become Assistant Dean of the Stanford Law School, and after eight years in that post

322. *National Bar Bulletin*, vol. 9, no. 6 (June 1977), p. 7.
323. *Who's Who in America 1980–81*, vol. 2, p. 2597.

resumed law practice as a partner in a three-lawyer firm until he left to ascend to the bench.

According to the 1981–82 statistics (see the following chart and Table 15), there are six black judges in San Francisco—two federal and four state and local, out of a total of eighty-four, which constitutes 7.1 percent. Only Columbus, Milwaukee, and Minneapolis have lower percentages of black judges than San Francisco.

Our 1980 survey of San Francisco's law firms found one black partner in its large firms and none in its medium-size firms. Its percentage of associates in both large and medium-size firms is higher, which may well be an indicator of future partnership status. San Francisco does not compare poorly with Philadelphia, which has a much larger black population and black lawyer population as well as a longer history of black involvement in the legal profession.

As elsewhere, black lawyers in San Francisco have not only looked to the white firms but also branched out into federal, state, and local govern-

|  | San Francisco | Philadelphia |
|---|---|---|
| State & Local Judges | 69 | 110 |
| Black Judges | 4 (5.8%) | 21 (19.1%) |
| U.S. Court of Appeals & District Judges | 15 | 20 |
| Black Judges | 2 (13.3%) | 3 (15.0%) |
| Total Judges | 84 | 130 |
| Total Black Judges | 6 (7.1%) | 24 (18.5%)[324] |

Federal judges as of April 1982, 527 F. Supp. XIX–XXI, X–XI; State and local judges as of November 1981.

| Large Firms* | Total Lawyers | Black Lawyers | Total Partners | Black Partners | Total Associates | Black Associates |
|---|---|---|---|---|---|---|
| San Francisco | 927 | 14 (1.5%) | 397 | 1 (0.2%)* | 520 | 13 (2.5%) |
| Philadelphia | 1,094 | 26 (2.4%) | 531 | 4 (0.8%) | 563 | 22 (3.9%) |
| Medium-size Firms* | | | | | | |
| San Francisco | 727 | 5 (0.6%) | 312 | 0* | 415 | 5 (1.2%) |
| Philadelphia | 550 | 6 (1.1%) | 288 | 1 (0.3%) | 262 | 5 (1.9%)[325] |

*According to the 1980 survey conducted by the author. Since then a second black partner was added to the large firms and one to the medium-size firms.

324. For detailed statistics on black and white judges in all cities surveyed, including U.S. bankruptcy judges and magistrates, see Appendix 12.

325. For detailed statistics on black and white lawyers in all cities surveyed, see Appendices 13 and 14.

ment posts. Especially significant, in addition to those already mentioned, are G. William Hunter, formerly Deputy District Attorney of San Francisco, who resigned as United States Attorney on September 30, 1981, to join an all-white law firm; Judith Ford, former Chief of the Consumer Fraud Unit of the San Francisco District Attorney's Office, who has been promoted to Regional Director of the Federal Trade Commission; Joseph B. Williams, Regional Administrator for the General Services Administration; and Alice Lytle, Secretary of the California State and Consumer Services Agency, the only black serving in the governor's office.

Particularly noteworthy is the election of Willie L. Brown, Jr. as the first black Speaker of the California State Assembly, one of the most powerful posts in the government of California. An able lawyer, Brown is in demand as one of the area's most entertaining and forceful speakers.

Another first of a different kind was achieved by Robert L. Harris, who, although only admitted to the bar in 1972, served as President of the National Bar Association in 1979–80. Harris was not only the first California lawyer to occupy the post but also the first west of the Mississippi. He is a member of the corporate law department of the Pacific Gas and Electric Company.

According to the records of the State Bar of California, there are 9,034 active practicing lawyers at the San Francisco Bar in 1981. Shelley E. Wheeler, President of the California Association of Black Lawyers and an assistant United States attorney in San Francisco, reports that the best estimate reached by her and associate officers of the California Association of Black Lawyers, after consulting other knowledgeable sources, is that there are approximately thirty black lawyers in San Francisco. Accordingly, it would appear that the black lawyers comprise a little more than three-tenths of one percent of the total lawyer population of the city. Wheeler points out that a similar estimate for the surrounding area, including the East Bay of the San Francisco Bay area would be approximately 150 black lawyers. Other black members of San Francisco's legal community have expressed the view that both these estimates are too low.

(Although the author is aware of the close relationships between the legal communities of San Francisco and of the Bay Area, this section is almost exclusively concerned with San Francisco. Such close relationships of contiguous communities are not unique in a number of the sixteen cities under consideration, and therefore in order to delineate the subject uniformly in all cities, the accounts are essentially restricted to the cities selected according to the criteria described in the introduction to this chapter.) For blacks on law school faculties, see Appendix 18.

# Washington, D.C. ─────────────────────────────

Before 1951, when a court suit was filed, black lawyers were barred from the law library in the federal courthouse in Washington, D.C.[326] For six more years blacks were excluded from the review courses offered prior to bar examinations, so that Howard Law School Librarian A. Mercer Daniel had to fill the void by tutoring small groups of students in his home.

The Bar Association of the District of Columbia (the only general bar association in Washington until the integrated, unified District of Columbia Bar came into being in 1972) was itself segregated until 1956. When Charles S. Rhyne (later President of the American Bar Association) was elected president of the association in 1955, after having promised to integrate it if he became president, he ruled at a membership meeting that a voice vote had approved his integration plan. A group of lawyers filed a court suit to stop the program, but no local federal judge would agree to hear the case. After a federal judge from Ohio, assigned to preside in the United States District Court for the District of Columbia, ordered a new membership vote, color discrimination finally was eliminated, and by November 1959, some 25 black lawyers had been admitted to join the 2,500 lawyers in the Bar Association of the District of Columbia.[327]

The Washington Bar Association, formed in 1925 by black lawyers, could find no restaurant or hotel in Washington willing to serve dinner to its six hundred conventioneers, so the convention was held instead in the Interior Department auditorium, where the principal speaker was the Attorney General of the United States. Even as late as 1959, the United States Attorney's Office had to hold a party at Bolling Air Force Base Officers' Club in order to accommodate three black prosecutors.[328]

Yet for a century prior to that, Washington was the magnet that drew many black students who aspired to become lawyers. The reason for this was the Howard University School of Law. Chartered by the federal government in 1869, Howard has been responsible for the education of a large portion of black lawyers who practice today throughout the United States, and virtually all of those who came to the bar before 1950 (see Introduction).

Among the earliest black pioneers in the legal profession in Washington was Richard Theodore Greener (1844–1922). Born in Philadelphia, Greener moved to Boston in 1849 and became in 1870 the first black to receive a degree from Harvard College. Following a series of academic

326. *U.S. ex rel. Robinson v. Bar Association of the District of Columbia,* 197 F.2d, 408 (D.C. Cir. 1952).

327. Eugene L. Meyers and Joseph D. Whitaker, "Blacks Moving into Key Posts," *Washington Post,* April 11, 1976, p. A-18.

328. Ibid.

positions, including that of Dean of Howard University Law School, he turned to politics and became an active campaigner for Republican candidates who sought black votes in the near-western and near-southern states. In July 1898 he accepted appointment as the first United States Consul to Vladivostok, where he remained until 1905.[329]

In 1872 Charlotte E. Ray became not only the first female graduate of the Howard Law School but also the first black female graduate of any law school in the country. She also was the first woman admitted to the District of Columbia Bar[330] and the first woman admitted to practice before the Supreme Court of the District of Columbia.[331] Ollie May Cooper, a 1921 Howard Law School graduate, was the first female black lawyer in the country to practice as a partner in an all-female law firm, a firm in the District.[332] When she died at the age of ninety-four, she was the oldest-known black woman lawyer in the country.

Prior to the late 1950s after *Brown v. Board of Education,* and the early 1960s when the civil-rights movement was gathering momentum, black lawyers in Washington, as in Philadelphia, were relegated primarily to criminal defense work, domestic relations cases, and a variety of small negligence, insurance, contract, and other petty actions. They had virtually no white clientele and were not represented in the white law firms.

From the ranks of those local black practitioners emerged half a dozen lawyers who have been, since the 1930s, at the forefront of the early and subsequent civil-rights litigation in behalf of blacks—George E. C. Hayes, James Madison Nabrit, Jr., Charles H. Houston, William B. Bryant, Frank D. Reeves, and Joseph C. Waddy.

The late George E. C. Hayes, a 1918 graduate of Howard Law School, was a highly respected figure in the legal life of Washington, having played a key role in the development of the civil rights battle in the courts. Like numerous black lawyers in the nation's capital, Hayes had a stint of government service when he was Chairman of the District of Columbia Public Utilities Commission from 1955 to 1962.[333]

Another towering figure in the history of the black lawyer in Washington is James Madison Nabrit, Jr. As far back as 1938 he was, with Charles H. Houston and George Hayes, one of the original architects of

329. Bergman, *The Negro in America,* p. 180. See also Allison Blakely, "Richard T. Greener and the 'Talented Tenth's' Dilemma," *Journal of Negro History,* vol. 59, no. 4 (October 1974), pp. 307–8.

330. Bergman, *The Negro in America,* p. 271; Styles, *Negroes and the Law,* p. 15.

331. Gilbert Ware, *From the Black Bar: A Cry for Equal Justice* (New York: G. P. Putnam's Sons, 1976), p. xxviii; Styles, *Negroes and the Law,* p. 15.

332. *National Bar Bulletin,* vol. 11, no. 2 (February, 1979), p. 6.

333. J. Clay Smith, Jr., "The First Recipients of the Charles Hamilton Houston Medallion of Merit," *Howard Law Journal,* vol. 20, no. 1 (1977), pp. 16–17.

civil-rights litigation as we know it today. Nabrit argued a portion of *Brown v. Board of Education* in the Supreme Court and also played a significant role in the modern development of the Howard University Law School, instituting the first course in civil rights in the late 1940s. Later he became Dean of Howard Law School and, after a few years, President of Howard University.[334]

Charles H. Houston, discussed more extensively in Chapter 10, was a local practitioner who became nationally eminent as a trial and appellate lawyer in the 1930s and 1940s, particularly in civil-rights cases. In 1935 he left the deanship of Howard Law School to direct the NAACP's legal campaign. G. Franklin Edwards pronounced him the most outstanding black lawyer of his time.[335] The late Associate Justice William O. Douglas said that Houston was one of the ten best lawyers ever to appear before the Supreme Court in Douglas's thirty-one years on that bench.[336]

Houston practiced for many years, until his untimely death in 1950, in the firm of Houston and Houston, founded in 1892 by his father, William LePré Houston. The oldest and most prestigious black law firm in Washington, Houston and Houston attracted a number of other civil-rights activists and outstanding black members of the legal profession.

One of them was Joseph C. Waddy. Graduating in 1939 from Howard Law School with the highest academic average in the class, Waddy immediately joined Houston and Houston as an associate, the firm name becoming Houston, Houston, Hastie and Waddy after he was made a partner. From 1954 to 1962 Waddy, by then a highly regarded practitioner, was a senior member of Houston, Waddy, Bryant and Gardner, which developed into Washington's most prestigious black law firm. In 1962 he was appointed an associate judge of the Domestic Relations Branch of the Municipal Court (now Superior Court) for the District of Columbia, and in 1967 became a judge of the United States District Court for the District of Columbia.[337]

Another of those who affiliated with Houston's firm was William B. Bryant. When Bryant graduated from Howard Law School in 1936 at the top of his class, the only job he could get was operating an elevator. From 1951 to 1954, as government posts began to open up for blacks, he served as Assistant United States Attorney for Washington, D.C. For the next eleven years Bryant practiced law in the firm of Houston, Bryant and

334. Ibid., pp. 15–16.

335. G. Franklin Edwards, *The Negro Professional Class* (Glencoe, Ill.: Free Press, 1959), p. 137. See also Geraldine R. Segal, *In Any Fight Some Fall* (Rockville, Md.: Mercury Press, 1975), for a biography of Charles H. Houston.

336. Letter from J. Clay Smith quoting a statement made by Justice William O. Douglas, *Washington Post*, January 29, 1980, p. 22.

337. *Washington Post*, April 12, 1976, p. A-21; Smith, "The First Recipients," p. 15.

Gardner,[338] maintaining an active involvement in civil-rights litigation. In 1960 he became the first black lawyer in Washington to be appointed to distribute the assets of a major estate—eight million dollars in cash and property. At that time it was still most unusual for a black lawyer to appear in a court case in which a substantial economic interest was involved.[339] In 1965 Bryant was appointed to the United States District Court for the District of Columbia,[340] and in 1977 became chief judge of that court, the first black to hold that office in any United States district court.[341]

Also involved in the continuing civil rights struggle, including presentation of the school desegregation cases before the Supreme Court of the United States (1953–55), was Charles T. Duncan. Duncan was admitted to the New York Bar in 1951 and practiced for three years as an associate in a leading large New York law firm. In 1953 he moved to Washington, formed a small law firm, and began teaching at the Howard Law School. In 1974 he returned to serve as its dean until 1977, having before that been principal Assistant United States Attorney for the District, General Counsel of the Equal Employment Opportunity Commission, and Corporation Counsel of the District. While Dean at Howard, he had been President of the District of Columbia Bar (1973–74) and had also been Chairman of the District of Columbia Judicial Nomination Commission and a member of the United States Commission on Executive, Legislative, and Judicial Salaries by appointment of the Chief Justice. After his deanship and professorship at Howard, he returned to the practice of law with a predominantly white law firm in Washington and continues to participate actively in the public sector.[342]

Frank Reeves's concern with civil rights for blacks eventually expressed itself in political involvements. While he was engaged in private practice, Reeves developed an interest in politics, and as early as 1948 he became active in the affairs of the Democratic Party. A member of the District of Columbia's delegation to the Democratic National Convention of 1960, he was one of the three persons selected to second John F. Kennedy's nomination for President. That year he was the first black to be elected a Democratic national committeeman from anywhere in the United States. In 1961 he was named Special Assistant to the President.[343]

High in the ranks of local black lawyers whose careers led to government posts is Patricia Roberts Harris, who, admitted to the bar in 1960, was

338. *Who's Who in America 1980–81*, vol. 1, p. 467.

339. Joseph D. Whitaker, "Judge Bryant Struggles to Reach His High Post," *Washington Post*, April 15, 1976, p. A-14.

340. *Who's Who in America 1980–81*, vol. 1, p. 467.

341. *National Bar Bulletin*, vol. 9, no. 4 (April 1977), p. 1.

342. *Who's Who in America 1980–81)*, vol. 1, p. 935.

343. *New York Times*, June 29, 1961, p. 19; April 11, 1973, p. 50.

appointed Ambassador to Luxembourg in 1965. After serving as Dean of the Howard Law School, she engaged in active practice as a partner, later as managing partner, in the Washington office of a large, predominantly white New York and Washington law firm. In 1977 she was appointed Secretary of Housing and Urban Development (HUD) in the cabinet of President Jimmy Carter and, two years later, Secretary of Health, Education, and Welfare (HEW).[344]

In 1967 Walter E. Washington left the practice of law in Washington to become the first mayor of the city, initially by presidential appointment and then by reappointment. In 1975, when the system of selection was changed, he was elected Mayor and served until 1979, when he was defeated for reelection. He then became the Washington resident partner of a predominantly white New York–based law firm.[345]

Several local black lawyers also have been appointed to judgeships in Washington. The first was Robert Herberton Terrell, who was named to the Municipal Court of the District of Columbia in 1909 and reappointed by Presidents Roosevelt, Taft, and Wilson.[346] During his seventeen-year tenure he was the only black judge in Washington.[347]

The next black appointment to that court was James A. Cobb in 1926. Cobb had served as Special Assistant to the Attorney General of the United States from 1907 to 1915. He served on the Municipal Court for ten years until 1936.[348]

In 1969 William S. Thompson became the first of four black lawyers appointed to the Superior Court of the District of Columbia during the succeeding decade. Thompson has served as Secretary-General of the World Peace Through Law Center from the time of its creation in 1963. Since then he has played important roles at that organization's world conferences held biennially in various countries in Europe, Africa, and South America, as well as in Washington, D.C.[349]

William C. Gardner, the only black in the 1951 class of 585 students at the Harvard Law School,[350] immediately upon passing the bar in that year became a member of Houston, Waddy, Bryant and Gardner. He has been a member of many civic and government bodies, and in April 1980

344. Burke, *Civil Rights*, p. 2.

345. Ibid., pp. 116–17; *Who's Who in America 1980–81*, vol. 2, pp. 3440–441.

346. M. Sammy Miller, "Robert H. Terrell: First Black D.C. Municipal Judge," *The Crisis*, vol. 83, no. 6 (June–July 1976), pp. 209–10.

347. Joseph D. Whitaker and Eugene L. Meyer, "Moving Up to the Bench," *Washington Post*, April 15, 1976, p. A-14.

348. Walter J. Leonard, "The Development of the Black Bar," *The Annals of the American Academy of Political and Social Science*, May 1973, p. 138.

349. *National Bar Bulletin*, vol. 11, no. 7 (July 1979), p. 12.

350. *Washington Post*, April 12, 1976, p. A-21.

became a judge of the District of Columbia Superior Court. In 1979 Gardner was named the District of Columbia Bar Association's Outstanding Lawyer for 1979.[351]

Another member of the Houston and Gardner firm, Theodore R. Newman, Jr., became a judge of the District of Columbia Superior Court in 1970, serving in that capacity until 1976, when he was appointed the first black chief judge of the District of Columbia Court of Appeals.[352]

H. Carl Moultrie was appointed an associate judge of the District of Columbia Superior Court in 1972. Six years later he became the first black chief judge of that court.[353]

In addition to the many local black lawyers who have risen to prominence, numerous others have been brought to Washington by the voters and by presidents to serve in government and judicial posts. Perhaps the most famed of these is Supreme Court Justice Thurgood Marshall. From 1965 to 1967, by appointment of President Lyndon B. Johnson, Marshall served as the first black Solicitor General of the United States. In 1967 Johnson appointed him the first, and he remains the only, black justice of the Supreme Court of the United States.[354] (See the New York section for information on Marshall's prior career, e.g., as a chief litigator for the NAACP.)

The first black to sit on any federal court was William H. Hastie. A native of Philadelphia, Hastie practiced law in Washington with Charles Houston before entering government service in 1932 as Assistant Solicitor in the Department of the Interior. In 1940 he became Civilian Aide to Secretary of War Stimson but resigned that post in protest over continued segregation of training facilities in the Air Force. In 1937, only six years after his admission to the bar, he received his landmark appointment by President Franklin D. Roosevelt to the United States Territorial District Court of the Virgin Islands. After nine years on that court, he became Governor of the Virgin Islands, the first of his race to attain so high a position in the executive branch of the federal government. In 1949 he returned to Philadelphia to serve on the United States Court of Appeals for the Third Circuit, the first black to be appointed to a United States Court of Appeals.[355] (See Chapter 6 for full details of Hastie's distinguished career.)

The first black judge on the federal bench in the nation's capital was Spottswood William Robinson III, who was appointed to the United States

351. Diana Huffman, "Minority Firms Look for Share of Uptown Practice," *Legal Times of Washington,* January 21, 1980, p. 17.

352. *Who's Who in America 1980–81,* vol. 2, p. 2455.

353. Ibid., p. 2390.

354. Ibid., p. 2158.

355. Bergman, *The Negro in America,* pp. 458, 480, 501, 513, 521.

District Court for the District of Columbia in 1964. Robinson had graduated from Howard Law School in 1939 with the highest academic average in its history, practiced law briefly in Richmond, and served as a teacher and as dean at Howard Law School until his appointment to the District Court. In 1966 he was elevated to the United States Court of Appeals for the District of Columbia, becoming the first black to sit on that bench as well. On May 7, 1981, he became chief judge of that court, the second black to hold that position in any circuit, the first having been William H. Hastie in the Third Circuit.[356]

Wade H. McCree, Jr., who had served on the United States District Court for the Eastern District of Michigan (1961–66) and on the United States Court of Appeals for the Sixth Circuit (1966–77), entered the Washington scene in 1977 when he became the second black Solicitor General of the United States.[357] (See the Detroit section for more details on McCree's distinguished career.)

Another black member of Detroit's legal community, Hobart Taylor, Jr. came to Washington in 1964 to serve in a series of government posts —first as Special Counsel to, then as Executive Vice-Chairman of, the President's Committee on Equal Opportunity. His subsequent positions included Associate Counsel to President Johnson. He served as a director of the board of large corporations, including, among others, Eastern Airlines, Great Atlantic and Pacific Tea Company, and Standard Oil Company. Taylor died on April 2, 1981.[358]

Another Johnson appointee was Wiley A. Branton, who was Special Assistant to the Attorney General of the United States from 1965 to 1967. Branton came to Washington from his native Pine Bluff, Arkansas, where he practiced at the bar from 1952. He also served in executive capacities for various civil-rights and social-action organizations, including Director of the Voter Education Project and the Southern Regional Council Organization. In Washington he practiced for six years in a firm that he formed before embarking on his academic career. In 1976 he became Dean of the Howard Law School. Dean Branton has been the recipient of numerous awards, including those for his active and effective participation in civil rights litigation.[359]

Clifford L. Alexander, Jr. came to Washington from New York City during the Johnson years, served first in the White House, and then was appointed Chairman of the Equal Employment Opportunity Commission

356. Laura A. Kiernan, "The Fire Still Burns," *Washington Post,* May 27, 1981, p. A-4; *Legal Times of Washington,* January 19, 1981, p. 3.

357. *Who's Who in America 1980–81,* vol. 2, p. 2219.

358. Ibid., p. 3257; *Afro-American,* week of February 6–10, 1979.

359. *Who's Who in America 1980–81,* vol. 1, p. 399.

in 1967. He resigned in 1969 in protest over President Richard Nixon's EEO policies. He was appointed Secretary of the Army in 1977.[360]

C. Clyde Ferguson, Jr., former Dean of the Howard Law School, was United States Representative to the Economic and Social Council of the United Nations in 1974, having before that been General Counsel to the United States Civil Rights Commission. He was the first black president of the American Society of International Law.[361]

Benjamin L. Hooks was appointed the first black member of the Federal Communications Commission in 1972. After leaving the commission, he became Executive Director of the NAACP in 1977, a post he continues to occupy.[362]

William T. Coleman, Jr., for many years a leading Philadelphia practitioner and a lawyer of national standing, went to Washington in 1975 to serve as Secretary of the Department of Transportation. In 1977 he became a senior partner in the Washington office of one of the two largest firms in Los Angeles.[363] (See Chapter 1 for further details.)

Edward W. Brooke, who came to Washington as a United States Senator from Massachusetts, also became a partner in a predominantly white Washington law firm.[364] (See the Boston section for further details concerning Senator Brooke's career.)

In 1981 the Chairman of the Equal Employment Opportunity Commission, Dr. J. Clay Smith, Jr., completed his term as President of the 15,000-member Federal Bar Association. He was the first black to hold that office in the FBA's sixty-year history.[365] Smith came to Washington in 1964 from Omaha, Nebraska, to attend Howard Law School. In Omaha he was the first black American to be elected Governor of Boys' State, sponsored by the American Legion. In 1960 Governor Ralph G. Brooks of Nebraska designated Smith, who was then eighteen years of age, to serve as chairman of the Nebraska delegation to the White House Conference on Children and Youth. As EEOC acting chairman, Smith has become a highly regarded lecturer and writer on the status of black lawyers, as well as a spokesman for them.

According to Smith's recent estimates, there are between 1,300 and 2,000 black lawyers in Washington, D.C. Some 1,000 are members of the Washington Bar Association, but its president believes there are an additional 1,000 black lawyers in the metropolitan area, or a total of 2,000.

360. Burke, *Civil Rights*, p. 2. *Who's Who in America 1980–81*, vol. 1, p. 39.
361. Ibid., p. 46.
362. Ibid., pp. 63–64.
363. *Who's Who in America 1980–81*, vol. 1, p. 674.
364. *Martindale-Hubbell 1981*, vol. 2, p. 1546B.
365. Resumé of Dr. J. Clay Smith, June 30, 1980; *National Law Journal*, September 1, 1980, p. 17.

Others, including Smith, Charles Duncan, and Wiley Branton, have estimated only a few hundred more than one thousand. Thus, black lawyers constitute between 5.3 percent and 8.1 percent of the approximately 24,500 active, resident members of the District of Columbia bar.

Smith and Duncan also concur, although there are no hard figures available, that the government employs the largest percentage of the black lawyers in Washington. Though black lawyers are present throughout the federal agencies, the numbers in any one office are small. According to Duncan, the largest concentrations of black attorneys are in local law enforcement or criminal justice agencies in the District of Columbia agencies, such as the United States Attorney's Office, the District of Columbia Corporation Counsel, and the Public Defender, which have especially aggressive programs to recruit minority lawyers.

In percentage of black judges, Washington leads the sixteen cities (see Table 15). While its overall 28.6 percent is only slightly above Detroit's 25 percent, it exceeds most of the other cities, including Philadelphia, by significant margins.

On May 7, 1981, Chief Judge Carl McGowan of the United States Court of Appeals for the District of Columbia reached his seventieth birthday, and Spottswood Robinson succeeded to the post. Thus began a brief period in judicial history when every federal and local trial and appellate court in the nation's capital was presided over by a black chief judge. Serving as Chief Judge at the same time as Robinson were William B. Bryant on the United States District Court for the District of Columbia, Theodore R. Newman, Jr., on the District of Columbia Court of Appeals, and H. Carl Moultrie on the District of Columbia Superior Court.[366] (In September 1981 Bryant turned seventy and stepped down from the chief judgeship.)

|  | Washington, D.C. | Philadelphia |
|---|---|---|
| State & Local Judges | 53 | 110 |
| Black Judges | 15 (28.3%) | 21 (19.1%) |
| U.S. Court of Appeals & District Judges | 24 | 20 |
| Black Judges | 7 (29.2%) | 3 (15.0%) |
| Total Judges | 77 | 130 |
| Total Black Judges | 22 (28.6%) | 24 (18.5%)[367] |

Federal judges as of April 1982. 527 F. Supp. VII, X–XI; State and local judges as of November 1981.

366. Kiernan, "The Fire Still Burns," p. A-1.

367. For detailed statistics on black and white judges in all cities surveyed, including U.S. bankruptcy judges and magistrates, see Appendix 12.

Despite the high level of representation and the lofty achievements of blacks in the courts of Washington, the 1980 survey demonstrates that black representation in the leading private firms is low. In comparison with Philadelphia, as the following chart shows, the large and medium-size firms of Washington have a slightly higher percentage of black partners, while the large firms of Philadelphia have a slightly higher percentage of black associates. One would have been justified in expecting a greater differential, since Washington has a much larger percentage of blacks in the total population (68.4% compared with Philadelphia's 36.5%).

Thus, while the doors of the top Washington firms are no longer closed to blacks, the numbers are still extremely low. There may be a dozen black lawyers with incomes over $100,000 but the vast majority, most of whom are still sole practitioners or in practice with one or two other blacks, probably earn less than the median income for lawyers generally.[368]

Of all the sixteen cities in the 1980 survey, Washington had the highest percentage black population (68.4%), a total of 448,229 blacks with no more than 2,000 black lawyers. Asked if there are enough practitioners to service the needs of Washington's large black community, Charles Duncan observed that the situation there is probably no different from the one nationally: Those who can pay get legal help; those who are indigent get legal services; and in between are those who cannot afford to pay but do not qualify for assistance. "If you separate the black population out by economic class," Duncan believes, "the situation in Washington reflects the pattern you see nationwide." For blacks on law school faculties, see Appendix 18.

| Large Firms* | Total Lawyers | Black Lawyers | Total Partners | Black Partners | Total Associates | Black Associates |
|---|---|---|---|---|---|---|
| Washington | 861 | 22 (2.5%) | 352 | 4 (1.1%) | 509 | 18 (3.5%) |
| Philadelphia | 1,094 | 26 (2.4%) | 531 | 4 (0.8%) | 563 | 22 (3.9%) |
| Medium-size Firms* | | | | | | |
| Washington | 1,867 | 36 (1.9%) | 877 | 7 (0.8%) | 990 | 29 (2.9%) |
| Philadelphia | 550 | 6 (1.1%) | 288 | 1 (0.3%) | 262 | 5 (1.9%)[369] |

*According to the 1980 survey conducted by the author.

368. Observations of Charles Duncan.

369. For detailed statistics on black and white lawyers in all cities surveyed, see Appendices 13 and 14.

# 10

## Blacks in the Legal Profession Today

"It is from numberless diverse acts of courage and belief that human history is shaped," said Robert Kennedy at the University of Capetown in 1966. With words that two years later were chosen for the eulogy to him in St. Patrick's Cathedral, the Senator and former Attorney General added:

> Each time a man stands up for an ideal, or acts to improve the lot of others, or strikes out against injustice, he sends forth a tiny ripple of hope, and crossing each other from a million different centers of energy and daring those ripples build a current that can sweep down the mightiest walls of oppression and resistance.[1]

The "ripple," or multiplier effect, is manifest in the history of blacks in the legal profession.[2] In each of the fields of law surveyed in Philadelphia and the fifteen additional cities, there have been many diverse acts of courage and belief, and from thousands of centers of energy and daring a current has swelled that may some day be strong enough to sweep down the remaining walls of resistance to blacks in American law.

The Philadelphia account of blacks in the law shows the multiplier effect of a few ambitious and courageous men (and later women) who broke through barriers of prejudice and tradition to become members of the legal profession. As the facts from the fifteen other cities demonstrate, this story has taken place throughout the United States, although in different circumstances and at varying rates. An overview of the national scene finds the same essential pattern of pioneering repeated not only geographically but also in each of the main fields of legal endeavor—in private practice, corporations, and government as attorneys; in the judiciary as federal, state, and local judges; and in law schools as teachers, administrators, and, recently, deans.

The progression from slavery to the various branches of the legal

---

1. Arthur M. Schlesinger, Jr., *Robert Kennedy and His Times* (Boston: Houghton-Mifflin Co., 1978), pp. 745–46.
2. For an account of the role of black lawyers in the struggle for justice in America, see *From the Black Bar: Voices for Equal Justice*, ed. Gilbert Ware (New York: G.P. Putnam's Sons, 1976).

207

profession began with no blacks trained in law or admitted to the bar. Thus it is natural that the early pioneers among blacks, in Philadelphia and elsewhere, tended to cut across the various categories of professional endeavor, overcoming obstacles and opening paths for blacks in more than one field. Each was indeed a center of energy and daring, having a multiple effect.

For example, as the section on Boston recounts, according to the best available records the first black to be admitted to the bar anywhere in the United States was Macon B. Allen, in 1844 in Maine. Allen soon moved to Massachusetts, where he practiced law from 1845 through the Civil War. During Reconstruction he went to practice in South Carolina, where in 1873 he was chosen by the state legislature as an inferior court judge.[3] The second black lawyer noted in the records, Robert Morris, Jr., was admitted in Massachusetts in 1846 or 1847, and in 1849 helped to bring and argue a suit challenging (unsuccessfully) the constitutionality of Boston's system of segregated schools.[4] About 1850, when the governor of Massachusetts appointed him a magistrate, Morris became the first recorded black to exercise judicial power in the United States.[5]

John S. Rock became the first black admitted to the bar of the United States Supreme Court in 1865. When Chief Justice Salmon Chase administered the oath to the then Boston lawyer, it was said that "the grave to bury the *Dred Scott* decision was in that sentence dug."[6] Another pioneer black, John Mercer Langston, started practice in Ohio in 1854, was admitted to the Supreme Court Bar in 1867 (on motion of James Garfield, later President of the United States), and went on to become Congressman from Virginia, Dean of Howard Law School, Acting President of Howard University, and United States Minister to Haiti.[7]

The first black to graduate from an American law school, George

3. Based on rolls of attorneys in Maine and Massachusetts courts, Anton-Hermann Chroust, *The Rise of the Legal Profession in America* (Norman, Okla.: University of Oklahoma Press, 1965), vol. 2, p. 90, states that Allen was the first black admitted to the bar and that Robert Morris, Jr., was the second. But J. Clay Smith, Jr., in his paper "The Afro-American Lawyer: Their Beginning," p. 2, asserts that Morris was the first ("about 1843"). That 1843 date is also given by Fitzhugh Lee Styles in *Negroes and the Law* (Boston: Christopher Publishing Co., 1937), pp. 14, 115. Allen's South Carolina judgeship is noted in the *National Roster of Black Judicial Officers 1980* (Chicago: American Judicature Society, 1980), p. 1.

4. *Roberts v. City of Boston,* 59 Mass. (5 Cush.) 198 (1849).

5. *National Roster of Black Judicial Officers,* p. 1. According to Chroust, Morris studied law in the office of Ellis Loring Gray in Boston and was appointed magistrate by Governor George N. Briggs (*Rise of the Legal Profession,* p. 90). The *National Roster* gives 1852 as the date of Brigg's appointment of Morris (p. 1), but Briggs's governorship ended in 1851. See also Styles, *Negroes and the Law,* pp. 115–16.

6. Styles, *Negroes and the Law,* p. 14.

7. Ibid., pp. 14–15, 117–20.

Lewis Ruffin, was later, as reported in the Boston section, the first black outside the southern states (during Reconstruction) to hold a judicial post above that of magistrate.[8] In 1869 Ruffin received his degree from Harvard Law School; in 1883 he was appointed Judge of the Charlestown District Court. The career of the first black to receive a B.A. degree from Harvard (in 1870), Richard T. Greener of Philadelphia, is described in the Washington section. Greener graduated from Howard Law School, served as its dean, practiced law before the Supreme Court of South Carolina, and finished his career with high posts in the United States Government and Foreign Service.[9]

In the first two decades of this century the examples become more numerous. Throughout the fifteen cities surveyed in Chapter 9 we find one after another pioneering black who succeeded in several areas of the legal profession and created currents of change in his or her own city and even nationally. These figures include Austin T. Walden in Atlanta, Earl B. Dickerson in Chicago, L. A. Ransom in Columbus, Harold E. Bledsoe in Detroit, Thomas Benjamin Dyett in New York, Homer S. Brown in Pittsburgh, and Oliver W. Hill in Richmond, and of course Charles Houston, of Washington, whose exemplary career is discussed in detail below.

In the Philadelphia story we saw other early examples of black legal pioneering. Aaron Mossell, Jr., was the first black graduate of the University of Pennsylvania Law School (in 1888). His daughter, Sadie Tanner Mossell Alexander, was the first black woman to graduate from that law school (in 1927) and the first black woman to be admitted to practice in Pennsylvania (where she is still active in public affairs). Her husband, Raymond Pace Alexander, became the first black judge on Philadelphia's Court of Common Pleas, the trial court of general jurisdiction. The Alexanders were among the total of twenty-one blacks admitted to the Philadelphia Bar between 1920 and 1945. Though their numbers were few, the multiplying power of these twenty-one was considerable. Most of them succeeded in legal practice, and more than half became judges or were appointed to distinguished government posts.[10]

On the national scene, the life of Charles Hamilton Houston shows

8. Charles Sumner Brown, "The Genesis of the Negro Lawyer in New England, Part II," *Negro History Bulletin,* vol. 22, no. 8 (1958), p. 173. See also Styles, *Negroes and the Law,* p. 15.

9. Styles, *Negroes and the Law,* pp. 131–32.

10. *The University of Pennsylvania Law School Black Law Alumni Directory* (Philadelphia: Black Law Students Union, Class of 1981, Fall 1979), p. 1; Raymond Pace Alexander, "A View from the Bench," *Verdict,* vol. 6, no. 4 (September 1970), p. 3; Walter J. Leonard, *Black Lawyers* (Boston: Senna & Shih, 1977), p. 147; and Fleming D. Tucker, comp., *A Directory of the Colored Members of the Philadelphia Bar, Including a List of the Pioneer Members)* revised to April 1, 1964 (n.p., n.d.).

how one man, as practicing lawyer, law teacher, law dean, and civil-rights attorney, inspired generations of blacks in the law. His legal secretary, Juanita Kidd Stout, who later went to law school and became the first black woman elected to the office of judge in the United States (the Municipal Court of Philadelphia in 1959), recalls Houston's relentless insistence upon excellence and hard work. He advised her and all his students, "Regardless of how small a case may be, act as though it will end in the Supreme Court of the United States." That is where a number of Houston's most important cases did end—successfully.[11]

Charles H. Houston was the grandson of slaves. His father, William LePré Houston, worked his way through Howard University's night law school, started one of the first black law firms in Washington, D.C., and at the same time taught law at Howard. Houston entered Amherst College at age sixteen and graduated in 1915 as class valedictorian and a member of Phi Beta Kappa. In 1922 he graduated from Harvard Law School in the top 5 percent of his class, having been the first black elected to the editorial board of the *Harvard Law Review.* He stayed on to become the first black to earn a Doctor of Judicial Science degree, and after a year of overseas study, he received the degree of Doctor of Civil Law from the University of Madrid.[12]

After entering into partnership with his father, he taught at Howard Law School, became Vice-Dean in 1929, and was soon put in charge of the school. In two years he turned that institution from a mediocre night school into a full-time, and fully accredited, day law school. One of his first full-time students was Thurgood Marshall, who joined in dubbing him "Iron Shoes" because of his high standards and heavy demands. Houston wanted "no coddling" of blacks, only a fair chance and advancement "on the basis of merit . . . or not at all." He instilled in Howard students and his faculty and other legal colleagues the idea that they ought to become effective social engineers and use the law to end segregation and achieve equal rights for blacks.[13]

In 1935 Houston left the deanship to direct the NAACP's legal campaign and soon collaborated with Thurgood Marshall in a suit to desegregate the University of Maryland Law School. As the NAACP brought lawsuits to end discrimination in higher education and in voting, they turned to members of the Howard Law School faculty—and to its gradu-

11. Geraldine R. Segal, *In Any Fight Some Fall* (Rockville, Md.: Mercury Press, 1975), pp. 72–73.

12. Ibid., pp. 17, 22–24, 29–30. See also Genna Rae McNeil, "Charles Hamilton Houston," *Black Law Journal,* vol. 3, nos. 2 and 3 (1975), where McNeil reports that in 1943 Justice Felix Frankfurter commented that Houston was one of the "most brilliant and able students at Harvard" within his memory (p. 123, n. 1).

13. Segal, *In Any Fight Some Fall,* pp. 33–34, 67.

ates in private practice—as central resources. Houston also enlisted as a key adviser a recent member of Houston and Houston, his second cousin William H. Hastie, who had followed him to Amherst and Harvard Law School with an equally outstanding record. By their efforts the talents of many black lawyers were mobilized, the number of civil-rights suits was multiplied, and the walls of segregation began to fall, in one institution after another, in one field after another, and in one state after another.[14]

Charles Houston worked himself to death of a heart attack in 1950, at age fifty-four. In a final message to his six-year-old son he wrote: "Tell Bo I did not run out on him, but went down fighting that he might have better and broader opportunities than I had, without prejudices or bias operating against him. In any fight some fall."[15] Houston fell, but he did not fail. The era of civil-rights litigation that he initiated and led, and the record of the NAACP Legal Defense and Educational Fund, Inc., which grew out of his work, stand as an extraordinary historical success. One by-product was the appointment of Houston's NAACP successor, Thurgood Marshall, as the first black justice of the United States Supreme Court, three decades after Houston and Marshall started work together and after Marshall had served as the first black solicitor general.

His other close colleague, William H. Hastie, called Houston "the effective leader of the essential first stage" of the twentieth-century struggle for civil rights in America.[16] He wrote, in 1950, that Houston "led us through the legal wilderness of second-class citizenship. He was truly the Moses of that journey."[17]

Houston's partnership with his father and Hastie, and his collaboration with Marshall and the faculty of Howard Law School, are exemplary demonstrations of the multiplier factor that has been at work among blacks in American law.

Decade-by-decade statistics on the number of blacks in the profession give much the same picture as the stories of early pioneers: the smallest possible beginning, a long period of slow growth, and then in recent times a quantum jump—with greater growth to be expected in the coming decades. The imponderable is the rate at which this growth will take place.

Of all blacks gainfully employed in the United States in 1890, only

14. Ibid., pp. 35, 37, 42–45. Houston's first case with Marshall was *University of Maryland v. Murray*, 169 Md. 478 (1936), which resulted in opening the University of Maryland to blacks. Several years before this, Marshall himself had found the door closed to his admission to this school. See also Margaret Bush Wilson and Duane Ridely, "A New Birth of Liberty," *Black Law Journal*, vol. 6, no. 1 (1978), p. 77.

15. Segal, *In Any Fight Some Fall*, p. 75.

16. Ibid., p. 6.

17. Ibid., p. 88.

431 were reported to be lawyers. By 1910 the number of black lawyers had increased to 779. By 1960 the census reported 2,004.[18] In 1970 the total was 3,406.[19] The 1980 census figures on the number of blacks who are lawyers have not yet been released, but the Bureau of Labor Statistics estimated that in 1979 there were 12,000 blacks out of a total of 478,000 Americans employed as lawyers. Thus, while in 1970 blacks comprised about 1.0 percent of the total number of American lawyers, by 1979 they comprised about 2.5 percent.[20]

This multiplication in one decade of the total number of black lawyers by a factor of more than three and a half was predictable as a result of the prior increase in the total number of black law students described in the Introduction to this volume: from about 700, or less than one percent of all law students, in 1965, to more than 5,500, or nearly 5 percent, in 1976.

Even with the difficulties many black law graduates have had in passing state bar examinations, the number of black members of the bar has far outpaced the growth of the legal profession as a whole. American Bar Foundation studies show that the total number of United States lawyers in 1980 was almost twice the number in 1960, and one and a half times as many as there were in 1970.[21] The number of black lawyers in 1980 was more than five times the number in 1960, and more than three and a half times the number in 1970. However, since blacks constitute about 11 percent of the total population and still provide less than 3 percent of the lawyers, one wonders how much more time must elapse before black lawyers will constitute a more representative percentage of the lawyer population.

Among black lawyers, only a small proportion are women. As noted in the Washington section, the first black woman to graduate from any law school was Charlotte E. Ray, who in 1872 received an LL.B. from Howard

18. U.S. Bureau of the Census, *1890 Census,* vol. 16, pt. 2, table 89, p. 402; *1910 Census,* vol. 4, table 6, p. 429; *1960 Census,* vol. 1, pt. 1, table 205, pp. 1–544.

19. U.S. Bureau of the Census, *1970 Census of Population: Subject reports, Final Report P.C. (2)-7A, Occupational Characteristics* (1973), table 2, p. 12. The census may underestimate these totals because of errors in its survey methods and the difficulty of identifying or locating blacks. The Judicial Committee of the National Bar Association reported that there were 3,845 black lawyers in 1970, nearly 13% more than the 3,406 reported by the 1970 census.

20. Bureau of Labor Statistics, U.S. Department of Labor, *Employment and Earnings,* vol. 27, no. 1 (January 1980), table 23, p. 174. This is in accord with the 12,000 total reported by the president of the National Bar Association in 1981. See *New York Times,* July 29, 1981, p. A-20. The government figures also appear to underestimate the number of white lawyers. According to an American Bar Foundation study using information from Martindale-Hubbell, as of April 1980 there were approximately 535,000 lawyers in the United States.

21. Barbara A. Curran, "Lawyer Demographics," paper read at the American Bar Association Annual Meeting, New Orleans, August 8, 1981, p. 3.

Law School and was admitted to the District of Columbia Bar.[22] Between then and 1926 there were reportedly no more than 25 black women lawyers in the United States. But this picture has changed. As of 1979 it was estimated that approximately 1,800 to 2,000 black women had graduated from the nation's law schools, most of them in the last few decades.[23]

The upsurge between 1960 and 1980 in the number of women (including black women) law students, graduates, and practicing lawyers was spurred by both the civil-rights movement and the women's movement. From a 1970 census estimate of a total of 12,655 women lawyers in the United States, or about 4.5 percent of a total of 264,752 persons employed as lawyers, the number of women lawyers has grown, according to the Bureau of Labor Statistics, to 61,000 in 1980, or about 13.0 percent of the estimated total of 478,000 lawyers.

This nearly fivefold increase in women lawyers in one decade compares with the estimated nearly fourfold increase in the number of black lawyers, while the total for all lawyers did not quite double. The proportion of women in the legal profession had remained about the same for the previous twenty years (2.5% in 1950 to 2.8% in 1970); then, in the 1970s the number increased dramatically to 7.5 percent of all lawyers. As of August 1981, women are estimated to account for one-third of the lawyers graduating from law schools. As Tables 4, 5, and 6 in Chapter 4 show, of the black students enrolled in Philadelphia-area law schools in the 1981–82 school year, a majority are women. At the University of Pennsylvania, this has been so since the 1978–79 school year; at Temple, for two years; and at Villanova this year only.

When it is released, the 1980 census breakdown of lawyers by race, geography, and fields of employment will indicate some of the changes that have occurred or are beginning to occur as the number of black lawyers multiplies. The 1970 breakdown by race and geography, disclosing the ratio of black lawyers to the black population in each state, compared with the ratio of white lawyers to the white population of those states, is given in Appendix 15. That table cannot be brought up-to-date until the detailed 1980 census breakdowns are available, but from totals already given certain overall figures can be stated.[24]

In 1980 there was approximately one white lawyer for every 360 white persons in the United States. Using the estimate of 12,000 black lawyers and the total reported black population of 26.5 million, in 1980 there was

22. *Negro Women in the Judiciary,* Alpha Kappa Alpha Sorority Heritage Series 1 (Chicago, 1968), p. 15.

23. From a speech by Dr. J. Clay Smith, Jr., before the National Conference of Black Lawyers, Washington, D.C., March 13, 1980.

24. *1970 Census,* table 2, p. 12; U.S. Department of Labor, *Employment and Earnings,* Table 23, p. 174; Curran, "Lawyer Demographics," pp. 15–16.

approximately one black lawyer for every 2,208 black Americans.[25] The 1980 ratios are major improvements over the overall 1970 estimates (in Appendix 15) of one black lawyer for every 5,790 black Americans and one white lawyer for every 635 white Americans.

To some extent, the geographical distribution of black lawyers follows the pattern of all lawyers, but there are notable differences. For example, as of 1980 almost one-fourth of all lawyers were located in New York and California, each having about 12 percent of the total lawyer population. According to the 1970 estimates, just over one-fourth of black lawyers were in those two states, but California had 373 black lawyers to New York's 650.[26] Also, from the 1970 figures the differences between the North and the South in the distribution of black and white lawyers were the most notable. For example, looking again to Appendix 15, we note the differences in the nine states with more than one million blacks:

|  | No. blacks per black lawyer | No. whites per white lawyer |
| --- | --- | --- |
| California | 3,754 | 736 |
| Florida | 17,493 | 749 |
| Georgia | 39,693 | 844 |
| Illinois | 2,137 | 622 |
| Louisiana | 40,324 | 697 |
| New York | 3,334 | 396 |
| North Carolina | 16,252 | 1,306 |
| Pennsylvania | 7,209 | 961 |
| Texas | 12,496 | 799 |

Consider also the six states with the next largest black populations (see chart on next page).

The history of slavery and racial discrimination is embedded in these disparities. Will the admission of black students in all the nation's law schools make inroads on this pattern of concentration of black lawyers in the North and West? Will the economic prosperity of the sunbelt and the increase of black political power, including the growing number of black public officials, attract more black lawyers to the southern states, where they are so underrepresented? Will that new black political power cause

25. The 1980 total of all lawyers, according to Martindale-Hubbell, was 535,000. Curran, "Lawyer Demographics," p. 3. The 1980 total of all U.S. whites: 188,340,790; of blacks: 26,488,218. *1980 Census of Population, Supplementary Reports,* PC 80-31-3 (July 1981), p. 1.

26. Curran, "Lawyer Demographics," pp. 2–3. Some 4% to 6% of all American lawyers are located in each of six jurisdictions: Florida, Illinois, Ohio, Pennsylvania, Texas, and the District of Columbia. Together they account for 30% of the lawyer population. Including California and New York, over half of all lawyers in 1980 were in these eight jurisdictions.

| | No. blacks per black lawyer | No. whites per white lawyer |
|---|---|---|
| Alabama | 37,844 | 1,026 |
| Michigan | 3,964 | 944 |
| Mississippi | 35,468 | 749 |
| Ohio | 2,333 | 843 |
| South Carolina | 71,731 | 1,066 |
| Virginia | 8,402 | 456 |

law firms and corporations in the states with few black lawyers to recruit more of them? These are critical questions for the years ahead.

The employment opportunities in each of the fields of law in each state will of course be a dominant factor affecting the future geographical distribution. The division of black lawyers among the separate fields of endeavor is an important measure of their status within the profession. It reflects their progress and their frustrations. According to a 1979 presentation by J. Clay Smith, Jr., Acting Chairman of the Equal Employment Opportunity Commission, the 11,000 black lawyers he estimated to exist at that time were divided, in their fields of employment, as follows:[27]

| | | |
|---|---|---|
| Private practice | 1,500 | 13.6% |
| Public-interest law firms | 500 | 4.5% |
| Corporations (legal and nonlegal posts) | 2,300 | 20.9% |
| Federal or state government lawyers | 3,500 | 31.8% |
| Federal or state judges | 400 | 3.6% |
| Law teachers | 300 | 2.7% |
| Nonlegal jobs or unemployed | 2,500 | 22.7% |

The 1980 census figures may modify these estimates, but the orders of magnitude of the black lawyers in these several categories of employment appear to portray the present general pattern. The above distribution of black lawyers should be compared with the figures for the total legal population. According to the Martindale-Hubbell data for 1980, 70 percent of all lawyers were in private law practice, 25 percent were working for the government or for corporations or were otherwise employed, and 5 percent reported themselves as retired or inactive. These figures contrast sharply with the less than 14 percent of all black lawyers in private practice and

27. J. Clay Smith, Jr., "The Future of the Black Lawyer in America," speech before the Annual Convention of the Old Dominion Bar Association, May 26, 1979, p. 2. In 1980 Smith became the first black president of the Federal Bar Association.

the more than 56 percent in government or corporations. Of the 25 percent of all lawyers working but not in private practice, approximately one-half (or 13% of the total number of lawyers) were in government, including federal, state, and local judiciaries, and nearly one-third (or 9% of all lawyers) were in private industry.

Other comparisons are also revealing. One percent of all lawyers work in education, including both law schools and other educational institutions; J. Clay Smith, Jr. estimates that 2.7 percent of black lawyers are law teachers. One percent of all lawyers work in legal aid and public defender programs; Smith reports that 4.5 percent of black lawyers are in public-interest firms. One percent of all lawyers are reported to work for various nonprofit institutions, including bar groups, unions, trade associations, political action groups, and religious and charitable organizations; there is no estimate of the proportion of blacks in this category.[28]

The following pages review in more detail facts and trends regarding black representation in the major areas of the legal profession.

## Black Lawyers in Private Practice, Corporations, and Government

Earlier in this century, as in the nineteenth century, the majority of those blacks who succeeded in becoming lawyers were in private practice, generally in small black firms or as sole practitioners, representing black clients. Such representation was primarily in everyday legal matters of a minor nature, most often petty criminal, accident, and domestic relations cases.

In recent decades there has been a trend among black lawyers away from such private practice to government and corporate positions, often nonlegal ones. J. Clay Smith, Jr., attributes this to two major factors. First, more and more blacks have been attending predominantly white law schools. Some of these students, after being "exposed to different legal philosophies and living in a more prosperous era" do not "have any desire to return to the black community to do time representing the interest of the poor."[29] Second, established white firms have not hired blacks in substantial numbers, although they have begun to seek outstanding black law graduates as associates. This has meant that for most black lawyers government and corporations have been the major sources of available and well-paying jobs.

Smith's view that recent black law graduates from predominantly white law schools have become disenchanted with serving the needs of the poor may do them and their schools an injustice. The five hundred black

28. Curran, "Lawyer Demographics," pp. 11–13.
29. Smith, "Future of the Black Lawyer," pp. 4–5.

lawyers whom he found to be working in public-interest law firms represented nearly 5 percent of his total for all black lawyers. That proportion is much higher than the equivalent proportion of white lawyers in public-interest firms, and the same appears to be true of the larger field of legal services for the poor, including legal aid and public defender programs.[30] The lack of opportunities in established white firms, for all but high-ranking law-school graduates and the readiness of public-interest firms and other legal services programs to employ black lawyers provide part of the explanation for the relatively high proportion of blacks attracted to such work. But whatever the factors, and however highly one must regard Smith's knowledge of the black bar, these figures do not support Smith's hypothesis that blacks have turned away from representing the poor because of attendance at predominantly white law schools with "different legal philosophies." The surge of student attraction to public-interest law took place in those very law schools during the late 1960s and the 1970s, just as black students were entering those schools in larger numbers.

The surge to legal services for the poor and other public-interest work seems to have receded generally by the 1980s, among whites as well as blacks, but this probably reflects a national mood and the reduction in secure funding for these programs more than any specific change of attitude among blacks. Moreover, in past decades the numbers of black lawyers engaged in civil-rights litigation was never as large as civil-rights leaders wished. The representation of the poor by black lawyers was probably more by necessity than by principle or by any philosophy learned in law schools, despite Charles Houston's urgings and hopes. Houston's father was more concerned than his son with making ends meet and serving clients who could pay; when asked, "Where's Charley?" he would say, "He's off saving the race."[31] This may have been part compliment, part complaint. In any case, saving the race and serving the poor, by dedication, has always been the exception rather than the rule, not only among black lawyers but among all other parts of the population, white and black. Indeed, some black lawyers who were seeking clients among the

30. Altogether there are approximately 6,000 legal-aid lawyers supported by the Federal Legal Services Corporation (*New York Times,* September 10, 1981, p. B-15). In 1980 the Legal Services Corporation reported that it was funding 5,325 lawyers in service to the poor, of which 565 (or more than 10%) were black (and 512 were Hispanic). The 4,145 white lawyers working with the Legal Services Corporation comprised less than 1% of white lawyers in the U.S.; the 565 black lawyers working in the program comprised nearly 5% of all U.S. black lawyers. A smaller number of lawyers work in the category of public-interest law firms, and others work as public defenders. According to a National Association for Law Placement survey for law school graduates of 1979, about 5.4% went into public-interest work. Larry Bodine, "Scrambling for Jobs in the J.D. Rat Race," *National Law Journal,* April 27, 1981, p. 12.

31. Segal, *In Any Fight Some Fall,* p. 51.

poor in order to make ends meet (like some white lawyers) have viewed the increase of free legal services for the poor as unfair competition.

Smith's second explanation for the trend among black lawyers away from private practice is no doubt accurate: the slowness of established white firms in hiring black lawyers as associates and in making them partners. In all the cities surveyed for this book, almost all the white firms were closed to black lawyers until at least the 1950s or early 1960s, some later. Only after the rise of the civil-rights movement and the graduation of substantial numbers of black law students from predominantly white law schools did major white law firms begin to employ black lawyers. Later, after the customary six- or seven-, and with some today eight-, year trial period before consideration for partnership, firms have made partners of a few black associates. Since the 1960s a momentum has begun to develop in the recruitment, employment, and promotion of blacks by formerly all-white firms, but the increase in the number of black associates and partners has not kept pace with the large relative increase in the total number of black lawyers.

There is, of course, a complex interplay of factors affecting the employment pattern. Along with undoubted racial discrimination in numerous instances, there are nonracial considerations that have diminished the employment of blacks by law firms. For example, the large firms, and many others as well, tend to employ only lawyers with relatively high ranking in law schools, which further reduces the pool of available black candidates. As of 1980 only 8 percent of all black lawyers in private practice were in firms with 25 to 99 lawyers, and only 3 percent were in firms with 100 or more lawyers. Three percent of the total black lawyers in 1980 would be only 360.[32]

A detailed account of the situation of black lawyers in Philadelphia and a survey of black lawyers' employment in 325 large and medium-size firms in sixteen cities (including Philadelphia) have been reported in the preceding chapters. From these studies and from a smaller sample of black employment in the nation's 50 largest firms, taken by the *National Law Journal* (April 20, 1981), an overview of the nationwide pattern and trends clearly emerges.

In the late 1940s a *summa cum laude* graduate of the University of Pennsylvania, *magna cum laude* graduate of Harvard Law School, and editor of the *Harvard Law Review* states that he could not, as a black, get a job as an associate in a major law firm in Philadelphia. After serving as the first black law clerk to a Supreme Court Justice, William T. Coleman, Jr., went to work with what was then said to be the only large interfaith, interracial law firm in New York City. Coleman returned to Philadelphia in 1952 to

32. Curran, "Lawyer Demographics," p. 9.

become an associate in an established white, medium-size firm, and in 1956 became a partner. From this base, he developed his distinguished career, which is detailed in Chapter 1. Today he practices in Washington, D.C., as the ranking partner of one of the two largest law firms in Los Angeles.[33]

Coleman's experience indicates the pattern of most of the outstanding black lawyers. The *National Law Journal* survey, published in April 1981, found only twenty black partners in the fifty largest firms in the nation (with 150 or more lawyers in each firm). These blacks comprised 0.5 percent of the firms' 4,271 partners. Of the 6,408 associates in those firms, 151, or 2.4 percent, were black. Together, black associates and partners made up 171, or 1.6 percent, of the 10,679 lawyers in these firms. Only one large firm (in Omaha, Nebraska) had more than two black partners. Two of the firms (one in Philadelphia and one in New York) had no black lawyers at all.[34]

These figures, plus the fact that black lawyers in the fifty firms had increased by only 0.1 percent over the previous year's percentage of 1.5 percent out of the total number of lawyers in those firms, are disappointing to those who had hoped for faster progress. Yet the multiplier factor, even with these small beginnings, is taking effect. The move from 15 to 20 black partners in one year is an increase of 33.3 percent, and the pool of 151 black associates is many times that of a few years ago.

One of the first blacks to become a partner (in 1973) in a major New York firm, Samuel C. Jackson, commented:

> There is no doubt in my mind as to why there are only 20 black partners at the majors. . . . It is due to historic racism. But the pattern is changing . . . , and certainly in the last five years there is evidence that there will be stepped-up opportunity for partnerships.[35]

A black partner in a large Chicago firm, Charles E. Lomax, said:

> I think everybody's shooting for minority hiring. We've gone so far as to talk to the law school professors about likely students, just like they do for athletes. Find me one, I'll hire him.[36]

With the growing pool of black law students, he should more readily be able to find one—and more.

Robert Kutak, a partner in the Omaha firm (with offices in Atlanta, Denver, and Washington, D.C.) that, according to the *National Law Journal,*

33. Richard Kluger, *Simple Justice* (New York: Vintage Books, 1977), pp. 292–93.
34. Edward J. Burke and Connie Johnson, "More Women on the Way Up," *National Law Journal,* April 20, 1981, pp. 1, 10–11.
35. "Data on Law Firms Raises Racial Issue," *New York Times,* July 29, 1981, p. A-20.
36. Burke and Johnson, "More Women," p. 11.

has had the strongest overall record in hiring and advancing blacks—four black partners and five associates—explained that firm's approach as a policy of "hiring lawyers, not clients." He said, "We ignore their immediate potential to draw clients or to frighten them off." Kutak added:

> We've found that if you go out and get really good lawyers, the clients will follow. There's a natural tendency to hire traditionally, and that means giving in to subtle discrimination. I wanted to hire intelligently. You have to keep hammering away until you bring together a wide variety of experience and outlook.[37]

At the time, the Kutak firm had, in addition to the cities mentioned above, an office in Minneapolis, which closed in 1981. The black partners and associates comprise nearly 5 percent of the lawyers in the five offices of the firm (before the Minneapolis closing).[38]

Many other firms that state they are working diligently to recruit blacks report recurring obstacles and setbacks. Respondents to the questionnaires for the survey of cities in this book registered similar complaints from all regions. From the East:

> This record [no black partners and only one black associate] has been a great disappointment. We have been repeatedly frustrated in our efforts to improve.

From the Midwest:

> We don't seem to be able to attract good blacks.

From the West:

> Extremely difficult to attract qualified black associates.

From the South:

> We have been actively searching for black associates for at least a decade. Unfortunately all we have hired left of their own volition.

There is no doubt that subtle, and sometimes not so subtle, discrimination still prevails in many places. But it is also a fact that highly qualified black law graduates find themselves sought after and welcomed by most of the major firms in large cities and that most of them receive one or more job offers. This generally appears to be the case in the firms of Philadelphia and the fifteen cities considered in Chapter 9. However, as in the case of most young white lawyers, the overwhelming majority of young black lawyers do not have the qualifications sought by major firms and are

37. Ibid., p. 10.
38. Ibid. Women make up more than 20% of the firm's lawyers.

therefore left with the alternatives of becoming sole practitioners, entering a firm with a few partners and associates, seeking a legal post in government or in a corporate law department, or leaving the bar.[39]

Accordingly, more and more young black lawyers have been finding their first employment not in private firms but in government service, at the federal, state, or local level, or in legal or nonlegal positions with business corporations. This trend has also been encouraged and accelerated by the active recruitment of blacks by corporations and by government. That new effort was mandated by the programs for affirmative action initiated by federal (and in some instances by state and local) executive action, accepted by business corporations, and finally established by legislation.[40]

After affirmative action was instituted by Presidential Order in 1961, Attorney General Robert Kennedy played a driving role in the effort to recruit blacks in all the higher echelons of government and in all departments, including first of all his own. He found that only 10 out of the more than 950 attorneys in the Department of Justice in Washington and only 9 out of 742 lawyers in the United States Attorneys' Offices around the country were black, although all 56 department messengers were black.[41]

The achievements of affirmative action, in both government agencies and business corporations (as well as colleges and universities and other institutions), have been documented in many studies, and some of the pitfalls of this approach have been pointed to and disputed.[42] Beyond dispute, however, is the fact that opportunities have greatly increased for blacks, notably including black lawyers in all these sources of employment.

The impact of affirmative action was clearly felt in Philadelphia. In the 1978 Philadelphia survey, none of the oldest cohort of lawyers (born between 1895 and 1920) listed corporations or the federal government as his or her first employer. Of the younger cohorts (born between 1938 and 1954), 25 percent or more went to work for the federal government, the

39. Of the 70% of all lawyers in private practice in 1980, 47% were reported to be sole practitioners, 17% to be in firms of 2 to 3 lawyers, and 16% to be in firms of 4 to 9 lawyers. Only 20% of all private practitioners were in firms of 10 or more lawyers (Curran, "Lawyer Demographics," p. 9). In 1981 there were 34,000 graduates from the 171 accredited law schools, a number expected to remain constant in the next few years, and the U.S. Department of Labor estimates that only 26,400 legal jobs will open in each of the years from 1981 through 1985. Bodine, "Scrambling for Jobs," p. 12.

40. For a history of federal affirmative-action programs, see U.S. Commission on Civil Rights, *Statement on Affirmative Action*, Clearinghouse Publication 54, October 1977.

41. Harris Wofford, *Of Kennedys and Kings* (New York: Farrar, Straus & Giroux, 1980), p. 141.

42. See Thomas Sowell, "Affirmative Action Harms the Disadvantaged," *Wall Street Journal*, July 28, 1981, p. 28.

largest category of employer. Corporate opportunities for black lawyers had only begun to open for the middle cohort (born between 1921 and 1937), but that source of employment accounted for 10 percent of the youngest group. Employment in the state government also rose from none in the oldest cohort to 14 percent in the youngest.

With employment in white law firms rising to 17 percent for the youngest cohort in the Philadelphia survey, and with the increases in the proportion of black lawyers going into corporations and city and state governments, the proportion of those joining black law firms had dwindled from 29 percent of the oldest cohort, to none of the youngest. The other earlier large category of black employment—that of the sole practitioner —also went down drastically, from 29 percent of the oldest to 6 percent of the youngest. Although accurate figures are difficult to secure for the current status of black sole practitioners and small black law firms across the nation, the surveys of the large and the medium-size firms in fifteen other cities confirm that the trends found in Philadelphia are prevailing elsewhere.

There is reason to believe that all levels of government and the large business corporations with public constituencies will continue to attract black lawyers. With the right to vote now secured for blacks throughout the country, with blacks playing a major role in the politics and adminis-tration of most of the nation's large cities, and with blacks exercising a balance of power in many local, state, and national elections, there is also likely to be a political compulsion to hire, appoint, or elect blacks in increasing numbers. Since lawyers have proven their ability in a variety of fields of public administration and corporate leadership, it is probable that government and corporations will continue to increase as sources of em-ployment for black lawyers.

In politics itself, from the Constitutional Convention that founded this nation to the present Congress of the United States, lawyers (most of them white) have played a disproportionately large part in legislative bodies throughout the country, and among elected officials. In the mid-nineteenth century, Alexis de Tocqueville observed that lawyers were the natural aristocracy of a democracy since in a government of law, not men, it is the men of law who govern.[43]

After the Civil War, blacks served in southern legislatures and repre-sented southern states in Congress, and a considerable portion of these were lawyers.[44] With the end of the Reconstruction period, there was a

43. Alexis de Tocqueville, *Democracy in America* (1859), p. 258. See Edgar S. and Jean Cahn, "Power to the People or to the Profession?—The Public Interest in Public Interest Law," *Yale Law Journal,* vol. 79, no. 6 (May 1970), p. 1007.

44. Styles, *Negroes and the Law,* p. 17. Between the end of the Civil War and 1936, 24 blacks served in the U.S. Congress; 9 of these were lawyers.

long hiatus in the election of black officials. Then, in the latter half of the twentieth century, blacks increasingly began to win places in legislative bodies and appointment and election to executive and judicial posts. This movement is seen repeatedly in the discussion of Philadelphia in Part One and of the fifteen cities in Chapter 9.

In 1981, according to the Joint Center for Political Studies, there were 5,038 elected black officials in the United States, including 18 members of Congress, 333 state legislators, 204 mayors, 1,818 members of municipal governing bodies, and 274 elected judges (not including magistrates).[45] Aside from the judges (and 6 of the 18 Congressmen), just how many of these nearly 5,000 officials are lawyers is not known, but the number is substantial. Since the total of elected black officials has been multiplying in each of the recent decades, this should remain another promising field for black lawyers in the future.

## Blacks in the Judiciary

In terms of prestige and legal power, the judiciary is recognized as the pinnacle of the legal profession, although this is not reflected in the financial compensation of our judges. The lack of black judges throughout most of American history added to the conviction among blacks that there was an inherent injustice toward them built into the "system." The courthouse, especially in southern states, has historically been viewed by blacks as an alien setting and often an agency of discrimination. The story is told of the black mother warning her child to walk on the other side of the street when passing the courthouse. Not until the successful civil-rights litigation in the middle of the twentieth century did this attitude start to change, and then the federal judiciary became the branch of government to which blacks could best look to secure their rights.

One recites the list of first appointments of blacks in the judiciary with a certain ambivalence, as in the case of black "firsts" in other sought-after fields. The individual achievements are encouraging; yet it is discouraging that these "firsts" should have come at such late dates, so long after the Emancipation.

With rare exceptions, judges in the United States, excluding justices of the peace and local magistrates of limited jurisdiction, have always been drawn from the pool of lawyers. Since there were barely a handful of black lawyers before the Civil War, and their experience was extremely limited, it is not surprising that it was not until 1850 that the first reported black American magistrate—Robert Morris of Massachusetts—was appointed

45. *National Roster of Black Elected Officials 1981*, Joint Center for Political Studies, Washington, D.C.

and that he was one of the first two recorded black lawyers in the country. The first black lawyer, Macon B. Allen, also became a judge in South Carolina, but that was not until almost a quarter of a century later—in 1873.[46]

Under the domination of Reconstruction forces, the South Carolina State Legislature in 1870 elected the first black state supreme court justice, Jonathan J. Wright, who wrote approximately two hundred opinions before he had to resign in 1877 after the resurgence of white supremacy.[47] In 1872 the South Carolina legislature elected a black, George Lee, as the first southern inferior court judge, and when he died within the year, Macon B. Allen was elected to take his place.[48] In 1873 Mifflin Wister Gibbs, a black law graduate of Oberlin College, served on the municipal court in Little Rock; he has been regarded as the nation's first black judge of a trial court of general jurisdiction.[49] During Reconstruction black lawyers were elected to a number of southern legislatures, but very few secured judicial appointments.[50] It was not until 1883, when George Ruffin was appointed Judge of the Charlestown District Court in Massachusetts, that a black in the North held a judicial post higher than magistrate.[51] North or South, there is no record of many more judicial posts for blacks during the nineteenth century.

After Reconstruction, it was more than eight decades before a black became a state supreme court justice in any state when, in 1961, Otis M. Smith was appointed to fill an unexpired term on the Supreme Court of Michigan. He was defeated for election to a full term and, as the Detroit section tells, went on to become General Counsel of General Motors Corporation. It was not until a century after Reconstruction that a black was again appointed to a state supreme court in the South, when Joseph W. Hatchett was chosen in 1975 for the Florida Supreme Court—also filling an unexpired term. He was reelected to a full term in 1976, and in 1979, when appointed to the United States Court of Appeals for the Fifth (now the Eleventh) Circuit, he became the first black federal circuit judge in the South.[52]

Whether the system of choosing state and local judges is by popular election, as in a majority of states, or by appointment by the governor, prejudice has been, and may continue to be, a significant limitation on the number of blacks who become judges. Such racial discrimination is not, of course, restricted to the South. The first black judge to be elected in the North is said to be Albert B. George, who won a municipal court judgeship

46. See note 2 of this chapter.
47. Styles, *Negroes and the Law*, pp. 123–24; *National Roster of Black Judicial Officers*, p. 2.
48. *National Roster of Black Judicial Officers*, p. 1.
49. Styles, *Negroes and the Law*, p. 125.
50. Ibid., p. 20.
51. Brown, "Genesis of the Negro Lawyer," p. 173.
52. *National Roster of Black Judicial Officers*, p. 2.

in Chicago in 1924.[53] Since then, in most of the places where blacks have been elected judges, the constituencies have been predominantly black or at least the proportion of black voters has been relatively large. The number of state and local judges who are black has increased dramatically in the last two decades, but the majority of black judges in the South are elected in small, rural, overwhelmingly black communities, and black judges in the North are generally concentrated in the lower courts of major metropolitan areas with large black populations. More than half of all black state judges are in the cities of Chicago, Detroit, Los Angeles, New York, Philadelphia, and Washington, D.C.[54]

Still, the increase in the total number of state and local judges who are black is impressive. In 1970 a report based on information from the governors of the fifty states named 195 state and municipal court judges who were black, including 15 who were part-time or special judges and many who were local magistrates. This was up from a total of fewer than 100 just four years before.[55] By 1980 the *National Roster of Black Judicial Officers* listed 505 black judges in state judiciaries:[56]

| | |
|---|---|
| 21 | on appellate courts (including 4 on courts of last resort) |
| 204 | on courts of general jurisdiction |
| 233 | on courts of limited jurisdiction |
| 47 | serving in quasi-judicial capacities |

Appendix 16 shows the distribution of these judgeships by states, excluding the 47 listed in the quasi-judicial category. These figures for blacks should be compared with the total of approximately 26,650 judges of all races in the same categories:[57]

| | |
|---|---|
| 926 | on appellate courts (including 341 on courts of last resort) |
| 7,127 | on courts of general jurisdiction |
| 18,597 | (approximate) on courts of limited jurisdiction |

53. Edward B. Toles, "A Short History of Black Lawyers in Illinois," in *History of the National Bar Association, Fifty Years of Progress for Black Lawyers,* souvenir booklet distributed at the annual meeting of the National Bar Association, Chicago, 1974, p. 24.

54. *National Roster of Black Judicial Officers,* p. 4. See also Beverly Blair Cook, "Black Representation in the Third Branch," *Black Law Journal,* vol. 1, nos. 2 and 3 (1971), p. 260.

55. *National Roster of Black Judicial Officers,* p. 5 (citing Edward Toles, "The Negro Lawyer in the United States: A 1966 Report," *Congressional Record,* Appendix, A5458, October 20, 1966).

56. *National Roster of Black Judicial Officers,* p. 5.

57. Statistics on state and local judges supplied by the National Center for State Courts, Williamsburg, Va. It is interesting to note that approximately the same disparities in the regional distribution of black judges are found in Appendix 16 as those found shown in Appendix 15 on the regional distribution of black lawyers. Black judges, like black lawyers, are found in proportionally large numbers in states with larger black populations, except in southern states, where they are found in disproportionately smaller numbers despite large black populations.

It is clear that blacks are still substantially underrepresented on state and local courts. Although constituting more than 11 percent of the population, they comprise less than 2 percent of the judges on these courts. Nevertheless, the trend has been sharply upward.[58]

Blacks are also underrepresented on the federal bench, but much less so than on state and local courts. Blacks now hold about 5 percent of all federal judgeships, magistrates, and other judicial posts. This is more than double their proportion in the state and local judiciaries (and ten times the proportion of black partners in the largest private firms).[59]

As of 1980 there were 94 black judges and magistrates serving in the federal judiciary, distributed as follows:[60]

| | |
|---|---|
| 1 | Justice of the Supreme Court |
| 10 | Judges of Circuit Courts of Appeals |
| 40 | Judges of District Courts (with lifetime tenure) |
| 2 | Judges of the U.S. Court of International Trade |
| 1 | Judge of the District Court for the Virgin Islands (eight-year term) |
| 6 | Judges of U.S. Bankruptcy Courts |
| 7 | Magistrates |
| 11 | Administrative law judges |
| 4 | Appellate judges of the District of Columbia |
| 12 | Trial court judges of the District of Columbia |
| Total 94 | |

Excluding the local courts of the District of Columbia and courts of special or limited jurisdiction, blacks in 1980 accounted for 51, or nearly 8 percent, of the total of 657 lifetime federal justices and judges. These 51 judges, (including one Supreme Court Justice) and their black predecessors, are listed, with their dates of appointment, in Appendix 17. The District of Columbia, as the nation's capital and having a black majority population, is a unique case. For a period in 1981, as the Washington section notes, all four chief judges of the courts sitting in the District were black.[61]

It took a long time to reach this level of black representation in the

58. *National Roster of Black Judicial Officers,* pp. 1, 5.

59. Ibid. Only 0.5% of the partners in the 50 largest law firms in the U.S. are black. Burke and Johnson, "More Women," p. 10.

60. From *National Roster of Black Judicial Officers,* pp. 15–25, and later information provided by Solicitor General Wade H. McCree, Jr.

61. They were William B. Bryant (went on Senior Status in 1981), U.S. District Court for the District of Columbia; Theodore R. Newman, Jr., D.C. Court of Appeals; H. Carl Moultrie, Superior Court of the District of Columbia; and Spottswood W. Robinson, U.S. Court of Appeals for the District of Columbia.

federal judiciary. One might have expected that the responsibility of presidents to act in terms of a national constituency would have resulted in a far more representative federal judiciary a great deal earlier.

From the Civil War until 1900, blacks received no presidential encouragement that judicial opportunities would be open to them as their legal experience increased. In 1901 President Theodore Roosevelt appointed a black, Robert H. Terrell, to be a judge of the District of Columbia Municipal Court, the first black appointed to any judgeship by a president. Thereafter, this local District of Columbia term-judgeship became in effect a black post, and in 1950 President Harry S. Truman appointed two other blacks to the same court.[62]

When President Franklin Delano Roosevelt appointed Charles Houston's partner, William H. Hastie, to the United States District Court for the Virgin Islands in 1937, this too was a term, not a lifetime, appointment (and in a territory that was indigenously black). Hastie's successors were black, and that judgeship also became in effect a black post.

No other black federal judges were appointed until after World War II, when Truman selected Irvin C. Mollison, in 1945, as a judge on the United States Customs Court (now the Court of International Trade). This was the first lifetime black judge on the federal bench, but it was a special court, not a constitutional trial or appellate court of general jurisdiction. That very significant breakthrough for a black occurred in 1949 when Truman appointed Judge Hastie to the United States Court of Appeals for the Third Circuit.[63]

No black was appointed as a lifetime United States district judge until 1961, when President John F. Kennedy named James B. Parsons to the United States District Court for the Northern District of Illinois. A month later Kennedy appointed a second black district court judge, Wade H. McCree, Jr., who in 1966 was elevated by President Lyndon B. Johnson from the District Court of the Eastern District of Michigan to the United States Circuit Court of Appeals for the Sixth Circuit. Judge McCree resigned the latter post in 1977 to accept President Jimmy Carter's appointment as Solicitor General, only the second black to occupy this important office.

Although Kennedy was the first president to pledge the active recruitment and appointment of blacks to the federal bench, in the less than three years of his presidency he appointed only the above two blacks to district courts and Thurgood Marshall to the Second Circuit Court of Appeals. In

62. See M. Sammy Miller, "Robert H. Terrell: First Black D.C. Municipal Court Judge," *The Crisis*, vol. 83, no. 6 (June–July 1976), pp. 209–10.

63. Peter M. Bergman, *The Negro in America* (New York: Harper & Row, 1969), pp. 480, 509, 521.

addition, he nominated Spottswood Robinson to the United States District Court of the District of Columbia, but confirmation did not come until after Kennedy's death. This made three blacks out of a total of 130 Kennedy appointments to district and appellate courts. Further, a number of appointments of black judges in succeeding administrations were given their start by Kennedy. Nevertheless, in retrospect, the number of black appointments as lifetime judges by Kennedy does not seem impressive.[64] But at the time, those lifetime black federal judges represented important steps, and Thurgood Marshall's long-delayed confirmation by the Senate required difficult negotiations with the chairman of the powerful Judiciary Committee, Senator James Eastland of Mississippi.[65]

With President Johnson the pace quickened. During his five years in office, he appointed seven black district judges, including A. Leon Higginbotham, Jr. (whose name had first been projected for a district court judgeship by President Kennedy), Spottswood Robinson (whom he renominated after Kennedy's death), and Constance B. Motley, another former NAACP attorney (the first black woman to become a federal judge). He also promoted two black district judges—Robinson and Wade McCree—to the courts of appeals for the District of Columbia Circuit and for the Sixth Circuit, respectively. And it was President Johnson who appointed the first black justice of the Supreme Court of the United States, Thurgood Marshall.[66]

President Kennedy had committed himself to making such an appointment, and Attorney General Robert Kennedy had initially proposed Judge Hastie to be the first Kennedy nominee for the Supreme Court. But in his oral history interview with Anthony Lewis, Robert Kennedy reports that they were discouraged from appointing Hastie by Chief Justice Earl Warren, who argued strongly with him against Hastie's selection on the ground that the black circuit judge was too conservative.[67]

Under Presidents Richard M. Nixon and Gerald R. Ford the pace of black judicial appointments slackened, with no new black judges for appellate courts and altogether between 1969 and 1977 only ten black judges

64. Harold W. Chase, *Federal Judges: The Appointing Process* (Minneapolis: University of Minnesota Press, 1972), pp. 49, 77–79. Chase states that 5 of the 130 Kennedy appointments were Negroes.

65. Schlesinger, *Robert Kennedy,* pp. 308, 372–73.

66. When appointed a circuit judge, Marshall had briefed or argued 62 cases before the Supreme Court. Of the 32 NAACP cases he argued before the court, he won 29. In this century, only Justices Brandeis, Reed, Frankfurter, and Jackson have had comparable experience before their appointments to the court. Irving Kaufman, "Thurgood Marshall: A Tribute from a Former Colleague"; and Kenneth Karst, "Justice Marshall and the First Amendment," in *Black Law Journal,* vol. 6, no. 1 (1978), p. 43.

67. Wofford, *Of Kennedys and Kings,* p. 169.

for district courts (seven by Nixon and three by Ford) being appointed. Then, to the surprise of many, President Jimmy Carter, a former governor of Georgia, appointed more black federal judges in one term than the combined total by all his predecessors. Carter appointed 9 black circuit judges (including the first female black appellate judge, Amalya Kearse) and 29 black district judges. That made a total of 38 black judges—or nearly 15 percent—out of the total of 258 federal judgeships filled by President Carter. This extraordinary record was made possible by Congressional enactment in 1978 of an omnibus judgeship bill providing for 152 new federal judgeships. President Carter had the opportunity to appoint more judges than any other president, by a large margin. As of 1981 his appointees comprised about 40 percent of the federal judiciary.[68]

The large number of total judgeships open to President Carter accounts only in part for this unusual number of blacks. In terms of race, ethnic background, and gender, the pattern of his appointments was very different from those of any previous president. Carter determinedly sought to make the federal bench more representative by selecting an unprecedented proportion of blacks, Hispanics, and women. He seemed to take particular relish as a southerner in pointing out the black judges he had chosen. His record in this respect is seen in the following figures:[69]

|  | Total Carter Appointments | Black Appointments | % Blacks |
|---|---|---|---|
| District Courts | 202 | 28 | 14 |
| Courts of Appeals | 56 | 9 | 16 |

Carter nominated at least one black to the district courts sitting in ten southern and two border states. Of the eleven states of the Confederacy, Mississippi was the only state for which Carter did not nominate a black to the district court, and it remains (along with Virginia) without a black federal judge, although Mississippi continues to be the state with the largest proportion of blacks in its population.

Of the forty-one nominations of circuit and district court judges made by President Ronald Reagan during his first eleven months in office, no black district judge, and only one black circuit judge (Lawrence W. Pierce) has been nominated. Since Judge Pierce was a district judge prior to being

68. Sheldon Goldman, "Carter's Judicial Appointments: A Lasting Legacy," *Judicature,* vol. 64, no. 8 (March 1981), pp. 344, 349, 351.

69. Ibid., pp. 345, 348–51. These figures include only those judges who were confirmed by the Senate. As for women and Hispanics, Carter appointed 28 women (including 6 blacks) and 14 Hispanics (including 1 woman) to district courts, and 11 women (including 1 black) and 2 Hispanics to courts of appeals.

sworn in on December 7, 1981 as a circuit judge (Court of Appeals for the Second Circuit), the number of black federal judges was unchanged.

A storm of controversy swirled around three of Carter's last nominations—the first blacks nominated for district courts in Alabama and Virginia. The American Bar Association Standing Committee on Federal Judiciary had rated the Virginia nominee "Qualified," but the staff investigators for the Senate Judiciary Committee turned up information that undermined support for him in the Senate Committee. The confirmation hearings were postponed, and the nomination was effectively buried. The ABA committee had rated both Alabama nominees "Not Qualified." One of the Alabama nominees was nominated by the President and confirmed by the Senate despite the ABA rating, an extremely infrequent occurrence, but derogatory information on the other nominee led to his withdrawing himself from consideration and the substitute nomination of a young, Yale-educated black attorney who was given a "Qualified" rating by the ABA committee and was quickly confirmed.[70]

In the wake of this controversy, unjustified charges of prejudice were made against the ABA Standing Committee, which has been consulted by every administration by direction of the President with respect to almost every federal judicial appointment since 1952 and has been consulted by the Senate Judiciary Committee on every federal judicial nomination since 1948.[71] Its advice, including its formal ratings of "Qualified," "Well Qualified," "Exceptionally Well Qualified," and "Not Qualified" have carried very great weight with Presidents, Attorneys General, and the Senate Judiciary Committee.

In the first years of the committee's work, the memory of the ABA's long tradition of excluding blacks from its membership (effectively remedied only in 1943) justified skepticism about the ability of white leaders of the bar—on an all-white committee—to free themselves from prejudice in considering prospective black nominees. But some outstanding civil-rights leaders have served as chairmen and members of the committee, and an examination of the ratings that it has given black (and Hispanic and female) nominees clearly does not support a charge of prejudice.

As already noted, two of Carter's black nominees were rated "Not Qualified" (one of these then being confirmed by the Senate). Four of his white male nominees were similarly rated. Thirty-eight of Carter's black nominees were accorded a rating of "Qualified" or better.

Finding nominees "Not Qualified" is not a new practice for the Stand-

---

70. Ibid., pp. 349, 353–54. The Alabama black nominee who was first confirmed was U. W. Clemon; the second nominee confirmed was Myron H. Thompson.

71. American Bar Association, *Standing Committee on Federal Judiciary—What It Is and How It Works* (1980), p. 1.

ing Committee, nor has it been related to race. Before the first black lawyer was nominated for a lifetime district court judgeship, the committee had made as many as twenty-seven unfavorable reports in a single year (all on white nominees); and also, before 1961, the committee, particularly with regard to nominees for district courts, had taken a firm position that no one should be nominated who had not had a reasonable amount of trial experience.[72]

Until the two black nominees in 1980, the ABA Standing Committee, in its almost four decades of investigations and reporting on the qualification of persons under consideration for federal judicial appointment, had never found a proposed black to be "Not Qualified." Indeed, in order to take into account the special difficulties that blacks, Hispanics, and women had faced in acquiring experience and reputation, and thus to make possible the appointment of more blacks and women, who might otherwise have been unacceptable, the committee in 1977, upon announcement by President Carter of his minority appointment program, revised its guidelines.[73] The earlier rebuttable presumption that a nominee should have practiced before the bar for at least fifteen years had already been reduced to twelve years. Faced with Carter's determination to appoint many more blacks, Hispanics, and women, the committee responded with further flexibility. Its Chairperson, Brooksley E. Landau, explained the new approach:

> The ABA has been concerned for some time about the low number of women and minorities on the federal bench and has recognized the need for greater diversity. . . . Nevertheless, our Committee recognizes that some of the criteria we use to evaluate prospective nominees could work to the disadvantage of women and minority candidates. For example, the Committee believes that ordinarily a prospective nominee should have been admitted to the Bar for 12 years to ensure that the person has had adequate professional experience. However, an inflexible 12-year rule would limit the number of eligible women and minority appointees, since relatively few of them have had such lengthy experience.[74]

Therefore, she reported, in order "to ensure that women and minority candidates are given full and fair consideration even if their legal experience may have been limited," the Standing Committee had expressly

---

72. Bernard G. Segal, "Federal Judicial Selection—Progress and the Promise of the Future," Address to the American College of Trial Lawyers, March 28, 1961.

73. Brooksley E. Landau, Remarks to the New Orleans ABA Conference on the Role of the Judge in the 1980s, Washington, D.C., June 20, 1981, pp. 7–8.

74. Ibid., pp. 6–7.

adopted new guidelines that "permit a finding of qualified based on less experience than had traditionally been required." One woman appointee, under this new policy, was found qualified even though she had been a member of the bar for only five years (three of which were as a well-respected state court judge).[75]

In 1981 there were two black members and one Hispanic member of the fourteen-member ABA Standing Committee, and a woman as chairperson. The Committee's new approach helps to explain another matter of concern to some observers: the high proportion of blacks (and Hispanics and women) given the rating of "Qualified," in contrast to the higher proportion of white male nominees given ratings of "Well Qualified" or "Exceptionally Well Qualified." Table 17 gives the white/black breakdown of the ABA ratings for Carter nominees.

A closer look makes the disparities understandable, without any factor of prejudice. According to the ABA committee standards,[76] in order to merit "the sparingly awarded" rating of "Exceptionally Well Qualified" the prospective nominee "must stand at the top of the legal profession in the community involved and have outstanding legal ability, wide experience, and the highest reputation for integrity and temperament." Everything in this study explains why relatively few blacks have yet had the opportunity to reach the top of the profession and have the wide experience called for to be deemed "Exceptionally Well Qualified." To be "Well Qualified," the prospective nominee must be "one of the best available for the vacancy from the standpoint of competence."[77]

One black appointment to the Court of Appeals, A. Leon Higginbo-

Table 17
**Racial Breakdown of ABA Ratings for Carter Judicial Nominees**

| Rating | White Men | White Women | Black Men | Black Women |
|---|---|---|---|---|
| Qualified | 62 (32.3%) | 24 (70.5%) | 21 (63.6%) | 5 (71.4%) |
| Well Qualified | 111 (57.8%) | 9 (26.5%) | 9 (27.2%) | 2 (28.5%) |
| Exceptionally Well Qualified | 15 (7.8%) | 1 (2.9%) | 1 (3.0%) | 0 |
| Not Qualified | 4 (2.1%) | 0 | 2 (6.0%) | 0 |
| Totals | 192 | 34 | 33 | 7 |

75. Ibid., p. 8. See also Brooksley E. Landau, Remarks to the Federal Judicial Selection Workshop of the National Association of Women Judges, Washington, D.C., October 4, 1980, p. 9.

76. American Bar Association, *Standing Committee on Federal Judiciary*, pp. 4–5.

77. Many of the same factors apply to the experience of Hispanic nominees. Carter's Hispanic nominees received the following ratings: qualified—9; well qualified—1; exceptionally well qualified—0; not qualified—0.

tham, Jr., previously discussed, received the rating of "Exceptionally Well Qualified" in 1977. Of Carter's other eight black appointments to circuit courts, five received ratings of "Well Qualified" and three of "Qualified."

Judge Higginbotham is a noteworthy example. In an early stage of the Kennedy administration, the Attorney General indicated to the chairman of the ABA Standing Committee that President Kennedy would like to nominate the thirty-three-year-old Higginbotham to the United States District Court (for the Eastern District of Pennsylvania). The committee chairman subsequently advised that because of Higginbotham's limited experience the committee's vote of "Qualified" had been by a divided vote. In those days a divided rating by the ABA Committee on a black nominee might well enable one or more members of the Senate Judiciary Committee to block confirmation. In response to Attorney General Robert Kennedy's queries, the ABA Committee chairman, expressing confidence in Higginbotham's inherent ability and promise, suggested that the president appoint Higginbotham to a national quasi-judicial post where he could speedily gain special experience and broader exposure and thereby enhance his professional standing. President Kennedy appointed Higginbotham a commissioner of the Federal Trade Commission.[78] Two years later, prior to his nomination by President Johnson, the ABA Committee unanimously found him "Qualified" for a district court judgeship. In 1968 President Johnson proposed nominating Higginbotham for the Court of Appeals (for the Third Circuit). The ABA Committee promptly reported him as "Well Qualified," meaning that in three years on the bench he had already proven to be among the best qualified of those available. Johnson, however, left office before the appointment could be made. Then came the "Exceptionally Well Qualified" rating for Higginbotham at the start of the Carter administration.

A study by the ABA Standing Committee found that the median years at the bar for all 286 Carter nominees was twenty-four. The pool of black lawyers with that much experience at the bar is very small, and most of the black lawyers practicing in the 1940s and 1950s were prevented from having the kind of professional experience likely to qualify them for a judgeship. Since about three out of every four black lawyers as of 1981 were admitted to the bar during the last ten years, only a few thousand of them were old enough to have gained the experience necessary, excluding the other questions of education, integrity, temperament, and ability.

Flexibility in the number of years at the bar is only one aspect of the ABA Standing Committee's new approach. In fact, far from opening the floodgates to a wave of judges with very limited experience, the revised

78. Information from Bernard G. Segal, who was at that time chairman of the Standing Committee on Federal Judiciary.

policy led to only thirteen Carter nominees who had less than twelve years at the bar, and eight of these had eleven years. Of the thirteen, four were black (one of whom the committee found "Not Qualified"), four were women (including one black), three were Hispanic (two of whom the ABA Committee found "Well Qualified"), and three were white men (one of whom the ABA Committee found "Not Qualified"). In view of their shorter experience at the bar and of other factors related to their limited opportunities, the large number of women and minority group nominees found "Qualified" by the Standing Committee is evidence of the committee's broader, more constructive approach and of the absence of prejudice of any kind. Under rules in force in times past, many of these candidates would almost certainly have been rated "Not Qualified."

As with so many aspects of racial disadvantage, the relative youth of black lawyers is double-edged. The encouraging side is that the rapidly increasing pool of young black lawyers assures that, as the years pass and they gain experience, the black proportion of the total pool of lawyers in the nation available to be considered for judgeships, and assured of satisfactory ratings, will also increase.[79]

## Black Law Teachers

In *Sweatt v. Painter,* the Supreme Court of the United States in 1950 emphasized the need for law schools to be representative. The court did not consider the "law school for Negroes," to which Mr. Sweatt had been referred under the state law, to be equal to the University of Texas Law School, which had denied him admission, since the Negro school excluded from its student body "members of the racial groups which number 85% of the population of the State and include most of the lawyers, witnesses, jurors, judges and other officials with whom petitioner will inevitably be dealing when he becomes a member of the Texas Bar." As Chief Justice Fred Vinson put it for a unanimous court:

> The law school, the proving ground for legal learning and practice, cannot be effective in isolation from the individuals and institutions with which the law interacts. Few students and no one who has practiced law would choose to study in an academic vacuum, removed from the interplay of ideas and the exchange of views with which law is concerned.[80]

79. A former chairman of the Standing Commitee, as well as its published material, contributed to the data on judicial selection in this chapter, within the limits of the confidentiality required by the rules of the Committee. (Judge Higginbotham authorized the use of the items pertaining to Judge Higginbotham which are not a matter of record.)

80. *Sweatt v. Painter,* 339 U.S. 629, 634 (1950).

The decision in *Sweatt v. Painter* is rightly credited with ending the era of *de jure* segregation in legal education. The aspirations and opportunities of black students no longer could be constrained by the number of seats in the few historically black law schools. In theory, black students now could compete for a seat in any law school in the country.

Little, if any, attention was paid to the fact that those black students venturing beyond the black law schools would be confronted by faculties that were populated almost exclusively by white males. In the year *Sweatt* was decided, there was only one black in the entire country who held a full-time teaching position at a law school other than an historically black institution. For almost a decade after William Ming, Jr., started teaching at the University of Chicago Law School in 1947, becoming a full professor in 1951, he was the first and the only black law teacher at a predominantly white law school (see the Chicago section).

If the access to traditionally white law schools that was promised by *Sweatt* was at first illusory for most black law students, for many years it was virtually nonexistent for black law teachers. As late as 1968 there were fewer than ten black members of law faculties who held full-time positions leading to academic tenure other than at the four historically black institutions—Howard, North Carolina Central, Texas Southern, and Southern (at Baton Rouge). Even this is a generous estimate. Research thus far has revealed only five in addition to Ming: Kenneth R. Callahan (Wayne State, Michigan), Ronald R. Davenport (Duquesne), Charles Quick (Wayne State, Illinois), George Strait (Northeastern), and John Wilkens (Boalt Hall, Berkeley).

This situation changed dramatically in the next decade. The five years from 1969 to 1974 saw a substantial increase in the employment of minority faculty in law schools. In 1969 Harvard Law School appointed Derrick A. Bell, Jr., then a civil rights attorney. By selecting Bell and advancing him to tenured status the next year, Harvard reinforced what was until then a very tentative effort by many of the nation's law schools to find a black or other minority faculty member. Within the next two years a number of the leading law schools had added a minority member to their faculties: Columbia—Kellis E. Parker; Michigan—Harry T. Edwards; California at Berkeley (Boalt Hall)—Henry Ramsey, Jr.; Stanford—William Benjamin Gould; and Yale—John Baker.

Many of the other national law schools kept pace. In 1969, when UCLA hired both Reginald H. Alleyne, Jr., and Henry W. McGee, Jr., that institution became the first predominantly white law school to have more than one black faculty member. Rutgers, which had pioneered by appointing Clarence Clyde Ferguson, Jr. (referred to later in this chapter) a professor in 1955, a post he retained until 1963 when he became Dean at Howard Law School, took on in 1970 Charles H. Jones, Jr., and Alfred Anson

Slocum. New York University, with Leroy D. Clark and Napoleon Williams, and Temple, with H. Patrick Swygert and Handsel B. Minyard, were not far behind. The majority of law schools secured at most one black faculty member, but by 1974 the total number of blacks teaching on the nation's law faculties had grown to more than one hundred. Over seventy-eight were teaching at once all-white institutions.[81]

How and why did this turnabout occur? While it was no doubt partly due to the forces that were producing greatly increased admissions of black law students and other minorities, a major reason for the urge to seek blacks and other minorities for faculty positions seems to be directly related to the changing nature of the student population. In 1964, when there were only seven hundred black law students enrolled in ABA-approved law schools, there appeared to be little or no interest in seeking black faculty. By 1969, when the black student population had virtually doubled, law schools had an incentive for considering a larger number of blacks for the faculty. Anecdotes abound about minority faculty prospects who were suddenly "discovered" by former teachers and classmates. Harvard Professor (now Dean of the University of Oregon Law School) Derrick Bell's reminiscence of the "before and after" attitude at Harvard Law School is illustrative of a not uncommon experience:

> By this time in late 1968, the efforts to recruit more minority students into the nation's law schools were well underway, and several schools were becoming aware of the hoped-for value of having a black faculty member to help handle the problems presented by the recruited minority members, many of whom refused to express their appreciation by settling down to their studies and ignoring the racism that continued to flourish all around them. Recognizing this racism, they were determined to fight it.
>
> Suddenly, I was besieged with teaching offers, all from top schools. As much as I enjoyed working with the Western Center, I decided to accept one of the teaching offers before the crusading mood of the law schools changed—as it later did. I accepted Harvard's offer because it was generous, and I greatly enjoyed my interview visit with students and faculty. In addition, a few years before, after a visit there, during which I gave a lecture to a civil rights class taught by a young Harvard graduate with one year of civil rights experiences, I inquired about the possibility of a teaching post. I received the response, "We

81. Presentation by Professor Harry Edwards of the University of Michigan Law School, in "Report of Minority-Group Law Teachers Planning Conference," Harvard Law School, September 19–20, 1974, pp. 6–7, reprinted in *Black Law Journal*, vol. 4, no. 3 (1974), pp. 575, 580.

have no openings for a person of your experience." Coming to Harvard represented a personal challenge that I could not resist.[82]

With few exceptions, in hiring black faculty the early schools all had a relatively larger minority student population. Even in the 1980s minority faculty are most likely to be found in those law schools with more than an insignificant number of minority students. A 1981 study by Professor Ralph R. Smith of the University of Pennsylvania Law School shows that while some 41 percent of the nation's law schools had no minority faculty members, schools designated as "high minority" in terms of the number of minority students were not in this category.[83] Moreover, while 69 percent of all law schools had no more than one minority faculty member, 75 percent of the "high minority" schools had two or more minority faculty members. Just one of the "elite" schools, Harvard, had as many as three minority faculty members, and this was only during a two-year period when Derrick Bell, Harry T. Edwards (now Judge of the United States Court of Appeals for the District of Columbia Circuit), and Clarence Ferguson, Jr. (after extended public service, including as United States Ambassador to Uganda and Dean of Howard Law School), were there together. With six black law teachers in 1981, Temple University Law School (with 104 black students comprising nearly 9% of the total enrollment) continued to have more black faculty than any other predominantly white law school in the country.

By the 1981–82 academic year there were some 224 full-time black law teachers (173 men, 51 women) on the faculties of law schools approved by the American Bar Association. Moreover, in 1981 black law professors were deans of three predominantly white law schools: Derrick Bell, of the University of Oregon Law School; Elwin Griffith, of De Paul; and Ronald R. Davenport, of Duquesne. Even with this considerable progress, blacks remained vastly underrepresented among legal educators, constituting about 4 percent of the nationwide total of more than 5,000 teachers and administrators in legal education.[84]

Harry T. Edwards has offered some of the reasons the total of black teachers remains relatively low, including, first of all, the still "very small pool of blacks and other minorities with traditional qualifications, i.e., high grades, prestigious law school diploma, law review, Supreme Court clerk-

82. The Derrick Bell quote is a mildly edited (by Mr. Bell himself) version. An article included in *Minority Opportunities in Law for Blacks, Puerto Ricans, and Chicanos,* ed. Christine Philport Clark (Law Journal Press, 1974).
83. Ralph Smith, "Great Expectations and Dubious Results: A Pessimistic Prognosis for the Black Lawyer," *Black Law Journal,* vol. 7, no. 1 (1981).
84. 1981–82 Directory of Minority Law Faculty Members, Section on Minority groups, Directory of Law Teachers, Association of American Law Schools.

ship, association with a large law firm, etc."[85] These "traditional qualifications" for employment on law faculties and for tenure are indeed a serious limitation on the pool of possible black teachers.

James J. Jones, Jr., Professor of Law at the University of Wisconsin Law School, suggests that, in reviewing qualifications, "most schools would discover some 'B' students who went on to become excellent teachers" and find "renowned legal scholars who are just as renowned as abominable teachers." Jones argues that, "if put to it, the law teaching community might be hard pressed to convince a skeptical court of the job-relatedness of the top 5 to 10 percent of the class, law review, and a judicial clerkship to the teaching of law."[86]

Therefore, it has been proposed that law schools should develop new job-related qualifications for law teaching that would give greater emphasis to teaching and somewhat less emphasis to scholarship. The issue of research and writing versus classroom teaching is, of course, a general one, affecting all prospects for appointment and tenure on law faculties, not just blacks. But such a shift of emphasis might well have the effect of enlarging the pool of black candidates.

Even with the present limitations, however, law teaching has now become a real career option for a significant number of black lawyers. The increases in the ranks of black law teachers during the 1970s, together with the wider distribution of such teachers among the nation's law schools, represents progress. But there have been some complicating ramifications, with at least one negative aspect. Spread out over so many law schools across the country, black law teachers are not able to benefit from the collegiality and cross-fertilization among fellow black faculty members that previously were the hallmarks of black law schools, especially Howard. Moreover, there is considerable support for the proposition that the black presence on white law faculties has come at the expense of a "brain-drain" from the historically black law schools. Partly for these reasons, and perhaps partly because of changed times, today's black law teachers are not viewed as playing as pivotal a role in shaping civil rights strategy as that of their predecessors on the Howard law faculty three, four, and five decades ago.

Black law teachers, however, still spend an impressive portion of their time handling public-interest and civil-rights litigation, particularly at the

85. "Report of Minority-Group Law Teachers Planning Conference," pp. 6–7. According to the summary of his remarks, Professor Edwards added: "The good black practitioners are not available. They like the work they are doing, they are making money, and they simply don't want to be hassled in order to get into a teaching position. . . . Minority-group students are usually in heavy debt after seven years of college education, and the money attractions of practice are very appealing."

86. Ibid., p. 493.

appellate level. Moreover, some individual law teachers have played more than a mere supporting role. Temple Law School Professor Drew S. Days III served as United States Assistant Attorney General, Civil Rights Division, before resuming his law teaching career at Yale. Temple Law Professor H. Patrick Swygert also served in the Carter administration as General Counsel of the United States Civil Service Commission, then as Special Counsel of the Merit Systems Protection Board before returning to teach at Temple. New York University Professor Leroy Clark was General Counsel to the Equal Employment Opportunity Commission and then joined the law faculty of Catholic University of America. Professor Patricia King added to her already formidable array of public-service ventures by serving as United States Deputy Assistant Attorney General in the Civil Division while on leave from her teaching duties at Georgetown Law Center. Professor Ralph Smith, of the University of Pennsylvania, served as Chairman of the National Conference of Black Lawyers Task Force on Legal Education and from that position played a significant role in the planning of the national strategy around the Bakke case. Professor Denise Carty-Bennia, of Northeastern University, has only recently completed a two-year term as Co-Chairperson of the National Conference of Black Lawyers. Professor Alfred Slocum was the Executive Director of the Council on Legal Education Opportunity for three years before returning to the Rutgers faculty. Many other black law faculty members have contributed significantly both in their teaching and in public activities.

These contributions notwithstanding, black law teachers as a group have not had as great an impact on legal institutions as they may have wished. There are two obvious reasons: first, despite their increase in numbers, black law teachers still constitute less than four percent of the nation's law faculties; second, a substantial number of black law teachers are junior faculty who are either untenured or only recently tenured.[87]

Another reason has been suggested. Unlike their counterparts in medical education, black law teachers have chosen not to develop an independent organizational base. Despite occasional musings about the possibilities, black law teachers have not formed a separate organization, nor have they expressed interest in establishing a law teachers' division or caucus within either the National Conference of Black Lawyers or the National Bar Association. Blacks in legal education, along with other minority law teachers, have continued to function under the auspices of the Section on Minority Groups of the Association of American Law Schools. Established in 1968 as the Committee on Minority Groups, the Section has evolved into the primary vehicle for minority law teachers to

87. 1981–82 *Directory of Minority Law Faculty Members,* Section on Minority Groups, and *Directory of Law Teachers,* Association of American Law Schools.

express collectively their concerns and examine their status. This goal has been pursued through an active program of panels, workshops, and conferences.

More recently a new note was struck. In 1980 the substantive session of the Section's annual meeting revolved around the thesis of "The Declining Significance of Race."[88] The 1981 Section meeting also revolved around an issue broader than legal education: "Polarization Between the Black Managerial Elite and the Black Underclass."[89]

The choice of these subjects appears to represent a growing awareness that the most crucial issue to be faced by those seeking equal justice is the matter of the black underclass. The challenge of poverty may indeed involve a declining significance of race. It is ironic that progress in surmounting and breaking down the barriers of race leads not to rest in the promised land of equal rights but to a new vision of the difficulties and more complex economic challenges to be met before those rights become a reality for all Americans.

As this national overview shows, there is still a long way to go before bias and the effects of long-standing prejudice are finally overcome. Taking full note of the arduous journey ahead, we should not, however, minimize the milestones already passed. Encouragement should come from a deeper appreciation of the distance traveled since the early days of American law when the first blacks set forth to become lawyers. For example, it is worth recalling the move of the Ruffin family from Richmond to Boston, before the Civil War, to escape the Virginia law making it a crime—"to be punished by stripes not exceeding thirty-nine"—for any "slaves, free negroes or mulattoes" to assemble "at any meeting house or other place . . . for the purpose of instruction in reading or writing."[90]

88. The substantive session of the 1980 Section meeting focused on a paper by Dr. William Julius Wilson, a black University of Chicago sociologist, reprinted as, "The Political Economy of Race: Reflections on the Declining Significance of Race," *Black Law Journal,* vol. 7, no. 1 (1981), p. 6.

89. Paper by Dr. William Darrity, a black economist, reprinted in *Black Law Journal,* vol. 7, no. 1 (1981), p. 21.

90. The Virginia statute also made it a crime for a white person to teach a black to read or write. Pertinent sections follow:

"39. Every assemblage of slaves, free negroes or mulattoes, at any meeting house or other place . . . for the purpose of instruction in reading or writing, by whomsoever conducted, . . . shall be an unlawful assembly, and it shall be the duty of all magistrates to suppress all such assemblies which occur within their respective jurisdictions . . . and seize any slave, free negro or mulatto there found, and . . . to order any slave, free negro or mulatto so seized to be punished by stripes not exceeding thirty-nine.

"40. Any white person who shall assemble with slaves, free negroes or mulattoes for the purpose of instructing them to read or write . . . shall be punished by confine-

Without his family's move North, George Lewis Ruffin would not have had the education to qualify for admission to Harvard Law School to become in 1869 the nation's first black law graduate. Previous pages have recounted his later role, and that of many other pioneer blacks, in opening opportunities for millions of Americans.

Few may have had the chance individually to shape history to the extent done by the first black lawyers, or by later leaders such as Charles Houston and Thurgood Marshall and William Hastie. The time of the early pioneers has passed. Nevertheless, black lawyers—as teachers, attorneys, administrators, and judges—have together, in relatively few decades, done much to change the course of American law. The total of all the achievements recorded in this study, against such massive resistance, is far more than the sum of its parts. In the light of this record, it is not hard to believe, as Martin Luther King, Jr. predicted on the first night of the Montgomery bus boycott in 1956, that "when the history books are written in future generations, the historians will have to pause and say, 'There lived a great people—a black people—who injected new meaning and dignity into the veins of civilization.' "[91] Certainly, blacks in the law will have made their enormous contribution to this achievement.

---

ment in the jail not exceeding six months, and by fine not exceeding one hundred dollars. . . ." (Acts of the General Assembly of Virginia, 1848 Chap. 12, p. 120.) A. Leon Higginbotham, Jr., in his *In the Matter of Color* (New York: Oxford University Press, 1978), pp. 199, 200–201, 250, 258, cites similar laws relating to slaves enacted dating back to 1740 in South Carolina and to 1755 in Georgia.

91. Wofford, *Of Kennedys and Kings*, p. 114.

# Epilogue

I complete this investigation and analysis with a multitude of conclusions, impressions, and unanswered questions. Initially, I embarked upon the project in order to construct a profile of blacks in the law in Philadelphia, then I expanded the study to cover a representative sample of the nation in order to determine the proper context in which to place the experience of black lawyers in Philadelphia; I examined other cities as sources of comparison, and I found Philadelphia to be, in significant ways, prototypical of the black experience in the legal sector of American metropolitan life. Along the way, however, much emerged concerning important issues apparently general to the status of black lawyers in the United States.

Two countervailing phenomena have come into focus. On the one hand, it is clear that many black men and women have succeeded, have attained their goals despite the fact that the road has been enormously difficult—uphill, fraught with obstacles, unjustly barricaded. The success of these attorneys and judges is a tribute to the endurance such a road demands.

On the other hand, the data force me to conclude that blacks in this country have not acquired their fair share of the opportunities and rewards potentially available from the pursuit of law. Findings regarding law-school admissions, acceptance to the bar, membership in large or medium law firms, and advancement in law-school faculties and in the judiciary demonstrate that blacks have a long way to go.

There is no simple explanation for the continuing disparity between whites and blacks, and contributing causes of this multidimensional phenomenon are numerous. Some pertain to the minds and experience of the blacks, some to the patterns and dynamics of the larger culture. In the first category, one must examine a broad range of factors, including the trauma of discrimination from birth, community patterns, educational opportunities, self-perception, motivational issues, and a great deal more. Clearly, many black Americans are at present less prepared than many whites for the highly specific reward system inherent in the American legal ascendancy. As for the society's role, it is apparent that predominantly white institutions in America—including institutions of the law—have been neither adequately welcoming to blacks nor sufficiently comprehending of their capacities and needs. A thorough discussion of this matter would require consideration of historical, economic, sociocultural, and attitudinal matters. The responsibility for the status quo and for altering it does not rest with only one group in this pluralistic society. For example, black commercial entities—individuals and corporations—must increase the frequency with which they retain and employ capable black lawyers. It is beyond question that the success of each black lawyer contributes to the general welfare of the black community; justice requires reciprocity.

What of the role of the white community, the sector that dominates virtually every aspect of America's legal world? The preceding chapters discuss, by implication, white legal institutions and their impact upon the lives of black lawyers. In a more general if less verifiable way, I must acknowledge my belief that diverse investigators from Myrdal to Kerner, from Allport to Higginbotham, are substantially correct—that, put succinctly, who has and who has not made it in America has been, with disturbing frequency, "a matter of color." This is not the place to discuss in detail the nature and effect of American racial attitudes, but to overlook the part that American racism—individual and institutional—has played in creating the problems encountered by blacks in the law would be naive.

I wish I could conclude this study greatly encouraged; however, the mixed nature of the past coalesces with the ill-conceived and worrisome policies emerging from Washington at this historical moment to make my outlook guarded and my heart heavy. In the end, nonetheless, there is hope. I find it in reflecting upon the inspiring lives of individual lawyers and judges: Houston, Marshall, Hastie; and continuing the tradition today: McCree, Coleman, Higginbotham—giants in American law. Such men, and many less renowned figures, have with courage and perseverance found their greatness in the dual success they have achieved, in the brilliance of their careers in American law, and in the incalculable contributions they have made to the black struggle, both to the black lawyers who have followed them and to the black community in general. In such contributions, they have gained distinction as figures of awesome importance in the best traditions of American constitutional law. It is more than merely ironic that in utilizing legal channels to oppose, transcend, and change unjust practices, they have helped the American legal system move closer to the realization of its own ideals.

There will always be such heroes, for groups which endure adversity always produce them, and for four centuries blacks in this country have had to learn to survive. Hence, after all the questionnaires, the interviews, the data, the analyses, it is through contemplating such people that I can put down my pen with a sense of great admiration and a rekindled spirit of hope.

# Appendix 1

## Questionnaire for the Philadelphia Study

The information sought by this questionnaire is in connection with a Ph.D dissertation on the subject *Black Members of the Philadelphia Bar—History, Progress and the Road Ahead*. Your cooperation is greatly appreciated.

It is not necessary for you to sign this questionnaire. I am interested in statistical and sociological findings only.

Please answer *yes* or *no* or *use check marks* wherever possible.

If you do not have an answer to a question or if you do not feel that it is applicable to you, please so indicate.

I. *Family and Personal Information*
   A. Your sex. M____ F____
   B. Year of your birth_____
   C. Your birthplace. Town or city_____State_____
   D. Birthplace of your father. Town or city_____State_____
   E. Birthplace of your mother. Town or city_____State_____
   F. Birthplace of your father's father. Town or city____State____
   G. Birthplace of your father's mother. Town or city____State____
   H. Birthplace of your mother's father. Town or city____State____
   I. Birthplace of your mother's mother. Town or city____State____
   J. Number of brothers_____Older_____Younger_____
   K. Number of sisters_____Older_____Younger_____

II. *Household Set-up*
   In the household in which you lived when you entered college, what was the relationship of each person to you there? (For example, mother, father, sister(s), brother(s), grandmother on father's side, aunt on mother's side, uncle on father's side.)

III. *Religion*
   A. Father's father_____
   B. Father's mother_____
   C. Mother's father_____
   D. Mother's mother_____
   E. Father_____
   F. Mother_____
   G. Yours_____

IV. *Your Home When You Entered College*
  A.  Rented house
    1.  City_____
    2.  Suburbs_____
  B.  Family-owned house
    1.  City_____
    2.  Suburbs_____
  C.  Apartment
    1.  City_____
    2.  Suburbs_____
  D.  Rooming house
    1.  City_____
    2.  Suburbs_____
  E.  Farm
    1.  Rented_____
    2.  Family-owned_____

V.  *Parents' Education*
  Please check highest grade attained.
  A.  Father
    1.  Elementary school_____Years of school completed_____
    2.  Secondary school_____Years of school completed_____
    3.  Undergraduate school_____What degree_____Without degree_____
    4.  Graduate school_____What degree_____Without degree_____
    5.  Professional school_____What degree_____Without degree_____
  B.  Mother
    1.  Elementary school_____Years of school completed_____
    2.  Secondary school_____Years of school completed_____
    3.  Undergraduate school_____What degree_____Without degree_____
    4.  Graduate school_____What degree_____Without degree_____
    5.  Professional school_____What degree_____Without degree_____

VI. *Parents' Occupation*
  This question applies to your parents' occupation at the time you entered college.
  A.  Father
    1.  Lawyer_____
    2.  Dentist_____

3. Physician_____
4. Clergyman_____
5. Teacher_____Elementary school_____Secondary school_____
    College or University_____
6. Funeral director_____
7. Railroad conductor_____
8. Insurance agent_____
9. Mail carrier_____
10. Clerk_____
11. Cabinet maker_____
12. Carpenter_____
13. Electrician_____
14. Mechanic_____Garage_____Other_____
15. Bus driver_____
16. Conductor or motorman, urban rail transit_____
17. Taxicab driver_____
18. Chauffeur_____
19. Truck driver_____
20. Construction laborer_____
21. Garbage collector_____
22. Farmer (owner)_____
23. Farm laborer_____
24. Janitor_____
25. Cook_____
26. Waiter_____
27. Baggage porter_____
28. Barber_____
29. Elevator operator_____
30. Fireman_____
31. Policeman_____
32. Other_____

B. Mother
1. Lawyer_____
2. Librarian_____
3. Physician_____
4. Dietitian_____
5. Registered nurse_____
6. Dental hygienist_____
7. Social worker_____
8. Teacher_____Elementary school_____Secondary
    school_____College or University_____
9. Bank teller_____
10. Bookkeeper_____

11. Cashier_____
12. Clerk in store_____
13. File clerk_____
14. Keypunch operator_____
15. Secretary_____
16. Stenographer_____
17. Typist_____
18. Dressmaker_____
19. Milliner_____
20. Food counter and fountain worker_____
21. Practical nurse_____
22. Elevator operator_____
23. Hairdresser_____
24. Private household worker-cook_____Maid_____
    Laundress_____
25. Housewife_____
26. Other_____

VII. *Your Education*
  A. In what region of the country did you attend grade school? Please give city and state, if possible_____
  B. What type of grade school did you graduate from?
     1. Public_____
     2. Private_____
     3. Parochial_____
     4. If mixed, what was the approximate percentage of black students?_____
  C. In what region of the country did you attend high school? Please give city and state, if possible_____
  D. What type of high school did you graduate from?
     1. Public_____
     2. Private_____
     3. Parochial_____
     4. If mixed, what was the approximate percentage of black students?_____
  E. In what region of the country did you attend undergraduate school? Please give city and state, if possible_____
     1. From what undergraduate school did you receive a degree?_____
        a. What degree_____
        b. Day school or night school_____
     2. Year of graduation_____

3. Approximately what percentage of the student body was black?_____

4. Approximately what percentage of the faculty was black?_____

5. Tuition payments. Please check basis on which tuition was paid; if a combination, check more than one category.
   a. Personal funds_____
   b. Family funds_____
   c. Scholarship_____
   d. Loan grant_____
   e. Veterans' benefits_____
   f. Worked way through undergraduate school_____
      1. Type of work_____

6. Residence at undergraduate school
   a. On campus
      1. Integrated dormitory_____
      2. Segregated dormitory_____
      3. Fraternity house_____Integrated_____
         Segregated_____
   b. Off campus
      1. Alone_____
      2. With spouse_____
      3. With roommate_____
      4. With parents and other members of the household_____
      5. With others_____
         a. Black_____
         b. White_____
         c. Mixed_____

7. Social activities
   a. Of your friends in college, were any of them white?_____
      1. Did you visit them socially?_____
      2. Did they visit you socially?_____
      3. Have you remained friends?_____

F. Career Decisions
   1. What motivating factors inspired you to study law?
      a. Aptitude for the law_____
      b. Interest in the law_____
      c. Inspiration of outstanding lawyers. Black_____White_____
         If possible, please specify_____
      d. Desire to help achieve justice for minority groups_____
      e. Economic benefits of the practice of law_____
      f. Family direction and encouragement_____

        1.    Did any one particular member of the family motivate you?_____

      g.    Other. Please specify_____

    2.    After leaving college and before enrolling in law school, did you pursue any other career or line of work? Please specify_____

G.    In what region of the country did you attend law school? Please give city and state_____

    1.    From what law school did you receive a degree?_____

      a.    What degree?_____

      b.    Day school or night school?_____

    2.    Year_____

    3.    Approximately what percentage of the student body was black?_____

    4.    Approximately what percentage of the faculty was black?_____

    5.    Tuition payments. Please check basis on which tuition was paid; if a combination, check more than one category.

      a.    Personal funds_____

      b.    Family funds_____

      c.    Scholarship_____

      d.    Loan grant_____

      e.    Veterans' benefits_____

      f.    Worked way through law school_____

        1.    Type of work_____

    6.    Residence at law school

      a.    On campus

        1.    In integrated dormitory_____

        2.    In segregated dormitory_____

      b.    Off campus

        1.    Alone_____

        2.    With spouse_____

        3.    With roommate_____

        4.    With parents and other members of the household_____

        5.    With others_____

          a.    Black_____

          b.    White_____

          c.    Mixed_____

          d.    Other_____

    7.    Social activities

      a.    Of your friends in law school, were any of them white?____

        1.    Did you visit them socially?_____

  2.  Did they visit you socially?_____
  3.  Have you remained friends?_____

8.  Activities in law school
  a.  Law Review_____
  b.  Order of Coif_____
  c.  Other. Please specify_____
9.  Will you please comment about Bar Examinations.
  a.  Date of admission to the Bar_____
10. Career Plans
  a.  Did you receive offers of employment while at law school
      from any of the following?
      1.  White sole practitioner_____
      2.  Black sole practitioner_____
      3.  White firm_____
      4.  Black firm_____
      5.  Mixed firm_____
      6.  Corporation_____
      7.  Federal government_____
      8.  State government_____
      9.  City government_____
      10. Law school_____
      11. Other. Please describe_____
  b.  Did you accept an offer in any of the above
      categories?_____
      1.  If yes, please describe _____
          _____
          _____

  c.  If you did not receive an offer, did you actively seek
      employment from any of the following?
      1.  White sole practitioner_____
      2.  Black sole practitioner_____
      3.  White firm_____
      4.  Black firm_____
      5.  Mixed firm_____
      6.  Corporation_____
      7.  Federal government_____
      8.  State government_____
      9.  City government_____
      10. Law school_____
      11. Other. Please describe _____
          _____
          _____

    d. In which of the above categories was your first
employer?_____

VIII. *Professional Life*

  A. Are you still with your original employer?_____
  B. If not, why did you leave?_____
  C. What type or types of practice have you engaged in since you began
the practice of law? Please note in chronological order, if possible.
    1. Personal injury_____
    2. Civil rights_____
    3. Criminal law_____
    4. Litigation_____
    5. Labor law_____
      a. Labor union representation_____
      b. Employer representation_____
    6. Domestic relations_____
    7. Tax law_____
    8. Corporation law_____
    9. Estates and Trusts_____
    10. Real estate_____
    11. Research and briefing_____
    12. Other_____
      a. If possible, will you please comment upon and describe the
racial mixtures in your various places of employment? _____
_____
_____

  D. Description of present employment.
    1. Are you a sole practitioner?_____
    2. Private law firm_____What is the percentage blacks?_____
    3. Corporation_____What is the percentage blacks?_____
    4. Federal government_____
    5. State government_____
    6. City government_____
    7. Law school teacher_____
    8. Public interest law firm_____What is percentage of
blacks_____
    9. Corporate law department_____What is percentage of
blacks_____
    10. Member of federal judiciary_____
    11. Member of state judiciary_____
  E. Details of present employment, applying only to membership in a
private law firm.
    1. Size of firm_____

2. Racial mixture
   a. Black_____
   b. White_____
   c. Integrated_____
      1. Percentage of black members_____
3. Number of partners_____
   a. Black_____
   b. White_____
4. Number of associates_____
   a. Black_____
   b. White_____
5. Your rank
   a. Partner_____
   b. Associate_____
6. Your professional specialty
   a. Personal injury_____
   b. Civil rights_____
   c. Criminal law_____
   d. Litigation_____
   e. Labor law_____
      1. Labor union representation_____
      2. Employer representation_____
   f. Domestic relations_____
   g. Tax law_____
   h. Corporate law_____
   i. Estates and trusts_____
   j. Real estate_____
   k. Research and briefing_____
   l. Other_____
7. Is your present annual income established by a fixed formula applying to all members of the firm?_____
   a. If not, are you satisfied with the method of distribution?_____
8. Has your practice developed in accordance with your expectations?_____
   a. If not, will you comment as to reasons? _____
   _____
   _____
   _____
9. Is your social relationship with other members of your firm satisfactory?_____
   a. If not, have you resisted social overtures?_____
   b. Have social overtures not been forthcoming?_____

10. Does your firm represent mixed clientele?_____
   a. If so, do you personally represent both white and black clients?_____

F. Are you a member of:
   1. A bar of any state other than Pennsylvania_____
   2. Philadelphia Bar Association_____
   3. Pennsylvania Bar Association_____
   4. American Bar Association_____
   5. National Bar Association_____
   6. Barristers Association of Philadelphia, Inc._____
   7. Federal Bar Association_____
   8. Other professional organizations_____ Please give names and description _____

   9. Has membership in any or all of these organizations been helpful to you professionally_____
   a. If so, please name the organization(s) _____

   b. If so, please comment upon the helpfulness of the organization(s) _____

   10. If you do not belong to any of the above organizations, will you please give your reasons? _____

G. How do you appraise the status of the black lawyer in Philadelphia as compared with white lawyers? _____

   1. How do you appraise the attitude of clients or prospective clients toward representation by black lawyers? _____

   2. How do you envision the future of black lawyers? _____

    a.   Will they join white firms in increasing numbers?_____

    b.   Will they join black firms in increasing numbers?_____

    c.   Will they be sole practitioners in increasing
       numbers?_____

    d.   Will they establish their own firms?_____

H.  Do you consider Philadelphia a satisfactory city for the black lawyer's
professional progress? _____

_____

_____

## Birthplaces of Respondents by Region Numbers and Percentages

Cohort 1 (1890–1920) 17 respondents

|  | R | M | F | PGF | PGM | MGF | MGM |
|---|---|---|---|---|---|---|---|
| Pennsylvania | 6 (35%) | 3 (18%) | 1 (6%) | 0 | 0 | 1 (6%) | 1 (6%) |
| South | 9 (52%) | 11 (64%) | 14 (82%) | 14 (82%) | 10 (58%) | 8 (47%) | 10 (58%) |
| North, East, West | 2 (12%) | 1 (6%) | 0 | 0 | 0 | 1 (6%) | 1 (6%) |
| Outside U.S. | 0 | 1 (6%) | 2 (12%) | 2 (12%) | 1 (6%) | 2 (12%) | 1 (6%) |

One did not answer.

Cohort 2 (1921–1937) 30 respondents

|  | R | M | F | PGF | PGM | MGF | MGM |
|---|---|---|---|---|---|---|---|
| Pennsylvania | 20 (67%) | 6 (20%) | 9 (30%) | 5 (16%) | 3 (10%) | 2 (7%) | 2 (7%) |
| South | 7 (23%) | 22 (73%) | 18 (60%) | 17 (56%) | 17 (56%) | 19 (63%) | 18 (60%) |
| North, East, West | 3 (10%) | 1 (3%) | 0 | 0 | 0 | 0 | 0 |
| Outside U.S. | 0 | 1 (3%) | 2 (7%) | 2 (7%) | 2 (7%) | 0 | 1 (3%) |

Cohort 3 (1938–1954) 93 respondents

|  | R | M | F | PGF | PGM | MGF | MGM |
|---|---|---|---|---|---|---|---|
| Pennsylvania | 40 (43%) | 15 (16%) | 17 (18%) | 4 (4%) | 4 (4%) | 2 (2%) | 3 (3%) |
| South | 30 (32%) | 54 (90%) | 62 (68%) | 51 (56%) | 50 (50%) | 50 (54%) | 48 (53%) |
| North, East, West | 18 (19%) | 12 (13%) | 5 (5%) | 2 (2%) | 1 (1%) | 3 (3%) | 7 (8%) |
| Outside U.S. | 5 (5%) | 8 (9%) | 5 (5%) | 10 (10%) | 8 (9%) | 9 (10%) | 7 (8%) |

Key:
R = Respondent
M = Mother
F = Father

PGF = Paternal grandfather
PGM = Paternal grandmother
MGF = Maternal grandfather
MGM = Maternal grandmother

# Appendix 3

## Undergraduate Schools of Respondents

| | Cohort 1 | | Cohort 2 | | Cohort 3 | |
|---|---|---|---|---|---|---|
| | Male | Female | Male | Female | Male | Female |
| Albright | | | 1 | | | |
| Amherst | | | | | 1 | |
| Augustana | | | | | | 1 |
| Bennett | | | | | | 1 |
| Berkeley | | | | | 1 | |
| Boston University | | | | | 1 | |
| Bowdoin | 1 | | | | | |
| Brown | | | | | | 1 |
| California, University of So. | | | | | 1 | |
| California, University of at L.A. | | | | | | 1 |
| Case | | | | | 1 | |
| Central State | | | | | 3 | |
| Chestnut Hill | | | | | | 1 |
| Cheyney State | 1 | | | | 3 | |
| Clark | | | 1 | | | |
| Columbia | | | | | 1 | |
| Delaware State | | | | | 1 | |
| Delaware, University of | | | | | 1 | |
| Dickinson | | | | | | 1 |
| Fairleigh-Dickinson | | | | | | 1 |
| Fisk | 1 | | | | 1 | 1 |
| Hampton Institute | | | | | 1 | 1 |
| Harpur | | | | | 1 | |
| Hartford, University of | | | | | 1 | |
| Harvard | 1 | | 1 | | 2 | |
| Howard | 1 | | 3 | 1 | 9 | 3 |
| Indiana | | | | | | 1 |
| Iowa, University of | 1 | | | | | |
| Johnson C. Smith | | | | | | 1 |
| LaSalle | | | 1 | | 1 | |
| Lincoln | 2 | | 5 | | 8 | 1 |
| Marygrove | | | | | | 1 |
| Merchant Marine Academy | | | | | 1 | |
| Michigan, University of | 1 | | | | | |
| Morgan State | | | 1 | | 1 | 1 |
| New York | | | 1 | | 1 | |
| North Carolina Central | | | 1 | | 2 | 1 |
| North Carolina, University of | | | | | 1 | |
| Oakwood | | | | | 1 | |
| Penn State | | | | | 4 | |
| Pennsylvania, University of | 3 | 1 | 2 | | 3 | 1 |
| Pittsburgh, University of | | | | | 1 | |
| Princeton | | | | | 1 | |
| Rochester, University of | | | | | | 1 |

257

| | Cohort 1 | | Cohort 2 | | Cohort 3 | |
| --- | --- | --- | --- | --- | --- | --- |
| | Male | Female | Male | Female | Male | Female |
| Rutgers | | | | | 1 | |
| St. Bonaventure | | | | | 1 | |
| St. Johns | | | | | 1 | |
| Talledega | | | | | 1 | |
| Temple | | 1 | 7 | | 10 | |
| Ursinus | | | | | 1 | |
| Villanova | | | 2 | | 1 | |
| Virginia State | | | | | 1 | |
| Virginia Union | | | 1 | | | |
| Wayne State | | | | | | 1 |
| Wesleyan | | | | | 1 | |
| West Virginia State | | | 1 | | | |
| West Virginia | | | 1 | | | |
| Williams | | | | | 1 | |
| Yale | | | | | 1 | |

One did not attend and one did not reply.

# Appendix 4

## Repondents' Undergraduate Scholarships

| | Cohort 1 | | Cohort 2 | | Cohort 3 | |
|---|---|---|---|---|---|---|
| | Male | Female | Male | Female | Male | Female |
| Amherst | | | | | 1 | |
| Augustana | | | | | | 1 |
| Bennett | | | | | | 1 |
| Brown | | | | | | 1 |
| Chestnut Hill | | | | | | 1 |
| Cheyney | | | | | 3 | |
| Columbia | | | | | 1 | |
| Delaware, University of | | | | | 1 | |
| Dickinson | | | | | | 1 |
| Hampton Institute | | | | | 1 | |
| Harpur | | | | | 1 | |
| Hartford, University of | | | | | 1 | |
| Harvard | | | 1 | | 1 | |
| Howard | | | 1 | 1 | 3 | 1 |
| Johnson C. Smith | | | | | 1 | |
| LaSalle | | | | | 1 | |
| Lincoln | 2 | | 3 | | 7 | |
| Marygrove | | | | | | 1 |
| Merchant Marine | | | | | 1 | |
| Morgan State | | | 1 | | 1 | 1 |
| New York | | | | | 1 | |
| North Carolina Central | | | | | 1 | |
| North Carolina, University of | | | | | 1 | |
| Penn State | | | | | 6 | |
| Pennsylvania, University of | 1 | | 1 | | 1 | 1 |
| Pittsburgh, University of | | | | | 1 | |
| Princeton | | | | | 1 | |
| Rochester, University of | | | | | | 1 |
| Talledega | | | | | 1 | |
| Temple | | | 2 | | 7 | |
| Ursinus | | | | | 1 | |
| Villanova | | | 1 | | 1 | |
| Virginia State | 1 | | | | | |
| Virginia Union | | | 1 | | | |
| Wayne State | | | | | | 1 |
| Wesleyan | | | | | 1 | |
| Williams | | | | | 1 | |
| Yale | | | | | 1 | |

These range from partial to full scholarships.
Two respondents said they received scholarships but did not identify the schools.

# Appendix 5

## CLEO Participant Data Report (1979)

1. Number of students participating in CLEO since its inception:

| 1968 | 1969 | 1970 | 1971 | 1972 | 1973 | 1974 | 1975 | 1976 | 1977 | 1978 | 1979 | Total |
|---|---|---|---|---|---|---|---|---|---|---|---|---|
| 161 | 448 | 212 | 221 | 217 | 233 | 225 | 251 | 220 | 221 | 217 | 224 | 2,850 |

2. Number of students successfully completing the summer institute program:

| 1968 | 1969 | 1970 | 1971 | 1972 | 1973 | 1974 | 1975 | 1976 | 1977 | 1978 | 1979 | Total |
|---|---|---|---|---|---|---|---|---|---|---|---|---|
| 151 | 444 | 197 | 210 | 213 | 229 | 225 | 244 | 216 | 208 | 213 | 222 | 2,772 |

3. Number of summer institute graduates entering law school:

| 1968 | 1969 | 1970 | 1971 | 1972 | 1973 | 1974 | 1975 | 1976 | 1977 | 1978 | 1979 | Total |
|---|---|---|---|---|---|---|---|---|---|---|---|---|
| 131 | 400 | 191 | 207 | 210 | 218 | 219 | 234 | 205 | 197 | 203 | 214 | 2,629 |

4. Number of students who have graduated from law school:

| 1968 | 1969 | 1970 | 1971 | 1972 | 1973 | 1974 | 1975 | 1976 | 1977 | 1978 | 1979 | Total |
|---|---|---|---|---|---|---|---|---|---|---|---|---|
| 83 | 292 | 130 | 138 | 142 | 158 | 161 | 157 | 149 | NA | NA | NA | 1,410 |

5. Number of law school graduates who have passed the bar examination:

| 1968 | 1969 | 1970 | 1971 | 1972 | 1973 | 1974 | 1975 | 1976 | 1977 | 1978 | 1979 | Total |
|---|---|---|---|---|---|---|---|---|---|---|---|---|
| 69 | 176 | 83 | 63 | 56 | 53 | 55 | 47 | 3 | NA | NA | NA | 605 |

6. Number of law school graduates for whom CLEO has no bar data:

| 1968 | 1969 | 1970 | 1971 | 1972 | 1973 | 1974 | 1975 | 1976 | 1977 | 1978 | 1979 | Total |
|---|---|---|---|---|---|---|---|---|---|---|---|---|
| 8 | 85 | 38 | 71 | 81 | 97 | 98 | 98 | 145 | NA | NA | NA | 721 |

7. Number of law school graduates who failed the bar examination:

| 1968 | 1969 | 1970 | 1971 | 1972 | 1973 | 1974 | 1975 | 1976 | 1977 | 1978 | 1979 | Total |
|---|---|---|---|---|---|---|---|---|---|---|---|---|
| 7 | 30 | 10 | 3 | 5 | 8 | 6 | 12 | NA | NA | NA | NA | 81 |
| | | | 1 | (Didn't Take) | 2 | | (Didn't Take) | | | | | 3 |

NOTE: Bar information is grossly understated. The CLEO National Office has been conducting an extensive survey over the past year of *all* CLEO law school graduates to determine more accurate bar statistics. This information is not generally known by the law schools and can only be ascertained with accuracy if it is known in which of the fifty (50) jurisdictions an individual sat for an examination. The survey, when completed, will hopefully provide more satisfactory statistical results.

8. Number of students enrolled in law school receiving CLEO stipends:

| 1968 | 1969 | 1970 | 1971 | 1972 | 1973 | 1974 | 1975 | 1976 | 1977 | 1978 | 1979 | Total |
|---|---|---|---|---|---|---|---|---|---|---|---|---|
| 0 | 0 | 0 | 0 | 0 | 0 | 0 | 0 | 6 | 152 | 159 | 206 | 523 |

9. Number of students enrolled in law school *not* receiving CLEO stipends:

| 1968 | 1969 | 1970 | 1971 | 1972 | 1973 | 1974 | 1975 | 1976 | 1977 | 1978 | 1979 | Total |
|---|---|---|---|---|---|---|---|---|---|---|---|---|
| 0 | 0 | 0 | 0 | 0 | 0 | 0 | 0 | 10 | 2 | 7 | 7 | 26 |

10. Total number of students enrolled in law school:

| 1968 | 1969 | 1970 | 1971 | 1972 | 1973 | 1974 | 1975 | 1976 | 1977 | 1978 | 1979 | Total |
|---|---|---|---|---|---|---|---|---|---|---|---|---|
| 0 | 0 | 0 | 0 | 0 | 0 | 0 | 0 | 16 | 154 | 166 | 213 | 549 |

11. Number of male students in law school receiving CLEO stipends:

| 1968 | 1969 | 1970 | 1971 | 1972 | 1973 | 1974 | 1975 | 1976 | 1977 | 1978 | 1979 | Total |
|---|---|---|---|---|---|---|---|---|---|---|---|---|
| 0 | 0 | 0 | 0 | 0 | 0 | 0 | 0 | 4 | 83 | 84 | 102 | 273 |

12. Number of female students in law school receiving CLEO stipends:

| 1968 | 1969 | 1970 | 1971 | 1972 | 1973 | 1974 | 1975 | 1976 | 1977 | 1978 | 1979 | Total |
|---|---|---|---|---|---|---|---|---|---|---|---|---|
| 0 | 0 | 0 | 0 | 0 | 0 | 0 | 0 | 2 | 69 | 75 | 104 | 250 |

13. Unknown Academic Status: Some law schools became reluctant in 1978/1979 to release academic data on CLEO students. The academic status of the following students is presently unknown:

| 1968 | 1969 | 1970 | 1971 | 1972 | 1973 | 1974 | 1975 | 1976 | 1977 | 1978 | 1979 | Total |
|------|------|------|------|------|------|------|------|------|------|------|------|-------|
| 0 | 0 | 0 | 0 | 0 | 0 | 0 | 25 | 6 | 5 | 4 | 0 | 40 |

14. Number of students who have deferred entrance, withdrawn, or failed law school:

| | 1968 | 1969 | 1970 | 1971 | 1972 | 1973 | 1974 | 1975 | 1976 | 1977 | 1978 | 1979 |
|---|------|------|------|------|------|------|------|------|------|------|------|------|
| Deferred entrance | — | — | — | — | — | — | — | — | — | 4 | 3 | 5 |
| Leave of Absence | — | — | — | — | — | — | — | 4 | 1 | 3 | — | — |
| Academic Dismissal | 21 | 52 | 43 | 49 | 31 | 30 | 31 | 29 | 24 | 23 | — | — |
| Withdrew–good standg. | 1 | 7 | 10 | 10 | 7 | 1 | 4 | — | — | — | — | — |
| Withdrew–failing | 8 | 18 | 7 | 5 | 1 | 3 | 3 | — | — | — | — | — |
| Withdrew–military | 5 | 6 | — | — | — | — | 1 | — | — | — | — | — |
| Withdrew–illness/death | 1 | 4 | — | 1 | — | 3 | 2 | 1 | 1 | 2 | 1 | — |
| Withdrew–financial | — | 2 | — | 1 | 2 | — | — | — | — | 1 | — | — |
| Withdrew–unknown | 12 | 18 | 1 | 4 | 28 | 23 | 18 | 18 | 10 | 11 | 9 | 1 |
| | 48 | 107 | 61 | 70 | 69 | 60 | 59 | 52 | 36 | 44 | 13 | 6 |

15. Number of students presently receiving CLEO stipends—by ethnic breakdown:

| | 1976 | 1977 | 1978 | 1979 | Total |
|---|------|------|------|------|-------|
| American Indian | — | — | — | 3 | 3 |
| Appalachian | 1 | — | — | 1 | 2 |
| Asian American | — | 5 | 4 | 5 | 14 |
| Black | 8 | 80 | 102 | 111 | 301 |
| Black Panamanian | — | — | 1 | — | 1 |
| Black West Indian | — | 1 | — | — | 1 |
| Caucasian | — | 2 | 2 | 6 | 10 |
| Chicano | 6 | 44 | 34 | 55 | 139 |
| Cuban American | — | 3 | 2 | 5 | 10 |
| Dominican American | — | — | 1 | 0 | 1 |
| Filipino American | — | — | — | 1 | 1 |
| Hawaiian | — | — | 1 | — | 1 |
| Italian American | — | — | 1 | — | 1 |
| Puerto Rican | 1 | 17 | 16 | 18 | 52 |
| Spanish Surname | — | 2 | 2 | 2 | 6 |
| Other Groups | — | — | — | 5 | 5 |
| TOTAL | 16 | 154 | 166 | 212 | 548 |

16. Number of students who audited the summer institute programs:

| 1968 | 1969 | 1970 | 1971 | 1972 | 1973 | 1974 | 1975 | 1976 | 1977 | 1978 | 1979 | Total |
|------|------|------|------|------|------|------|------|------|------|------|------|-------|
| 0 | 1 | 6 | 3 | 1 | 16 | 23 | 5 | 9 | 11 | 10 | 6 | 91 |

17. Anticipated law school enrollment of CLEO participants in 1979–80: 220

18. Number of law schools who have participated by accepting CLEO students: 144

## Law Schools Attended (According to Cohort and Sex)

| | Cohort 1 | | Middle 2 | | Youngest 3 | |
|---|---|---|---|---|---|---|
| | Male | Female | Male | Female | Male | Female |
| Boston College | | | | | 1 | |
| Boston University | 1 | | | | 1 | |
| California, University of | | | | | 2 | |
| Cincinnati, University of | | | | | | 1 |
| Columbia University | | | | | 2 | |
| Connecticut, University of | | | 1 | | 1 | |
| Dickinson College of Law | | | | | 1 | |
| George Washington University | | | | | 1 | 1 |
| Harvard University | 2 | | 1 | | 1 | |
| Howard University | 4 | | 6 | | 12 | 4 |
| Illinois, University of | | | | | 1 | |
| Indiana, University of | | 1 | | | | |
| Kentucky, University of | | | | | 1 | |
| Michigan, University of | | | | | 1 | |
| New York University | | | | | | 2 |
| North Carolinia Central University | | | 1 | | 4 | |
| North Carolina, University of | | | | | | 1 |
| Notre Dame, University of | | | | | 1 | |
| Pennsylvania, University of | 3 | 1 | 2 | 1 | 14 | 4 |
| Pittsburgh, University of | | | | | | 1 |
| Robert Terrell Law School | 1 | | | | | |
| Rutgers University | | | | | 2 | |
| Temple University | 1 | 1 | 17 | | 15 | 2 |
| Villanova University | | | 2 | | 6 | |
| Virginia, University of | | | | | | 1 |
| Wayne State University | | | | | | 1 |
| Western Reserve University | 1 | | | | | |
| Yale University | 1 | | 1 | | 4 | 1 |

141 respondents.
139 answered this question.
1 did not answer this question.
1 did not attend law school.

# Appendix 7

## Law School Scholarships (According to Cohort and Sex)

|  | Cohort 1 | | Cohort 2 | | Cohort 3 | |
|---|---|---|---|---|---|---|
|  | Male | Female | Male | Female | Male | Female |
| Boston College |  |  |  |  |  | 1 |
| Boston University |  |  |  |  |  | 1 |
| California, University of |  |  |  |  | 2 |  |
| Cincinnati, University of |  |  |  |  |  | 1 |
| Columbia University |  |  |  |  | 2 |  |
| Connecticut, University of |  |  |  |  | 1 |  |
| Dickinson College of Law |  |  |  |  | 1 |  |
| George Washington University |  |  |  |  | 1 | 1 |
| Harvard University | 1 |  | 1 |  | 1 |  |
| Howard University | 1 |  | 3 |  | 10 | 3 |
| Illinois, University of |  |  |  |  | 1 |  |
| Michigan, University of |  |  |  |  | 1 |  |
| New York University |  |  |  |  |  | 2 |
| North Carolinia Central University |  |  |  |  | 1 | 1 |
| North Carolinia, University of |  |  |  |  |  | 1 |
| Notre Dame, University of |  |  |  |  | 1 |  |
| Pennsylvania, University of | 1 |  | 1 | 1 | 11 | 3 |
| Pittsburgh, University of |  |  |  |  | 1 |  |
| Rutgers University |  |  |  |  | 2 |  |
| Temple University | 1 | 1 | 3 |  | 10 | 2 |
| Villanova University |  |  |  |  | 2 |  |
| Virginia, University of |  |  |  |  | 1 |  |
| Wayne State |  |  |  |  |  | 1 |
| Yale University |  |  |  |  | 4 | 1 |

141 respondents.
139 answered this question.
1 did not answer this question.
1 did not attend law school.

# Appendix 8

---

## Estimated "Pass" Rates of Graduates of Howard University Law School on Several States' Bar Examinations, 1965–70

This table appears as table 7 in "Philadelphia Bar Association Special Committee Report," *Temple Law Quarterly,* vol. 44 (1971), pp. 177–78. The committee's note follows:

"Because of the unusually low 'pass' rate on the Pennsylvania Bar examination of graduates of A.A.L.S. member school Howard University Law School, which is predominantly Black, we have gathered data concerning Howard graduates' 'pass' rates in other Bar examinations. In such fact finding, we have not had the leverage outside Pennsylvania that we did in this Commonwealth. The data we have compiled comes from three sources: (1) certification (for Bar examination eligibility) records of [Howard Law School's] Vice Dean Elwood Chisholm, which exaggerate the probable number of actual takers of a particular Bar exam since a Howard student may apply for the D.C., Maryland and Virginia Bar exam and actually take only one of them. Vice Dean Chisholm's certification records have therefore been adjusted downwards for this Table, but only by twenty percent and only for the D.C., Maryland and Virginia exams; (2) correspondence between State Board of Law Examiners and Deans' office and (3) interviews we conducted with the Deans' office and (3) interviews we conducted with the Dean and Vice Dean of Howard University Law School."

D.C.
    Howard (estimated 220 papers, actual 88 passed) . . . . . . . . . . . . 40.0%
    All candidates . . . . . . . . . . . . . . . . . . . . . . . . . . . . . . . . . 61.5%

Florida
    Howard (20 papers, 13 passed) . . . . . . . . . . . . . . . . . . . . . 65.0%
    All candidates . . . . . . . . . . . . . . . . . . . . . . . . . . . . . . . . . 88.0%

Maryland
    Howard (estimated 28 papers, actual 9 passed) . . . . . . . . . . . . 32.2%
    All candidates . . . . . . . . . . . . . . . . . . . . . . . . . . . . . . . . . 44.0%

New York
    Howard (estimates by Vice-Dean Chisholm: 30 papers, 21 passed) . . 70.0%
    All candidates . . . . . . . . . . . . . . . . . . . . . . . . . . . . . . . . . 71.0%

Ohio
    Howard (16 papers, 11 passed) . . . . . . . . . . . . . . . . . . . . . 68.8%
    All candidates . . . . . . . . . . . . . . . . . . . . . . . . . . . . . . . . . 86.6%

Pennsylvania
Howard (44 papers, 5 passed) . . . . . . . . . . . . . . . . . . . . . . . 11.4%
All candidates . . . . . . . . . . . . . . . . . . . . . . . . . . . . . . . . 77.9%

Tennessee
Howard (6 papers, 4 passed). . . . . . . . . . . . . . . . . . . . . . . 66.7%
All candidates . . . . . . . . . . . . . . . . . . . . . . . . . . . . . . . . 81.0%

Virginia
Howard (estimated 27 papers, actual 13 passed) . . . . . . . . . . . 48.1%
All candidates . . . . . . . . . . . . . . . . . . . . . . . . . . . . . . . . 73.5%

# Appendix 9

**Comparing "Pass" Rates of Black and Nonblack Graduates of Philadelphia Area Law Schools 32 Examinations (January 1955–July 1970)**

| | Total Papers Examined | Number Failed | Number Passed | % Papers Passed |
|---|---|---|---|---|
| **Temple Law School** | | | | |
| All graduates | 2,035 | 709 | 1,326 | 65.1 |
| Blacks (who eventually passed the bar exam) | 68 | 42 | 26 | 38.3 |
| **Penn Law School** | | | | |
| All graduates | 1,599 | 316 | 1,283 | 80.2 |
| Blacks (who eventually passed the bar exam) | 13 | 6 | 7 | 53.8 |
| **Villanova Law School** | | | | |
| All graduates | 847 | 207 | 640 | 75.5 |
| Blacks (who eventually passed the bar exam) | 8 | 4 | 4 | 50.0 |
| All other black candidates (whether or not they eventually passed the bar exam) | 217 | 169 | 48 | 22.1 |

# Appendix 10

**Employment Offers and Decisions of Respondents by Cohort**

### Cohort 1
### (1890–1920)

No Offers
10

| Offers from | Number of Offers | Number of Acceptances | Number of Rejections |
|---|---|---|---|
| White sole practitioner | 0 | 0 | 0 |
| Black sole practitioner | 3 | 2 | 1 |
| White firm | 0 | 0 | 0 |
| Black firm | 3 | 3 | 0 |
| Mixed firm | 0 | 0 | 0 |
| Corporation | 0 | 0 | 0 |
| Federal government | 0 | 0 | 0 |
| State government | 0 | 0 | 0 |
| City government | 2 | 1 | 1 |
| Law school | 1 | 0 | 1 |
| Other | 2 | 2 | 0 |
| | 11 | 8 | 3 |

### Cohort 2
### (1921–1937)

No Offers
17

| Offers from | Number of Offers | Number of Acceptances | Number of Rejections |
|---|---|---|---|
| White sole practitioner | 2 | 0 | 2 |
| Black sole practitioner | 7 | 2 | 5 |
| White firm | 1 | 1 | 0 |
| Black firm | 5 | 2 | 3 |
| Mixed firm | 1 | 1 | 0 |
| Corporation | 1 | 1 | 0 |
| Federal government | 6 | 2 | 4 |
| State government | 0 | 0 | 0 |
| City government | 3 | 2 | 1 |
| Law school | 0 | 0 | 0 |
| Other | 0 | 0 | 0 |
| | 27 | 12 | 15 |

Of those who did not accept any offer, one later obtained a position with a black firm, another became a sole practitioner.

Cohort 3
(1938–1954)

No Offers
12

| Offers from | Number of Offers | Number of Acceptances | Number of Rejections |
|---|---|---|---|
| White sole practitioner | 1 | 0 | 1 |
| Black sole practitioner | 11 | 1 | 10 |
| White firm | 26 | 13 | 13 |
| Black firm | 9 | 2 | 7 |
| Mixed firm | 4 | 2 | 2 |
| Corporation | 17 | 5 | 12 |
| Federal government | 40 | 22 | 18 |
| State government | 17 | 9 | 8 |
| City government | 16 | 11 | 5 |
| Law school | 6 | 3 | 3 |
| Other | 9 | 6 | 3 |
| | 156 | 74 | 82 |

Of those who did not accept any offer, one started his own firm and one went into the army.

# Appendix 11

## Membership of Respondents in Professional Organizations Other Than Those Mentioned in the Text

| | Cohort 1 | Cohort 2 | Cohort 3 |
|---|---|---|---|
| American Arbitration Association | | | 2 |
| American Bar Foundation (Fellow)* | | 1 | 2 |
| American Civil Liberties Union | | | 1 |
| American Judicature Society† | 1 | 5 | |
| American Law Institute | | 1 | |
| American Trial Lawyers Association | | 4 | 2 |
| Black American Law Students Association | | | 28 |
| Federal Communication Bar Association | | | 1 |
| Federal Power Bar Association | | | 1 |
| International Bar Association | | 1 | |
| Judicial Council | 1 | | |
| Lawyers Club of Philadelphia | | 4 | 4 |
| Lawyers Committee for Civil Rights Under Law | | 1 | |
| National Association of College and Universities Attorneys | | | 1 |
| National Association of Defense Lawyers | | 1 | |
| National Conference of Black Lawyers | | | 10 |
| National District Attorneys Association | | 1 | |
| National Lawyers Guild | | 1 | |
| National Trial Lawyers Association | | | 1 |
| National Women Lawyers Association | | | 1 |
| Philadelphia Trial Lawyers Association | | 1 | 1 |
| Pennsylvania Trial Lawyers Association | | 3 | 2 |
| Postal Bar Association | | | 1 |
| Socialegal Club‡ | | 1 | |
| Society of American Law Teachers | | | 1 |
| State Conference of Trial Judges | | 2 | |
| World Peace Through Law Center | | 1 | |
| Totals | 2 | 28 | 32 |

*Fellows of the American Bar Foundation are nominated by State Committees of the Fellows of the Foundation and elected by the Board of Governors. The Foundation was started in 1955, and the first meeting of the Fellows was in 1957.

†Here, too, membership is by election only. Until last year, the number of active members was restricted to 1,500; it is now 1,750.

‡Membership is by election.

# Appendix 12

## U.S., State, and Local Judges, Including U.S. Bankruptcy Judges and Magistrates (November 1981)

|  | State & Local | | | Federal | | | |
|---|---|---|---|---|---|---|---|
|  | Total State & Local Judges | No. Black Judges | % Black Judges | Total U.S. District & Appellate Judges | No. Black Dist. & Appellate Judges | % Black Judges | Total U.S. Bankruptcy Judges |
| ATLANTA | 50 | 11 | 22.0 | 13 | 2 | 15.4 | 4 |
| BOSTON | 76 | 9 | 11.8 | 11 | 1 | 9.0 | 3 |
| CHICAGO | 407 | 34 | 8.4 | 20 | 1 | 5.0 | 7 |
| CLEVELAND | 63 | 10 | 15.9 | 7 | 1 | 14.3 | 3 |
| COLUMBUS | 42 | 2 | 4.8 | 3 | 1 | 33.3 | 3 |
| DETROIT | 100 | 25 | 25.0 | 12 | 3 | 25.0 | 3 |
| HOUSTON | 104 | 9 | 8.7 | 10 | 1 | 10.0 | 3 |
| LOS ANGELES | 280 | 29 | 10.4 | 19 | 2 | 10.5 | 8 |
| MILWAUKEE | 40 | 2 | 5.0 | 4 | 0 | 0 | 3 |
| MINNEAPOLIS | 37 | 1 | 2.7 | 3 | 0 | 0 | 2 |
| NEW YORK | 442 | 47 | 10.6 | 39 | 6 | 15.4 | 9 |
| PHILADELPHIA | 110 | 21 | 19.1 | 20 | 3 | 15.0 | 2 |
| PITTSBURGH | 49 | 5 | 10.2 | 9 | 1 | 11.1 | 2 |
| RICHMOND | 24 | 2 | 8.3 | 3 | 0 | 0 | 1 |
| SAN FRANCISCO | 69 | 4 | 5.8 | 15 | 2 | 13.3 | 1 |
| WASHINGTON, D.C. | 53 | 15 | 28.3 | 24 | 7 | 29.2 | 1 |

Compiled in cooperation with the National Center for State Courts, Williamsburg, Virginia.

Federal judges as of April 1982 (527 F. Supp.); State and local judges as of November 1981

| | | | | | | Total | | |
|---|---|---|---|---|---|---|---|---|
| No. Black Bank- ruptcy Judges | Total U.S. Magis- trates | No. Black Magis. | Total Fed. Judges & Magis. | No. Black Fed. Judges & Magis. | % Black Fed. Judges & Magis. | Total State & Local & U.S. Dist. & App. & Bkpcy. Judges & Magis | No. Black | % Black |
| 0 | 4 | 0 | 21 | 2 | 9.5 | 71 | 13 | 18.3 |
| 0 | 4 | 1 | 18 | 2 | 11.1 | 94 | 11 | 11.7 |
| 1 | 3 | 0 | 30 | 2 | 6.7 | 437 | 36 | 8.2 |
| 0 | 2 | 0 | 12 | 1 | 8.3 | 75 | 11 | 14.7 |
| 1 | 1 | 0 | 7 | 2 | 28.6 | 49 | 4 | 8.2 |
| 1 | 4 | 1 | 19 | 5 | 25.0 | 119 | 30 | 25.2 |
| 0 | 3 | 1 | 16 | 2 | 12.5 | 120 | 11 | 9.2 |
| 1 | 6 | 0 | 33 | 3 | 9.1 | 313 | 32 | 10.2 |
| 1 | 2 | 0 | 9 | 1 | 11.1 | 49 | 3 | 6.1 |
| 0 | 2 | 0 | 7 | 0 | 0. | 44 | 1 | 2.3 |
| 0 | 10 | 1 | 58 | 7 | 12.1 | 500 | 54 | 10.8 |
| 0 | 5 | 1 | 27 | 4 | 14.8 | 137 | 25 | 18.2 |
| 0 | 2 | 0 | 13 | 1 | 7.7 | 62 | 6 | 9.7 |
| 0 | 2 | 0 | 6 | 0 | 0. | 30 | 2 | 6.6 |
| 0 | 4 | 0 | 20 | 2 | 10.0 | 89 | 6 | 6.7 |
| 0 | 3 | 1 | 28 | 8 | 28.6 | 81 | 23 | 28.4 |

# Black Representation in Large Law Firms in Sixteen Cities (1980)

| | Total Lawyers | No. White Partners | | No. Black Partners | | No. White Assoc. | | No. Black Assoc. | |
|---|---|---|---|---|---|---|---|---|---|
| | | M | F | M | F | M | F | M | F |
| Atlanta | 432 | 208 | 4 | 0 | 0 | 175 | 41 | 4 | 0 |
| Boston | 368 | 176 | 5 | 1 | 0 | 140 | 43 | 3 | 0 |
| Chicago | 1,691 | 782 | 28 | 2 | 0 | 690 | 169 | 18 | 2 |
| Cleveland | 536 | 240 | 4 | 2 | 0 | 237 | 47 | 5 | 1 |
| Columbus | 223 | 109 | 2 | 0 | 0 | 93 | 14 | 5 | 0 |
| Detroit | 212 | 98 | 5 | 0 | 0 | 83 | 18 | 7 | 1 |
| Washington, D.C. | 861 | 338 | 10 | 4 | 0 | 376 | 115 | 13 | 5 |
| Houston | 1,045 | 423 | 1 | 0 | 0 | 502 | 109 | 8 | 2 |
| Los Angeles | 716 | 243 | 5 | 2 | 0 | 366 | 86 | 8 | 6 |
| Milwaukee | 277 | 152 | 0 | 1 | 0 | 103 | 18 | 2 | 1 |
| Minneapolis | 272 | 144 | 1 | 0 | 0 | 95 | 30 | 1 | 1 |
| New York | 3,831 | 1,232 | 34 | 1 | 0 | 1,941 | 568 | 40 | 15 |
| Omaha | 96 | 35 | 6 | 0 | 0 | 29 | 21 | 2 | 2 |
| Philadelphia | 1,094 | 514 | 13 | 4 | 0 | 397 | 144 | 14 | 8 |
| Pittsburgh | 497 | 234 | 1 | 1 | 0 | 222 | 37 | 2 | 0 |
| Richmond | 276 | 132 | 2 | 0 | 0 | 111 | 28 | 3 | 0 |
| San Francisco | 927 | 387 | 9 | 1 | 0 | 389 | 128 | 7 | 6 |

| % White Partners | | % Black Partners | | % White Assoc. | | % Black Assoc. | | % Females | |
|---|---|---|---|---|---|---|---|---|---|
| M | F | M | F | M | F | M | F | Part. | Assoc. |
| 98.1 | 1.9 | 0 | 0 | 79.6 | 18.6 | 1.8 | 0 | 1.9 | 18.6 |
| 96.7 | 2.7 | 0.6 | 0 | 75.3 | 23.1 | 1.6 | 0 | 2.7 | 23.1 |
| 96.3 | 3.4 | 0.3 | 0 | 78.5 | 19.2 | 2.0 | 0.2 | 3.4 | 19.5 |
| 97.6 | 1.6 | 0.8 | 0 | 81.7 | 16.2 | 1.7 | 0.4 | 1.6 | 16.6 |
| 98.2 | 1.8 | 0 | 0 | 83.0 | 12.5 | 4.5 | 0 | 1.8 | 12.5 |
| 95.1 | 4.9 | 0 | 0 | 76.2 | 16.5 | 6.4 | 0.9 | 4.9 | 17.4 |
| 96.0 | 2.9 | 1.1 | 0 | 73.9 | 22.6 | 2.5 | 1.0 | 2.9 | 23.6 |
| 99.8 | 0.2 | 0 | 0 | 80.8 | 17.6 | 1.3 | 0.3 | 0.2 | 17.9 |
| 97.2 | 2.0 | 0.8 | 0 | 78.5 | 18.5 | 1.7 | 1.3 | 2.0 | 19.7 |
| 99.3 | 0 | 0.7 | 0 | 83.1 | 14.5 | 1.6 | 0.8 | 0 | 15.3 |
| 99.3 | 0.7 | 0 | 0 | 74.8 | 23.6 | 0.8 | 0.8 | 0.7 | 24.4 |
| 97.2 | 2.7 | 0.1 | 0 | 75.7 | 22.1 | 1.6 | 0.6 | 2.7 | 22.7 |
| 91.2 | 7.5 | 1.3 | 0 | 63.3 | 26.6 | 7.6 | 2.5 | 7.5 | 29.1 |
| 96.8 | 2.4 | 0.8 | 0 | 70.5 | 25.6 | 2.5 | 1.4 | 2.4 | 27.0 |
| 99.2 | 0.4 | 0.4 | 0 | 85.1 | 14.2 | 0.8 | 0 | 0.4 | 14.2 |
| 98.5 | 1.5 | 0 | 0 | 78.2 | 19.7 | 2.1 | 0 | 1.5 | 19.7 |
| 97.5 | 2.3 | 0.2 | 0 | 73.4 | 24.2 | 1.3 | 1.1 | 2.3 | 25.3 |

## Black Representation in Medium-size Law Firms in Sixteen Cities (1980)

| | Total Firm Members | No. White Partners M | F | No. Black Partners M | F | No. White Assoc. M | F | No. Black Assoc.* |
|---|---|---|---|---|---|---|---|---|
| Atlanta | 620 | 274 | 3 | 1 | 0 | 271 | 57 | 14 |
| Boston | 1,015 | 510 | 13 | 1 | 0 | 364 | 119 | 8 |
| Chicago | 2,050 | 975 | 24 | 1 | 0 | 846 | 186 | 18 |
| Cleveland | 584 | 265 | 1 | 2 | 0 | 258 | 48 | 10 |
| Columbus | 42 | 24 | 0 | 0 | 0 | 14 | 3 | 1 |
| Detroit | 368 | 200 | 4 | 2 | 0 | 130 | 24 | 8 |
| Washington, D.C. | 1,867 | 850 | 20 | 7 | 0 | 761 | 200 | 29 |
| Houston | 729 | 301 | 0 | 0 | 0 | 349 | 72 | 7 |
| Los Angeles | 1,444 | 660 | 17 | 5 | 0 | 583 | 158 | 21 |
| Milwaukee | 116 | 60 | 0 | 0 | 0 | 50 | 6 | 0 |
| Minneapolis | 184 | 101 | 0 | 0 | 0 | 67 | 16 | 0 |
| New York | 4280 | 1,524 | 38 | 3 | 0 | 2,077 | 601 | 37 |
| Omaha | 34 | 23 | 0 | 0 | 0 | 9 | 2 | 0 |
| Philadelphia | 550 | 286 | 1 | 1 | 0 | 202 | 55 | 5 |
| Pittsburgh | 145 | 62 | 0 | 0 | 0 | 70 | 13 | 0 |
| Richmond | 177 | 95 | 1 | 0 | 0 | 68 | 12 | 1 |
| San Francisco | 727 | 307 | 5 | 0 | 0 | 305 | 105 | 5 |

*Black associates not differentiated by sex.
†No black female partners.

| % White Partners | | % Black Partners | | % White Assoc. | | % Black Assoc.* | % Females† Part | Assoc. |
|---|---|---|---|---|---|---|---|---|
| M | F | M | F | M | F | | | |
| 98.5 | 1.1 | 0.4 | 0 | 79.2 | 16.7 | 4.1 | 1.1 | 16.7 |
| 97.3 | 2.5 | 0.2 | 0 | 74.2 | 24.2 | 1.6 | 2.5 | 24.2 |
| 97.5 | 2.4 | 0.1 | 0 | 80.6 | 17.7 | 1.7 | 2.4 | 17.7 |
| 98.9 | 0.4 | 0.7 | 0 | 81.6 | 15.2 | 3.2 | 0.4 | 15.2 |
| 100 | 0 | 0 | 0 | 77.8 | 16.6 | 5.6 | 0 | 16.6 |
| 97.1 | 1.9 | 1.0 | 0 | 80.2 | 14.8 | 5.0 | 1.9 | 14.8 |
| 96.9 | 2.3 | 0.8 | 0 | 76.9 | 20.2 | 2.9 | 2.0 | 20.2 |
| 100 | 0 | 0 | 0 | 81.5 | 16.8 | 1.7 | 0 | 16.8 |
| 96.8 | 2.5 | 0.7 | 0 | 76.5 | 20.7 | 2.8 | 2.5 | 20.7 |
| 100 | 0 | 0 | 0 | 89.3 | 10.7 | 0 | 0 | 10.7 |
| 100 | 0 | 0 | 0 | 80.7 | 19.3 | 0 | 0 | 19.3 |
| 97.4 | 2.4 | 0.2 | 0 | 76.5 | 22.1 | 1.4 | 2.4 | 22.1 |
| 100 | 0 | 0 | 0 | 81.8 | 18.2 | 0 | 0 | 18.2 |
| 99.4 | 0.3 | 0.3 | 0 | 77.1 | 21.0 | 1.9 | 0.3 | 21.0 |
| 100 | 0 | 0 | 0 | 84.3 | 15.7 | 0 | 0 | 15.7 |
| 99.0 | 1.0 | 0 | 0 | 84.0 | 14.8 | 1.2 | 0 | 14.8 |
| 98.4 | 1.6 | 0 | 0 | 73.5 | 25.3 | 1.2 | 1.6 | 25.3 |

# Appendix 15

## Ratios of Blacks and Black Lawyers to Whites and White Lawyers, by States (1970 and 1980)

| | | Black Lawyers | Black Population | Ratio: Black Lawyers to Black Population | White Lawyers | White Population | Ratio: White Lawyers to White Population |
|---|---|---|---|---|---|---|---|
| Alabama | 1970 | 24 | 908,247 | 1:37,844 | 2,471 | 2,535,918 | 1:1,026 |
| | 1980 | | 995,623 | | | 2,869,688 | |
| Alaska | 1970 | 1 | 8,911 | 1:8,911 | 290 | 293,262 | 1:1,011 |
| | 1980 | | 13,619 | | | 308,455 | |
| Arizona | 1970 | 2 | 43,403 | 1:21,702 | 1,888 | 1,649,597 | 1:873 |
| | 1980 | | 75,034 | | | 2,240,033 | |
| Arkansas | 1970 | 10 | 357,225 | 1:35,723 | 1,343 | 1,566,070 | 1:1,166 |
| | 1980 | | 373,192 | | | 1,890,002 | |
| California | 1970 | 373 | 1,400,143 | 1:3,754 | 25,179 | 18,552,991 | 1:736 |
| | 1980 | | 1,819,282 | | | 18,031,689 | |
| Colorado | 1970 | 10 | 66,411 | 1:6,641 | 3,161 | 2,140,848 | 1:677 |
| | 1980 | | 101,702 | | | 2,570,615 | |
| Connecticut | 1970 | 26 | 78,276 | 1:6,968 | 4,714 | 2,851,040 | 1:717 |
| | 1980 | | 217,433 | | | 2,799,420 | |
| Delaware | 1970 | 3 | 78,276 | 1:26,092 | 697 | 469,828 | 1:674 |
| | 1980 | | 95,971 | | | 488,543 | |
| Florida | 1970 | 60 | 1,049,578 | 1:17,493 | 7,661 | 5,739,865 | 1:749 |
| | 1980 | | 1,342,478 | | | 8,178,387 | |
| Georgia | 1970 | 30 | 1,190,779 | 1:39,693 | 4,025 | 3,398,761 | 1:844 |
| | 1980 | | 1,465,457 | | | 3,948,007 | |
| Hawaii | 1970 | 1 | 7,573 | 1:7,573 | 587 | 760,988 | 1:1,296 |
| | 1980 | | 17,352 | | | 318,608 | |
| Idaho | 1970 | 1 | 2,130 | 1:2,130 | 668 | 710,437 | 1:1,063 |
| | 1980 | | 2,716 | | | 901,641 | |
| Illinois | 1970 | 667 | 1,425,674 | 1:2,137 | 15,555 | 9,688,302 | 1:622 |
| | 1980 | | 1,675,229 | | | 9,255,575 | |
| Indiana | 1970 | 56 | 357,464 | 1:6,383 | 4,359 | 4,836,205 | 1:1,109 |
| | 1980 | | 414,732 | | | 5,004,567 | |
| Iowa | 1970 | 15 | 32,596 | 1:2,173 | 2,571 | 2,792,445 | 1:1,086 |
| | 1980 | | 41,700 | | | 2,838,805 | |
| Kansas | 1970 | 30 | 106,977 | 1:3,566 | 2,839 | 2,142,094 | 1:754 |
| | 1980 | | 126,127 | | | 2,167,752 | |
| Kentucky | 1970 | 22 | 241,292 | 1:10,968 | 2,688 | 2,978,019 | 1:1,107 |
| | 1980 | | 259,490 | | | 3,379,648 | |
| Louisiana | 1970 | 27 | 1,088,734 | 1:40,324 | 3,662 | 2,554,446 | 1:697 |
| | 1980 | | 1,237,263 | | | 2,911,243 | |
| Maine | 1970 | 0 | 2,800 | 0:2,800 | 720 | 989,248 | 1:1,373 |
| | 1980 | | 3,128 | | | 1,109,850 | |
| Maryland | 1970 | 32 | 518,410 | 1:16,200 | 8,855 | 3,246,590 | 1:366 |
| | 1980 | | 958,050 | | | 3,158,412 | |
| Massachusetts | 1970 | 50 | 175,817 | 1:3,516 | 8,924 | 5,513,353 | 1:617 |
| | 1980 | | 221,279 | | | 5,362,836 | |
| Michigan | 1970 | 250 | 991,066 | 1:3,964 | 8,347 | 7,884,017 | 1:944 |
| | 1980 | | 1,198,710 | | | 7,868,956 | |
| Minnesota | 1970 | 14 | 34,868 | 1:2,491 | 4,267 | 3,770,201 | 1:883 |
| | 1980 | | 53,342 | | | 3,396,948 | |
| Mississippi | 1970 | 23 | 815,770 | 1:35,468 | 1,869 | 1,401,142 | 1:749 |
| | 1980 | | 887,206 | | | 1,615,190 | |
| Missouri | 1970 | 64 | 480,172 | 1:7,503 | 5,074 | 4,197,227 | 1:827 |
| | 1980 | | 514,274 | | | 4,346,267 | |
| Montana | 1970 | 1 | 1,995 | 1:1,995 | 750 | 692,414 | 1:923 |
| | 1980 | | 1,786 | | | 740,148 | |
| Nebraska | 1970 | 5 | 39,911 | 1:7,982 | 1,788 | 1,443,880 | 1:807 |
| | 1980 | | 48,389 | | | 1,490,569 | |
| Nevada | 1970 | 4 | 27,762 | 1:6,941 | 461 | 460,976 | 1:999 |
| | 1980 | | 50,791 | | | 669,377 | |
| New Hampshire | 1970 | 1 | 2,505 | 1:2,505 | 555 | 735,176 | 1:1,324 |
| | 1980 | | 3,990 | | | 910,099 | |

| | | Black Lawyers | Black Population | Ratio: Black Lawyers to Black Population | White Lawyers | White Population | Ratio: White Lawyers to White Population |
|---|---|---|---|---|---|---|---|
| New Jersey | 1970 | 65 | 770,292 | 1:11,851 | 10,870 | 6,397,872 | 1:588 |
| | 1980 | | 924,786 | | | 6,127,090 | |
| New Mexico | 1970 | 0 | 17,063 | 0:17,063 | 879 | 976,937 | 1:1,111 |
| | 1980 | | 24,042 | | | 976,465 | |
| New York | 1970 | 650 | 2,166,933 | 1:3,334 | 40,434 | 16,023,807 | 1:396 |
| | 1980 | | 2,401,842 | | | 13,961,106 | |
| North Carolina | 1970 | 70 | 1,137,664 | 1:16,252 | 3,019 | 3,944,395 | 1:1,306 |
| | 1980 | | 948,146 | | | 2,145,122 | |
| North Dakota | 1970 | 0 | 2,494 | 0:2,494 | 488 | 615,267 | 1:1,260 |
| | 1980 | | 2,568 | | | 625,536 | |
| Ohio | 1970 | 416 | 970,477 | 1:2,333 | 11,480 | 9,681,540 | 1:843 |
| | 1980 | | 1,076,734 | | | 9,597,266 | |
| Oklahoma | 1970 | 16 | 177,907 | 1:11,119 | 3,181 | 2,381,346 | 1:748 |
| | 1980 | | 204,658 | | | 2,597,783 | |
| Oregon | 1970 | 7 | 26,308 | 1:3,758 | 2,435 | 2,065,077 | 1:848 |
| | 1980 | | 37,059 | | | 2,490,192 | |
| Pennsylvania | 1970 | 141 | 1,016,514 | 1:7,209 | 11,213 | 10,777,395 | 1:961 |
| | 1980 | | 1,047,609 | | | 10,654,325 | |
| Rhode Island | 1970 | 2 | 25,338 | 1:12,669 | 1,094 | 924,385 | 1:844 |
| | 1980 | | 27,584 | | | 896,692 | |
| South Carolina | 1970 | 11 | 789,041 | 1:71,731 | 1,689 | 1,801,475 | 1:1,066 |
| | 1980 | | 948,146 | | | 2,145,122 | |
| South Dakota | 1970 | 0 | 1,627 | 0:1,627 | 610 | 663,880 | 1:1,088 |
| | 1980 | | 2,144 | | | 638,955 | |
| Tennessee | 1970 | 35 | 631,696 | 1:18,049 | 3,307 | 3,292,468 | 1:995 |
| | 1980 | | 725,949 | | | 3,835,078 | |
| Texas | 1970 | 95 | 1,187,125 | 1:12,496 | 12,510 | 9,999,875 | 1:799 |
| | 1980 | | 1,710,250 | | | 11,197,663 | |
| Utah | 1970 | 1 | 6,617 | 1:6,617 | 1,100 | 1,052,656 | 1:956 |
| | 1980 | | 9,255 | | | 1,382,550 | |
| Vermont | 1970 | 0 | 761 | 0:761 | 399 | 443,569 | 1:1,111 |
| | 1980 | | 1,135 | | | 506,736 | |
| Virginia | 1970 | 103 | 865,388 | 1:8,402 | 8,289 | 3,783,106 | 1:456 |
| | 1980 | | 1,008,311 | | | 4,229,734 | |
| Washington | 1970 | 20 | 71,308 | 1:3,565 | 3,759 | 3,337,861 | 1:887 |
| | 1980 | | 105,544 | | | 3,777,296 | |
| West Virginia | 1970 | 8 | 73,931 | 1:9,241 | 1,304 | 1,670,306 | 1:1,280 |
| | 1980 | | 65,051 | | | 1,874,751 | |
| Wisconsin | 1970 | 18 | 128,224 | 1:7,124 | 4,627 | 4,289,709 | 1:927 |
| | 1980 | | 182,593 | | | 4,442,598 | |
| Wyoming | 1970 | 1 | 2,568 | 1:2,568 | 331 | 329,848 | 1:996 |
| | 1980 | | 3,364 | | | 447,716 | |
| Washington, D.C. | 1970 | 503 | 537,712 | 1:1,069 | 3,578 | 218,798 | 1:61 |
| | 1980 | | | | | | |
| Totals | 1970 | 3,845 | 22,260,609 | 1:5,790 | 252,347 | 180,650,972 | |
| | 1980 | | 26,488,218 | | | 188,340,790 | |

# Appendix 16

## Representation of Blacks in State Judiciaries (1980)

| | Population | Judges in Courts of Last Resort | Judges in Intermediate Appellate Courts | Judges in General Jurisdiction Courts | Judges in Limited Jurisdiction Courts | Totals |
|---|---|---|---|---|---|---|
| **Alabama** | | | | | | |
| Total | 3,890,061 | 9 | 8 | 113 | 370 | 500 |
| Black | 995,623 (25.6%) | 0 | 0 | 1 | 9 | 10 (2.0%) |
| **Alaska** | | | | | | |
| Total | 400,481 | 5 | 3 | 21 | 69 | 98 |
| Black | 13,619 (3.4%) | 0 | 0 | 0 | 0 | 0 (0.0%) |
| **Arizona** | | | | | | |
| Total | 2,717,866 | 5 | 12 | 80 | 178 | 275 |
| Black | 75,034 (2.8%) | 0 | 0 | 0 | 0 | 0 (0.0%) |
| **Arkansas** | | | | | | |
| Total | 2,285,513 | 7 | 6 | 63 | 254 | 330 |
| Black | 373,192 (16.3%) | 1 | 1 | 0 | 0 | 2 (0.6%) |
| **California** | | | | | | |
| Total | 23,668,562 | 7 | 59 | 607 | 568 | 1,241 |
| Black | 1,819,282 (7.7%) | 1 | 4 | 27 | 34 | 65 (5.2%) |
| **Colorado** | | | | | | |
| Total | 2,888,834 | 7 | 10 | 106 | 353 | 476 |
| Black | 101,702 (3.5%) | 0 | 0 | 3 | 1 | 4 (0.84%) |
| **Connecticut** | | | | | | |
| Total | 3,107,576 | 6 | 3 | 110 | 130 | 249 |
| Black | 217,433 (7.0%) | 0 | 0 | 6 | 0 | 6 (2.4%) |
| **Delaware** | | | | | | |
| Total | 595,225 | 5 | 0 | 14 | 94 | 113 |
| Black | 95,971 (16.1%) | 0 | 0 | 0 | 5 | 5 (4.4%) |
| **Florida** | | | | | | |
| Total | 9,739,992 | 7 | 39 | 302 | 198 | 546 |
| Black | 1,342,478 (13.8%) | 0 | 1 | 7 | 4 | 12 (2.2%) |
| **Georgia** | | | | | | |
| Total | 5,464,265 | 7 | 9 | 110 | 2,318* | 2,444* |
| Black | 1,465,457 (26.8%) | 0 | 0 | 2 | 10 | 12 (0.49%) |
| **Hawaii** | | | | | | |
| Total | 965,000 | 5 | 3 | 25 | 18 | 51 |
| Black | 17,352 (1.8%) | 0 | 0 | 0 | 0 | 0 (0.0%) |
| **Idaho** | | | | | | |
| Total | 943,935 | 5 | 3 | 99 | 0 | 107 |
| Black | 2,716 (0.29%) | 0 | 0 | 0 | 0 | 0 (0.0%) |

| | Population | Judges in Courts of Last Resort | Judges in Intermediate Appellate Courts | Judges in General Jurisdiction Courts | Judges in Limited Jurisdiction Courts | Totals |
|---|---|---|---|---|---|---|
| **Illinois** | | | | | | |
| Total | 11,418,461 | 7 | 34 | 677 | 0 | 718 |
| Black | 1,675,229 (14.7%) | 0 | 3 | 35 | 0 | 38 (5.3%) |
| **Indiana** | | | | | | |
| Total | 5,490,179 | 5 | 12 | 171 | 155 | 343 |
| Black | 414,732 (7.6%) | 0 | 0 | 3 | 5 | 8 (2.3%) |
| **Iowa** | | | | | | |
| Total | 2,913,387 | 9 | 5 | 300 | 0 | 314 |
| Black | 41,700 (1.4%) | 0 | 0 | 1 | 2 | 3 (0.96%) |
| **Kansas** | | | | | | |
| Total | 2,363,208 | 7 | 7 | 211 | 356 | 581 |
| Black | 126,127 (5.3%) | 0 | 1 | 1 | 2 | 4 (6.9%) |
| **Kentucky** | | | | | | |
| Total | 3,661,433 | 7 | 14 | 91 | 123 | 235 |
| Black | 259,490 (7.1%) | 0 | 0 | 2 | 3 | 5 (2.1%) |
| **Louisiana** | | | | | | |
| Total | 4,203,972 | 7 | 33 | 161 | 711 | 912 |
| Black | 1,237,263 (29.4%) | 0 | 0 | 4 | 3 | 7 (0.77%) |
| **Maine** | | | | | | |
| Total | 1,124,660 | 7 | 0 | 14 | 38 | 59 |
| Black | 3,128 (0.28%) | 0 | 0 | 0 | 0 | 0 (0.0%) |
| **Maryland** | | | | | | |
| Total | 4,216,446 | 7 | 13 | 97 | 153 | 270 |
| Black | 958,050 (22.7%) | 0 | 2 | 5 | 6 | 13 (4.8%) |
| **Massachusetts** | | | | | | |
| Total | 5,737,037 | 7 | 10 | 264 | 0 | 281 |
| Black | 221,279 (3.9%) | 0 | 1 | 2 | 12 | 15 (5.3%) |
| **Michigan** | | | | | | |
| Total | 9,258,344 | 7 | 18 | 173 | 341 | 539 |
| Black | 1,198,710 (12.9%) | 0 | 0 | 22 | 10 | 32 (5.9%) |
| **Minnesota** | | | | | | |
| Total | 4,077,148 | 9 | 0 | 72 | 166 | 247 |
| Black | 53,342 (1.3%) | 0 | 0 | 2 | 0 | 2 (0.81%) |
| **Mississippi** | | | | | | |
| Total | 2,520,638 | 9 | 0 | 65 | 591 | 665 |
| Black | 887,206 (35.2%) | 0 | 0 | 1 | 1 | 2 (0.30%) |
| **Missouri** | | | | | | |
| Total | 4,917,444 | 7 | 30 | 300 | 0 | 337 |
| Black | 514,274 (10.5%) | 0 | 0 | 2 | 6 | 8 (2.4%) |
| **Montana** | | | | | | |
| Total | 786,690 | 7 | 0 | 32 | 192 | 231 |
| Black | 1,786 (0.23%) | 0 | 0 | 0 | 0 | 0 (0.0%) |
| **Nebraska** | | | | | | |
| Total | 1,570,000 | 7 | 0 | 45 | 65 | 117 |
| Black | 48,389 (3.1%) | 0 | 0 | 0 | 1 | 1 (0.85%) |

| | Population | Judges in Courts of Last Resort | Judges in Intermediate Appellate Courts | Judges in General Jurisdiction Courts | Judges in Limited Jurisdiction Courts | Totals |
|---|---|---|---|---|---|---|
| **Nevada** | | | | | | |
| Total | 779,184 | 5 | 0 | 29 | 81 | 115 |
| Black | 50,791 (6.5%) | 0 | 0 | 1 | 0 | 1 (0.87%) |
| **New Hampshire** | | | | | | |
| Total | 920,610 | 5 | 0 | 15 | 114 | 134 |
| Black | 3,990 (0.43%) | 0 | 0 | 0 | 1 | 1 (7.5%) |
| **New Jersey** | | | | | | |
| Total | 7,364,158 | 7 | 21 | 214 | 474 | 716 |
| Black | 924,786 (12.6%) | 0 | 0 | 5 | 12 | 17 (2.4%) |
| **New Mexico** | | | | | | |
| Total | 1,299,968 | 5 | 7 | 44 | 201 | 257 |
| Black | 24,042 (1.8%) | 0 | 0 | 0 | 0 | 0 (0.0%) |
| **New York** | | | | | | |
| Total | 17,557,288 | 7 | 33 | 367 | 3,037 | 3,444 |
| Black | 2,401,842 (13.7%) | 0 | 0 | 23 | 31 | 54 (1.6%) |
| **North Carolina** | | | | | | |
| Total | 5,874,429 | 7 | 12 | 66 | 136 | 221 |
| Black | 1,316,050 (22.4%) | 0 | 1 | 2 | 9 | 12 (5.4%) |
| **North Dakota** | | | | | | |
| Total | 652,695 | 5 | 0 | 24 | 279 | 308 |
| Black | 2,568 (0.39%) | 0 | 0 | 0 | 0 | 0 (0.0%) |
| **Ohio** | | | | | | |
| Total | 10,797,419 | 7 | 44 | 313 | 938 | 1,302 |
| Black | 1,076,734 (10.0%) | 0 | 1 | 5 | 14 | 20 (1.5%) |
| **Oklahoma** | | | | | | |
| Total | 3,025,266 | 12 | 6 | 198 | 553 | 769 |
| Black | 204,658 (6.8%) | 0 | 0 | 1 | 1 | 2 (0.26%) |
| **Oregon** | | | | | | |
| Total | 2,632,663 | 7 | 10 | 76 | 297 | 390 |
| Black | 37,059 (1.4%) | 0 | 0 | 1 | 1 | 2 (0.51%) |
| **Pennsylvania** | | | | | | |
| Total | 11,866,728 | 7 | 16 | 285 | 589 | 897 |
| Black | 1,047,609 (8.8%) | 1 | 1 | 21 | 4 | 27 (3.0%) |
| **Rhode Island** | | | | | | |
| Total | 947,154 | 5 | 0 | 19 | 68 | 92 |
| Black | 27,584 (2.9%) | 0 | 0 | 0 | 0 | 0 (0.0%) |
| **South Carolina** | | | | | | |
| Total | 3,119,208 | 5 | 5 | 31 | 672 | 713 |
| Black | 948,146 (30.4%) | 0 | 0 | 1 | 12 | 13 (1.8%) |
| **South Dakota** | | | | | | |
| Total | 690,178 | 5 | 0 | 141 | 0 | 146 |
| Black | 2,144 (0.31%) | 0 | 0 | 0 | 0 | 0 (0.0%) |
| **Tennessee** | | | | | | |
| Total | 4,590,750 | 5 | 21 | 116 | 362 | 504 |
| Black | 725,949 (15.8%) | 1 | 0 | 5 | 1 | 7 (1.4%) |

| | Population | Judges in Courts of Last Resort | Judges in Intermediate Appellate Courts | Judges in General Jurisdiction Courts | Judges in Limited Jurisdiction Courts | Totals |
|---|---|---|---|---|---|---|
| **Texas** | | | | | | |
| Total | 14,228,383 | 18 | 51 | 310 | 2,195 | 2,574 |
| Black | 1,710,250 (12.0%) | 0 | 1 | 4 | 18 | 23 (0.89%) |
| **Utah** | | | | | | |
| Total | 1,461,037 | 5 | 0 | 24 | 212 | 241 |
| Black | 9,225 (0.63%) | 0 | 0 | 0 | 0 | 0 (0.0%) |
| **Vermont** | | | | | | |
| Total | 511,456 | 5 | 0 | 38 | 33 | 76 |
| Black | 1,135 (0.22%) | 0 | 0 | 0 | 0 | 0 (0.0%) |
| **Virginia** | | | | | | |
| Total | 5,346,279 | 7 | 0 | 111 | 163 | 281 |
| Black | 1,008,311 (18.9%) | 0 | 0 | 1 | 11 | 12 (4.3%) |
| **Washington** | | | | | | |
| Total | 4,130,163 | 9 | 16 | 118 | 208 | 351 |
| Black | 105,544 (2.6%) | 0 | 0 | 1 | 1 | 2 (0.57%) |
| **West Virginia** | | | | | | |
| Total | 1,949,644 | 5 | 0 | 60 | 204 | 269 |
| Black | 65,051 (3.3%) | 0 | 0 | 0 | 2 | 2 (0.74%) |
| **Wisconsin** | | | | | | |
| Total | 4,705,335 | 7 | 12 | 190 | 216 | 425 |
| Black | 182,593 (3.9%) | 0 | 0 | 2 | 0 | 2 (0.47%) |
| **Wyoming** | | | | | | |
| Total | 470,816 | 7 | 0 | 15 | 124 | 146 |
| Black | 3,364 (0.71%) | 0 | 0 | 2 | 0 | 2 (1.4%) |
| **District of Columbia** | | | | | | |
| Total | 637,651 | 9 | 0 | 44 | 0 | 53 |
| Black | 448,229 (70.3%) | 4 | 0 | 12 | 0 | 16 (30.2%) |
| **States Only** | | | | | | |
| Total | 225,867,174 | 341 | 585 | 7,127 | 18,597* | 26,650* |
| Black | 25,977,989 (11.5%) | 4 | 17 | 201 | 232 | 453 (1.7%) |
| **States and D.C.** | | | | | | |
| Total | 226,504,825 | 350 | 585 | 7,171 | 18,597* | 26,703* |
| Black | 26,488,218 (11.7%) | 8 | 17 | 213 | 232 | 469 (1.8%) |

*Data from limited jurisdiction courts in Georgia do not include the judges of the criminal court, police court, and municipal court (other than the municipal courts in Savannah and Columbia). These data therefore are not included in any total figures.

The figures for limited jurisdiction courts include 15 magistrates: in Iowa (2), Louisiana (1), Pennsylvania (1), South Carolina (9), and West Virginia (2) and include 11 justices of the peace in Delaware (4), Indiana (1), Mississippi (1), and Texas (5) and 1 commissioner in Louisiana.

Figures for black state judges taken from *National Roster of Black Judicial Officers,* 1980, pp. 29–111.

Figures for black and total population in each state taken from U.S. Bureau of the Census, *1980 Census of Population,* Supplementary Reports P.C. 80-51-3, Race of Population by States: 1980 (Washington, D.C.: Government Printing Office, 1981), table 1, p. 6. Figures for state and local judgeships supplied by the National Center for State Courts, Williamsburg, Virginia.

# Appendix 17

## Presidential Appointments of Black Federal Judges

| Supreme Court | Year Appointed | President |
|---|---|---|
| Marshall, Thurgood | 1967 | Johnson |
| *Circuit Judges* | | |
| Hastie, William H.<br>Third | 1949 (Assumed senior status<br>1971. Deceased 1976.) | Truman |
| Marshall, Thurgood<br>Second | 1962 (Resigned in 1965 to accept<br>appointment as Solicitor<br>General.) | Kennedy |
| McCree, Wade H., Jr.*<br>Sixth | 1966 (Resigned in 1977 to accept<br>appointment as Solicitor<br>General.) | Johnson |
| Robinson, Spottswood, III*<br>D.C. | 1966 | Johnson |
| Higginbotham, A. Leon, Jr.*<br>Third | 1977 | Carter |
| Keith, Damon J.*<br>Sixth | 1977 | Carter |
| McMillian, Theodore<br>Eighth | 1978 | Carter |
| Kearse, Amalya<br>Second | 1979 | Carter |
| Hatchett, Joseph Woodrow<br>Eleventh (formerly Fifth) | 1979 | Carter |
| Jones, Nathaniel<br>Sixth | 1979 | Carter |
| Farris, J. Jerome<br>Ninth | 1979 | Carter |
| Poole, Cecil F.*<br>Ninth | 1979 | Carter |
| Edwards, Harry T.<br>D.C. | 1980 | Carter |
| Pierce, Lawrence W.<br>Second | 1981 | Reagan |
| *District Judges* | | |
| Parsons, James B. (Ill. N) | 1961 (Assumed senior status<br>1981) | Kennedy |
| McCree, Wade H., Jr. (Mich.<br>E.D.) | 1961 (Elevated to Circuit Judge<br>1966.) | Kennedy |
| Robinson, Spottswood, III (D.C.) | 1964 (Elevated to Circuit Judge<br>1966.) | Nominated by<br>Kennedy,<br>confirmed under<br>Johnson |

| | | |
|---|---|---|
| Higginbotham, A. Leon, Jr. (Pa. E.D.) | 1964 (Elevated to Circuit Judge 1977.) | Johnson |
| Bryant, William B. (D.C.) | 1965 (Assumed senior status 1982) | Johnson |
| Motley, Constance B. (N.Y. S) | 1966 | Johnson |
| Robinson, Aubrey E. (D.C.) | 1966 | Johnson |
| Waddy, Joseph C. (D.C.) | 1967 (Deceased 1978.) | Johnson |
| Keith, Damon J. (Mich. (E.D.) | 1967 (Elevated to Circuit Judge 1977.) | Johnson |
| Williams, David W. (Calif. C) | 1969 | Nixon |
| Parker, Barrington (D.C.) | 1969 | Nixon |
| Pierce, Lawrence W. (N.Y. S) | 1971 (Elevated to Circuit Judge 1981) | Nixon |
| Green, Clifford Scott (Pa. E) | 1971 | Nixon |
| Carter, Robert L. (N.Y. S) | 1972 | Nixon |
| Duncan, Robert M. (Ohio S) | 1974 | Nixon |
| Bramwell, Henry (N.Y. E) | 1974 | Ford |
| Leighton, George N. (Ill. N) | 1976 | Ford |
| Poole, Cecil F. (Calif. N) | 1976 (Elevated to Circuit Judge 1979.) | Ford |
| Simmons, Paul A. (Pa. W) | 1976 | Carter |
| Collins, Robert F. (La. E) | 1976 | Carter |
| Tanner, Jack E. (Wash. E & W) | 1976 | Carter |
| Lowe, Mary Johnson (N.Y. S) | 1978 | Carter |
| Cook, Julian A. (Mich. E) | 1978 | Carter |
| Nelson, Davis S. (Mass.) | 1979 | Carter |
| Penn, John G. (D.C.) | 1979 | Carter |
| McDonald, Gabrielle (Tex. S) | 1979 | Carter |
| Perry, Matthew (S.C.) | 1979 | Carter |
| Gibson, Matthew (S.C.) | 1979 | Carter |
| Howard, Joseph (Md.) | 1979 | Carter |
| Taylor, Anna (Diggs) (Mich. E) | 1979 | Carter |
| Hastings, Alcee (Fla. S) | 1979 | Carter |
| Thompson, Ann (N.J.) | 1979 | Carter |
| Giles, James (Pa. E) | 1979 | Carter |
| Ward, Horace B. (Ga. N) | 1979 | Carter |
| Hatter, Terry (Calif. C) | 1979 | Carter |
| Horton, Odell (Tenn. W) | 1980 | Carter |
| Johnson, Norma H. (D.C.) | 1980 | Carter |
| White, George (Ohio N) | 1980 | Carter |
| Cahill, Clyde (Mo. E) | 1980 | Carter |
| Clemon, U. W. (Ala. N) | 1980 | Carter |
| Henderson, Thelton E. (Calif. N) | 1980 | Carter |
| Gilliam, Earl (Calif. E) | 1980 | Carter |
| Howard, George (Ark. E) | 1980 | Carter |
| Marshall, Consuello (Calif. N) | 1980 | Carter |
| Erwin, Richard (N.C. M) | 1980 | Carter |
| Thompson, Myron H. (Ala. M) | 1980 | Carter |

*U.S. Court of International Trade (formerly U.S. Customs Court)*

| | | |
|---|---|---|
| Irvin C. Mollison | 1945 (Deceased 1962.) | Truman |
| Richardson, Scovel | 1957 | Eisenhower |
| Watson, James L. | 1966 | Johnson |

*Term Judges*

| | | |
|---|---|---|
| Hastie, William H. (V.I.) | 1937 (Resigned 1939.) | Roosevelt |
| Moore, Herman E. (V.I.) | 1939 (Retired 1957 after four successive terms.) | Roosevelt (2 terms) Truman (3rd term) Eisenhower (4th term) |
| Gordon, Walter A. (V.I.) | 1958 (Retired 1968; Deceased 1978.) | Eisenhower |
| Christian, Almeric L. (V.I.) | 1969 | Nixon |
| | 1978 | Carter |

*Former United States District Judge.

# Blacks on Law School Faculties in Sixteen Cities (1981–82)

| | Professors | Assoc. Professors | Asst. Professors | Adminis- trators | Teachers/ Administrators | Part-time All Categories | Teaching Fellows |
|---|---|---|---|---|---|---|---|
| **Atlanta** | | | | | | | |
| Emory U. | | | | | | 1 | |
| **Boston** | | | | | | | |
| Boston College | | | 1 | | | 1 | |
| Boston U. | | | | 1 | | 2 | |
| Harvard U. | 1 | | | | | 1 | |
| **New England** | | | | | | | |
| Northeastern U. | 2 | | | 1 | | | |
| Suffolk U. | | | 1 | | | | |
| **Chicago** | | | | | | | |
| Chicago-Kent | | | | | | | |
| De Paul U. | 1 | 2 | | | 1 | 1 | |
| John Marshall | | | | | | 1 | |
| Loyola U. | 1 | | | | | | |
| Northern Illinois | 1 | | | | | | |
| Northwestern U. | 2 | | | | | | |
| U. of Chicago | | | | | | | |
| **Cleveland** | | | | | | | |
| Cleveland State U. | | | 1 | | | | |
| Case Western Reserve U. | | | | | | | |
| **Columbus** | | | | | | | |
| Capital U. | | | | | | | |
| Ohio State U. | | 1 | | 1 | | | |
| **Detroit** | | | | | | | |
| Detroit College | | 1 | 1 | | | 1 | |
| Wayne State U. | 2 | | | | | | |
| U. of Michigan | | | | | | 1 | |
| **Houston** | | | | | | | |
| Texas Southern | | | | | | | |
| Thurgood Marshall | 6 | 7 | 4 | | | | |
| U. of Houston | | | | | | | |
| South Texas | | | 1 | | | | |
| **Los Angeles** | | | | | | | |
| Loyola | | | | | 1 | 1 | |
| Southwestern U. | 2 | | | | | | |
| Whittier College | | | | | | | |
| U. of California | 3 | | | | | | |
| U. of Southern California | | | 1 | | | | |
| **Milwaukee** | | | | | | | |
| Marquette U. | | | | | | | |
| **Minneapolis** | | | | | | | |
| U. of Minnesota | | 1 | | 1 | | | |
| **New York** | | | | | | | |
| Brooklyn | | | | | | | |

| | Professors | Assoc. Professors | Asst. Professors | Administrators | Teachers/ Administrators | Part-time All Categories | Teaching Fellows |
|---|---|---|---|---|---|---|---|
| Columbia U. | 1 | | | | | | |
| Fordham U. | | | | | | | |
| New York | | 1 | 1 | | | 1 | |
| Pace U. | | 1 | 1 | | | | |
| New York U. | 1 | | | | | 2 | |
| Hofstra U. | 2 | | | | | | |
| St. Johns U. | | | | | | 1 | |
| Yeshiva U. | 1 | | | | | | |
| Philadelphia | | | | | | | |
| U. of Pennsylvania | | | 2 | | | | |
| Temple U. | 3 | | | 1 | | 5 | |
| Villanova U. | 1 | | | | 1 | 1 | |
| Pittsburgh | | | | | | | |
| U. of Pittsburgh | | | 2 | | | | |
| Duquesne U. | 1 | | | | 1 | | |
| Richmond | | | | | | | |
| U. of Richmond | | | | | | | |
| San Francisco | | | | | | | |
| Golden Gate U. | | | 2 | | | | |
| U. of San Francisco | 1 | | | | | | |
| U. of California Hastings | | | 1 | | | | |
| U. of California Berkeley | 1 | | | | | | |
| Washington, D.C. | | | | | | | |
| American U. | 1 | | | | | | |
| Antioch | 1 | | | | | 1 | |
| Catholic U. | | | | 1 | | | |
| Georgetown U. | 4 | 1 | 1 | 2 | | | |
| George Washington U. | 1 | | | 1 | | 1 | |
| Howard U. | 11 | 7 | 3 | 2 | 11 | 5 | |

# Bibliography

Adams, Russell L. *Great Negroes Past and Present*. Chicago: Afro-American Publishing Co., 1969.

Allen, James E. *The Negro in New York*. Exposition Press, 1964.

Banfield, E., ed. *Urban Government*. New York: The Free Press, 1969.

Bardolph, Richard. *The Negro Vanguard*. Westport, Conn.: Negro University Press, 1959.

Beasley, Delilah L. *The Negro Trail Blazers of California*. Reprint ed. New York: Negro Universities Press, 1969.

Bergman, Peter M. *The Chronological History of the Negro in America*. New York: Harper and Row, 1969.

Brewer, J. Mason. *Negro Legislators of Texas*. Dallas: Mathas Publishing Co., 1935.

Britts, Maurice W. *Blacks on White College Campuses*. Minneapolis: Challenge Productions, Inc., 1975.

Broom, Leonard and Norval D. Glenn. *The Occupations and Incomes of Black Americans from Transformation of the Negro Americans*. New York: Harper and Row, 1965.

Burke, Joan Martin. *Civil Rights*. 2d ed. New York: Bowker and Co., 1974.

Cantor, Daniel J. & Co. "Negro Lawyers in the U.S., 1966: An Economic Study." A project of Howard University School of Law in cooperation with the National Bar Assn., October, 1966.

Carlin, Jerome E. *Lawyers on Their Own*. New Brunswick, N. J.: Rutgers University Press, 1961.

Chase, Harold W. *Federal Judges—The Appointing Process*. Minneapolis: University of Minnesota Press, 1972.

Chroust, Anton-Hermann. *The Rise of the Legal Profession in America*. Norman, Okla.: University of Oklahoma Press, 1965.

Daniels, John. *In Freedom's Birthplace. A Study of Boston Negroes*. Reprint ed. New York: Negro Universities Press, 1968.

Davis, John P., ed. *The American Negro Reference Book*. Englewood Cliffs, N.J.: Prentice-Hall, 1960.

de Tocqueville, Alexis. *Democracy in America*. Barnes and Co. 1859.

DuBois, W. E. B. *The Philadelphia Negro*. New York: Schocken ed. 1967.

Edwards, G. Franklin. *The Negro Professional Class*. Glencoe, Ill.: The Free Press, 1959.

Frazier, E. Franklin. *The Negro in the United States*. New York: Macmillan, 1957.

Goldman, Marion S. *A Portrait of the Black Attorney in Chicago*. Chicago: American Bar Foundation, 1972.

Groves, Harry E. *Opportunities for Negroes in the Law.* Washington, D.C.: American Association of Law Schools, 1967.

Haley, Alex. *The Autobiography of Malcolm X.* New York: Grove Press, 1964.

Higginbotham, A. Leon, Jr. *In the Matter of Color.* New York: Oxford, 1978.

Kluger, Richard. *Simple Justice.* New York: Vintage Books, 1977.

Leonard, Walter J. *Black Lawyers.* Boston: Senna and Shih, 1977.

Low, W. Augustus and Virgil Clift, eds. *Encyclopedia of Black America.* New York: McGraw Hill, 1981.

Mayer, Martin P. *The Lawyers.* New York: Harper and Row, 1966.

Morsbach, Mabel. *The Negro in American Life.* New York: Harcourt Brace and World, 1966.

Ploski, Harry A. and Warren Marr III, eds. *The Negro Almanac: The Afro-American.* 3d ed. New York: Bellweather Co., 1976.

Reasons, George and Sam Patrick. *They Had a Dream.* Los Angeles: Los Angeles Times Syndicate, 1970.

Reincke, Mary and Nancy Lichterman, eds. *The American Bench. Judges of the Nation.* 2d ed. Minneapolis: Reginald Bishop Forster and Associates, Inc., 1979.

Richardson, Julius, Associates. *Towards a Diversified Legal Profession.* San Francisco, 1981.

Saunders, John A. *100 Years After Emancipation: History of the Philadelphia Negro.* Philadelphia: F.R.S. Publishing Co., n.d.

Schlesinger, Arthur M., Jr. *Robert Kennedy and His Times.* Boston: Houghton-Mifflin Co., 1978.

Segal, Geraldine R. *In Any Fight Some Fall.* Rockville, Md.: Mercury Press, 1975.

Sherman, Joan R. *Invisible Poets* (City). Urbana: University of Illinois Press, 1974.

Spradling, Mary Mace, ed. *In Black and White.* Detroit: Gale Research Co., 1980.

Styles, Fitzhugh Lee. *Negroes and the Law.* Boston: The Christopher Publishing House, 1937.

Sunderland, Edson R. *History of the American Bar Association and Its Work.* 1953.

Vollmer, Howard M. and Donald L. Mills. *Professionalization.* Englewood Cliffs, N.J.: Prentice-Hall, Inc., 1966.

Ware, Gilbert, ed. *From the Black Bar: Voices for Equal Justice.* New York: G. P. Putnam's Sons, 1976.

Wesley, Charles H. *Negro Labor in the United States, 1850–1925.* New York: Vanguard Press, 1927.

Wofford, Harris. *Of Kennedys and Kings.* New York: Farrar, Straus and Giroux, 1980.

Woodson, Carter G. *The Negro Professional Man and the Community.* Washington, D.C.: The Association for the Study of Negro Life and History, Inc., 1934.

## Law School Publications

*Buffalo Law Review, Duke Law Journal, Harvard Law School Bulletin, Howard Law Journal, Marquette Law Review, Maryland Law Review, Mercer Law Review, Michigan Law Review, Temple Law Quarterly, University of Toledo Law Review, Villanova Law Review, Yale Law Journal.* (For specific dates, see footnotes)

# Newspapers

*Afro-American, Chicago Daily News, Chicago Sun Times, Christian Science Monitor, Cleveland Press, Legal Times of Washington, Milwaukee Journal, Milwaukee Sentinel, New York Times, Philadelphia Inquirer, Philadelphia Tribune, Plain Dealer, Wall Street Journal, Washington Post.*

## Periodicals and Other Publications

*Atlanta Lawyer, American Sociological Review, Annals of the American Academy of Political and Social Science, Bar Examiner, Black Law Journal, Crisis, Echo, Encyclopedia of Associations, Historical Statistics of the United States, Journal of American History, Journal of Comparative Family Studies, Journal of Legal Education, Journal of Negro Education, Journal of Negro History, Journal of Public Law, Journal of Social and Behavioral Sciences, Judicature, Martindale-Hubbell Law Directory, National Bar Bulletin, National Bar Journal, National Conference of Artists, National Law Journal, National Roster of Black Elected Officials, National Roster of Black Judicial Officers, Negro History Bulletin, New Encyclopaedia Britannica, Nexus, Pennsylvania Bar Association Quarterly, Reports of the American Bar Association, Social Problems, Student Lawyer, United States Bureau of the Census, Who's Who Among Black Americans, Who's Who in America, Who's Who in American Law, Who's Who in Harlem.*

# Index